Annual Editions:
The Family, 43/e

Patricia Hrusa Willi

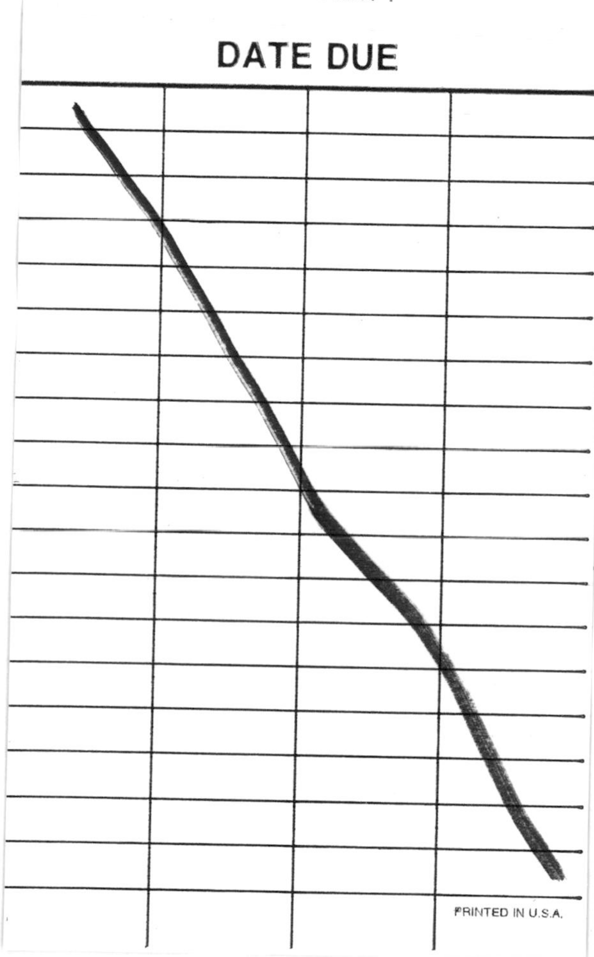

http://create.mheducation.com

ISBN-10: 1259910733 ISBN-13: 9781259910739

Contents

Detailed Table of Contents

Unit 1: Evolving Perspectives on the Family

Unit 2: Exploring and Establishing Relationships

to assume your partner gives consent to sex through their behavior; now consent needs to be explicitly and enthusiastically given. How will this change in the law influence the sexual behavior and experiences of young adults?

Unit 3: Family Relationships

Unit 4: Challenges and Opportunities

An Epidemic of Children Dying in Hot Cars, David Diamond, *The Conversation*, 2016
There has been a startling increase in the number of children who have been killed or injured after caregivers left them in a hot car. Why do caregivers sometimes make this deadly mistake? Should they be held criminally negligent?

Gluten-free Baby: When Parents Ignore Science, Aaron Hutchins, *Maclean's*, 2017
Parents are increasingly utilizing unconventional medical approaches and diets in caring for and raising their children. The efficacy and safety of many treatments are sometimes unproven and can have detrimental effects on children's health. The article asks "when does out of the box parenting end up going too far"?

Family Privilege, John R. Seita, *Reclaiming Children and Youth*, 2014
Family privilege is defined as "strengths and supports gained through primary caring relationships." Children reared in foster care often lack access to the privileges afforded by families. To promote resilience in the face of adversity, the author highlights the role of kin and communities in helping children build trust, find their talents, foster independence, and find purpose.

Terrorism in the Home, Victor M. Parachin, *The Priest*, 2013
What is domestic violence? The article discusses 11 common myths about domestic violence. Topics addressed include the signs of domestic violence, causes, and the challenges involved in assisting victims.

When Your Parents Are Heroin Addicts, Tracey Helton, *The Daily Beast*, 2016
Opioid addiction has become an epidemic in the United States. The National Survey on Drug Use and Health estimates 2.2 million children have parents who use illegal drugs. This article tells of the story of some of these families.

"We Never Talked About It": As Opioid Deaths Rise, Families of Color Stay Silent, Leah Samuel, *Stat News*, 2017
There is a stigma to addiction, and overdose deaths are often hidden by families who fear it reflects poorly on them. This article discusses why families of color and immigrant families often hide deaths due to overdose.

Growing Pains: Are Perfect Families a Recipe for Stress? Vanessa Thorpe, *The Guardian*, 2016
This article reports on the findings of a recent British study which finds almost one-third of modern families report feeling burned out from balancing work, children's activities, and domestic duties.

Your Kid Goes to Jail, You Get the Bill, Eli Hager, *The Marshall Project*, 2017
Most people don't realize that parents in 28 states can be billed for their children's incarceration or detention, even if later proven innocent. This article discusses the policy and the complexities of the juvenile justice system for families.

Separation Anxiety: How Deportation Divides Immigrant Families, Hank Kalet, *NJ Spotlight*, 2016
Immigration and border security are contentious issues in the United States. How does the fear of deportation and detention practices when families cross the border illegally affect parents and their children? U.S. policies, research findings, and the experiences of families are utilized to illustrate the challenges.

Myths about Military Families, Jennifer Woodworth, *Exceptional Parent Magazine*, 2016
This article works to dispel stereotypes held about military families including the idea that they have fewer economic worries than nonmilitary families, are only separated during deployment, and that all veterans experience Post-Traumatic Stress Disorder.

A Whole-family Approach to Workforce Engagement, Kerry Desjardins, *Policy & Practice*, 2016
What is a whole-family approach? How might it benefit low-income working families to promote economic self-sufficiency and upward mobility?

Working Hard, Hardly Working, Chris Sorenson, *Maclean's*, 2015
This article discusses the workaholic culture prevalent in North America. Does working all the time make us more or less productive? What are the ramifications for our well-being and family life?

Unit 5: Families, Now and into the Future

Relationships in the Melting Pot, Tina Livingstone, *Healthcare Counseling and Psychotherapy Journal*, 2015
This article considers issues faced when a partner in a relationship discloses their identity as a transidentified person. Topics explored include exposure and disclosure, distress, loss, and challenges in reframing the couple's relationship.

Family Diversity Is the New Normal for America's Children, Philip Cohen, *Council on Contemporary Families*, 2014
We know the families in which children live have changed since the 1950s. However, are families just different or instead so diverse that one model, pattern, or structure no longer predominates? Using demographic data, changes in family structure, living arrangements, and parental employment patterns are explored.

Family Strengths and Resilience, Eugene C. Roehlkepartain and Amy K. Syvertsen, *Reclaiming Children and Youth*, 2014
Using research data from a nationally representative sample of parents and their teens, the authors examine family assets with goal of identifying family characteristics and strategies which help promote resilience.

Strengthening Ties: The Case for Building a Social Policy Centered on Families, Phillip Longman et al., *New America*, 2015
As families have changed and evolved, have family and social policies kept pace? This article explores trends in modern families including their economic prospects, changes in family structure, and how technology is changing family life. Suggestions are then made as to how these trends can incorporated in developing programs and policies to strengthen and support families.

Preface

In publishing ANNUAL EDITIONS, we recognize the enormous role played by the magazines, newspapers, and journals of the public press in providing current, first-rate educational information in a broad spectrum of interest areas. Many of these articles are appropriate for students, researchers, and professionals, seeking accurate, current material to help bridge the gap between principles and theories and the real world. These articles, however, become more useful for study when those of lasting value are carefully collected, organized, indexed, and reproduced in a low-cost format, which provides easy and permanent access when the material is needed. That is the role played by ANNUAL EDITIONS.

The purpose of *Annual Editions: The Family, 43/e* is to bring to the reader the latest thoughts and trends in our understanding of the family. Articles consider current concerns, problems, potential solutions, and ways families remain resilient in the face of adversity. The volume also presents alternative views on family relationships, processes, patterns, and structures. The intent of this anthology is to explore family relationships and to reflect on the family's evolving function and importance. The articles in this volume are taken from professional journals as well as other professionally oriented publications and popular lay publications aimed at both special populations and a general readership. The selections are carefully reviewed for their currency and accuracy.

In the current edition, a number of new articles have been added to reflect reviewers' comments on the previous edition. As the reader, you will note the tremendous range in tone and focus of these articles, from first-person accounts to reports of scientific discoveries as well as philosophical and theoretical writings. Some are more practical and applications-oriented, while others are more conceptual and research-oriented. Together they highlight the multidisciplinary nature of the study of the family and the myriad of influences that shape the family as a social structure and unit of socialization.

This anthology is organized to address many important aspects of family and family relationships. The first unit takes an overview perspective and looks at varied viewpoints on the family. The second unit examines the beginnings of relationships as individuals go through the process of exploring and establishing connections. The third unit examines family communication, relationships, and interactions in various types of relationships including marital, parent–child, sibling, and intergenerational relationships. The fourth unit is concerned with crises and ways in which these can act as challenges and opportunities for families and their members. Finally, the fifth unit takes an affirming tone as it looks at family strengths, ways of empowering families, and emerging trends within families and their formation.

Annual Editions: The Family, 43/e is intended to be used as a supplemental text for lower-level, introductory marriage, family, or sociology of the family classes, particularly when they tie the content of the readings to essential information on marriages and families, however, they are defined. As a supplement, this book can also be used to update or emphasize certain aspects of standard marriage and family textbooks. Because of the provocative nature of many of the essays in this anthology, it works well as a basis for class discussion, debate, and critical thinking exercises about various aspects of marriages and family relationships. This edition of *Annual Editions: The Family* contains Internet References noted after each article that can be used to further explore topics addressed in the readings.

Patricia Hrusa Williams
University of Maine at Farmington

Editor of This Volume

Patricia Hrusa Williams is an associate professor in the Department of Early Childhood and Elementary Education at the University of Maine at Farmington. She received her BA in Health & Society and Psychology from the University of Rochester. Her PhD is in Applied Child Development from Tufts University. Dr. Williams' primary areas of interest are family support programs, parental involvement in early childhood education, infant-toddler development, service learning, and the development of writing and critical thinking skills in college students. She has authored, coauthored, or edited over 20 published articles in books, academic journals, and the popular press. Dr. Williams lives with her family in the mountains of western Maine.

Acknowledgments

We would like to thank everyone involved in the development of this volume. Our appreciation goes to those who provided comments on the previous edition as well as those who suggested articles to consider for inclusion in this edition.

Academic Advisory Board Members

Members of the Academic Advisory Board are instrumental in the final selection of articles for *Annual Editions* books. Their review of the articles for content, level, and appropriateness provides critical direction to the editor and staff. We think that you will find their careful consideration reflected in this edition.

Unit 1

UNIT

Prepared by: Patricia Hrusa Williams, *University of Maine at Farmington*

Evolving Perspectives on the Family

Our image of what family is and what it should be is a powerful combination of personal experience, family forms we encounter or observe, and attitudes we hold. Once formed, this image informs decision-making and interpersonal interactions throughout our lives with far-reaching effects. On an intimate level, it influences individual and family development as well as the relationships we create and maintain, both inside and outside the family. On a broader level, it affects legislation, social policy, and programmatic supports developed and offered to couples, parents, and families. In many ways, the images we build and hold can be positive. They can act to clarify our thinking and facilitate interaction with like-minded individuals. They can also be negative, narrowing our thinking and limiting our ability appreciate and see value in how others carry out family functions. Interaction with others can also be impeded because of contrasting views.

This unit is intended to meet several goals in exploring evolving perspectives on the family including: (1) sensitizing the reader to sources of beliefs about the "shoulds" of the family—what the family should be and the ways in which family roles and functions should be carried out, (2) showing how different views of the family can influence attitudes toward community responsibility and family policy, and (3) showing how changes in society are altering family characteristics, structures, relationships, and functions. Among the issues to be considered in this unit include how historical, demographic, social, and philosophical changes are influencing families, marriage, relationships, and the nature of family life in the United States and abroad.

Article

Prepared by: Patricia Hrusa Williams, *University of Maine at Farmington*

Five Reasons We Can't Handle Marriage Anymore

ANTHONY D'AMBROSIO

Learning Outcomes

After reading this article, you will be able to:

- Identify factors which contribute to marital stability and longevity.
- Analyze how changes in modern society may serve to promote marital dissolution.
- Suggest ways to strengthen relationships in a time of great technological and social change.

Marriages today just don't work. The million dollar question? Why not? It's a pretty simple concept—fall in love and share your life together. Our great grandparents did it, our grandparents followed suit, and for many of us, our parents did it as well. Why the hell can't we?

Many of you will ask what gives me the right to share my advice or opinions. I've been divorced myself. But I'm only one of the many people today that have failed at marriage. And while some of us have gone through a divorce, others stay in their relationships, miserably, and live completely phony lives. These same people, though, are quick to point the finger and judge others for speaking up.

I've spent the better part of the last three years trying to understand the dating scene again. Back when I met my ex-wife in 2004, things were just so different. Social media had yet to explode. I had this desire to ask her about her day simply because I didn't know. Texting was just starting to make its way into mainstream society, so if I wanted to speak to her, I had to call her. If I wanted to see her, I had to drive to her house and knock on her door. Everything required an action on my part, or hers. Today, things are different though.

To my ex-wife: I wish I would have held you tighter.

Looking back nearly 11 years, I began to wonder how different things were for the older generations. More importantly, I wonder how different they will be for my children.

Our generation isn't equipped to handle marriages—and here's why:

1) Sex Becomes Almost Non-Existent

I don't know about you, but I am an extremely sexual person. Not only do I believe it's an important aspect of a relationship, I believe it's the most important. Beyond being pleasurable, sex connects two individuals. There's a reason why it's referred to as making love. There's just something about touching someone, kissing someone, feeling someone that should make your hair stand up.

I'm baffled by couples who neglect having sex, especially younger ones. We all desire physical connection, so how does cutting that off lead you to believe your marriage will be successful? It's like telling someone you'll take them out to a restaurant but they can't order food.

Instead, we have sex once every couple of weeks, or when it's time to get pregnant. It becomes this chore. You no longer look at your partner wanting to rip their clothes off, but rather instead, dread the thought. That's not crazy to you?

It's not just boredom that stops sex from happening. Everywhere you look, there's pictures of men and women we know half naked—some look better than your husband or wife. So it becomes desirable. It's in your face every single day and changes your mindset. It's no wonder why insecurities loom so largely these days. You have to be perfect to keep someone attracted to you. Meanwhile, what your lover should really be attracted to is your heart. Maybe if you felt that connection beyond a physical level, would you realize a sexual attraction you've never felt before.

2) Finances Cripple Us

Years ago, it didn't cost upward of $200,000 for an education. It also didn't cost $300,000-plus for a home. The cost of living was very different than what it is now. You'd be naive to believe this stress doesn't cause strain on marriages today.

You need to find a job to pay for student loans, a mortgage, utilities, living expenses, and a baby. Problem is, it's extremely difficult to find a job that can provide an income that will help you live comfortably while paying all of these bills—especially not in your mid-20s.

This strain causes separation between us. It halts us from being able to live life. We're too busy paying bills to enjoy our youth. Forget going to dinner, you have to pay the mortgage. You'll have to skip out on an anniversary gift this year because those student loans are due at the end of the month. Vacations? Not happening. We're trying to live the way our grandparents and parents did in a world that has put more debt on our plate than ever before. It's possible, but it puts us in an awful position.

Part of life is being able to live. Not having the finances to do so takes away yet another important aspect of our relationships. It keeps us inside, forced to see the life everyone else is living.

3) We're More Connected than Ever Before, but Completely Disconnected at the Same Time

Let's face it, the last time you "spoke" to the person you love, you didn't even hear their voice. You could be at work, the gym, maybe with the kids at soccer. You may even be in the same room. You told your wife you made dinner reservations . . . through a text message. Your husband had flowers delivered to your job . . . through an app on his phone. You both searched for furnishings for your new home . . . on Pinterest. There's no physical connection attached to anything anymore.

We've developed relationships with things, not each other. Ninety-five percent of the personal conversations you have on a daily basis occur through some type of technology. We've removed human emotion from our relationships, and we've replaced it with colorful bubbles.

Somehow, we've learned to get offended by text on a screen, accusing others of being "angry" or "sad" when, in fact, we have no idea what they are feeling. We argue about this—at length. We've forgotten how to communicate yet expect healthy marriages. How is it possible to grow and mature together if we barely speak?

Years ago, my grandmother wouldn't hear from my grandfather all day; he was working down at the piers in Brooklyn. But today, if someone doesn't text you back within 30 minutes, they're suddenly cheating on you.

You want to know why your grandmother and grandfather just celebrated their 60th wedding anniversary? Because they weren't scrolling through Instagram worrying about what John ate for dinner. They weren't on Facebook criticizing others. They weren't on vacation sending Snapchats to their friends. No. They were too preoccupied loving and respecting one another. They were talking to each other at dinner, walking with each other holding hands instead of their phones. They weren't distracted by everything around them. They had dreams and chased them together.

4) Our Desire for Attention Outweighs Our Desire to be Loved

Even years ago, people would clamor over celebrities. When I think back, I can imagine young women wanting to be like Marilyn Monroe. She was beautiful, all over magazines, could have any man she wanted and, in fact, did.

But she was a celebrity. And in order to be a successful one, she had to keep all eyes on her. Same holds true for celebrities today. They have to stay in the spotlight or their fame runs out, and they get replaced by the next best thing.

Social media, however, has given everyone an opportunity to be famous. Attention you couldn't dream of getting unless you were a celebrity is now a selfie away. Post a picture, and thousands of strangers will like it. Wear less clothing, and guess what? More likes.

It's more than that though. What about the life you live? I see pictures of people decked out in designer clothes, posted up in some club with fancy drinks—people that I know are dead broke. But they portray themselves as successful because, well, they can. And they get this gratification from people who like and comment on their statuses or pictures.

If you want to love someone, stop seeking attention from everyone because you'll never be satisfied with the attention from one person.

Same holds true for love. Love is supposed to be sacred. You can't love someone when you're preoccupied with worrying about what others think of you. Whether it be posting pictures on social media, buying homes to compete with others, or going on lavish vacations—none of it matters.

5) Social Media Just Invited a Few Thousand People into Bed with You

We've thrown privacy out the window these days. Nothing is sacred anymore, in fact, it's splattered all over the web for the world to see. Everywhere we go, everything we do—made public. Instead of enjoying the moment, we get lost in cyberspace, trying to figure out the best status update, or the perfect filter. Something as simple as enjoying breakfast has become a photo shoot. Vacations are no longer a time to relax, but more a time to post vigorously. You can't just sit back and soak it all in.

There's absolutely nothing wrong with sharing moments of your life. I do it myself. But where do we draw the line? When does it become too much?

We've invited strangers into our homes and brought them on dates with us. We've shown them our wardrobe, drove with them in our cars, and we even showed them our bathing suits. Might as well pack them a suitcase, too.

The worst part about all this? It's only going to get worse.

Immediately, people will assume that my failed marriage is why I am expressing these emotions; that's not the case. It's what I see around me every single day that inspired me to write this article.

Marriage is sacred. It is the most beautiful sacrament and has tremendous promise for those fortunate enough to experience it. Divorced or not, I am a believer in true love and building a beautiful life with someone. In fact, it's been my dream since I was young.

I hope you never experience the demise of your love. It's painful, and life changing; something nobody should ever feel. I do fear, however, that the world we live in today has put roadblocks in the way of getting there and living a happy life with someone. Some things are in our control, and unfortunately, others are not.

People can agree or disagree. I'm perfectly okay with that.

Critical Thinking

1. The author states in the very beginning of the article "Marriages today just don't work." Do you agree or disagree with him? Why?
2. The article considers five stresses and strains which the author feels contribute to the failure of modern marriages. Evaluate each, considering their role in developing, maintaining, and dissolving relationships in the modern world.
3. Where do you feel marriage is going as a social institution? What are roadblocks to lifelong love and commitment with another person and how might they be overcome?

Internet References

National Healthy Marriage Resource Center
http://www.healthymarriageinfo.org/index.aspx

Psychology Today: Divorce
https://www.psychologytoday.com/basics/divorce

Two of Us
http://www.twoofus.org

ANTHONY **D'AMBROSIO**, 29, of Wall has built a large following after the success of his relationship columns that regularly appear on these pages. Today, he discusses why marriages just don't work for people of his generation. D'Ambrosio is now divorced after getting married in 2012.

Article

Prepared by: Patricia Hrusa Williams, *University of Maine at Farmington*

Family Matters

What's the Most Important Factor Blocking Social Mobility? Single Parents, Suggests a New Study.

W. Bradford Wilcox

Learning Outcomes

After reading this article, you will be able to:

- Identify community and family factors associated with social mobility in the United States.
- Describe how single parenthood may be linked with other factors that limit children's later economic outcomes.

Next week, in his State of the Union address, President Obama is expected to return to a theme he and many progressives have been hitting hard in recent months: namely, that the American Dream is in trouble and that growing economic inequality is largely to blame. In a speech to the Center for American Progress last month, Obama said: "The combined trends of increased inequality and decreasing mobility pose a fundamental threat to the American Dream." Likewise, [The] *New York Times* columnist Paul Krugman recently wrote that the nation "claims to reward the best and brightest regardless of family background" but in practice shuts out "children of the middle and working classes."

Progressives like Obama and Krugman are clearly right to argue that the American Dream is in trouble. Today, poor children have a limited shot at moving up the economic ladder into the middle or upper class. One study found that the nation leaves 70 percent of poor children below the middle class as adults. Equally telling, poor children growing up in countries like Canada and Denmark have a greater chance of moving up the economic ladder than do poor children from the United States. As Obama noted, these trends call into question the "American story" that our nation is exceptionally successful in delivering equal opportunity to its citizens.

But the more difficult question is: Why? What are the factors preventing poor children from getting ahead? An important new Harvard study that looks at the best community data on mobility in America—released this past weekend—suggests a cause progressives may find discomforting, especially if they are interested in reviving the American Dream for the 21st century.

The study, "Where is the Land of Opportunity?: The Geography of Intergenerational Mobility in the United States," authored by Harvard economist Raj Chetty and colleagues from Harvard and Berkeley, explores the community characteristics most likely to predict mobility for lower-income children. The study specifically focuses on two outcomes: absolute mobility for lower-income children—that is, how far up the income ladder they move as adults; and relative mobility—that is, how far apart children who grew up rich and poor in the same community end up on the economic ladder as adults. When it comes to these measures of upward mobility in America, the new Harvard study asks: Which "factors are the strongest predictors of upward mobility in multiple variable regressions"?

1) Family structure. Of all the factors most predictive of economic mobility in America, one factor clearly stands out in their study: family structure. By their reckoning, when it comes to mobility, "the strongest and most robust predictor is the fraction of children with single parents." They find that children raised in communities with high percentages of single mothers are significantly less likely to experience absolute and relative mobility. Moreover, "[c]hildren of married parents also have higher rates of upward mobility if they live in communities with fewer single parents." In other words, as Figure 1 indicates, it looks like a married village is more likely to raise the economic prospects of a poor child.

What makes this finding particularly significant is that this is the first major study showing that rates of single parenthood

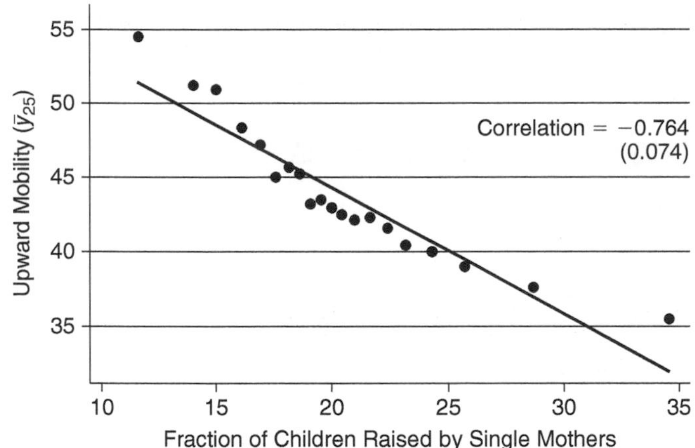

Figure 1 Upward Mobility by Share of Single Mothers in a Community A. Upward Mobility vs. Fraction Single Mothers in CZ

Source: Chetty et al. 2014

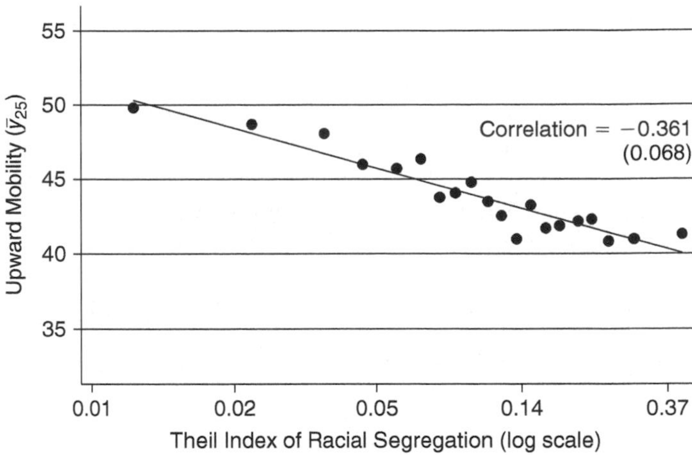

Figure 2 Upward Mobility by Racial Segregation in a Community A. Upward Mobility vs. Theil Index of Racial Segregation

Source: Chetty et al. 2014

at the community level are linked to children's economic opportunities over the course of their lives. A lot of research—including new research from the Brookings Institution—has shown us that kids are more likely to climb the income ladder when they are raised by two, married parents. But this is the first study to show that lower-income kids from both single- and married-parent families are more likely to succeed if they hail from a community with lots of two-parent families.

2) Racial and economic segregation. According to this new study, economic and racial segregation are also important characteristics of communities that do not foster economic mobility. Children growing up in communities that are racially segregated, or cluster lots of poor kids together, do not have a great shot at the American Dream. In fact, in their study, racial segregation is one of only two key factors—the other is family structure—that is consistently associated with both absolute and relative mobility in America. Figure 2 illustrates the bivariate association between racial segregation and economic mobility.

3) School quality. Another powerful predictor of absolute mobility for lower-income children is the quality of schools in their communities. Chetty et al. measure this in the study by looking at high-school dropout rates. Their takeaway: Poor kids are more likely to make it in America when they have access to schools that do a good job of educating them.

4) Social capital. In a finding that is bound to warm the heart of their colleague, Harvard political scientist Robert Putnam, Chetty and his team find that communities with more social capital enjoy significantly higher levels of absolute mobility for poor children. That is, communities across America that have high levels of religiosity, civic engagement, and voter involvement are more likely to lift the fortunes of their poorest members.

5) Income inequality. Finally, consistent with the diagnosis of Messrs. Obama and Krugman, Chetty and his team note that income inequality within communities is correlated with lower levels of mobility. However, its predictive power—measured in their study by a Gini coefficient—is comparatively weak: According to their results, in statistical models with all of the five factors they designated as most important, economic inequality was *not* a statistically significant predictor of absolute or relative mobility.

Chetty, who recently won the John Bates Clark Medal for his achievements as an economist under the age of 40, has been careful to stress that this research cannot prove causation—that removing or adding these factors will cause mobility in America. The study also acknowledges that many of these key factors are correlated with one another, such as income inequality and the share of single mothers in a community. This means that economic inequality may degrade the two-parent family *or* that increases in single parenthood may increase economic inequality. But what does seem clear from this study of the "land[s] of opportunity" in America is that communities characterized by a thriving middle class, racial and economic integration, better schools, a vibrant civil society, and, especially, strong two-parent families are more likely to foster the kind of equality of opportunity that has recently drawn the attention of Democrats and Republicans alike.

Throughout his presidency, Barack Obama has stressed his commitment to data-driven decision-making, not ideology. Similarly, progressives like Krugman have stressed their scientific bona fides, as against the "anti-science" right. If progressives like the president and the Nobel laureate are serious about reviving the fortunes of the American Dream in the 21st century in light of the data, this new study suggests they will need to take pages from *both* left and right playbooks on matters ranging from zoning to education reform. More fundamentally, these new data indicate that any effort to revive opportunity in America must run through two arenas where government has only limited power—civil society and the American family. This is a tall order, to be sure, but unless President Obama, and progressives more generally, can enlist a range of political, civic, business, and cultural leaders—not to mention parents—in this undertaking, this new study suggests they will not succeed in achieving one of their most cherished goals: reviving America as a "land of opportunity."

Critical Thinking

1. How do you think growing up in a community with many single-parent families influences children's development, experiences, and future aspirations?
2. Why can't we say single parenthood causes children to remain mired in the cycle of poverty and unable to achieve social mobility?
3. What types of interventions and supports are needed to assist the children of single-parent families and those who reside in communities where single parents predominate?

Internet References

Child Trends
http://www.childtrends.org

Fragile Families and Child Wellbeing Study, Princeton and Columbia Universities
http://www.fragilefamilies.princeton.edu

World Family Map
http://worldfamilymap.org/2014/about

W. Bradford Wilcox is director of the National Marriage Project and a visiting scholar at the American Enterprise Institute. Follow him on Twitter.

Article Prepared by: Patricia Hrusa Williams, *University of Maine at Farmington*

The New Nuclear Family

What Gay Marriage Means for the Future of Parenthood.

SUZY KHIMM

Learning Outcomes

After reading this article, you will be able to:

- Explain the *Obergefell v. Hodges* ruling and its implications.
- Understand the challenges experienced by same-sex families.
- Discuss factors how we define family.

Just days after Shawn Davis and Richard Sawyers were married in September 2011, they started planning to have kids. "You started asking fast," Davis said, looking over at his husband. "Was it even on the honeymoon?"

"I think it was," Sawyers replied, recalling their time in Venice. We were sitting on the couch of their home in Washington, DC, in Brightwood, near the border of Maryland. Their two-year-old son, Levi, whom they adopted at birth, was napping upstairs.

The two had talked about parenthood for years before their honeymoon and had even taken a workshop that laid out the different paths to becoming parents: private adoption, public foster-care adoption, and surrogacy. But for Sawyers, tradition mattered. "It was important to be married and to be a family unit—I wanted that to happen first," he said.

The same was true for the Wesoleks, whom I met on the steps of the Supreme Court in June on the day that gay marriage became legal nationwide. "Other people do it in different orders, but for us it was get married, buy a house, have a baby," Danielle Wesolek told me. She and her wife, Amy Wesolek, moved to Maryland, got two Boston terriers, and then had their daughter, Lena, who's now 18 months old.

The landmark ruling in *Obergefell v. Hodges* paves the way for other same-sex couples to follow their lead. Most states permit only married couples or unmarried individuals to adopt, and some have laws that give married couples preference. If couples want to hire a surrogate to carry their child, many states require that they be hitched.

Prior to the Supreme Court's decision, the path to parenthood for gay couples was much more complicated. In states that prohibited same-sex marriage, couples could pursue single-parent adoption. But that allowed only one parent to be recognized legally; in the event of the illness, death, or separation of that parent, children could be removed from their families. Schools, hospitals, and other institutions could deny nonlegal parents the ability to make decisions about their children.

This shaky legal footing forced same-sex parents to seek various workarounds to protect their relationships with their children—drawing up paperwork like co-parenting or custody agreements. In 15 states and Washington, DC, individuals can petition for "second-parent" adoption of children who were conceived through assisted reproduction or adopted. It can be costly and time-consuming—frequently involving lawyers, criminal background checks, and a home study by a social worker—which can feel particularly invasive for new mothers and fathers who already consider themselves to be the parents of their children.

Even in states that recognized same-sex marriage, couples sought additional protection for when they traveled to areas of the country that didn't recognize their unions. When the Wesoleks went to South Carolina in May, they made sure to pack the paperwork confirming Danielle's parental status. "The thing that freaked me out was that this could be all down to one person—this could be down to one judge that said, 'You know what, I'm going to take a stand,'" said Amy Wesolek, Lena's birth mother, who conceived her through a sperm donor.

Obergefell has alleviated some of these anxieties and lowered the legal barriers to parenthood. Married gay couples are now allowed to adopt jointly in nearly every state, according to Emily Hecht-McGowan, director of public policy at Family Equality Council, an LGBT advocacy group. In June, a federal judge in Utah ordered that married lesbian couples who use sperm donors be recognized as legal mothers from birth, the same as with straight parents.

The decision hasn't cleared away all of the legal obstacles to same-sex parenthood, though. Michigan, Virginia, and North Dakota still allow child-welfare agencies to prohibit gay couples from adopting or fostering children for religious reasons. Mississippi prohibits same-sex couples from adopting altogether. And despite the ruling in Utah, there's still no guarantee in other states that couples using sperm donors will be automatically recognized as parents. States that allow surrogacy often lack clear laws delineating parental rights, and courts have repeatedly granted them to surrogate mothers over same-sex parents.

But there will be growing pressure to dismantle such barriers as same-sex marriage and parenthood become mainstream. "One of the reasons [same-sex] couples haven't been adopting is because they didn't have confidence in the system and the legality of it," said April Dinwoodie of the Donaldson Adoption Institute, a research and policy group. The Supreme Court's decision has proven to be reassuring: Post-*Obergefell*, one of the country's biggest surrogacy agencies is reporting a spike in interest from newly engaged and married LGBT couples.

So will same-sex parents simply become the new beacons of old family values? In his *Obergefell* decision, Supreme Court Justice Anthony Kennedy proclaimed that marriage is essential to parenthood and child-rearing. "Without the recognition, stability, and predictability marriage offers, children suffer the stigma of knowing their families are somehow lesser," his decision reads.

Danielle Wesolek jokes that she feels like an "old man Republican" when she talks to her younger brother, who's straight and had his first child around the same time as she did. "Don't you think you ought to be married?" she tells him. And that's what gay conservatives had hoped for in their push for gay marriage. "The intent of same-sex marriage is not to establish new family structures but to reaffirm the old one," writer Jonathan Rauch said in a 2004 talk at the University of Michigan.

But the rise of LGBT families could also affirm a more expansive and progressive notion of what it means to be a parent. As gay men and women come out earlier in life, fewer will have children from previous heterosexual relationships. As a matter of necessity, most gay parents have to use outside help—a donor, a surrogate, or adoption agency—to bring children into their lives. That's affirmed a model of parenting built on relationships, support, and commitment rather than on biology or predetermined gender roles. "We will have no choice but to see the law eventually evolve with us, and we are going to see an increased, expanding definition of who makes a family and what families look like," Hecht-McGowan said.

Those differences should be recognized and respected—not overlooked. Writer Andrew Solomon, who has a young son, recounted in the *New Statesman* how he and his husband are still asked "which of us is the mom," comparing his experience to a single mother being asked what it's like to be "both mom and dad."

"All men are created equal but not identical. New family structures are different from mainstream ones," he wrote. "We are not lesser, but we are not the same, and to deny the nuance of that asymmetry is to keep us almost as ensnared as we were when our marriages and families were impossible."

The nuclear family as ideal is itself a historical artifact that rose to greatest prominence in the 1950s, when psychologists encouraged couples to abandon their friendships to focus on their families, explains marriage historian Stephanie Coontz, whose work Kennedy cited in his opinion. "In the long run, it harms your ability to call on a larger network of social support that you might need personally from the stresses of life and that your family needs," Coontz told me. "The problem with elevating [the nuclear family] as the source of all of your strength is that it almost by definition is too small to carry all of life's burdens."

Even as people like Justice Kennedy praise the virtues of marriage and a two-parent household, the old nuclear ideal is already a fiction. Only 46 percent of children now live with married heterosexual parents, and a "record share of Americans have never married," according to Pew Research. "Legalizing same-sex marriage continues a trend toward more complex family relationships," said sociologist Andrew Cherlin of Johns Hopkins University. "We're becoming related to more and more people to whom we owe less and less."

Gay parenting simply adds another layer of complexity to what's already a diverse picture. In his book *Modern Families*, sociologist Joshua Gamson explains the ways that assisted reproductive technology and adoption have challenged traditional notions of kinship: A lesbian couple teamed up with a gay couple to adopt two children; a woman carried a child conceived from her partner's egg and a sperm donor. Gamson also tells his story. His first daughter was conceived through an egg donated by one friend and carried by another. His second daughter was born through a privately hired surrogate.

Our notions of what constitutes a family continue to expand and evolve: Already, open adoptions have become more popular for adoptive parents, gay and straight. When Levi's birth mother discovered she was having a boy, she personally called Davis and Sawyers to tell them. They save every text message and e-mail they receive from her to pass on one day to their son. So far, his birth mother hasn't taken up their invitation to see him, but they told her she'd always be welcome. "It's important for him to know where he comes from, to know who his people are, to know what that foundation is," said Sawyers. "As a parent, I'm going to do everything I can to foster that relationship."

With gay marriage now legal across the country, such complexity will become increasingly mainstream, making it harder to settle on a simple definition of what makes a family. "The challenges to the more conventional notions of kinship are going to come up more and more," Gamson told me. "There's just going to be more of us."

Critical Thinking

1. What is the *Obergefell v. Hodges* ruling and how has it influenced same-sex couples' paths to parenthood?
2. The article states that "The traditional view of what constitutes a family is already fiction" (p. 9). Explain what this means. How would you define the term "family"? Why?
3. Is same-sex marriage just a new take on the married two-parent family paradigm or is it creating something completely different? How and why are these paradigms the same? How are they different?

Internet References

LGBT Parenting in the U.S.: Williams Institute at the UCLA School of Law
https://williamsinstitute.law.ucla.edu/research/census-lgbt-demographics-studies/lgbt-parenting-in-the-united-states/

National Conference of State Legislators: Same-sex Marriage Laws By State
http://www.ncsl.org/research/human-services/same-sex-marriage.aspx

Obergefell v. Hodges Law Case
https://www.supremecourt.gov/opinions/14pdf/14-556_3204.pdf

Same-sex Couples in the U.S.: U.S. Census Bureau
https://www.census.gov/topics/families/same-sex-couples.html

Suzy Khimm is a journalist based in Washington, DC, and a former staff writer for the *New Republic, MSNBC, and The Washington Post.*

Article

Prepared by: Patricia Hrusa Williams, *University of Maine at Farmington*

Bridging Cultural Divides: The Role and Impact of Binational Families

SAMANTHA N.N. CROSS AND MARY C. GILLY

Learning Outcomes

After reading this article, you will be able to:

- Define the term "binational family."
- Explain trends and changes in the demographic composition of U.S. families.
- Understand how immigration, culture, and intermarriage influences family decision making.

The press has given considerable attention recently to what unites diverse groups within or between countries—groups separated by culture, ideology, race, religion, or economic status. Much of this talk has stemmed from the unique background of President Barack Obama (the product of a binational relationship), often presented as the rare candidate who could bridge barriers of race, culture, ideology, and party. However, the discourse is primarily at a macro level. In politics, as in marketing, it is often overlooked that for barriers to truly be breached, change and exchange also must occur at more micro levels. This essay argues that binational families (with partners from different countries) provide an important micro-setting for appreciating marketplace diversity and inclusion and the bridging of cultural divides.

Mélange, hotch-potch, a bit of this and a bit of that is how newness enters the world.

—Rushdie (1990)

Brown (1979) contends that two important changes have happened, at both micro and macro levels, that require a major reorientation in researchers' thinking: the change in the composition and structure of the American family and market globalization. Andreasen (1990, p. 848) also notes that accelerating rates of immigration have a considerable effect on the level of "intranational and international cultural interpenetration." He argues that it is the responsibility of consumer researchers to describe and explain both the nature of cultural interpenetration and the consequences for both the immigrant and the penetrated cultural groups (Andreasen 1990). This is important for both advancement of knowledge and societal benefit.

The foreign-born population in countries worldwide has increased; for example, the United States saw an increase of 85% between 1990 and 2009, from 19.8 million to 36.7 million (U.S. Census Bureau 2010). Similarly, in the United Kingdom, the foreign-born population almost doubled between 1993 and 2011, from 3.8 million to approximately 7.0 million (Rienzo and Vargas-Silva 2012). This growth in the number of immigrants inevitably has an impact on the growth of intermarriages (Bean and Stevens 2003). Yet marketing research studies that examine this notion of cultural interpenetration, though growing, remain limited. More work is needed to explore the nature and consequences of cultural interpenetration, within both the family and society.

In this essay, the driving questions are as follows: What is the role of the binational family and what are the implications for marketplace diversity, inclusion, and creativity? We begin with a brief overview of studies in family decision making and cultural interpenetration. This is followed by a discussion of the role of the binational family as a familial and societal force. We end with implications for marketing, public policy, and society.

Studies in Family Decision Making

Over the past 50 years, research in household decision making has predominantly focused on gender roles in the purchase or consumption of a particular product or service. The emphasis has been on which partner has the most influence, the factors contributing to the differing levels of influence, and how that influence has changed over time (e.g., Belch and Willis 2002; Blood and Wolfe 1960; Commuri and Gentry 2005; Davis and Rigaux 1974; Ford, LaTour, and Henthorne 1995; Qualls 1987; Spiro 1983; Wolfe 1959).

Several theories have evolved to explain the bases of power and influence in the home. Blood and Wolfe's (1960) resource theory proposes that as women became more educated and contributed more income, decision-making processes became more egalitarian. Raven, Centers, and Rodrigues (1975) later applied social power theory, developed by French and Raven (1959), to the family decision-making process. Qualls (1987) concludes that family decision making should be viewed as a network of household relationships rather than as a series of static independent actions. Webster (2000) notes that the particular cultural characteristics of the society determine individual behavior and the type of decision making prevalent in households.

Nevertheless, Commuri and Gentry (2000) insist that the definition of the family must be enlarged, with more studies examining family composition, nontraditional family structures, and cross-cultural comparisons. They note a tendency to emphasize family member characteristics and the effect on relative household influence rather than the characteristics and identity of the household itself. Epp and Price (2008) offer insights into family identity and consumption practices and consider nontraditional family forms, including divorced couples and their children. However, they do not consider binational families, in which members face challenges from the outset with defining and reconciling their disparate identities (Cross and Gilly 2012).

We also argue that it is important to understand how the family functions as a unit or group. While an important foundational knowledge has been developed, the family decision-making literature to date and the critiques of it (Commuri and Gentry 2000; Olsen and Cromwell 1975) have taken a predominantly inward focus. The emphasis has been on the internal impact of influence strategies, decision processes, and identity on household purchase choices. Yet given the importance of the family as a key social and consumption unit (Davis 1970), researchers also must appreciate the wider role of evolving nontraditional family units within diverse societies. We address this gap by examining the role and influence of the binational family.

In addition, in studies of the family or household, researchers draw parallels between the family and other social or structured groups. The family is often described as an institution (Laslett 1973): a collective entity with members who participate and contribute within and outside its social structure or system. Researchers discuss issues of household production, family dynamics, decision-making roles, responsibilities and tasks, housework, conflict, management of domestic labor, expertise, resource allocation, and influence strategies (Commuri and Gentry 2000, 2005). Researchers tend to view spousal relations as partnerships and the family as a unit whose members engage in family planning. The family as an entity also goes through different stages, described as the family life cycle (Gilly and Enis 1982; Murphy and Staples 1979; Wagner and Hanna 1983). These parallels allow additional analogies between the inclusive role of binational families and diversity inclusion in other settings.

Studies in Cultural Interpenetration

While the family decision-making literature has considered culture (Davis and Rigaux 1974; Ford, LaTour, and Henthorne 1995; Green et al. 1983; Wallendorf and Reilly 1983; Webster 1994, 2000), it mainly makes comparisons of culturally homogeneous households in one country with culturally homogeneous households in another country. This research indicates that culture affects family decision-making styles, but it offers little insight into cultural differences *within* families (Cross 2007). Research on immigrants bringing their own culture to another country is also fairly common in consumer behavior, marketing, anthropology, and sociology research. However, this cultural interpenetration research focuses on the individual and/or group experience rather than the experience of two cultures within one household.

Stewart (1999, pp. 40–41) argues that anthropology researchers' increased interest in cultural interpenetration has resulted in critiques of earlier views of "'culture' that cast it as too stable, bounded, and homogeneous to be useful in a world characterized by migrations (voluntary or forced), cheap travel, international marketing, and telecommunications." He suggests that cultural interpenetration and borrowing are now viewed as "part of the very nature of cultures" because of their porousness. Although the studies he cites involve subgroups navigating the majority culture (e.g., Anglo-Indians in Madras), his conclusion that syncretism (mixing of different beliefs) is not eliminated as assimilation occurs suggests that cultural mixing occurs at the binational household level. Craig and Douglas (2006) go further to advocate that cultural mixing enriches both cultures. Thus, we infer that families also benefit from cultural mixing.

Appadurai (1990) identifies five global "flows" that affect cultural interpenetration. One, ethnoscapes, is relevant here. He argues that the flow of people (including immigrants, students, and tourists) helps transmit cultural content. Several empirical studies of immigrant groups support this idea. For example, Peñaloza and Gilly (1999) find that Mexican immigrants' consumption behavior is affected by living in the United States and that the marketers serving them alter product offerings and ways of doing business.

Immigrants must adopt products and practices in their country of residence, but research indicates that they are not wholly assimilated and keep some of their own cultural traditions, adopt some traditions of the host culture, and combine cultures in creative ways (Oswald 1999). While studies of immigrants reveal that most intend to return to their native country (Oswald 1999; Peñaloza 1994), intermarriage makes such a return much less likely. Thus, while immigrants in binational relationships may share some attributes with other immigrants, if they live in their partner's country, they are expected to establish deeper roots within that culture.

The Role of Binational Families

In this essay, the term "binational family" refers to a family with partners born and raised in different countries of origin. Several other terms are also prevalent in the literature (e.g., "bicultural," "biethnic," "interethnic"). "Bicultural" often refers to a person's ability to comfortably navigate life in two different cultures and implies familiarity with the language and customs in two different cultural contexts (e.g., Lau-Gesk 2003; Luna, Ringberg, and Peracchio 2008). In a binational family, at least one of the partners is an immigrant to the country of residence and is considered bicultural. Similarly, "biethnic" or "interethnic" specifically refer to familiarity within, or a combination of, two different ethnic groups (i.e., a crossing of ethnic lines), even for participants born and reared in the same country (Alba and Nee 2003; Freeman 1955). Binational families may also be biethnic or biracial, which refers to the crossing of racial boundaries. We focus on the dynamics within the binational family—dynamics that often encompass the nuances of other mixed families, whether bicultural, biethnic, or biracial.

As a unit comprising family members with ties both within and outside their country of residence, the binational family, and the individual partners within the family, play an intermediary role. They provide a conjugal and communal link between different cultural norms and perspectives. Through that link, each partner also gains access and exposure to the history, traditions, social norms, and consumption experiences of the country from which his or her partner originated. When the family resides in the native country of one of the spouses, this connection is particularly important for the immigrant spouse trying to navigate the vagaries of an unfamiliar host culture. Meng and Gregory (2005) argue that the immigrant spouse gains an economic labor advantage through intermarriage—an "intermarriage premium." Cross and Gilly (2012) also posit that the native spouse functions as a cultural intermediary and navigator for the immigrant spouse. Although Wamwara-Mbugua (2007) did not study binationals, she finds that Kenyan immigrant couples delegated initial decision making to the spouse who had been in the United States longer, even when it conflicted with traditional Kenyan gender roles. Lauth Bacas (2002) notes that cross-border marriage partners perform the role of gatekeeper to each cultural context. This gatekeeping role moves beyond that of the "kinkeeper"—the role ascribed to the individual family member responsible for maintaining kinship ties (Leach and Brathwaite 1996; Rosenthal 1985). Although not explored in this essay, the kin-keeping role in binational families should be inherently more complex, given the cross-cultural dynamics.

However, the influence goes beyond the household. The binational family unit is often viewed as atypical or novel, inciting curiosity and drawing attention from the wider community in which the family resides. This, and other nontraditional family structures, may initially exacerbate cultural and societal divides, leading to negative consequences such as prejudice, stigmatization, and even threat. Yet we argue that, over time, the increased presence of binational and other culturally heterogeneous families eventually provides a starting point for greater tolerance and appreciation of voluntarily formed diverse unions. These families allow people with disparate backgrounds to meet and exchange perspectives. This cultural exchange provides opportunities for growth in knowledge and understanding, to enhance the range of experiences, and to create new customs and novel consumption relationships.

The Binational Family as Bridge, Broker, and Boundary Spanner

The exposure gained through the marriage of people with differing cultural backgrounds affects the entire unit—the partners, children, and members of family and social networks, as well as the surrounding community. In the management innovation literature, several terms have been used to describe people who provide a link between different individuals, groups, and experiences.

Wasserman and Faust (1994, p. 114) describe one of these terms, "bridge," as a "critical tie" and note that "the removal of a bridge leaves more [disparate] components than when the bridge is included." Lin (1999) highlights the importance and usefulness of accessing and extending bridges in networks to obtain missing resources and facilitate information and influence flows. Another metaphor is that of a "broker." Hargadon and Sutton (1997, p. 716) note that the product design firm IDEO acts as a technology broker by introducing unknown solutions and creating new products "that are original combinations of existing knowledge from disparate industries." The authors also distinguish the firm acting as technology broker and the engineers within IDEO, who themselves act as "individual technology brokers." Williams (2002) uses the term "boundary spanner" to describe people who manage across divides. He believes that more focus is needed on the nature and behavior of these boundary spanners, also described as "diversity seekers" (Brumbaugh and Grier 2013), constructs that should be explored within different institutional and contextual situations.

These terms ("bridge," "broker," "boundary spanner," and "diversity seeker") refer to the person who is able to link otherwise disconnected groups. Individual members of binational families *do* play key parts in maintaining harmonious and continuous links between family members in the different cultures. However, we argue that *both* the binational family unit and its members play a similar structural and symbolic role in binding disparate families, networks, cultures, and communities. In the binational family structure, the union itself, not just a single person, functions as "a bridge between cultures," allowing cultural exchange between the partners, who are themselves cultural bridges (Lauth Bacas 2002). This unconventional union of culturally dissimilar partners unifies the two cultures and support structures of the partners in different countries. Prior existence of this link is slim to unlikely, given the geographical, cultural, and other boundaries between the partners. Thus, in the early stages of the household, this central position is unifying. As time passes and the partnership and families evolve, the link persists, even if the binational household dissolves. This is a bridge that binds and is practically irrevocable, particularly when children result. Thus, the impact of the binational union is pervasive and inclusive as social and family networks become interconnected.

The Binational Family as a Venue for Creative Consumption

Foner (1997, p. 961) notes that first-generation immigrants who relocate from one county to another "fuse . . . the old and the new to create a new kind of family life." Foner, a sociologist, points out that for these immigrants, the family is a place where "creative culture-building takes place." In the lingusitics literature, Baron and Cara (2003, pp. 6–7) describe a similar process as the "creative response" of people encountering one another and new situations. They refer to this as a creolization process that can occur whenever members of different cultures meet in "expressive interaction . . . [allowing] us to see cultural encounters as a process of continuous creative exchange." This process is often central to the maintenance and evolution of society.

As a unit in which cultural encounters occur daily, the binational family can also be viewed as a unique setting for creative culture building. It can even be argued that this creative process is vital to the maintenance of harmonious relations within the household and the very longevity of the family unit. Ultimately, the binational family lies at the intersection of the cultures of the two spouses. At this intersection, cross-cultural interactions, unique blending processes, and creative consumption experiences thrive. This cross-fertilization process between the different cultures occurs through conflict and compromise and through simultaneous fusion and diffusion. It eventually leads to a merging of meaning systems, to create new variations that transcend the individual preferences of the spouses. As a deviation from the traditional family structure, in this kind of family, deviation from norms and "inventive combination" (Hargadon and Sutton 1997) most likely occur. This process inevitably extends beyond the binational family unit and has an impact on the diversity of marketplace offerings, societal tolerance for difference, and the cultural flexibility of the surrounding communities.

Implications for Marketing and Public Policy

Binational families are a growing and inevitable phenomenon. This familial structure accommodates diversity and shapes the preferences, choices, experiences, and perspectives of the family members and those whom they encounter. We advocate that the existence of these families offers several societal and public policy implications.

Research suggests that for immigrant spouses, social and economic adaptation is enhanced when immigrants and natives intermarry (Cross and Gilly 2012; Meng and Gregory 2005). This enhanced participation and contribution strengthens the family and the immigrant partner's commitment to and identification with the new home country, which leads to greater engagement in prosocial behaviors. Immigrants who intermarry are also less likely to segregate in immigrant enclaves. Their inclusion in the wider, dominant community has a positive influence on public perception of immigrants, providing an alternate community perspective to national political sensationalism about immigration. Binational families also include same-sex couples. Yet in countries in which same-sex unions are not legally recognized, exclusionary immigration policies continue to be a threat that policy makers must acknowledge.

In communities in which binational and immigrant families co-reside with native families, immigrant spouses may seek marketplace offerings from their home countries. The acquisition of less accessible, preferred items is influenced by and affects export/import laws and customs restrictions. When natives and immigrants intermarry, members of their social networks are also exposed to these items. Norms slowly change about the acceptability and co-consumption of initially novel products with more familiar items. Vendors in these communities can capitalize on increased opportunities to meet changing marketplace expectations with creative product combinations and service experiences. Both partners in binational families also tend to take an active role in food shopping, to meet their differing cultural preferences (Cross and Gilly 2012). This has implications for grocery store vendors, who typically focus their marketing efforts on females and mono-national families, rather than on both genders and culturally mixed families.

Members of binational families, particularly the children, acquire a level of intercultural competence (Demangeot et al. 2013) and flexibility through the ongoing cross-cultural interactions within the home. They thus provide a potential recruitment pool for public and private employers seeking employees to participate in cross-cultural teams, who can lead an increasingly diverse workforce and serve a multicultural domestic and global population.

Conjugal tolerance eventually leads to societal tolerance. The insights gained from studying the processes and interactions within binational families move beyond prior notions of the "melting pot" or "salad bowl" concepts of assimilation, toward more fluid alternatives for harmonious cross-cultural coexistence and the resolution of intercultural conflict. In the United States, policies on individual self-classification on the census and elsewhere have changed. As the presence of binational families expands, so too will other perceptions of normalcy (Baker 2006) evolve, leading to a more dynamic, innovative, inclusive marketplace and global society.

References

Alba, Richard and Victor Nee (2003), *Remaking the American Mainstream.* Cambridge, MA: Harvard University Press.

Andreasen, Alan R. (1990), "Cultural Interpenetration: A Critical Consumer Research Issue for the 1990s," in *Advances in Consumer Research*, Vol. 17, Marvin E. Goldberg, Gerald Gorn, and Richard W. Pollay, eds. Provo, UT: Association for Consumer Research, 847–49.

Appadurai, Arjun (1990), "Disjuncture and Difference in the Global Cultural Economy," in *Media and Cultural Studies*, Meenakshi Gigi Durham and Douglas M. Kellner, eds. Malden, MA: Blackwell.

Baker, Stacy M. (2006), "Consumer Normalcy: Understanding the Value of Shopping Through Narratives of Consumers with Visual Impairments," *Journal of Retailing*, 82 (1), 37–50.

Baron, Robert and Ana C. Cara (2003), "Introduction: Creolization and Folklore—Cultural Creativity in Process," *Journal of American Folklore*, 116 (459), 4–8.

Bean, Frank D. and Gillian Stevens (2003), *America's Newcomers and the Dynamics of Diversity*. New York: Russell Sage Foundation.

Belch, Michael A. and Laura A. Willis (2002), "Family Decision at the Turn of the Century: Has the Changing Structure of Households Impacted the Family Decision-Making Process?" *Journal of Consumer Behaviour*, 2 (2), 111–24.

Blood, Robert O. and Donald Wolfe (1960), *Husbands and Wives.* New York: The Free Press.

Brown, Wilson (1979), "The Family and Consumer Decision Making: A Cultural View," *Journal of the Academy of Marketing Science*, 7 (4), 335–45.

Brumbaugh, Anne M. and Sonya A. Grier (2013), "Agents of Change: A Scale to Identify Diversity Seekers," *Journal of Public Policy & Marketing*, 32 (Special Issue), 144–55.

Commuri, Suraj and James W. Gentry (2000), "Opportunities for Family Research in Marketing," *Academy of Marketing Science Review*, 8 (accessed October 15, 2012), [available at http://www.amsreview.org/articles/commuri08-2000.pdf].

——— and ——— (2005), "Resource Allocation in Households with Women as Chief Wage Earners," *Journal of Consumer Research*, 32 (September), 185–95.

Craig, C. Samuel and Susan P. Douglas (2006), "Beyond National Culture: Implications of Cultural Dynamics for Consumer Research," *International Marketing Review*, 23 (3), 322–42.

Cross, Samantha N.N. (2007), "For Better or for Worse: The Intersection of Cultures in Binational Homes," in *Advances in Consumer Research*, Vol. 35, A.Y. Lee and D. Soman, eds. Duluth, MN: Association for Consumer Research, 162–65.

——— and Mary C. Gilly (2012), "Cultural Competence, Cultural Capital and Cultural Compensatory Mechanisms in Binational Households," working paper, Iowa State University.

Davis, Harry L. (1970), "Dimensions of Marital Roles in Consumer Decision Making," *Journal of Marketing Research*, 7 (May), 168–77.

——— and Benny P. Rigaux (1974), "Perception of Marital Roles in Decision Processes," *Journal of Consumer Research*, 1 (1), 51–62.

Demangeot, Catherine, Natalie Ross Adkins, Rene Dentiste Mueller, Geraldine Rosa Henderson, Nakeisha S. Ferguson, James M. Mandiberg, et al. (2013), "Toward Intercultural Competency in Multicultural Marketplaces," *Journal of Public Policy & Marketing*, 32 (Special Issue), 156–64.

Epp, Amber M. and Linda L. Price (2008), "Family Identity: A Framework of Identity Interplay in Consumption Practices," *Journal of Consumer Research*, 35 (June), 50–70.

Foner, Nancy (1997), "The Immigrant Family: Cultural Legacies and Cultural Changes," *International Migration Review*, 31 (4, Special Issue: Immigrant Adaptation and Native-Born Responses in the Making of Americans), 961–74.

Ford, John B., Michael S. LaTour, and Tony L. Henthorne (1995), "Perception of Marital Roles in Purchase Decision Processes: A Cross-Cultural Study," *Journal of the Academy of Marketing Science*, 23 (2), 120–31.

Freeman, Linton (1955), "Homogamy in Interethnic Mate Selection," *Sociology and Social Research*, 39, 369–77.

French, John R.P., Jr., and Bertram Raven (1959), "The Bases of Social Power," in *Studies in Social Power*, Dorwin Cartwright, ed. Ann Arbor, MI: Research Center for Group Dynamics, Institute for Social Research, University of Michigan, 150–67.

Gilly, Mary C. and Ben M. Enis (1982), "Recycling the Family Life Cycle: A Proposal for Redefinition," *Advances in Consumer Research*, Vol. 9, Andrew Mitchell, ed. Ann Arbor: Association for Consumer Research, 271–76.

Green, Robert T., Jean-Paul Leonardi, Jena-Louis Chandon, Isabella C.M. Cunningham, Bronis Verhage, and Alain Strazzieri (1983), "Societal Development and Family Purchasing Roles: A Cross-National Study," *Journal of Consumer Research*, 9 (March), 436–42.

Hargadon, Andrew and Robert I. Sutton (1997), "Technology Brokering and Innovation in a Product Development Firm," *Administrative Science Quarterly*, 42 (4), 716–49.

Laslett, Barbara (1973), "The Family as a Public and Private Institution: An Historical Perspective," *Journal of Marriage and the Family*, 35 (3, Special Section: New Social History of the Family), 480–92.

Lau-Gesk, Loraine G. (2003), "Activating Culture Through Persuasion Appeals: An Examination of the Bicultural Consumer," *Journal of Consumer Psychology*, 13 (3), 301–315.

Lauth Bacas, Jutta (2002), "Cross-Border Marriages and the Formation of Transnational Families: A Case Study of Greek–German Couples in Athens," Transnational Communities Programme Working Paper Series (accessed October 15, 2012), [available at www.transcomm.ox.ac.uk/working%20papers/WPTC-02-10%20Bacas.pdf].

Leach, Margaret S. and Dawn O. Brathwaite (1996), "A Binding Tie: Supportive Communication of Family Kinkeepers," *Journal of Applied Communication Research*, 24 (3), 200–216.

Lin, Nan (1999), "Building a Network Theory of Social Capital," *Connections*, 22 (1), 28–51.

Luna, David, Torsten Ringberg, and Laura A. Peracchio (2008), "One Individual, Two Identities: Frame Switching Among Biculturals," *Journal of Consumer Research*, 35 (2), 279–93.

Meng, Xin and Robert G. Gregory (2005), "Intermarriage and the Economic Assimilation of Immigrants," *Journal of Labor Economics*, 23 (1), 135–75.

Murphy, Patrick E. and William A. Staples (1979), "A Modernized Family Life Cycle," *Journal of Consumer Research*, 6 (1), 12–22.

Olson, David H. and Ronald E. Cromwell (1975), "Methodological Issues in Family Power," in *Power in Families*, Ronald E. Cromwell and David H. Olson, eds. New York: Sage Publications, 131–50.

Oswald, Laura R. (1999), "Culture Swapping: Consumption and the Ethnogenesis of Middle-Class Haitian Immigrants," *Journal of Consumer Research*, 25 (March), 303–318.

Peñaloza, Lisa N. (1994), "Atravesando Fronteras/Border Crossings: A Critical Ethnographic Exploration of the Consumer Acculturation of Mexican Immigrants," *Journal of Consumer Research*, 21 (June), 32–54.

——— and Mary C. Gilly (1999), "Marketer Acculturation: The Changer and the Changed," *Journal of Marketing*, 63 (July), 84–104.

Qualls, William J. (1987), "Household Decision Behavior: The Impact of Husbands' and Wives' Sex Role Orientation," *Journal of Consumer Research*, 14 (2), 264–79.

Raven, Bertram H., Richard Centers, and Aroldo Rodrigues (1975), "The Bases of Conjugal Power," in *Power in Families*, Ronald E. Cromwell and David H. Olson, eds. New York: Sage Publications, 217–32.

Rienzo, Cinzia and Carlos Vargas-Silva (2012), "Migrants in the UK: An Overview," *The Migration Observatory*, (May 15), (accessed June 30, 2012), [available at http://migrationobservatory.ox.ac.uk/briefings/migrants-uk-overview].

Rosenthal, Carolyn J. (1985), "Kinkeeping in the Familial Division of Labor," *Journal of Marriage and Family*, 47 (4), 965–74.

Rushdie, Salman (1990), *In Good Faith.* London: Granta.

Spiro, Rosann L. (1983), "Persuasion in Family Decision-Making," *Journal of Consumer Research*, 9 (4), 393–402.

Stewart, Charles (1999), "Syncretism and Its Synonyms: Reflections on Cultural Mixture," *Diacritics*, 29 (Autumn), 40–62.

U.S. Census Bureau (2010), "2010 Census Data," [available at http://www.census.gov/2010census/data].

Wagner, Janet and Sherman Hanna (1983), "The Effectiveness of Family Life Cycle Variables in Consumer Expenditure Research," *Journal of Consumer Research*, 10 (3), 281–91.

Wallendorf, Melanie and Michael D. Reilly (1983), "Ethnic Migration, Assimilation, and Consumption," *Journal of Consumer Research*, 10 (3), 292–302.

Wamwara-Mbugua, L. Wakiuru (2007), "An Investigation of Household Decision Making Among Immigrants," in *Advances in Consumer Research*, Vol. 34, Gavan Fitzsimons and Vicki Morwitz, eds. Valdosta, GA: Association for Consumer Research, 180–86.

Wasserman, Stanley and Katherine Faust (1994), *Social Network Analysis*. Cambridge, UK: Cambridge University Press.

Webster, Cynthia (1994), "Effects of Hispanic Ethnic Identification on Marital Roles in the Purchase Decision-Process," *Journal of Consumer Research*, 21 (2), 319–31.

——— (2000), "Is Spousal Decision Making a Culturally Situated Phenomenon?" *Psychology & Marketing*, 17 (12), 1035–58.

Williams, Paul (2002), "The Competent Boundary Spanner," *Public Administration*, 80 (1), 103–124.

Wolfe, Donald M. (1959), "Power and Authority in the Family," in *Studies in Social Power*, Dorwin Cartwright, ed. Ann Arbor, MI: Research Center for Group Dynamics, Institute for Social Research, University of Michigan, 99–117.

Critical Thinking

1. Why do you think the authors have chosen to use the term "binational family" instead of referring to these families using some other terms mentioned in the article such as bicultural, biethnic, or interethnic?
2. How do you think being a binational family influences family dynamics and interactions between couples and family members?
3. What are special considerations and things to keep in mind when working with binational families?

Internet References

Family and Culture
http://familyandculture.com/index.html

World Fact Book
https://www.cia.gov/library/publications/the-world-factbook

World Family Map
http://worldfamilymap.org/2014/about

Samantha N.N. Cross is Assistant Professor of Marketing, College of Business, Iowa State University.

Mary C. Gilly is Professor of Marketing, Paul Merage School of Business, University of California, Irvine. Financial support to the first author through the Ray Watson Doctoral Fellowship at the University of California, Irvine; the Academy of Marketing Science Jane K. Fenyo Best Paper Award for Student Research; and the ACR/Sheth Foundation Dissertation Grant is gratefully acknowledged.

Cross, Samantha N.N.; Gilly, Mary C. "Bridging Cultural Divides: The Role and Impact of Binational Families." From *Journal of Public Policy and Marketing,* vol. 32, May 2013, pp. 106–111.

Article

Prepared by: Patricia Hrusa Williams, *University of Maine at Farmington*

Migration and Families Left Behind

Families that Stay Behind when a Member Migrates do not Clearly Benefit.

SYLVIE DÉMURGER

Learning Outcomes

After reading this article, you will be able to:

- Define terms including labor migration and remittances.
- Explain the pros and cons of labor migration for both the worker and the family that stays behind.
- Identify potential supports needed by families when labor migration occurs.

About a billion people worldwide live and work outside their country of birth or outside their region of birth within their own country. Labor migration is conventionally viewed as economically benefiting the family members who are left behind through remittances. However, splitting up families in this way may also have multiple adverse effects on education, health, labor supply response, and social status for family members who do not migrate. Identifying the causal impact of migration on those who are left behind remains a challenging empirical question with inconclusive evidence.

Introduction

The number of people migrating from their country of origin or from one region to another within it has been growing dramatically in recent decades. The UN estimates that about 232 million people live and work outside their country of birth and that 763 million people live and work outside their region of birth within their home country. Since 2000, the international migrant stock has been growing faster than the total world population, and it now accounts for 3.2 percent of the world population.

International migrants and internal migrants together account for one in seven people worldwide. These migrants do not always move with their entire family. More often, they leave the rest of their family behind: their spouse, children, and parents. Rigid migration policies, uncertain living conditions in the destination country or region, and the high cost of migration are among the reasons why many people migrate alone. In China, individuals who have migrated from rural areas to cities have left behind an estimated 61 million children, 47 million wives, and 45 million elderly relatives [1]. In the Philippines, one of the largest sources of migrant laborers worldwide, around nine million children are growing up without at least one of their parents because of migration.

The impact of migration on sending communities, especially on family members left behind, has long been debated. On the one hand, labor migration is viewed as economically benefiting the family in the home country through financial transfers. Remittances can ease liquidity and budget constraints and thereby improve households' long-term welfare through investments in health care and education. On the other hand, many studies have pointed out the social cost that migration imposes on families left behind. In particular, the physical absence of the migrant may have multiple adverse effects on family members' education, health, labor supply response, and social status. Thus, identifying the impact of migration on family members who remain is an open empirical question with inconclusive evidence.

Discussion of Pros and Cons

The Main Channels: Remittances and Household Time Allocation

When people migrate for work, the groups that are most likely to be left behind are women, children, and the elderly. Two primary mechanisms associated with migration can affect those staying behind. Most important, the migration of a family member usually brings additional income to the family through remittances and can therefore ease the budget constraint for family members in the home country or region. In particular, the income effect can enable larger investments in education and health care, create new opportunities to invest in businesses, and raise the reservation wage (the lowest wage at which a person is willing to accept a job) of family members who remain behind. Yet migration also entails the absence of an economically active family member and the loss of that member's time inputs to both market and household production. In particular, this absence may translate into disrupted personal care for dependent family members, including children and the elderly, and a greater burden of responsibility for work and household chores among family members. The forgone market and household production (including both labor force participation and care) may be substantial and may outweigh the gains from remittances. Since these two mechanisms work in opposite directions, the impact of migration on family members left behind can only be determined empirically.

Another dimension to consider when assessing the relationship between migration and the family left behind is the duration of migration [2]. The expected impact is ambiguous in both the short term and the long term. In the short term, migration may have a disruptive effect on the family because of reduced inputs to market and household production. As migration is costly and does not necessarily lead to immediate employment at destination, it may even translate into reduced income for the family that has to finance the migrant. In the long term, the forgone market and household production may be compensated for by a reallocation of labor among family members who stay behind. Yet, whether financial transfers rise or fall with the duration of migration is uncertain. Long-term migrants are likely to earn a higher income and as a consequence may be able to afford to send larger remittances. However, their commitment to their family may weaken over time, leading to reduced financial transfers.

Thus, the impact of migration on the family in the home country or community is complex, multichanneled, and context-dependent. It ultimately depends on who migrates and who is left behind (gender and age are key dimensions here) and on the duration of migration. Given the complexity of the relationship, empirical studies are needed to clarify a net impact that is ambiguous a priori.

Measuring the Causal Impact of Migration Is Challenging

Empirical work is made possible by the availability of household survey data that account for internal and international migration flows. The standard research strategy is to compare outcomes of interest for migrant-sending households and for nonmigrant-sending households. But there are important methodological problems that may limit the scope of the findings and to some extent explain their inconclusiveness. The main difficulty arises from the fact that migration is a choice variable, which plagues the empirical literature with important selection and reverse causality problems.

Selection bias, which complicates analyses of migration, can arise for a number of reasons: individuals (or households) are not randomly selected but self-select into migration; they choose how many family members will migrate; they choose when to migrate and for how long (including whether to return); and they choose whether to send remittances and how much to send. In this context, omitted variables that are correlated with both the migration decision and its outcomes for family members who are left behind may cause endogeneity problems and bias estimates of the impact of migration on the family left behind [2]. For instance, wealthier households may be able to afford to send family members abroad for work and still have enough money to pay for the education or health care expenses of the rest of the family. In that case, comparing migrant-sending households with nonmigrant-sending households may capture differences in wealth rather than the effect of migration. In addition, endogeneity may also result from reverse causalities between some of the outcomes of interest and migration. Because parental health can be part of the migration cost, having parents in poor health may outweigh the economic benefit of migration and may therefore reduce the likelihood that their children will migrate. A careful identification strategy that takes into account this possible reverse causality is required in order to estimate the causal impact of children's migration on parental health.

. . .

Evidence of the Impacts on Education

The impact of migration on the school attainment and education performance of children left behind is the most documented dimension of the link between migration and the family left behind. One difficulty in measuring this impact is that parental migration is likely to be correlated with unobserved factors that may also explain the education outcomes of the children. For instance, if migrants are positively selected (more skilled and educated than the average person in the home country or community), households with migrants may have stronger preferences for investment in education, in which case the analysis may be identifying the effect of education preferences rather than of migration.

There are several main channels where a parent's migration may affect children's education. On the positive side, remittances sent back home can ease the household budget constraint by making more resources available. As a direct consequence, families have less need of child labor, which frees up children's time for school. On the negative side, the disruption to family life as a result of a parent's migration, especially the lack of a parent's care and supervision, might negatively affect children's school performance.

A third, complementary channel is the possibility of a child's own (future) migration, which might either encourage or discourage a child's education, depending on perceived returns to education in prospective jobs. Studies for Mexico have pointed out that families with higher probabilities of migrating to the US invest less in education, an outcome that is attributed to the low return to Mexican education in the US labor market.

Finally, a parent's migration may lead to a redistribution of decision-making and responsibilities within the household, which can affect child schooling, either because the new decision maker (e.g., the other parent or an older child) cares more or less about investment in education than the migrating parent or because the redistribution of roles puts more pressure on children to help in the household.

The literature offers inconclusive evidence on whether migration has a net positive or net negative impact on education outcomes of children who are left behind [1], [3]. Most empirical studies highlight heterogeneous impacts that depend on the gender, age, and sibling birth order of the children left behind, as well as on the gender of the parent migrant and whether one or both parents are absent.

Focusing on the short-term direct effect of remittances on household decisions, some studies provide evidence of a positive impact of remittances on schooling in the Philippines [4] and in Mexico [5]. Other studies that have assessed the negative consequences of parental absence have found that parental migration increases the probability of a child's dropping out of school and of delayed school progression and has a negative impact on children's school performance.

Evidence for Mexico also reveals gender-based differences [6]. Parental migration significantly increases educational attainment for girls, lowers the probability of boys completing junior high school and of boys and girls completing high school, and, when the migrant was a caregiver, raises the probability that boys and girls will have academic difficulties. For girls, especially in developing countries, the income effect appears to dominate: remittances, by easing family budget constraints, open up greater education opportunities for girls, who are more likely to be deprived of educational investments when family finances are constrained. For older boys, however, alternatives to education, particularly their own migration, tend to overcome the income effect and drive boys away from school.

Evidence of the Impacts on Health

The impact of migration on the health of family members left behind has received relatively little attention. Estimating health effects also faces selection and reverse causality problems. For instance, adult children whose parents are in bad health and in need of care might be less likely to migrate. At the other end of the health spectrum, migrants may share a genetic predisposition to good health with their children and their parents.

The channels through which migration behavior may affect the health and nutrition status of family members left behind are similar to those highlighted for education. In the long term, the income effect of remittances may be large if they contribute to better sanitation, improved food habits, and more health-seeking behaviors. In the short term, migrants may also make up for missing formal health insurance mechanisms by sending larger financial transfers back home when they are needed.

Working in the opposite direction, however, is the household time reallocation necessitated by a migrant's absence, which may negatively affect the health of family members left behind. Family members may have to take on more housework (including farm work in rural areas), may suffer greater psychological pressure, or may eat more poorly, especially in the case of children, because of the absence of the main caregiver. In rural societies, migration may also disrupt traditional kinship systems and care structures, to the detriment of the most vulnerable groups. And as in the case of education, the relationship between migration and the health status of those who are left behind also differs by gender and age.

A growing literature is analyzing the causal effect of parental migration on children's health and nutrition. Migration seems to improve the nutritional status of very young children, measured by birth weight, infant mortality rate, or weight-for-age [7]. However, a study that exploits New Zealand's migration lottery program to capture the causal effect of migration from Tonga finds worse diets and lower height-for-age in the short term among children under the age of 18 who are left behind when a parent migrates compared with children whose parents applied but did not win the migration lottery [8].

Another set of studies, some using careful instrumental variable approaches, has empirically assessed the impact of the migration of adult children on the health of their elderly parents. Again, the evidence is mixed. In both China and Mexico, the migration of adult children has been found to result in lower self-reported health status among elderly parents. In contrast, a study for Moldova finds evidence of a beneficial impact of the migration of adult children on the physical health of elderly family members who stay behind and finds no significant impact on their mental health or cognitive capacity. These findings are attributed mostly to a strong income effect: remittances contribute to a more diversified diet and allow for changes in household time allocation toward more leisure and sleep. If anything, the inconclusiveness of the recent empirical literature on the health effects of migration reveals that whether migration is detrimental or beneficial to the health of those who are left behind is deeply context-dependent.

Evidence on the Labor Supply Response to Migration

As with education and health, migration affects the labor allocation decisions of the family members left behind through two main channels. First, the availability of remittances may change labor supply responses in potentially competing ways. On the one hand, financial transfers from migrants can enable family members who stay behind to enter riskier, higher-return activities by easing household financial constraints. If this effect dominates, then migration will lead to a diversification of economic activities among family members who are left behind and possibly to increased income from local activities in the long term. On the other hand, the increase in disposable income brought by remittances may dampen the incentives to work of nonmigrating family members, in particular if the financial transfers raise the reservation wage of family members and lower the opportunity cost of leisure [9]. In that case, the increase in income from remittances may reduce the labor force participation of family members, and in the long term, it may create dependency on income from remittances.

Second, migration results in the loss of the migrant's local labor, which may strongly constrain the labor supply response of nonmigrating members in the short term. In particular, when labor markets are imperfect, as is typically the case in developing countries, family members who are left behind may not be able to hire labor to compensate for the lost contributions from the migrant. In rural areas, this lost labor may force other family members to increase the time devoted to (subsistence) farming.

In addition to these two main channels, migration may also affect a spouse's labor market participation by affecting productivity in the home. If the inputs of spouses in the home production function are complements, then migration will lower the productivity of the spouse who remains behind; if the inputs are substitutes, the opposite will hold. As is the case for education and health, the net effect of migration on labor supply depends on the relative magnitudes of the remittances-related effect and the lost-labor effect. Moreover, the net effect may vary across different subgroups of people, depending on the age and the gender of the household members, their employment sector, the seasonal or permanent nature of migration, the household's assets, and on how binding liquidity constraints are for the household [10].

Research on the labor supply responses of family members to international migration consistently finds evidence of decreasing labor force participation of women who are left behind, be they Albanian, Egyptian, Mexican, or Nepalese [9]. The only increase in labor supply comes from an increase in unpaid family work and subsistence work, particularly in rural areas. In rural China, internal migration is found to increase farm work for all family members who remain behind (women, the elderly, and children), and return migration does not seem to reverse these labor allocation changes [10].

Evidence of Impacts on Intrafamily Roles and the Transfer of Norms

A straightforward extension of the analysis of the labor supply responses of family members left behind is to investigate the reallocation of intrafamily roles and the possible strengthening of the bargaining power of certain members who stay behind, as this affects decision-making and the control and allocation of resources.

In patriarchal societies, where most migrants are men, migration may influence not only the labor supply in communities of origin but also the position of women who remain behind [11]. In Albania, less educated women in households from which men have migrated are more likely than their peers in households without a male migrant to gain access to remunerative employment, which could empower them to make resource-allocation decisions within the household. Changes in intrafamily roles can also be observed among siblings: in China, older sisters are found to have a positive influence on their younger siblings in households from which a parent has migrated.

Finally, a recent strand of the literature focuses on the transfer of norms, looking in particular at how political norms and behavior at home change with migration. Migrants may transfer not only financial resources to the family left behind but also political knowledge, preferences, and practices absorbed in their host country. In transition or developing countries, where institutions are weak, the diffusion of political norms through communication between migrants and their family back home has the potential to boost demand for political accountability and promote democracy. Using a voting experiment to capture the individual demand for better governance in Cape Verde, a study provides evidence of a positive impact of the proportion of international migrants in an individual's locality on the demand for political accountability. International migration is also found to affect political behavior and voting: in Mexico and Moldova, there is evidence of a positive impact of migration on votes for opposition parties.

Limitations and Gaps

The literature on migration and the family left behind recognizes the difficulty of measuring a causal impact. This is both a clear limitation and a major challenge to researchers. Most studies rely on data from home-country household surveys, making it difficult to overcome the problem of the nonrandom selection of individuals into migration. . . . Collecting such data is particularly challenging, however, and often depends on the willingness of policy makers to share the data with researchers.

There is also a need for better survey data, notably for richer longitudinal data sets that simultaneously survey migrants abroad and sending households. Although studies using such data sets would still not be as good as randomized controlled studies, they would help researchers and policy makers learn more about the mechanisms through which migration affects family members who do not migrate.

Another limitation is that most studies have investigated specific settings, so the results may not be generalizable. In particular, the impact of migration may vary considerably depending on the type of migration and on the source and destination countries analyzed. For instance, the loss of parental supervision and interaction might be much more detrimental for international migration, with long-distance travel and infrequent returns, than for short-distance internal migration.

Another source of cross-study variability may be the family's income level before migration, which can influence whether the net effects are positive or negative. In particular, for poor households in poor countries the income effect of remittances would be expected to be stronger and more likely to counteract the negative effects associated with the absence of the migrant.

Summary and Policy Advice

With about one billion international and internal migrants worldwide, the relationship between migration and the family left behind is an important policy question. Labor migration is conventionally viewed as economically benefiting the family left behind. Remittance transfers can ease budget constraints and thereby increase spending on health care and education, improving households' long-term welfare in the source country. However, the migrant's absence might also have negative consequences for nonmigrants, be they children, the elderly, or a spouse.

Policy makers need to account for differences in the situations of migrants and their families who stay behind and bolster support systems in education and health care to help families cope with the detrimental effects of migration on the accumulation of human capital. If migration implies lower education or health status or more child labor, the potentially long-term costs of migration need to be mitigated through appropriate home country policies. Population aging is another issue to consider.

Many migrant-sending developing countries have inadequate social safety nets, especially in rural areas. Countries may need to establish supportive institutions that can help families who stay behind adapt to the loss of an economically active member or caregiver through migration. Policy options for developing countries include improving the functioning of labor markets (notably in rural areas, to facilitate the hiring of local labor when a family member migrates), strengthening formal insurance and credit markets, facilitating the transmission of remittances by lowering remitting costs, and increasing access to education and health care. More specifically, ways to mitigate the impact of migration on human capital include offering access to better education locally at primary and secondary school levels, including providing additional tutoring for children left behind, and building social safety nets to provide pensions and affordable health care for the elderly.

References

Further reading

Adams, R. H. (2011). "Evaluating the economic impact of international remittances on developing countries using household surveys: A literature review." *Journal of Development Studies* 47:6: 809–828.

Ratha, D., Mohapatra, S., and Scheja, E. (2011, February). *Impact of Migration and Economic and Social Development: A Review of Evidence and Emerging Issues*. World Bank Policy Research Working Paper No. 5558.

Key References

[1] Ye, J., C. Wang, H. Wu, C. He, and J. Liu. (2013). "Internal migration and left-behind populations in China." *The Journal of Peasant Studies* 40:6: 1119–1146.

[2] Gibson, J., D. McKenzie, and S. Stillman. (2013). "Accounting for selectivity and duration-dependent heterogeneity when estimating the impact of emigration on incomes and poverty in sending areas." *Economic Development and Cultural Change* 61:2 (2013): 247–280.

[3] Antman, F. M. (2013). "The impact of migration on family left behind." In: Constant, A. F., and K. F. Zimmermann (eds). *International Handbook of the Economics of Migration*. Cheltenham, UK: Edward Elgar; pp. 293–308.

[4] Yang, D. (2008). "International migration, remittances, and household investment: Evidence from Philippine migrants' exchange rate shocks." *The Economic Journal* 118:528: 591–630.

[5] Alcaraz, C., D. Chiquiar, and A. Salcedo. (2012). "Remittances, schooling, and child labor in Mexico." *Journal of Development Economics* 97:1: 156–165.

[6] Antman, F. M. (2012)."Gender, educational attainment, and the impact of parental migration on children left behind." *Journal of Population Economics* 25:4: 1187–1214.

[7] Mu, R., and A. de Brauw. (2013, June). *Migration and Young Child Nutrition: Evidence from Rural China*. IZA Discussion Paper No. 7466.

[8] Gibson, J., D. McKenzie, and S. Stillman. (2011)."What happens to diet and child health when migration splits households? Evidence from a migration lottery program." *Food Policy* 36:1: 7–15.

[9] Amuedo-Dorantes, C., and S. Pozo. (2006). "Migration, remittances, and male and female employment patterns." *American Economic Review* 96:2: 222–226.

[10] Démurger, S., and S. Li. (2013). "Migration, remittances and rural employment patterns: Evidence from China." *Research in Labor Economics* 37:1: 31–63.

[11] de Haas, H., and A. van Rooij. (2010). "Migration as emancipation? The impact of internal and international migration on the position of women left behind in rural Morocco." *Oxford Development Studies* 38:1: 43–62.

The full reference list for this article is available from the iZA World of labor website (http://wol.iza.org/articles/migration-and-families-left-behind).

Critical Thinking

1. You have been asked by your employer to spend six months working overseas. What might be the benefits and challenges presented by this situation for you and your family?
2. What factors are important to consider when making the decision to migrate to another area for work?
3. Identify two to three supports which families impacted by labor migration might need to promote their well-being while separated due to work commitments. How and why are these supports important?

Internet References

International Labour Organization: Labour Migration
http://www.ilo.org/global/topics/labour-migration/lang–en/index.htm

International Organization for Migration: The United Nations Migration Organization
https://www.iom.int/labour-migration

When a Parent Has to Travel for Work: Parents' Magazine
http://www.parents.com/parenting/work/how-to-prepare-kids-when-parents-travel-for-work/

Article

Prepared by: Patricia Hrusa Williams, *University of Maine at Farmington*

American's Think Their Own Families Are Great But Like Judging Other People's, A New Report Suggests

Most Americans are happy with their families—so why is there so much judgment about other people's choices?

Amanda Marcotte

Learning Outcomes

After reading this article, you will be able to:

- Define what is meant by the term "success sequence."
- Identify trends in Americans' attitudes about families and how they have changed over time.
- Discuss differences in attitudes about marriage and family by generation and political affiliation.

Americans think their families are doing pretty well, but they think other people are screwing things up. That's a major takeaway from this year's American Family Survey, an annual nationwide poll created by the Deseret News and the Center for the Study of Elections and Democracy to track trends in people's family lives and attitudes about relationships and families.

As was the case with last year's survey, researchers found that while most people think their marriages and families are stable or even getting stronger, when asked about other people, they think those fools are falling apart.

Researchers found a similar discrepancy when respondents were asked about their families. A whopping 87 percent of respondents felt their families were stable or getting stronger, but 34 percent of those surveyed felt that other people's families were weakening.

Americans "feel good about their marriages and families, for the most part," Christopher Karpowitz, the co-director of the Center for the Study of Elections and Democracy at Brigham Young University, explained in a phone interview. "It's the disparity between how they feel about their own relationships and families and how they see everyone else's relationships and families that's interesting."

"It just points to the way people can be quite judgmental about a number of things," agreed Jeremy Pope, the center's other co-director.

Pope pointed out another question in the survey had asked respondents about what they think are the most important issues facing Americans today. Even though researchers found that 4 in 10 of the Americans in the study have faced serious economic challenges in the past year, respondents were still more likely to rate poor discipline for children as a more serious problem for families than economic problems.

"What they mean by that is that other people are not disciplining their children," Pope cracked.

But while this widespread tendency to judge others may be amusing, there are serious reasons to care about this disparity between how people are feeling about their own lives and how

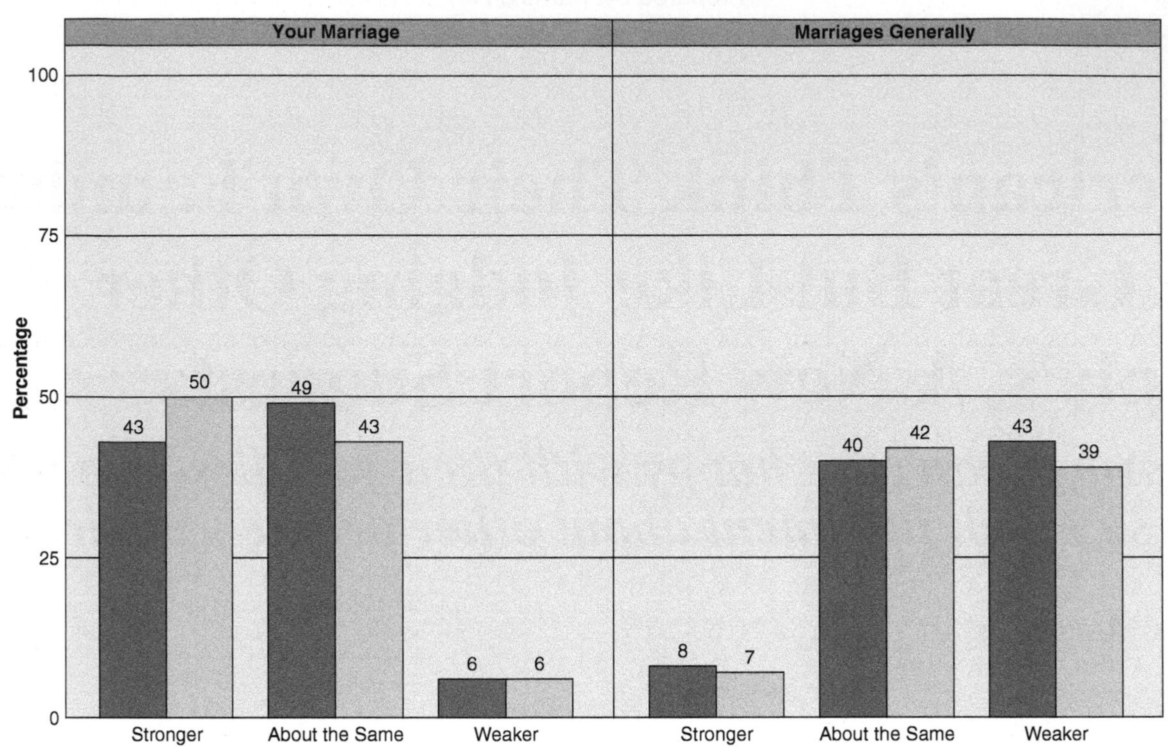

Graph from the American Family Survey 2016.

The Most Important Issues

	2015	2016	Difference
Economics			
The costs associated with raising a family	26	32	+6
High work demands and stress on parents	21	27	+6
The lack of good jobs	19	22	+3
Lack of government programs to support families	8	10	+2
Culture			
The widespread availability and use of drugs and alcohol	27	22	−5
Sexual permissiveness in our society	25	18	−7
Decline in religious faith and church attendance	23	22	−1
Crime and other threats to personal safety	19	20	+1
Family Structure and Stability			
Parents not teaching or disciplining their children sufficiently	53	52	−1
More children growing up in single-parent homes	25	25	0
Difficulty finding quality time with family in the digital age	21	21	0
Change in the definition of marriage and family	16	15	−1

Note: Cell entries indicate the percentage of the sample selecting that item as one of the three "most important issues facing families today."
Table from the American Family Survey 2016.

they feel about others'. The blunt truth, as this survey shows, is that American practices around marriage and childbearing are changing dramatically, and this lack of empathy and swiftness to judge is getting in the way of helping people understand the changes and adapt to them

The most headline-worthy change the researchers found was about the timing of marriage and childbearing.

"Over 90 percent of parents over age 65 were married when they first had children, but only 30 percent of those younger than 30 were married when their first child was born," the researchers wrote. "In addition, younger people tend to have different attitudes about the meaning and value of marriage. Though they do not oppose the idea of marriage, they are more likely than their older counterparts to believe that personal commitment to a partner is more important than the legal fact of marriage."

Karpowitz and Pope hastened to note that there's not a lot of information out there about what this shift means for Americans and getting a handle on the impact of this shift will require more research. But the ugly fact of the matter is that, for years now, Republicans have been arguing that nonmarital childbearing is the cause of every social problem you can imagine, from poverty to gun violence.

Republicans have grown increasingly attached to the notion that marriage is a cure-all for all that ails you. In June, House Speaker Paul Ryan and a Republican-led task force on poverty released a report called "A Better Way to Fight Poverty" that purported to offer a superior alternative to the social safety net. Rather than receiving food, shelter and health care, Ryan argued that lower-income people need to keep their knickers on and get married as quickly as they can.

The report observed:

Marriage is one component of what has been called the "success sequence": three key achievements that are associated with low poverty rates. People who graduate high school, work full-time, and delay having children until they are married are much less likely to live in poverty. Only 2 percent of people who do these three things are in poverty, compared to almost 80 percent of people who have done none of them. Unfortunately, our current welfare system may be exacerbating this problem, as many means-tested welfare programs penalize marriage—because when low-income fathers and mothers marry, their combined income from welfare and wages will almost certainly be lower than the amount they had separately.

This sort of rhetoric has a clear electoral appeal because it justifies cutting spending and appeals to the older Republican demographic. As the American Family Survey has found, older Americans are more likely than younger Americans to think there's something wrong with having children outside of marriage. But this overly simplistic attitude about marriage is not justified by the evidence.

The American Family Survey did find that married people were less likely to have had an economic crisis in the past year than people in a relationship or cohabiting. As Pope explained, however, "You should not attribute much causality to anything in the study because causality in the area of family life is extremely difficult to measure."

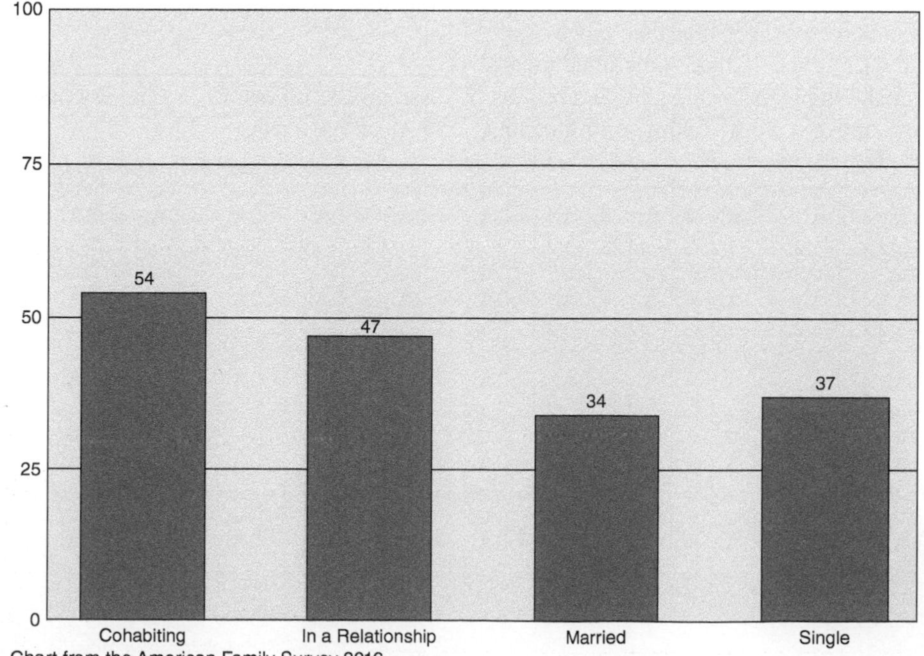

Chart from the American Family Survey 2016.

Pope also pointed out that the differences between different groups were not as significant as conservative rhetoric might lead you to believe, as shown by this chart.

There's probably a bit of the chicken-and-egg dynamic when it comes to the relationship between marriage and financial stability. Marriage may make people more stable, but people might wait until they're financially stable to get married.

"Young people have a sense that they should wait until they're more financially stable," Karpowitz said. "Older generations didn't necessarily do that. They were more willing to jump right in."

He noted that this tendency to wait might also explain why people in their 20s who have children are so much less likely to be married than in previous generations.

"The ages at which people are getting married are increasing," he explained. "It's possible that there's a group of people out there who have not had children and are waiting to get married to have children."

In other words, if you do have a kid in your 20s, you are more likely to not be married. But it's also quite possible that more people are putting off childbearing until their 30s, after they have established themselves in a career and married.

One thing's certain is that younger generations are not shunning marriage, as conservative rhetoric often implies.

"The millennial generation cares a lot about having strong relationships and they don't feel marriage is out-of-date or old-fashioned necessarily," Karpowitz explained. "In fact, young people and liberal respondents to our survey are the most optimistic about the health of marriages and families more generally in the United States, relative to conservatives."

It's possible that this great respect for marriage is why people are marrying later in life, even if that sometimes means having kids before they make the leap. Young people take marriage seriously and want to make it work. Taking your time and making sure you have the right person and right financial setup make it likelier that your marriage will be a strong one.

"Though an important goal of this report has been to describe the objective public opinion about family and family policy," the report concluded, "we do believe that American families of all types would be normatively better off if they understood one another better."

Critical Thinking

1. Why do you think Americans view their families and marriages more positively than their friends or neighbors?
2. What are some of the reasons for generational and political differences regarding attitudes toward marriage in our society? How are some of your ideas about marriage and family different from your grandparents?
3. Do you think the so-called "success sequence" influences the economic health and well-being of families in the United States today? What can we do to strengthen the economic prospects of families in the face of changes in family structure and attitudes?

Internet References

Center for the Study of Elections and Democracy: The American Family Survey

http://csed.byu.edu/american-family-survey/

Deseret News: American Family Survey

http://www.deseretnews.com/american-family-survey

Pew Research Center: Social and Demographic Trends

http://www.pewsocialtrends.org/attitudes-about-the-changing-american-family/

Amanda Marcotte is a politics writer for Salon. She's on Twitter @AmandaMarcotte.

Article Prepared by: Patricia Hrusa Williams, *University of Maine at Farmington*

Why We Need to Separate Kids from Tech—Now

Martha Ross

Learning Outcomes

After reading this article, you will be able to:

- Discuss how and why technology use has increased.
- Identify potential ways technology use may benefit and harm the functioning of individuals and families.
- Understand the differing perspectives of parents and their children about the meaning and use of technology in their lives.

It doesn't seem that long ago that many parents felt guilty for using even the highly acclaimed "Sesame Street" to babysit their kids while they cooked dinner.

But a not-so-funny thing happened on our way to our high-tech-enamored world of 2015: children's recreational use of screens, phones, and entertainment media has exploded.

"It's up considerably from years past," says Richard Freed, a Walnut Creek child and adolescent psychologist, in his new book, "Wired Child: Debunking Popular Technology Myths." Digital entertainment is now the "dominant activity in their lives," says Freed, who is also the father of two daughters, 11 and 7.

And that's not a recipe for a balanced, well-adjusted life, he and other media and educational experts say. Emerging research shows that kids' overuse of TV, computers, video games, tablets, and smartphones hinders their physical, intellectual, social, and emotional development.

Nonetheless, achievement-oriented parents, who a decade ago would have strictly limited their children's TV viewing, seem eager to equip their kids with the latest laptops, tablets, and smartphones. Freed and others blame an industry spin that says that early, regular and, in some cases, unlimited use of technology is essential for kids to be technically proficient and academically competitive in the 21st century.

Sharael Kolberg admits she was one of those parents. The former Silicon Valley web producer and author of "A Year Unplugged: A Family's Life Without Technology," recalls how she salivated over the latest laptops at the Apple store when she bought her young daughter an iMac.

Several years after her family's tech-free experiment, Kolberg agrees with Freed that there is nothing wrong with kids watching limited amounts of age-appropriate entertainment, going online to do school research or having cellphones to reach their parents.

"Technology isn't the problem," says Freed, whose daughters don't have smartphones and use computers for schoolwork. The problem comes when screen time is overused and displaces family, school and other experiences that Freed says are "fundamental to a strong mind and a happy, successful life."

This overuse is documented in a study by the Kaiser Family Foundation. It showed that 8- to 18-year-olds spend up to six total hours a day watching TV, playing computer games, or immersed in social media, YouTube videos, and movies on their iPads and phones. This daily habit rises to 7½ hours if kids are multitasking—posting on Instagram while watching TV, for example. Teenagers may spend an additional 2½ hours a day texting or talking on the phone. Meanwhile, kids spend only about 16 min a day using a computer at home for homework.

When Kolberg's daughter Katelyn was five, she used her iMac and her mother's iPhone to play games. She also watched TV an hour a day and movies after dinner.

But Katelyn wasn't the only tech-dependent member of the family. One day, it dawned on Kolberg that she and her husband had issues, too. "We had gotten into the habit of spending our evenings with the TV on while simultaneously checking e-mail or seeing what our Facebook friends were up to," she says.

So in late 2009, Kolberg and her family started their tech-free year. They removed TVs, computers, smartphones, the Internet, e-mail, and social media from their home. They kept a cellphone for emergencies.

Still, Kolberg felt worried that sticking her daughter's iMac in the garage would somehow make her fall behind. "As a child growing up in Silicon Valley, it just (didn't) seem right to take her computer away."

Like Kolberg, Freed challenges the idea that technology brings families together. In his book, he says this myth is perpetuated by such ads as a TV commercial for an Apple iPhone. As the ad starts, a teen's focus on his phone is revealed to be him actually videotaping family moments; the ad ends with the family together, watching his creation.

"The message is . . . buy your kids iPhones, and they will be closer to you, even if it looks like they're ignoring you in favor of their phones," Freed says.

In fact, kids' top uses for smartphones have nothing to do with interacting with family or doing research for school. Instead, they're playing games, texting, and watching TV—a lot of TV, according to the Kaiser Family Foundation study.

Americans have long had a reverence for technology, which Freed believes has been exploited by tech and gaming companies to market their products as essential educational tools or cool, engaging—and benign—entertainment, he says.

As parents hear education pundits pushing for more science, technology, engineering, and math programs in American schools, they are exhorted by app developers telling them their products can help their babies and preschoolers get a head start on math and reading. Never mind that many of the educational claims made by app developers "don't hold up," says Caroline Knorr, the parenting editor at the San Francisco-based non-profit Common Sense Media.

"A lot of products marketed to parents overpromise what they can do and are not age-appropriate," she says, adding that it's the rare preschooler who is developmentally ready to start reading or doing math. The real concern is kids' constant exposure to entertainment media, Freed says. In his more than 20 years of practice, he has seen hundreds of young patients who struggle academically and tested a number of them for ADHD. He says their symptoms, failing grades, and difficulty completing homework often are caused by too much screen time.

In fact, technology overuse could be rewiring kids' developing brains in ways that could explain the growing number of kids diagnosed with anxiety and other psychiatric disorders. Brain imaging techniques also show that video gaming stimulates the same pleasure pathways as drugs and alcohol. Video or Internet game addiction, which is gaining recognition by mental health professionals, can be devastating. One of Freed's patients, 15, threatened suicide when his parents announced he couldn't play his video games until his grades improved.

For both Freed and Kolberg, the strongest statements about limiting kids' technology use come from industry leaders like Bill Gates and Steve Jobs. Gates reportedly set strict time limits for his son and daughters' video gaming and screen time.

And in 2010, Jobs revealed to a journalist that his children had not used his company's recently released first-generation iPad. "We limit how much technology our kids use at home," Jobs said, according to a 2014 New York Times article.

In fact, low-tech learning definitely appeals to a small number of Silicon Valley executives who send their children to the Waldorf School of the Peninsula, where kids don't use computers in the classroom until seventh grade, says Lisa Babinet, the dean of students for the school's high school and chair of the math department.

In the Waldorf program, learning is hands-on in the purest sense. Kids garden, sew, make music, do lots of imaginative play, and use pencil and paper to master their handwriting. These methods are designed to teach students to concentrate deeply, master human interaction, and think creatively, Babinet explains.

The school's tech-savvy parents understand that gadgets should have a limited place in a well-balanced life, Babinet says. "In a (media) interview, one parent said 'power tools are amazing, but I wouldn't give a power tool to a kindergartner.'"

When Kolberg's family went tech-free, Katelyn complained almost daily. On day 365, Kolberg, whose family has since relocated from Los Gatos to Southern California, contemplated slowly reintegrating devices back into their lives. While relieved to resume technology use for convenience, she was, however, "disappointed to no longer live a life of simplistic communication and family bonding."

The sabbatical definitely benefited Katelyn, Kolberg says. Without tech, the youngster spent time reading, painting, drawing, and gardening. And somehow, removing the TV "dramatically" reduced the anxiety she had exhibited since she was a toddler.

Katelyn also became more adventurous about leaving the safe cocoon of her home. Instead of watching cartoons on Sunday mornings and resisting pleas to go out for a hike, she became "a confident, adventure-seeking nature lover in a matter of months."

Now 11, Katelyn has a smartphone but rarely uses it and generally has a healthy perspective on technology, her mother says. More than anything, Kolberg says, the no-tech approach taught her daughter to appreciate life's "simple pleasures."

Critical Thinking

1. What factors are behind tech use and overuse in families? Where do we draw the line between healthy use of technology and overuse?
2. Do you think you could go tech free for a year, like the Kolberg family did? Why or why not?
3. How do you feel the use of technology tools such as cellphones, computers, the Internet, and video games have benefitted you as an individual? How have the influenced your connection with your family?

Internet References

Child Mind Institute
https://childmind.org/article/big-disconnect-how-tech-changes-families-2/

Family Internet Safety Institute
www.fosi.org

Pew Research Center: Internet and Technology
http://www.pewinternet.org/

Martha Ross is a features writer who covers everything and anything related to popular culture, society, health, women's issues, and families. A native of the East Bay and a graduate of Northwestern University and Mills College, she's also a former hard news and investigative reporter, covering crime, and local politics.

Unit 2

UNIT

Prepared by: Patricia Hrusa Williams, *University of Maine at Farmington*

Exploring and Establishing Relationships

By and large, we are social animals, seeking out meaningful connections with other humans. John Bowlby, Mary Ainsworth, and others have proposed that this drive toward deep connections is biologically based and is at the core of what it means to be human. However, it plays out in childhood and adulthood, the need for connection, to love and be loved, is a powerful force moving us to establish and maintain close relationships. As we explore various possibilities, we engage in the complex business of relationship building. In doing this, many processes occur simultaneously. Messages are sent and received; differences are negotiated; assumptions and expectations are or are not met. The ultimate goals are closeness and continuity. How we feel about others and what we see as essential to these relationships play important roles as we work to establish and maintain these connections.

In this unit, we look at factors that underlie the establishment and beginning stages of relationships. Among the topics to be covered in this unit are an exploration of factors that influence how and why connections are built. Factors explored include biology, emotions, physical attraction, sex, personality, and the context in which relationships are established and developed. Changing views and practices in sex education, mating, relationships, marriage, commitment, family formation, procreation, and early family development are explored. Together, the chapter tries to investigate and understand the evolution of intimate and family relationships in our ever-changing society.

Article

Prepared by: Patricia Hrusa Williams, *University of Maine at Farmington*

What Schools Should Teach Kids About Sex

In America, the subject is often limited to "a smattering of information about [humans'] reproductive organs and a set of stern warnings about putting them to use."

JESSICA LAHEY

Learning Outcomes

After reading this article, you will be able to:

- Understand the role of the federal government, states, local entities, and public schools in sex education.
- Identify the differences between the three basic forms of sex education offered in the United States: comprehensive, abstinence-based, and abstinence-only.
- Explain the reasons why sex education is such a controversial topic in the United States.

"There is probably no subject that has posed greater headaches to teachers than sex education," writes NYU history and education professor Jonathan Zimmerman in his new book, *Too Hot to Handle: A Global History of Sex Education.* And no other topic illustrates the complexity and emotion that lies at the heart of the debates about parental, local, and federal control over education.

While every state offers some form of sex education, the substance and style of the given curriculum can range from comprehensive to significantly circumscribed, largely depending on local politics and beliefs. In many of America's school districts, sex education looks a lot like the current "global norm," which is described by Zimmerman in his book as, "a smattering of information about their reproductive organs and a set of stern warnings about putting them to use."

The question of who should be teaching sex education, and what form that instruction should take, is increasingly problematic in this diverse and often ideologically divided nation. There's little agreement on what should be included in sex education courses, let alone how, and at what ages it should be taught. The author Alice Dreger, writing for the *Pacific Standard,* pointed out that 44 percent of Americans mistakenly believe sex education is already covered by the Common Core standard. So, she asks, "Why Isn't Sex Education a Part of the Common Core?" On the other hand, sex-advice columnist and author Dan Savage suggests that if the country can't offer effective sex education, maybe it should be looking to families, the Internet, or even independent sex instructors such as Dr. Karen Rayne of Unhushed, or Amy Lang of Birds + Bees + Kids.

Whatever the issue, American adolescents need comprehensive sex education, well, because American adolescents have sex. According to the CDC, almost half—47 percent—of all U.S. high school students have had sexual intercourse, 34 percent of them during the previous three months. And 41 percent of those kids admit they did not use a condom the last time they had sex even though such contraception is highly effective against pregnancy and the spread of sexually transmitted infections such as HIV. That statistic might help explain why the U.S. has the highest teen pregnancy rate in the developed world and why America's adolescents account for nearly half of the 19 million new cases of STIs each year—even though, as the CDC indicates, teens represent only a fourth of the nation's sexually active people.

It appears that America isn't alone in neglecting the sexual education of its teens. That's evidenced by findings from the

U.K.'s third national Survey of Sexual Attitudes and Lifestyles, which was conducted among 4,000 adolescents and young adults and released today by the country's Medical Research Council. The report reveals that in Britain, teens learn about sex from (in descending order of popularity) school, friends, the media, the Internet, and pornography. Despite access to these types of "information," approximately seven in 10 adolescents felt that they should have known more about sex before their first experience having intercourse. Specifically, they wished they knew more about contraception, how to reduce the health risks of sexual behavior, and "how to make sex more satisfying."

Meanwhile, the list of the most recently asked questions on Scarleteen.com, one of the most popular sex-education sites on the Internet, shows that these are the concerns of the 1 billion users (54 percent of whom are from the U.S.) who apparently visited the site since its launch in 2006:

> (Scarleteen's slogan? "Sex education for the real world: Inclusive, comprehensive and smart sexuality information and help for teens and 20s.")

The sex topics British teens want to know more about, and answers to the questions Scarleteen and Savage receive weekly, are inconsistently taught in U.S. schools—probably due to uneven requirements and the decentralization of policymaking. Because virtually every aspect of education, let alone that involving sex, does not fall under the control of the federal government, state, and more often local, entities decide what goes in—and what stays out—of the classroom. While every state engages in some form of sex education for public school children, only 13 of them have laws requiring that, if such a curriculum is offered, it must be medically accurate and based on scientific evidence. Meanwhile, just 18 states and the District of Columbia require that schools "provide instruction on contraception." While 26 states and the D.C. teach about healthy sexuality and decision-making, 19 states require that school-based sex education emphasize the importance of abstinence until marriage. Many of these standards, moreover, are open to interpretation.

Sex education takes three basic forms in the U.S.: comprehensive, abstinence-based, and abstinence-only. The comprehensive approach, according to the Sexuality Education and Information Council of the United States, provides "age- and developmentally appropriate sexual health information" that is medically accurate, informed by scientific evidence, and sensitive to the needs of all young people. Topics covered by such a curriculum include "human development, abstinence, contraception, disease and pregnancy prevention, as well as skill development for healthy relationships and decision-making."

Abstinence-based sex education, on the other hand, specifically promotes abstinence while providing some or all of the elements of the comprehensive approach; abstinence-only models, of course, teach only abstinence until marriage. Abstinence-only curricula don't provide any information on contraception beyond its failure rates.

Comprehensive programs are slowly gaining ground in the U.S. Still, abstinence-only programs have been well-funded over the years, beginning with the Reagan Administration and the federal block grant for maternal and child health services under Title V of the Social Security Act—despite evidence that these programs are ineffective when it comes to better sexual health. According to multiple peer-reviewed studies, abstinence-only programs do not delay the average age of the first time a person has sexual intercourse, nor do they prevent the spread of STIs or reduce the number of sexual partners someone has during adolescence. The peer-reviewed *Journal of Adolescent Health* came out against abstinence-only education in a 2006 position paper, stating that while abstinence is a healthy choice for teens, "Providing 'abstinence only' or 'abstinence until marriage' messages as a sole option for teenagers is flawed from scientific and medical ethics viewpoints."

Many advocates and experts agree. As Savage, a longtime critic of abstinence-only education, recently told me in a phone interview, he supports having sex education in schools but believes "[the country] should stop pretending what passes for sex education is sex education." Savage has been commentator and sex advice columnist since 1991, both in his Savage Love column and his extremely popular "Savage Love" podcast. He's thus familiar with the full range of questions Americans have about sex. Savage agrees that the topics most school programs cover, such as reproductive biology, are important [but] emphasized that curricula often ignore topics such as consent, pleasure, and effective communication about sex.

So I asked Savage to elaborate on what a comprehensive sex-education curriculum should cover:

> We should be teaching the real things that can trip people up, things that can ruin people's lives or traumatize them, like what is and isn't consent, and what is and isn't on the menu, and what are you or are you not comfortable with, and how do you advocate for yourself, and how do you draw someone out and solicit their active consent so that you don't accidentally traumatize someone? We need to talk about sex for pleasure, which is 99.99 percent of the sex that people have, and that's 99.99 percent of what's not covered in even what liberals and progressives would look at and say, "Oh, look at that good sex ed!"

Savage claims that despite the nation's outward appearance of progress on matters such as marriage and gender equality, "Sex education has gone backward. When it comes to our children, there is more information and more truthfulness out there about sex, sexuality, gender identity, everything, than there has ever been. Social conservatives know they can't undo the sexual revolution, or unmake gay people, or roll back women's empowerment—but they have it in their heads that they can reverse engineer the future by raising today's children in ignorance."

To illustrate the consequences of such ignorance, Savage analogized the state of sex education today to a driver's education class that focuses exclusively on the mechanics of the internal combustion engine, with no mention of brakes, steering, red lights, and stop signs. "That's sex ed in America. We hand kids the keys to the car, and when they drive straight into walls, we say, 'See? See? If we'd only kept them a little more ignorant, this wouldn't be happening!'"

But for Zimmerman, conservatives aren't the only culprits responsible for the country's failure to progress on sex education: "Dan is right to be sanguine about any kind of real substantial change, but it's actually because of our country's diversity. The more diverse the world becomes, and the more it globalizes, the faster people and ideas move across borders, the more difficult [agreeing how to teach] sex ed becomes."

Even proponents of progressive, comprehensive sex education disagree about what phenomena are hindering its development. While some advocates may like the idea of a comprehensive national standard for the subject, such as Alice Dreger's vision of sex education as a Common Core standard, Zimmerman believes allowing schools to experiment with content or format would be key to promoting innovation.

> The United States might be one of the places where we will see a little bit more variation and experimentation, and that's because we *don't* have a national system. There are compelling reasons to think about national standards and national curriculum, but where sex ed is concerned, you have to think about some of the downsides of that, too, which is how it might inhibit experimentation and variation.

That experimentation and variation flourishes in independent sex-education classes around the country, such as those that Rayne teaches at the Austin-based Unhushed. Rayne, an author, sex educator, and the chair of the National Sex Ed Conference, is doggedly optimistic in her predictions about the future of sex education in America, largely because she knows firsthand about the demand for progressive, comprehensive curricula. "I do think we've come a long way," she said in a phone interview. "I've seen a lot of change that's happened since I started in sex education [in 2007]. People are much more open to it. The laws are improving—I would not say that they are great—but they are improving. The Texas Freedom Network does really good research on sex education in Texas and its findings show a clear trajectory toward openness, honesty, and fact-based information, so I do see that happening here and also nationally."

Zimmerman doubts a comprehensive national sex ed curriculum will ever happen. To him, the U.S. is simply too diverse for one solution to fit all. As he concludes in *Too Hot to Handle,* sex education serves as "a mirror, reflecting all the flux and diversity—and the confusion and instability—of sex and youth in our globalized world." No matter how rapidly sex education evolves, he believes, it will always be playing catch-up—to the media, to the Internet, and to everything adolescents talk about when adults are not around.

Critical Thinking

1. Why is sex education such a controversial topic in the United States?
2. What do you think should be the basic components of a sex education program which is offered in public schools in the United States?
3. Sex education has moved from the classroom to the web. Review at least one site listed here (Go Ask Alice, Scarleteen, Unhushed). Identify strengths and weaknesses of web-based sex education resources.

Internet References

Go Ask Alice!
http://www.goaskalice.columbia.edu

AVERTing HIV and AIDS: Sex Education That Works
http://www.avert.org/sex-education-works.htm

Scarleteen
http://www.scarleteen.com

State Policies on Sex Education in Schools
http://www.ncsl.org/research/health/state-policies-on-sex-education-in-schools.aspx

Unhushed
http://www.unhushed.net

Article

Prepared by: Patricia Hrusa Williams, *University of Maine at Farmington*

Sex and the Class of 2020: How Will Hookups Change?

Conor Friedersdorf

Learning Outcomes

After reading this article, you will be able to:

- Understand the legal definition of affirmative consent.
- Analyze how affirmative consent law may impact the sexual behavior of college students.
- Recognize gender differences and stereotypes regarding consent, date rape, and sexual behavior.

As California's colleges and universities adjust to a new state law mandating a standard of "affirmative consent" in sexual assault and rape cases—as well as campus judicial proceedings with a "preponderance of the evidence" standard of guilt—observers are trying to anticipate how these policy changes will affect the lived culture of sexual acts among students, most in their late teens or early 20s. The law's effect on campus culture will determine whether it advances the ends sought by supporters, who hope to reduce the incidence of sex crimes. Yet there is broad disagreement about whether and how sexual culture will adapt to the new regime. Even those who agree that the law is good or bad disagree about its likely effects.

What follows are some of the wildly divergent forecasts, some hopeful, others cautionary. Taken together, they illuminate different notions of human nature, the reach of public policy, and what life on California's many college campuses is actually like. The scenarios that they anticipate are not always mutually exclusive.

It Will Be Harder to Get Away with Rape

In the 2008 essay collection *Yes Means Yes!: Visions of Female Sexual Power and a World Without Rape,* contributor Jill Filipovic captured something very much like what supporters of California law hope sex on campus will look like in the near future.

"Plenty of men are able to grasp the idea that sex should be entered into joyfully and enthusiastically by both partners, and that an absence of 'no' isn't enough—'yes' should be the baseline requirement," she wrote. "And women are not empty vessels to be fucked or not fucked; we're sexual actors who should absolutely have the ability to say yes when we want it, just like men, and should feel safe saying no—even if we've been drinking, even if we've slept with you before, even if we're wearing tight jeans, even if we're naked in bed with you. Anti-rape activists further understand that men need to feel empowered to say no also. If women have the ability to fully and freely say yes, and if we establish a model of enthusiastic consent instead of just 'no means no,' it would be a lot harder for men to get away with rape. It would be a lot harder to argue that there's a 'gray area.' It would be a lot harder to push the idea that 'date rape' is less serious than 'real' rape, that women who are assaulted by acquaintances were probably teases, that what is now called 'date rape' used to just be called seduction."

Sex Will Be Hotter and More Enjoyable

There is a long history, Ann Friedman writes in *New York,* of young women having sex "that's consensual but not really much fun," and as long a history "of their male partners walking home the next morning thinking, 'Nailed it.'" She believes that "these droves of sexually dissatisfied young women will be unwitting beneficiaries" of California's new law, because "confirming consent leads to much hotter sex." She doesn't anticipate that the law will thwart rapists, "who clearly don't care about consent, be it verbal or nonverbal." But she believes that "most young men . . . *are* worried about inadvertently doing something in bed that their partner doesn't welcome" and "actively thinking about whether their partner is enjoying herself." As a result, they'll now find life "easier for both them and the women they sleep with," because the law "creates a compelling reason for both parties to speak up and talk about what they like. In essence, the new law forces universities—and the rest of us—to acknowledge that *women like sex.* Especially sex with a partner who wants to talk about what turns them on."

Sex Will Be Scary and Anxiety-Inducing

If implemented as intended, California's affirmative-consent law will intrude on "the most private and intimate of adult acts," Ezra Klein posits. It will settle "like a cold winter on college campuses, throwing everyday sexual practice into doubt," creating "a haze of fear and confusion over what counts as consent" and causing men "to feel a cold spike of fear when they begin a sexual encounter." Meanwhile, "colleges will fill with cases in which campus boards convict young men (and, occasionally, young women) . . . for genuinely ambiguous situations" in cases that "feel genuinely unclear and maybe even unfair." Klein is a supporter of the law. His followup article on the *culture* of affirmative consent is worth your while.

Hookup Culture Will Wither under Neo-Victorianism

Heather MacDonald describes affirmative-consent laws and the activist movement that produced them as "a bizarre hybrid of liberationist and traditionalist values" that "carefully preserves the prerogative of no-strings-attached sex" but adds "legalistic caveats that allow females to revert at will to a stance of offended virtue." She regards the "assumption of transparent contractual intention" to be "laughably out of touch with reality," and believes it implicitly treats women as "so helpless and passive that they should not even be assumed to have the strength or capacity to say 'no'" to stop unwanted sexual encounters, ushering in "a neo-Victorian ethos which makes the male the sole guardian of female safety."

Judging that the policies ushered in by this neo-Victorian ethos misunderstand sex and will take the fun out of it, she tells her fellow conservatives, "What's not to like? Leave laments about the inhibition of campus sex to *Reason* magazine." As she sees it, "If one-sided litigation risk results in boys taking a vow of celibacy until graduation, there is simply no loss whatsoever to society and only gain to individual character. Such efforts at self-control were made before, and can be made again."

Another conservative, Conn Carroll, reaches a closely related conclusion. "If you are in a committed relationship there is very little chance each new amorous encounter with your partner will result in hard feelings either way," he declares. "But if you are constantly switching partners, each new pairing is a roll of the dice. You have no idea how each woman will react the next morning. If you sleep around there are simply way more opportunities for things to blow up in your face."

Misogyny on Campus Will Increase

Like supporters of affirmative-consent laws, Ross Douthat of *The New York Times* doesn't anticipate that disciplinary cases springing from them will be particularly common, at least not enough to affect the behavior of the average student. "It seems very unlikely that any campus policy is suddenly going to make assault allegations commonplace, in a way that would have them intruding frequently into the social life of the typical college-going male," he writes. "Instead, 'yes means yes' will create a kind of black swan situation, where only *every once in a while* a man gets expelled for rape under highly ambiguous circumstances. And because the injustices or possible injustices will be rare, that 'every once in while' will not actually have much of a deterrent effect on men confronted with an opportunity for a drunken hook-up, in the same way that other very occasional disastrous consequences of binge drinking (e.g., death) seem remote to young men (or young women) who head out to get hammered on a typical Saturday night."

But he isn't arguing that there will be no significant cultural impact. Rather, he believes college males will react sort of like cable news viewers who develop persecution complexes:

> It will be a distant-seeming outrage that mostly feeds a sense of grievance and persecution among the men who might (but mostly won't) suffer unjust treatment at the university's hands. Which means that rather than being a spur to some sort of reborn chivalry or new-model code of male decency, it will mostly encourage the kind of toxic persecution fantasies that already circulate in the more misogynistic reaches of male culture. See, *the feminazis really are out to get us,* the argument will go, and in bro lore the stories of men railroaded off campus won't be seen as cautionary tales; they'll be seen as war stories, martyrologies (in which even actual, clear-as-day predators are given the benefit of the doubt), the latest battle in the endless struggle between the *Animal House* gang and Dean Wormer . . . reincarnated now, in our more egalitarian feminist era, as a castrating Nurse Ratched.
>
> The new standard of consent, in this scenario, will be neither reasonable enough to be embraced as a model

nor consistently punitive enough to scare men away from drunken wooing. Instead, it will have a randomness, an arbitrariness, and an occasional absurdity that will encourage a mix of resentment and resistance. As such, it will lock in an aspect of contemporary sexual culture that social conservatives probably don't talk enough about: The kind of toxic misogyny that feminists rightly call out and critique, but that also exists in a kind of twisted symbiosis with certain aspects of feminist ideology–answering overzealous political correctness with reactionary transgressiveness, bureaucratic pieties with deliberate blasphemy, ideologies of gender with performative machismo.

Sexual Harassment Will Change

Hanna Rosin's *Atlantic* cover story on sexting among teens includes a passage about what prompts one young person to send a naked photo to another at one high school: "Boys and girls were equally likely to have sent a sext, but girls were much more likely to have been asked to—68 percent had been," she wrote. "Plenty of girls just laugh off the requests. When a boy asked Olivia, who graduated last year from Louisa County High, 'What are you wearing?,' she told me she wrote back, 'Stinky track shorts and my Virginity Rocks T-shirt.' A boy asked another student for a picture, so she sent him a smiling selfie. 'I didn't mean your face,' he wrote back, so she sent him one of her foot. But boys can be persistent—like, 20-or-30-texts-in-a-row persistent. 'If we were in a dark room, what would we do?' 'I won't show it to anyone else.' 'You're only sending it to me.' 'I'll delete it right after.'"

Today's male high-schooler pestering a classmates with 30 texts in a row asking to see her boobs is tomorrow's drunk freshman at a UC-Santa Barbara house party. It is conceivable that he will be acculturated into seeking affirmative-consent—and that he will seek it by asking for intercourse or a blow job *again and again and again.* At what point is he guilty of sexually harassing one or more of his new classmates? I suspect that's an issue campuses will face more frequently as consent-seeking becomes both affirmatively encouraged and more explicit than before. The spirit of the standard would of course preclude pestering one's way to "yes." But we're talking about regime created precisely to address the behavior of young men who'll adhere to the letter of the law or social norm *at most.* A new standard won't extinguish their impulse to push the limits as far as they can while avoiding punishable acts. Pestering may be their adaptation. And somewhere, sorority girls will arrive at a frat party where, upon entering (if not as a condition) they'll confront men pressuring them to preemptively consent. "This bracelet means you're good to hook up–and it comes with a free shot!"

Will that be tolerated?

Women Will Face Charges More Often Than Expected

Some opponents of California's law have argued that predatory men will "game" the new system by responding to an accusation of sexual assault with a countercharge of their own. Consider a case arising from drunken sex that one party regrets the next day. A college male is informed that charges are being brought against him. "She couldn't give consent? Neither could I. In fact, I felt uncomfortable too—she came to my room, neither asked for nor got a yes, and I was way more drunk." Such a case could present thorny issues for a campus tribunal.

But I'm imagining a different scenario, in which the affirmative-consent regime coincides with a noticeable increase in *earnest* complaints by men against women. It isn't that I foresee a monumental shift. At the same time, if campus norms about consensual sex change significantly and rapidly, just as traditional taboos against women initiating sex are waning and explicit efforts are made to diminish taboos against reporting sexual assaults, is it possible that a population acculturated to expect men always want sex will make and be called on more misjudgments?

Consider the following passage from the fascinating *New York Times Magazine* article on Wellesley, a women's college, and the growing number of trans men attending it:

> Kaden Mohamed said he felt downright objectified when he returned from summer break last year, after five months of testosterone had lowered his voice, defined his arm muscles and reshaped his torso. It was attention that he had never experienced before he transitioned. But as his body changed, students he didn't even know would run their hands over his biceps. Once at the school pub, an intoxicated Wellesley woman even grabbed his crotch and that of another trans man.
>
> "It's this very bizarre reversal of what happens in the real world," Kaden said. "In the real world, it's women who get fetishized, catcalled, sexually harassed, grabbed. At Wellesley, it's trans men who do. If I were to go up to someone I just met and touch her body, I'd get grief from the entire Wellesley community, because they'd say it's assault—and it is. But for some reason, when it's done to trans men here, it doesn't get read the same way. It's like a free pass, that suddenly it's O.K. to talk about or touch someone's body as long as they're not a woman."

How would a disciplinary panel at Wellesley react to a trans man charging a woman with sexual assault? How would UC-San Diego's student body react to a straight male bringing charges against a straight female for giving him a blow job when he was very drunk that he regretted the next day—or two weeks later upon realizing that he contracted an STD from the encounter? My guess is that, 10 years hence, such cases will be far from common, but still far more common than they currently are.

Sexual Assault Will Become a Sometimes Less Serious Charge

That isn't to say that *all* sexual assaults would be treated less seriously in this scenario. Some sex crimes will always strike people as maximally abhorrent and awful. But if a person can technically run afoul of sexual-assault rules by, say, misreading the vibe on a first date, leaning over during the movie, and initiating an unwanted kiss, there will be scenarios on the margin—perhaps not that one exactly, but you get the idea—where observers agree affirmative consent was violated *and* that some sanction is warranted, but nevertheless feel the incident is different in degree or kind than their bygone notion of what the crime "sexual assault" is.

There are two spins to put on this. On one hand, perhaps it is salutary to maintain undiminished taboos around *all* rape and sexual assault, preserving clarity about its awfulness, avoiding ignorant tropes like the canard that date rape isn't "as bad" as stranger rape, and conferring maximal opprobrium on those who act sexually without consent. Or perhaps a spectrum of opprobrium would be salutary, as in cases where the victim regards himself or herself as having been wronged, but eschews taking any action because he or she doesn't believe it was sexual assault, or want to be subjected to—or subject someone else to—a sexual-assault case. In some ways, this is similar to the tension between wanting racism to carry a powerful taboo and seeing situations where that very taboo makes it harder to call out and remedy conduct that is mildly racially offensive.

* * *

Though some of the foregoing scenarios are of my own creation, I don't have any idea how affirmative-consent laws will actually play out on California's college campuses, how variable the effect will be on different college campuses, or whether the overall change in sexual culture will be salutary, negative, or negligible. By temperament, I tend to worry about unintended consequences more than most, but the legislature has spoken and early results will be in soon enough. I hope to report on campuses and find out how they're working.

It is nevertheless worth thinking through scenarios like the ones above, for the law is very likely to have a mishmash of positive and negative consequences coexisting with one another—and perhaps anticipating potential pitfalls as well as opportunities for worthwhile change can help college students and administrators to steer things in a slightly better direction than they'd float on their own.

With that in mind, I hope current college students (or recent grads) who've made it through the musings of out-of-touch oldsters like me will reflect on their observations and experiences, and then send e-mail articulating how *they* think affirmative-consent laws will play out (or have played out) on campus. What are commentators who haven't themselves been college students for years or decades missing, or misunderstanding, about sexual culture on campus today or how it will change? Insightful e-mail sent to conor@theatlantic.com will published as reader letters.

Critical Thinking

1. What are the requirements of California's affirmative consent law?
2. If this law were enacted in your state and on your campus how might it change your sexual behavior and that of your fellow students? Do you think there would be gender differences in reactions and responses to the law? If so, how might the behavior of male versus female college students be differentially impacted?
3. How effective do you think the law will be in preventing sexual assault among college students? What else might be needed besides the legislation to decrease rates of date rape and sexual violence on college campuses?

Internet References

American College Health Association: Campus and Sexual Violence
http://www.acha.org/Topics/violence.cfm

California's Affirmative Consent Law
https://leginfo.legislature.ca.gov/faces/billNavClient.xhtml?bill_id=201320140SB967

National Sexual Violence Resource Center: Campus Sexual Violence Resource List
http://www.nsvrc.org/saam/campus-resource-list

Article

Prepared by: Patricia Hrusa Williams, *University of Maine at Farmington*

There's No Such Thing as Everlasting Love (According to Science)

EMILY ESFAHANI SMITH

Learning Outcomes

After reading this article, you will be able to:

- Understand differences in theoretical, practical, and scientific definitions of love.
- Explain the science, biochemistry, and physiological components behind love.

In her new book *Love 2.0: How Our Supreme Emotion Affects Everything We Feel, Think, Do, and Become,* the psychologist Barbara Fredrickson offers a radically new conception of love.

Fredrickson, a leading researcher of positive emotions at the University of North Carolina at Chapel Hill, presents scientific evidence to argue that love is not what we think it is. It is not a long-lasting, continually present emotion that sustains a marriage; it is not the yearning and passion that characterizes young love; and it is not the blood-tie of kinship.

Rather, it is what she calls a "micro-moment of positivity resonance." She means that love is a connection, characterized by a flood of positive emotions, which you share with another person—*any* other person—whom you happen to connect with in the course of your day. You can experience these micro-moments with your romantic partner, child, or close friend. But you can also fall in love, however momentarily, with less likely candidates, like a stranger on the street, a colleague at work, or an attendant at a grocery store. Louis Armstrong put it best in "It's a Wonderful World" when he sang, "I see friends shaking hands, sayin' 'how do you do?' / They're really sayin', 'I love you.'"

Fredrickson's unconventional ideas are important to think about at this time of year. With Valentine's Day around the corner, many Americans are facing a grim reality: They are love-starved. Rates of loneliness are on the rise as social supports are disintegrating. In 1985, when the General Social Survey polled Americans on the number of confidants they have in their lives, the most common response was three. In 2004, when the survey was given again, the most common response was zero.

According to the University of Chicago's John Cacioppo, an expert on loneliness, and his co-author William Patrick, "at any given time, roughly 20 percent of individuals—that would be 60 million people in the U.S. alone—feel sufficiently isolated for it to be a major source of unhappiness in their lives." For older Americans, that number is closer to 35 percent. At the same time, rates of depression have been on the rise. In his 2011 book *Flourish,* the psychologist Martin Seligman notes that according to some estimates, depression is 10 times more prevalent now than it was five decades ago. Depression affects about 10 percent of the American population, according to the Centers for Disease Control.

A global poll taken last Valentine's Day showed that most married people—or those with a significant other—list their romantic partner as the greatest source of happiness in their lives. According to the same poll, nearly half of all single people are looking for a romantic partner, saying that finding a special person to love would contribute greatly to their happiness.

But to Fredrickson, these numbers reveal a "worldwide collapse of imagination," as she writes in her book. "Thinking of love purely as romance or commitment that you share with one special person—as it appears most on earth do—surely limits the health and happiness you derive" from love.

"My conception of love," she tells me, "gives hope to people who are single or divorced or widowed this Valentine's Day to find smaller ways to experience love."

You have to physically be with the person to experience the micro-moment. For example, if you and your significant other are not physically together—if you are reading this at work alone in your office—then you two are not in love. You may feel connected or bonded to your partner—you may long to be in his company—but your body is completely loveless.

To understand why, it's important to see how love works biologically. Like all emotions, love has a biochemical and physiological component. But unlike some of the other positive emotions, like joy or happiness, love cannot be kindled individually—it only exists in the physical connection between two people. Specifically, there are three players in the biological love system—mirror neurons, oxytocin, and vagal tone. Each involves connection and each contributes to those micro-moments of positivity resonance that Fredrickson calls love.

When you experience love, your brain mirrors the person's you are connecting with in a special way. Pioneering research by Princeton University's Uri Hasson shows what happens inside the brains of two people who connect in conversation. Because brains are scanned inside of noisy fMRI machines, where carrying on a conversation is nearly impossible, Hasson's team had his subjects mimic a natural conversation in an ingenious way. They recorded a young woman telling a lively, long, and circuitous story about her high school prom. Then, they played the recording for the participants in the study, who were listening to it as their brains were being scanned. Next, the researchers asked each participant to re-create the story so they, the researchers, could determine who was listening well and who was not. Good listeners, the logic goes, would probably be the ones who clicked in a natural conversation with the story-teller.

What they found was remarkable. In some cases, the brain patterns of the listener mirrored those of the storyteller after a short time gap. The listener needed time to process the story after all. In other cases, the brain activity was almost perfectly synchronized; there was no time lag at all between the speaker and the listener. But in some rare cases, if the listener was particularly tuned in to the story—if he was hanging on to every word of the story and really got it—his brain activity actually *anticipated* the story-teller's in some cortical areas.

The mutual understanding and shared emotions, especially in that third category of listener, generated a micro-moment of love, which "is a single act, performed by two brains," as Fredrickson writes in her book.

Oxytocin, the so-called love and cuddle hormone, facilitates these moments of shared intimacy and is part of the mammalian "calm-and-connect" system (as opposed to the more stressful "fight-or-flight" system that closes us off to others). The hormone, which is released in huge quantities during sex, and in lesser amounts during other moments of intimate connection, works by making people feel more trusting and open to connection. This is the hormone of attachment and bonding that spikes during micro-moments of love. Researchers have found, for instance, that when a parent acts affectionately with his or her infant—through micro-moments of love like making eye contact, smiling, hugging, and playing—oxytocin levels in both the parent and the child rise in sync.

The final player is the vagus nerve, which connects your brain to your heart and subtly but sophisticatedly allows you to meaningfully experience love. As Fredrickson explains in her book, "Your vagus nerve stimulates tiny facial muscles that better enable you to make eye contact and synchronize your facial expressions with another person. It even adjusts the miniscule muscles of your middle ear so you can better track her voice against any background noise."

The vagus nerve's potential for love can actually be measured by examining a person's heart rate in association with his breathing rate, what's called "vagal tone." Having a high vagal tone is good: People who have a high "vagal tone" can regulate their biological processes like their glucose levels better; they have more control over their emotions, behavior, and attention; they are socially adept and can kindle more positive connections with others; and, most importantly, they are more loving. In research from her lab, Fredrickson found that people with high vagal tone report more experiences of love in their days than those with a lower vagal tone.

Historically, vagal tone was considered stable from person to person. You either had a high one or you didn't; you either had a high potential for love or you didn't. Fredrickson's recent research has debunked that notion.

In a 2010 study from her lab, Fredrickson randomly assigned half of her participants to a "love" condition and half to a control condition. In the love condition, participants devoted about one hour of their weeks for several months to the ancient Buddhist practice of loving-kindness meditation. In loving-kindness meditation, you sit in silence for a period of time and cultivate feelings of tenderness, warmth, and compassion for another person by repeating a series of phrases to yourself wishing them love, peace, strength, and general well-being. Ultimately, the practice helps people step outside of themselves and become more aware of other people and their needs, desires, and struggles—something that can be difficult to do in our hyper individualistic culture.

Fredrickson measured the participants' vagal tone before and after the intervention. The results were so powerful that she was invited to present them before the Dalai Lama himself in 2010. Fredrickson and her team found that, contrary to the conventional wisdom, people could significantly increase their vagal tone by self-generating love through loving-kindness meditation. Since vagal tone mediates social connections and bonds, people whose vagal tones increased were suddenly capable of experiencing more micro-moments of love in their days. Beyond that, their growing capacity to love more will translate into health benefits given that high vagal tone is associated with lowered risk of inflammation, cardiovascular disease, diabetes, and stroke.

Fredrickson likes to call love a nutrient. If you are getting enough of the nutrient, then the health benefits of love can dramatically alter your biochemistry in ways that perpetuate more micro-moments of love in your life, and which ultimately contribute to your health, well-being, and longevity.

Fredrickson's ideas about love are not exactly the stuff of romantic comedies. Describing love as a "micro-moment of positivity resonance" seems like a buzz-kill. But if love now seems less glamorous and mysterious than you thought it was, then good. Part of Fredrickson's project is to lower cultural expectations about love—expectations that are so misguidedly high today that they have inflated love into something that it isn't, and into something that no sane person could actually experience.

Jonathan Haidt, another psychologist, calls these unrealistic expectations "the love myth" in his 2006 book *The Happiness Hypothesis:*

> True love is passionate love that never fades; if you are in true love, you should marry that person; if love ends, you should leave that person because it was not true love; and if you can find the right person, you will have true love forever. You might not believe this myth yourself, particularly if you are older than thirty; but many young people in Western nations are raised on it, and it acts as an ideal that they unconsciously carry with them even if they scoff at it. . . . But if true love is defined as eternal passion, it is biologically impossible.

Love 2.0 is, by contrast, far humbler. Fredrickson tells me, "I love the idea that it lowers the bar of love. If you don't have a Valentine, that doesn't mean that you don't have love. It puts love much more in our reach everyday regardless of our relationship status."

Lonely people who are looking for love are making a mistake if they are sitting around and waiting for love in the form of the "love myth" to take hold of them. If they instead sought out love in little moments of connection that we all experience many times a day, perhaps their loneliness would begin to subside.

Critical Thinking

1. What is your definition of love? What are some similarities and differences between your definition and the ones presented in the article?
2. Explain the love myth.
3. Do you believe that people can be trained to be more loving, as the article implies? Why or why not?
4. What are some advantages and disadvantages of defining love as "micro-moments" of positive feelings and emotions?

Internet References

Go Ask Alice!
www.goaskalice.columbia.edu

The Kinsey Institute for Research in Sex, Gender, and Reproduction
www.kinseyinstitute.org

The Society for the Scientific Study of Sexuality
www.sexscience.org

The Electronic Journal of Human Sexuality
www.ejhs.org/index.htm

Article

Prepared by: Patricia Hrusa Williams, *University of Maine at Farmington*

Dating As If It Were Driver's Ed

Lisa Jander

Learning Outcomes

After reading this article, you will be able to:

- Recognize risks faced by dating teens.
- Explain why mandating relationship education programs for teens is difficult and controversial.
- Define the components needed for a comprehensive relationship education program for teens and their parents.

"So, what movie do you think I should take Emily to see?" I was sitting in the passenger seat next to my 16-year-old son while he practiced his parallel parking, hoping he would not hit anything. His question made me grip the armrest just a little bit tighter. My head was spinning and my heart was racing trying to block out the image of what "parking" meant for teens when I was in high school. How in the world was I going to prepare him for dating with no manual, instructor, or parental supervision? Just like driving, dating invites a very skewed notion of freedom if not approached with a solid set of guidelines.

Millions of parents watch like deer in the headlights as their kids accelerate into the teen dating years without a map and find themselves in the midst of a crisis: teen sex and pregnancy; couples drinking and doing drugs; dating violence and abuse; plus stress, anxiety, depression, and even suicide. Just sit on the beach during spring break or chaperone a school dance: the boundary lines are blurry at best and fading fast. Teen dating is not what it used to be; our culture and social media have changed the course of teen relationships forever.

Despite every effort to educate teens about the dangers associated with unhealthy choices, statistics indicate that the information may be falling on deaf ears (or maybe an underdeveloped prefrontal cortex). The inconsistent delivery of information on topics such as sex and drugs are proving to be less than effective compared to the cultural pressures that every teen faces. In addition, budget restrictions, limited access to resources, and negative or nonexistent parental influence can become roadblocks to the essential help and guidance teenagers need. Consequently, we have become a reactive society, throwing sandbags against the tide of influence where teens already are in way over their heads.

So, where is the hope for this generation and what are we teaching them about relationships? The reality is that only 22 states and the District of Columbia require sex education in public schools when more than 47 percent of high school students already have had sex, according to a survey by the Centers for Disease Control and Prevention (CDC). Conflicting messages about whether to have protected sex, or none at all, present choices that require a degree of logic and long-term planning that many teens do not possess. Without a proper foundation and ongoing support, teens are left to let their emotions drive them in the heat of the moment, which can result in life-altering consequences. Add social media and mass distribution of smart phones to the equation, and young people are on a collision course with visual imagery that heightens the senses and could make it much easier for them to get into trouble. The signs are there and the culture is paving the way.

With a stream of violent input from the world around them, teen brains also are being rewired and desensitized to the shock of abuse. The CDC provides education on dating violence and abuse through a program called "Dating Matters" in four high-risk communities in the country, and surveys show that 1 in 10 teenagers report experiencing abuse within the past 12 months. Hundreds of localized courses, along with a dozen national organizations, have made huge strides to squash bullying in an effort to minimize dating violence and abuse. Creative programs are introduced in schools during pep assemblies to encourage kindness and respect, as well as raise awareness of physical boundaries.

Dating under the influence also includes the abuse of drugs and alcohol. Thrill-seeking teens are bored with traditional highs and [are] lured into experimentation fueled by concoctions such as "Molly" and "Spice," as well as a new drinking game called NekNominate. Trying to stay ahead of the trend is a full-time job for most parents and educators who simply do not have the time nor information to steer teens away from the latest dangers. Educational programs warn against peer pressure when often the real push is from a "love" influence, which, for the adolescent brain, is much harder to resist.

According to the National Comorbidity Survey-Adolescent Supplement (NCS-A), about 11 percent of adolescents have a depressive disorder by age 18. The World Health Organization states that major depressive disorder is the leading cause of disability among Americans aged 15 to 44. For youth between the ages of 10 and 24, suicide is the third leading cause of death, maintains the National Institute of Mental Health. These troubling statistics have created a flurry of new medication trials, research, and therapies to understand and treat this growing trend. Whether temporary or long term, mild or severe, much of the teen stress in today's world is traced back to relational challenges, which certainly include dating. Teens ending their lives because of a "bad breakup" is becoming more and more common.

So, where does the responsibility for dating safety fall? Is it on the school, parents, community, law, or teen? Perhaps we can learn something from the Driver's Ed program that will help families navigate the teen dating years without a disaster. The evidence shows that very few teens fail Driver's Ed, but millions fail at dating. By looking at the history of driving, we can learn how to help steer teens away from the tragic dating accidents that take them off course.

In the summer of 1886, Karl Benz rolled his pride and joy—a three-wheeled motor car—through the streets of Mannheim, Germany. This "baby" was born seven months earlier, marked by a patent for the design that often is regarded as the "birth certificate of the automobile." Two years later, Benz's wife Bertha and her two sons took a road trip to prove the reliability and practical nature of the vehicle. Bertha traveled a full 112 miles with a maximum speed of 8 miles per hour. There was no seatbelt law, speed limit signs, nor traffic lights. Her daring journey sparked new growth for Benz & Cie. to become the world's largest automobile manufacturer.

In 1902, Ransom Olds opened the door to his large-scale, production line manufacturing of automobiles in Lansing, Mich. Now, vehicle speeds were exceeding 40 miles per hour and people were getting hurt. There was no formal training and drivers were notoriously reckless and unskilled. In the United Kingdom, efforts were made to regulate safety through the Motor Car Act in 1903 by requiring the first mandatory registering of every vehicle. At 17 years old, potential drivers could apply for this newfound freedom—agreeing to travel at a maximum speed of no more than 20 mph.

Over the next nine years, accidents and fatalities spiraled out of control until, finally, in 1913, New Jersey paved the way for mandated education followed by an exam before issuing a license. The timing could not have been more perfect, as Henry Ford significantly expanded the concept of mass production through manufacturing in 1914 and began turning out vehicles that could achieve speeds as high as 65 mph.

The common thread that followed was the undeniable need for the merging of proactive instruction for drivers along with safety measures for automobiles to minimize the ever-growing need for reactive solutions. As the auto industry soared, so did the accident rate. Safety became central to the manufacturing of vehicles backed by laws to improve safety ratings monitored by the Federal Motor Vehicle Safety Standards. There had to be a collective effort on the part of manufacturers, law enforcement, educators, parents, and even new teenage drivers to help them reach their destinations in one piece.

In recent decades, we have seen a surge of safety features developed for cars in an attempt to reduce risk and save the lives of teens who are fueled by dopamine, adrenaline, and an underdeveloped brain, driving a two-ton weapon at speeds of up to 70 mph (or more). Seatbelts, airbags, anti-lock brakes, and shatterproof glass give them far more protection in the event of a collision, but does not eliminate the reality that accidents happen. Every person knows a teenager who has had a close call, or worse.

The good news is that men and women committed to the auto industry work progressively and diligently to invent new security features in a race to get ahead of the tragedies. New laws are passed each year printed in neon yellow on every street comer to slow the speed of driving disasters. Driver's Ed programs are enforced not only to educate, but to give supervised experience to teens so that they have a chance of getting to school and back without getting hit—or hitting something or someone.

Turbo-charged Hormones

So, what is the educational program for teen dating? Parents give teens the thumbs up and a smile and send them off in a pack with turbo-charged hormones to the dark movie theater and hope they do not have an accident. What new safety features have been implemented in the past 50 years to give our teens a better chance at healthy relationships? What proactive laws are in place to protect these young lives from ending up in the junkyard of broken hearts? What can we do as a culture to minimize the risks and enforce education? For teenagers, it seems that "speed dating" is not an event, it is a lifestyle.

The answer may not be as clear as a windshield after a summer rain, but it certainly is becoming more and more obvious.

Social media is not going away and neither is the invention of the teenager. A negative cultural norm is growing more enticing to teenagers, which promotes entitled independence and an Autobahn, boundary-free approach to dating for which there seems to be no exit.

Part of parental responsibility is to provide the opportunity for children to learn which is diverted when smartphones, advertisements, and media are educating our kids without our knowledge. What teens learn about relationships will impact virtually every aspect of their lives: at home, school, work, and in the community and world. Just like a driving accident can min their lives, a dating accident can be just as tragic.

Driver's Education is the government's way of standardizing what all drivers should learn so that young drivers do as little damage to themselves or to others as possible. The state booklet says that parents or guardians are "often the best judge of your teen drivers' progress, skill, and maturity." That is the sugarcoating. Below that it says that "They [meaning the state of Michigan in this case] will notify you by letter if your teen driver is convicted of violating the terms of his or her Graduated Driver License."

To mandate social skills training, dating education, and marriage readiness would evoke a pushback more massive than the 1913 Driver's Ed course law in New Jersey. Nonetheless, how many statistics need to pile up before we gather all of the fantastic efforts of the mighty few that are making a difference and put them into a bill or, at the very least, a required course for parents and teens.

What would the data reveal in 10 years if, today, all eighth-graders and their parents were required to take an eight-week class on "healthy relationships" before the student could attend high school or apply for a driver's license? This course could combine the knowledge of specialists dedicated to their field of expertise in one central location to prepare them to navigate the high school years socially. A certificate of completion, just like a driver's permit, would show that the student had accomplished the work. Insurance companies might even be interested in sponsoring the course—after all, the desire to drive and date shift into gear at right about the same age.

Driver's Ed courses require parents to log 50 hours of supervised drive time with their teen before they are permitted to operate a vehicle alone. Parents do not think twice about monitoring teen driving, but the thought of riding along on a teen date is considered ludicrous. Chaperoning on dates is considered taboo these days, but maybe a contemporary version of this practice should emerge and be supported by parents, schools, and the community. What if parents were required to log 50 hours of community service with their teens prior to their graduation to encourage and foster compassion and kindness in a structured environment?

Teens make up nearly 47 percent of our population but are 100 percent of our future. Teens are not defective; they just are not done yet. There are values, beliefs, morals, habits, and knowledge that still need to be installed. Parents and other healthy adults bridge the gap between teen emotions and mature logic to help them cruise safely into adulthood. We enlist teachers, coaches, pastors, family members, and others to guide and encourage our children. Leaving them to find their own way is like putting them alone in a car blindfolded with no brakes, steering wheel, or GPS. We have the right and the privilege of sliding into that seat beside them and helping them through the obstacle course of relationships. Without our support, they very well could find themselves on a crash course.

Buckle up, parents. It is the law of attraction. Safe teen dating does not happen by accident.

Critical Thinking

1. Why do you feel states have not adopted relationship education programs in the same way they require drivers' education for teens?
2. What do you see as the most important challenges facing teens and their parents when they begin dating?
3. If you were to develop a relationship education program for teens, what would it look like and why? What do you think of the Dating Matters Program mentioned in the article (see http://www.cdc.gov/ViolencePrevention/DatingMatters/index.html)?

Internet References

Dating Matters
http://www.cdc.gov/ViolencePrevention/DatingMatters/index.html

Go Ask Alice!
www.goaskalice.columbia.edu

Love is Respect
www.loveisrespect.org

Two of Us
http://www.twoofus.org

LISA JANDER who calls herself the Teen Dating Mechanic, is author of *Dater's Ed: Driver's Ed Model for Dating* and the online teen curriculum TeenDatingLicense.com.

Article Prepared by: Patricia Hrusa Williams, *University of Maine at Farmington*

Sliding versus Deciding: How Cohabitation Changes Marriage

Galena Rhoades

Learning Outcomes

After reading this article, you will be able to:

- Describe the concept of "sliding versus deciding."
- Explain the difference between dedication commitment and constraint commitment.
- Understand factors important to marital quality in heterosexual couples.

My colleague Scott Stanley and I put out a report in the summer of 2014 that was called "Before I Do," sponsored by the National Marriage Project at the University of Virginia; that report is the foundation for this article [1]. A generation or two ago, people formed relationships and made commitments differently than they do now. We were interested in looking at the ways dating and commitment sequences have changed over the years, and how those sequences might be related to later marital quality.

One of the perspectives Scott Stanley and I have been working on is what we call "sliding versus deciding." This concept refers, in part, to the number of choices young people have today. This variety of choices might be one of the biggest differences between dating today and dating a generation or two ago; now, people have many more options, not just in the partners that they choose, but also in the paths that might or might not lead them to marriage. Our general premise is that we can expect better outcomes if people make conscious decisions rather than sliding into new circumstances.

"Sliding versus deciding" summarizes the distinction between "dedication" and "constraint" commitment. "Commitment" usually implies the idea of a relationship having a long-term future, and that is what we call "dedication." It is a sense that the couple is working together as a team; there is the expectation of a future together and of planning for the future. The flip side of dedication commitment is "constraint" commitment. Constraint commitment comes from things that build up and make it harder to leave the relationship. Some examples of constraints are buying a home together, having a child together (that one does not happen to be predictive of whether or not couples stay together if they are unmarried, interestingly) or adopting a pet together—things that might make it harder to end a relationship regardless of how committed or dedicated you feel to that relationship. In simpler terms, constraint commitment is sliding; dedication is deciding.

A generation or two ago, deciding was the norm. You felt love toward another person, you felt attracted to another person, you decided to be more committed to another person, commitment built, and then you built constraints. It was after you made a commitment that you moved in together, had a child together, changed your career, moved across the country, bought a house together, and adopted pets. In that case, it did not really matter that you had taken on those extra constraints because you already felt dedicated to this person. But when you slide through new circumstances or relationship transitions like moving in together or having sex in a relationship, you break up that traditional sequence. For example, you might feel attracted to someone, you might feel like you love someone, and then you start building constraints without really developing a sense of dedication to the relationship. You are still on this track toward staying together, however, because of those constraints. We think what happens when people slide into relationship transitions is that they may start building constraints before they have a chance to think about whether they want to be committed or dedicated to this person and this relationship; and this constraint before commitment could cause problems later on.

To look at some of these questions about experiences and sequences before marriage, Scott and I used a study that we had conducted with our colleague Howard Markman at the University of Denver, a study that was initially funded by the National Institute of Child Health and Human Development. We call it the relationship development study [2]. About 1,300 people started this study. They were recruited nationally, all of them unmarried English-speaking people in the United States. They completed surveys 30 to 35 pages long in 11 waves four to six months apart. We were interested in looking at these unmarried couples and following them over time to see what happened. (I am very grateful that these participants stuck with us long enough to complete this study because it was fairly time consuming and a little intrusive.) We focused only on people in opposite-sex relationships in this study. When the study started, about 2/3 of participants were dating, and the other third had already moved in with their partners. For this report, we chose people who got married during the course of the study so that we could examine the histories of those relationships and those individuals, maybe even before they got into the relationship that turned into marriage, and then we could look at their marital quality after marriage.

Here are some of the results. . . . We measured marital quality with a brief version of a widely used instrument called the Dyadic Adjustment Scale. This instrument asks people to rate their marital happiness, how often they confide in one another, how often they think things are going well, and how often they have thought of breaking up or getting a divorce. In this sample, people were relatively happy, reporting fairly high marital quality, which makes sense, since most of them had just gotten married. In order to continue with the study, they had to get married during the study period; and usually newlyweds have the highest level of marital quality they will ever experience. Marital quality tends to decline after marriage, but why wouldn't it? You are not going to get married if you are not pretty sure you are happy in the relationship.

We analyzed a number of background characteristics before we started looking at the main questions about different relationship experiences and transitions. . . . Not many background characteristics were related to marital quality, at least in these first couple of years into marriage. What we do see are associations between factors that are significant, significance that has been well replicated. For example, we know that people who have higher levels of education tend to report higher marital quality, and they are less likely to get a divorce. We know that people who were living with both of their biological parents when they were 14–years-old also report higher marital quality later on. (There is nothing magical about the number 14; it is just the age that was used in other research.) We know that people who come from more stable families tend to have more stability in their own relationships later on. Unfortunately, we also see some important gaps between African Americans and Caucasians in terms of stability and quality of relationships. In this study, we do not see that religiousness was associated with marital quality. That contradicts a number of findings in this field, however, and merits some explanation. I think the reason we do not see an association between religion and marital quality in this study is because we are looking at such an early segment of marital quality; the effects of religiousness might show up later in marriage, especially when couples are having children together. Similarly, we did not find that income was associated with marital quality in this study and that also contradicts other findings, especially about the way income is related to the risk for divorce. Here again, I think that is likely because we were looking at marital quality right after marriage.

In terms of the main findings, we focused on two broad categories of experiences people might have before getting married. One category is experiences from prior relationships. The other category is experiences with the person whom they eventually marry, the couple's history before marriage.

. . .

Regarding individuals' prior relationship experiences, here is what we have found. Most of the people in the study were entering a first marriage. People who were entering a first marriage reported higher marital quality than people who were entering a second or third or even fourth (there was ¼ marriage in this sample). Couples with children from prior relationships had lower marital quality later on. We also looked at their experiences with past sexual partners. People who had sex only with their future spouse and no one else reported higher marital quality later on. About 23 percent of this sample had sex only with the person they married. . . . Almost 40 percent of the sample had lived with a prior partner before they got together with the person they married; having had other cohabiting partners was associated with lower marital quality later on.

There were a couple of gender differences regarding prior relationship experiences as well as regarding children from prior relationships. Having children from a prior marriage made a bigger difference for women in terms of their later marital quality than it did for men. This can probably be explained in part by the fact that women are more likely to have custody of those children, so the woman's children are more likely to be involved in the new marriage. Women's own marital quality may be more affected by their own children than by their partner's children.

We also saw a gender difference when we looked at the number of prior sex partners these individuals had before they got together with the person they married. While it was true that men who had sex only with their future spouse experienced higher marital quality, among those who had had multiple partners, the number did not make as much difference as it did for women. . . . About ¼ of the sample, as mentioned earlier, had sex only with their future spouse; another ¼ of the sample had sex with two to four partners before marriage; and about ⅓ had sex with five to ten partners before marriage. The findings show that the group of women who had had sex with more than 10 partners before marriage reported the lowest marital quality later on. The average in the sample, about eight sexual partners before marriage, was similar for men and women. However, the median in this sample was five—the mean is skewed by people who reported many, many sexual partners before marriage. What we see here is that, at least for women, the more partners they have had, the lower their marital quality later on.

One of the most interesting things about these findings, which in many ways were new to this field, is that prior relationship experience really matters, but in a somewhat counterintuitive way. If you are hiring an architect, you want to hire someone who has a lot of experience. If you are going to see a doctor, you probably want a doctor who has a lot of experience in your illness. But in terms of relationships, we are seeing that the opposite is true. People with more experience might end up having more trouble later on in their marriages. There are a couple of potential explanations for this. One is that, if you have a lot of experience, you also have a greater sense of what the alternatives are, and you have more comparisons to make to other people. It also is true that the more experience you have in relationships, the more experience you have breaking up. That experience with breaking up might make it seem easier to break up later in a marriage or it may make you think about breaking up more and question the quality of the relationship more. We also see that more experience means you are more likely to have children before you get married, and we saw the effect of that earlier.

More than 40 percent of babies born in the United States today are born to unmarried parents. We used to say they were born to single mothers, but they are not "single" mothers, for the most part. The mothers are often partnered with the baby's father or with someone else when the baby is born. We also know that those families tend to be quite fragile, and we are seeing some of that fragility carried over in these findings about marriage as well: children from prior relationships tend to be difficult on a marriage. Having children is hard, and it is especially hard to start a marriage already having children.

It is interesting to think about the messages young people hear today about relationship experience, messages like, "Don't settle down too soon." "Make sure you get everything out of your system." "Your 20s are a time for great exploration." "What happens in Vegas stays in Vegas." "Those things won't affect your future marital quality or outcomes." In fact, what we are seeing here seems to be the opposite. Those experiences do impact us in some important ways and may lead to us having a more difficult time later on in marriage. Scott Stanley talks about the "duct-tape hypothesis," which is the idea that, if you have a piece of duct tape and you keep sticking it to things, it gets less sticky over time. Applied to relationships, the idea is that the more relationships you have, the harder it may be to really commit to another partner going forward.

After looking at prior relationships, we looked at experiences the couple had together before they got married. For example, we looked at how long they had been together. Remarkably, in this sample, time together was not associated with their marital quality later on. There may be some extremes. Getting married very quickly could be a negative, or, in some cases, a positive. On the other hand, for people who have been together a very long time maybe there would be some circumstances where that was a negative. There is no magic number for how long you need to be together before getting married, at least according to these data.

We also looked at the age at which a couple married and found that getting married older was associated with lower marital quality, which again goes against some conventional wisdom.

We asked people if their relationship started with "hooking up," and we let them self-define what "hooking up" meant. About 32 percent of the sample did start that way, and we found that those couples had lower marital quality later on.

Couples who had children together already or who were pregnant before they got married also had lower marital quality. This finding may reflect the fact that having kids is hard, but it also may be a result of sliding into marriage. Hooking up, having sex before getting into a relationship, before feeling committed in a relationship, and having children or becoming pregnant before getting married may also reflect that sliding mentality to some degree.

However, education level was also related to how strongly being pregnant before marriage was associated with later marital quality. People who had a college degree were much less likely to be in the top marital quality group if they had a child together before they got married. For people who did not have a college degree, we hardly saw any difference at all in their marital quality based on whether they had a child before they got married. That difference is important for us to think about in future work and in public policy as well. In part, what this reflects are the norms. People who do not graduate from high school are much more likely to have a child outside of marriage than people who graduate from college. It is really quite outside the norm for people who do graduate from college to have a baby or become pregnant, or to let anyone know about that before getting married. Those social norms might affect later marital quality.

We also tried to look at some potential red flags in a relationship before getting married. We asked people in the study if they had ever had a sexual relationship with someone other than their partner while they were dating that person; in other words, had this person ever cheated on their partner before getting married. In our sample, 16 percent said yes, but this was only very weakly related to marital quality later on. Again, this is not a great message for us to be telling young people. Many dating relationships where there is infidelity end long before they would turn into marriage. About 10 percent of our sample knew that their partner had had a sexual relationship with someone else while the two of them were dating, and that was related to lower marital quality later on.

We also asked many questions about physical aggression in these relationships, and this data is staggering. Of people who got married in this sample, 53 percent reported that there had at some point been physical aggression in their relationship. It could be as minor as throwing something at your partner that could hurt, all the way up to very severe aggression, coercion, or sexual coercion. In marriage and couple research, we tend to ignore aggression, but this number says that we cannot. This is something we really need to be talking about and helping to educate people about: how to make sure conflict does not get to that level and how to get people out of very unsafe relationships. I imagine only a few of these in our study really represented very unsafe relationships, but there are some unsafe relationships within this sample. Probably not surprisingly, people who reported some physical aggression in their relationships also reported lower marital quality later on.

Aggression is also involved in some other findings that are coming out of our research lab at the University of Denver. A graduate student there has been looking at how infidelity and aggression in one relationship are associated with infidelity and aggression in the next relationship. She finds that you are much more likely to experience infidelity or aggression if you have had that in your just-prior relationship. This fits with the idea that the more experience you have, the more likely you are to repeat some of those negative patterns. Part of what is interesting here is that it goes both ways. That is, if you cheated in your last relationship, you are more likely to cheat in your next relationship; but also, unfortunately, if you were cheated on in your last relationship, you are also more likely to be cheated on in your next relationship.

We asked a number of questions about commitment and cohabitation. We asked people about the timing of moving in together and whether they had committed to marriage before they moved in together. About 70 percent of this sample had lived together before they got married. We found that people who had lived together before they were committed to marriage together, before they had a mutual and clear plan to get married, reported lower marital quality later on. About 70 to 75 percent of people now live together before they get married. The most common answer to the question "Why did you move in together?" is "It just kind of happened." And that it was more convenient. What we are seeing here is that, if a couple has already made the commitment to marry, if they are already dedicated to one another, moving in together is not associated with lower marital quality. However, moving in is associated with lower marital quality among those couples that slide into living together but then maybe build a number of those constraints. For some of them, it may be the constraints that lead them to get married, when they otherwise maybe would not have married this partner after all. That is also an important finding to consider, because a lot of young people today really like the idea of collecting lots of data before making the big decision of getting married. What better way to do that than by moving in with this person? You want to know if this person is going to leave the toilet seat up, or you want to know how she handles money. You want to find out all these things about this person. This desire may come from a really good place, but the problem is that moving in together may put couples on a track toward getting married that is hard to get off. It is harder to end a relationship once you have moved in together, even if the relationship fails that test, essentially.

We asked people who did live with their partners before they got married how it happened. Was it a slide, or did you make the decision together? We found that people who said they made a decision together reported higher marital quality, which supports the idea that deciding is generally associated with better outcomes. We also asked people at every wave to rate their own commitment on a 1–7 scale, and then immediately afterward to rate their partner's commitment on the same 1–7 scale. Interestingly, across those waves, before they got married, if they ever thought they were more committed than their partner was, they had lower marital quality later on. The results reflect the idea that, if there are major differences between a couple in how they like to make decisions and what commitment means to them, those differences may continue to cause problems.

We asked about the wedding and whether people got any kind of premarital education. An amazing 43 percent of people said that they got some kind of premarital education together. That education could range from something like meeting with the pastor at the church one time to talk about wedding plans to something much more intensive, like a 30-hr workshop on relationships. There is good evidence that premarital education—especially the kind that teaches couples communication skills and gets them talking about differences and expectations—is associated with a lower risk for divorce later on. We asked if people had a wedding, and about 90 percent said yes. Those who were in the minority on that question reported lower marital quality later on. We also asked how many people attended the wedding. The mean number of people was 116 in this sample, and the more people you had at your wedding, the higher your marital quality later on.

Further research that has come out recently has looked at this question of wedding attendance more carefully, and they also find that the more people who attend your wedding, the higher your marital quality and the lower your risk for divorce—and it is not related to how much money you spend on the wedding [3]. There are some really good theoretical reasons to think that the number of people who attend might actually be important. One reason is that the more public your commitment is, the more likely you are to follow through on that. If you stand up and tell 100 or 200 people that you are promising to spend the rest of your life with this person in sickness and in health, it is going to be a little harder for you to break that promise because it has been such a public commitment. The other reason is that the large group likely reflects a greater social system and social network that supports your marriage. It may be that people who have more wedding attendees simply also have greater social networks. There may also be a causal relationship there as well, because it means that this entire audience of people has also committed to you to help protect your marriage and support you in this marriage. We were a little nervous about the implications of these findings at first, and I think this is a great area to do more research to really understand what these dynamics mean before we start sending the message, "Go have a big wedding and make your parents spend lots of money on it." This is, however, an interesting finding to think about in terms of sliding versus deciding, of commitment and what it means.

So what does this all mean for educating people about relationships? One thing is clear: there are some experiences and background characteristics people have that they cannot change. We cannot go back and change whether we were living with both our biological parents at age 14, but there may be some ways we can change the dynamics that those kinds of background characteristics initiate. We also see that there are many things young people have some control over that may be related to later marital quality and outcomes. We really need to start thinking about ways that we can impact people and help them make good relationship decisions earlier. The field of relationship education has focused on couples and premarital couples. It seems important to teach people how to communicate better, but I think we could have a much greater impact if we helped people think about their relationship experiences before they have them—when they are teenagers, when they are young adults, when they are in the middle of making some of these decisions or sliding through things. These are the times to think about whether they should hook up with somebody, whether they should get pregnant, whether they should move in with someone. There is a great amount of education that we could be doing long before a couple is about to walk down the aisle.

References

1. Galena K. Rhoades and Scott M. Stanley. 2014. "Before 'I Do': What Do Premarital Experiences Have to Do with Marital Quality among Today's Young Adults?" The National Marriage Project, the University of Virginia, available at http://before-i-do.org/.
2. Scott Stanley et al., "The Relationship Development Study," University of Denver, available at http://www.du.edu/relationshipstudy/index.html.
3. Andrew M. Francis and Hugo M. Mialon. 2015, October. "'A Diamond is Forever' and Other Fairy Tales: The Relationship between Wedding Expenses and Marriage Duration." *Economic Inquiry* 53.4: 1919–1930.

Critical Thinking

1. What does it mean to slide versus decide in relationship transitions and making commitments? Do you agree with the author's assertion that this generation is more likely to slide into new circumstances than make conscious relationship decisions? Why?
2. The "Before I Do" study examined how relationship experiences and the couple's history before getting married were related to marital quality. List some factors which were "red flags" or factors which were related to unhappy marriages.
3. Do you agree or disagree with the author's assertion that cohabitation is a form of sliding which brings with it with constraint commitment and results in lower marital quality? How strong is their evidence to support this? How could their study be improved?

Internet References

National Healthy Marriage Resource Center
http://www.healthymarriageinfo.org

Smart Marriages: The Coalition for Marriage, Family, and Couples Education
http://www.smartmarriages.com/index.html

The Fragile Families and Child Wellbeing Study at Princeton/Columbia
http://www.fragilefamilies.princeton.edu/

The National Marriage Project at the University of Virginia
http://nationalmarriageproject.org/wordpress/

Galena Rhoades, PhD, is a research associate professor and an associate clinical professor in the Department of Psychology at the University of Denver.

Article

Prepared by: Patricia Hrusa Williams, *University of Maine at Farmington*

Is There a Shortage of Marriageable Men?

ISABEL SAWHILL AND JOANNA VENATOR

Learning Outcomes

After reading this article, you will be able to:

- Define terms such as marriageable male, marriageability, marriage markets, and associative mating.
- Identify differences in men's versus women's mate selection patterns and preferences.
- Discuss the role which economic and cultural factors have on men's and women's marriageability and marriage rates.

Summary

In the last half century, marriage rates have fallen dramatically. In this paper, we explore possible drivers of this trend, including declining economic prospects among men, an increase in unwed births that constrain women's later marriageability, rising rates of incarceration, and a reversal of the education gap that once favored men and now favors women. We estimate that the decline in male earnings since 1970 among both black and less-educated white men can explain a portion of the decline in marriage, but that cultural factors have played an important role as well. We argue that the ratio of marriageable men to women depends critically on how one defines "marriageable." Looking just at current data rather than historical trends and using different definitions of marriageability, we find that there are shortages of marriageable men among the black population, but not among the white population (except among the best educated).

The Relationship between Male Economic Prospects and Marriage Rates

The possible effects of male employment and earnings on marriage have a long history in academic thought, starting as early as the 1965 Moynihan Report. In 1987, sociologist William Julius Wilson coined the term "marriageable male" in his book The Truly Disadvantaged.

Wilson posited that falling marriage rates and the rise of female-headed families within the black community were attributable to the poor economic opportunities available to black males. A sizeable literature in economics and sociology since then has suggested that Wilson's hypothesis has merit; that is, that the employment rate and the earnings of men within a local marriage market affect marriage. More specifically, based on the magnitude of this relationship found in five such studies, we estimate that the change in men's employment and earnings can explain around 27 percent of the decline in marriage rates since 1980.

We also conducted our own analysis of this relationship. In an unpublished working paper (available upon request), we estimate the relationship between male earnings and marriage rates over a 40-year period (1970–2010), using data from the Current Population Survey and the General Social Survey. We focus on marriage markets characterized by age (between 25 and 35), geographic area (metropolitan area), race (white or black), and education (college or less than college). We examine the effects of three key variables on marriage: changing attitudes, women's earnings, and men's earnings. Different models produce very different results, but we estimate that the decline in male earnings for less skilled men can explain anywhere from none to almost half of the decline in marriage rates since 1970. The midpoint of these different estimates and the one that accords with our own best judgment about the most appropriate model to use both suggest that the decline in earnings among noncollege-educated white men can explain about one-quarter of the decline in marriage rates between 1970 and 2010. The effects for black men (all education levels) are comparable or smaller than that of noncollege-educated whites. For college-educated whites, the effects are smaller still. For blacks and the college-educated of both races, there is a negative relationship between female earnings and marriage rates.

What Do We Mean by Marriageable?

William Julius Wilson's original definition of "marriageability" was the ratio of employed men to all women of the same age. Most of the subsequent literature has focused on indicators of male economic potential, including employment, earnings, and not being incarcerated. Similarly, a recent Pew Research Center report looking at marriage rates among young Americans found that over three-quarters of women surveyed cited having a partner with a stable job as a very important attribute they look for in someone to marry.

The assumption built into this definition is that marriageability is specific to men, but that all women are equally marriageable, regardless of employment status or other characteristics. However, this comparison does not reflect modern realities about the role that women's earnings play in family finances; they are now the primary breadwinner in 41 percent of all families. In addition, rising rates of unwed parenthood mean that a growing proportion of young women of marriageable age already have children from a prior relationship. Not only are many men understandably reluctant to take responsibility for someone else's child, but the single parents themselves have less time, and perhaps less inclination, to look for a new partner, given their childcare responsibilities and prior experience with relationships that didn't work out. Women who had their first child outside of marriage are more likely to cohabit and less likely to marry than comparable women without children, and when they do marry, they do not marry as well (i.e., their marital partners are less educated and older).

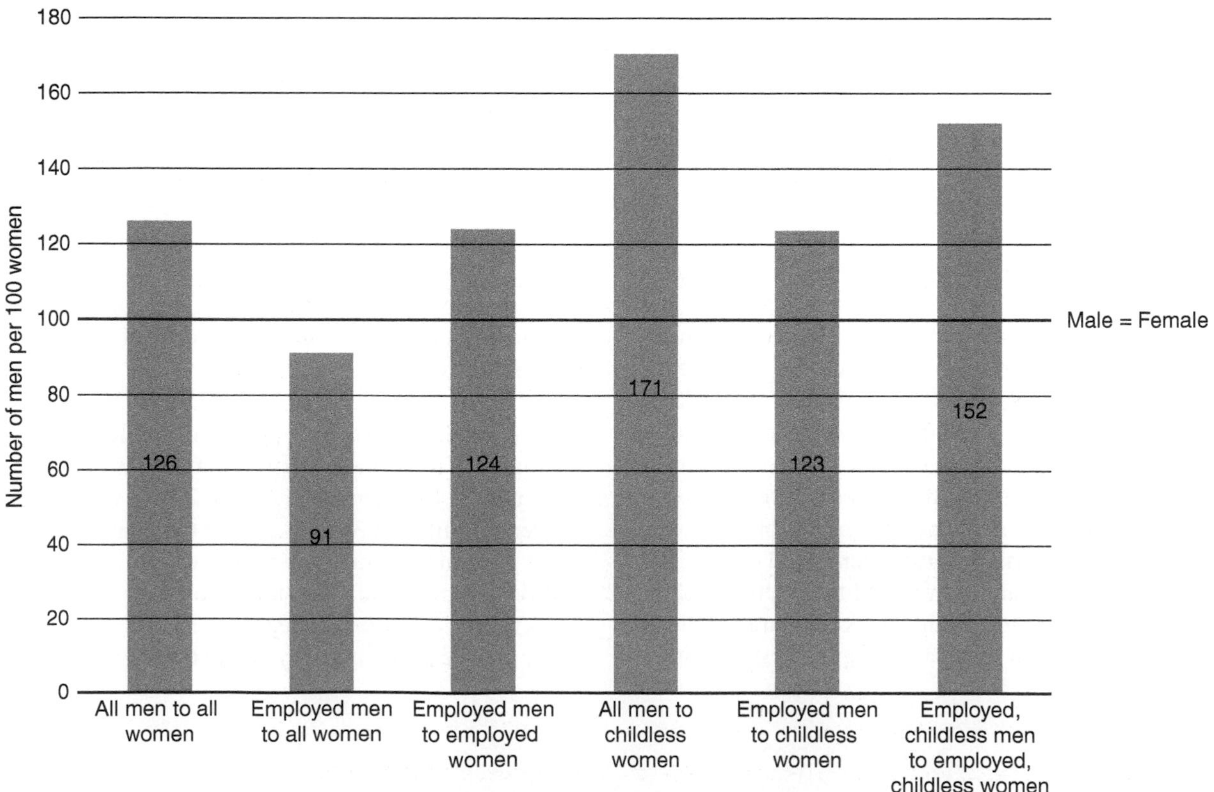

Figure 1 Marriage markets for never-married 25- to 34-year-olds, 2012

Source: Author's tabulations of 2012 Amercian Community Survey IPUMS data.

With these considerations in mind, we examined gender ratios that consider the employment of both men and women, as well as whether there are children from previous relationships, as indicators of marriageability. As Figure 1 shows, only one definition of marriageability—the original definition used by Wilson comparing employed men to all women—shows a lack of eligible men for women to marry. (Note that the ratio of all single men to all single women shows an excess of men, primarily because of women's earlier age at marriage.)

Looking at these gender ratios in the aggregate does not tell the whole story, of course. Assortative mating—marrying someone from a similar background—is the norm in the United States. A recent study from Jeremy Greenwood and colleagues finds that not only are Americans more likely to marry someone with the same level of education or income, but also that this tendency has increased since 1960. Similarly, though interracial marriage is on the rise, white Americans still primarily marry white Americans, and black Americans still primarily marry black Americans. Therefore, it makes sense to examine marriageability ratios within education group (Figure 2) and within race (Figure 3).

Breaking down marriage markets by education tells a somewhat surprising story: it is the group of women who have the highest marriage rates—college-educated women—who are facing the greatest "shortage" of men. In fact, using the conventional measure of marriageability—the ratio of employed men to all women—there are only 85 men for every 100 women among 25- to 35-year-old college-educated adults. In contrast, for every employed, childless woman with a high school diploma, there are over 2.5 comparable men. These disparities are the result of women's rising education levels. Women are now more educated than men, meaning that they will necessarily face a shortage of marriage partners with the same level of education. What we are likely to see in the future, then, is either women marrying "down" educationally, or not marrying at all.

Among black Americans, concerns about a shortage of marriageable men are much more consistent with the evidence. Only when we look at the number of men compared to childless women (whether employed or not) is the gender ratio among black Americans favorable to women. In contrast, white women have no shortage of options—even the ratio of employed men to all women is slightly more favorable to women than to

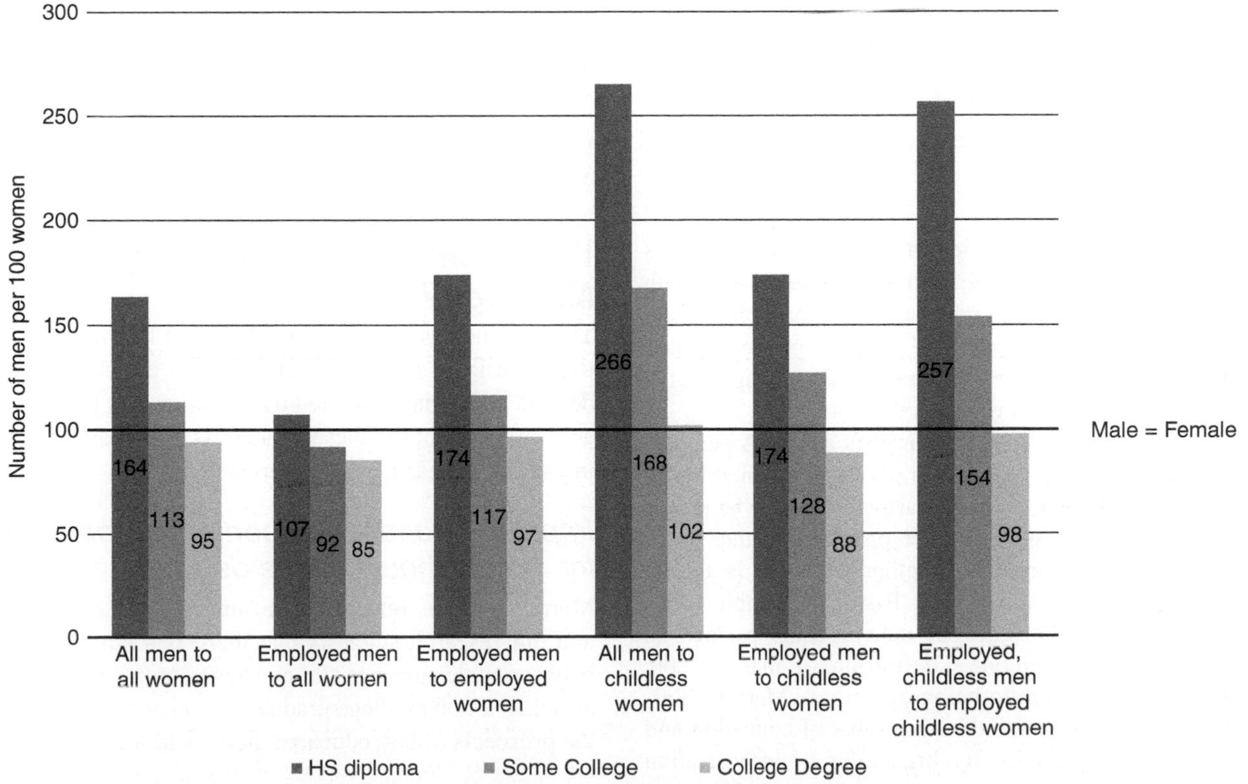

Figure 2 Marriage markets for never-married 25- to 34-year-olds, by education

Source: Author's tabulations of 2012 Amercian Community Survey IPUMS data.

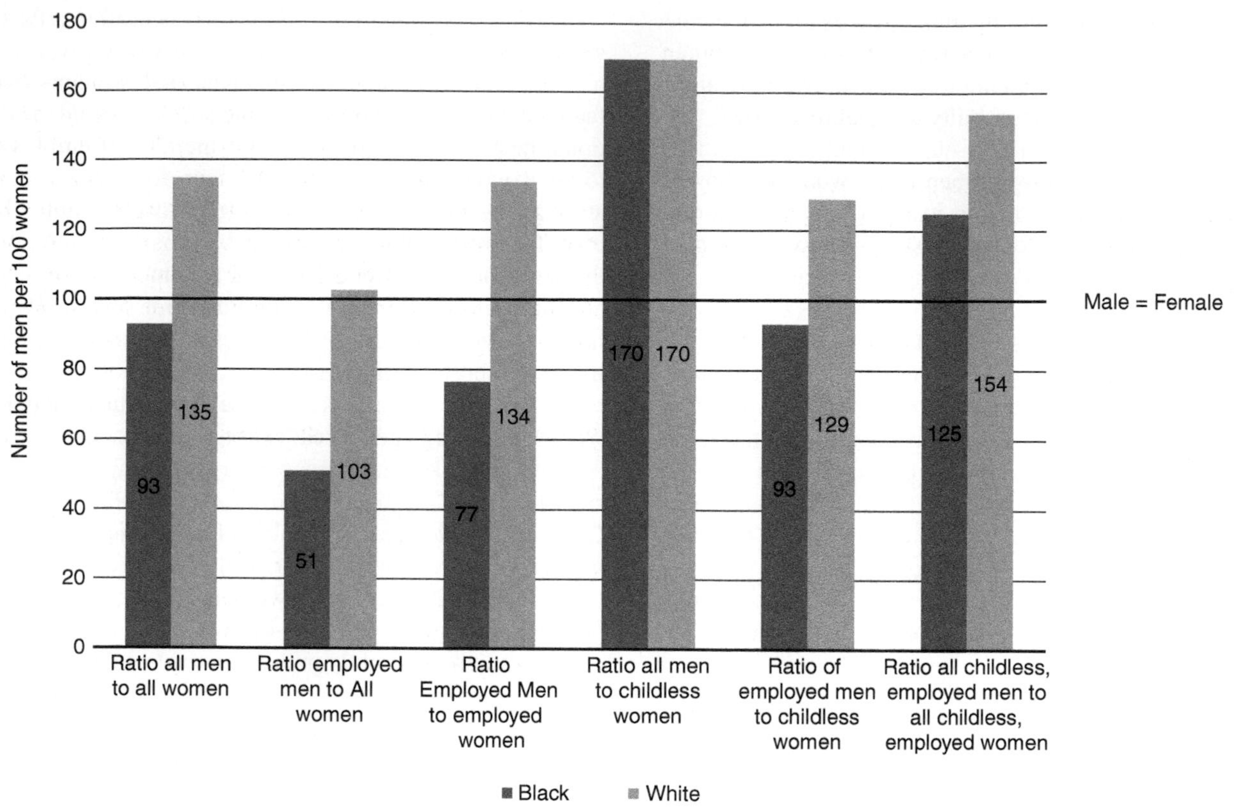

Figure 3 Marriage markets for never-married 25- to 34-year-olds, by race

Source: Author's tabulations of 2012 Amercian Community Survey IPUMS data.

men. The lack of marriageable men in the black community is affected by the very high rates of incarceration and early death among black men compared to white men. Among black male high school dropouts, 60 percent will be dead or incarcerated before the age of 35. Sentencing reform or other changes to the criminal justice system could improve this picture.

These tabulations are, of course, simplifications. A person's decision to marry is based on many traits that have nothing to do with the earning power of one's partner, whether he or she already has had children with another partner, whether he or she has been married before, and whether he or she is a good match in terms of race or education. But these simple ratios demonstrate that any "shortage" of marriageable partners is heavily dependent both on one's definition of marriageable and on the demographic group being examined. Marriageability may have as much to do with rising rates of education and employment among women, very high rates of incarceration among young black males, and high rates of unwed childbearing among young women as it does with a simple definition focused only on male employment and earnings.

What Can Be Done to Support Marriage?

There is increasing agreement between liberals and conservatives that there are both economic and cultural aspects to the decline in marriage. While no one policy will be a silver bullet, a combination of policies that address both may help bolster the institution of marriage in America.

Improve economic opportunities, particularly for men without college degrees

Marriage rates remain high among the college-educated, and our research suggests that there is a stronger association between male earnings and marriage among noncollege graduates than among college graduates. Policy measures to improve the prospects of less educated men could include:

- Creating more career and technical education and apprenticeships by expanding successful programs such as Small Schools of Choice, Talent Development, and Career Academies, and making access to technical training at the community college level more affordable.

- Making work pay through a more generous Earned Income Tax Credit for single adults and raising the minimum wage.
- Reforming the criminal justice system to reduce the size of the prison population, especially among black males, and better prepare inmates to reintegrate into society once their sentence is served.

Reduce the number of out-of-wedlock and unintended pregnancies

Around 40 percent of new mothers are unmarried at the time of birth, and the majority of these births are unplanned. Unmarried mothers are less likely to marry than women of the same age and demographic background without children. Delaying childbearing is thus a good way to increase marriage rates, and whatever marriages are formed are likely to be more stable if the partners are older and have had time to complete their educations and find steady work. Reversing the trends in out-of-wedlock childbearing will require that we:

- Encourage young adults to think more about whether, when, and with whom to have children, through cultural messages and social marketing campaigns that emphasize a new ethic of responsible parenthood.
- Improve women's educational and employment opportunities so that they will have greater motivation to delay childbearing.
- Increase knowledge about and access to effective methods of contraception, such as long-acting reversible contraception (the IUD and the implant).

Conclusion

If there is a shortage of marriageable men, it is most apparent among blacks and the highly educated of both races. That shortage is likely related to high rates of incarceration and early death among black men, and a growing education gap in favor of women among both races. Surprisingly, we find no shortage of marriageable men among less-educated whites based on various definitions of "marriageability." Among the college educated, on the other hand, there is a shortage that is likely to discourage marriage unless women are more willing to "marry down" or men catch up to women in terms of education.

Looking back over the past 40 or more years, we find that male earnings have affected marriage rates, but the magnitude of this effect is not huge and may diminish over time as women's education and earnings increase and gender roles evolve toward a more egalitarian state.

Finally, the question of whether marriage can be restored may be the wrong question. What matters for children is the stability of relationships, the maturity of their parents, and their desire to take on one of the most important tasks any adult ever undertakes. Historically, marriage has been the institution which promoted these goals. For some, it will continue to do so. But it is only a proxy for what matters more: the quality of parenting, the stability of a child's environment, and the circumstances of her birth.

Additional Reading

Autor, David and Melanie Wasser. 2013. "Wayward Sons: The Emerging Gender Gap in Labor Markets and Education." Third Way, March. http://economics.mit.edu/files/8754.

Charles, Kerwin Kofi and Ming Ching Luoh. 2010. "Male Incarceration, the Marriage Market, and Female Outcomes." Review of Economics and Statistics 92(3): 614–627.

Ellwood, David T. and Christopher Jencks. 2004. "The Uneven Spread of Single-Parent Families: What Do We Know? Where Do We Look for Answers?" In Social Inequality, edited by Kathryn M. Neckerman, 3–78. New York: Russell Sage Foundation.

Kearney, Melissa S. and Phillip B. Levine. 2012. "Income Inequality and Early Non-Marital Childbearing: An Economic Exploration of the 'Culture of Despair'." NBER Working Paper No. 17157: 1–60.

Lerman, Robert and W. Bradford Wilcox. 2014. "For Richer, For Poorer: How Family Structures Economic Success in America." American Enterprise Institute, October 28. https://www.aei.org/wp-content/uploads/2014/10/IFS-ForRicherForPoorer-Final_Web.pdf.

Qian, Zhenchao, Daniel Lichter, and Leanna Mellott. 2005. "Out-of Wedlock Childbearing, Marital Prospects and Mate Selection." Social Forces 84(1): 473–491.

Sawhill, Isabel V. 2014. Generation Unbound: Drifting Into Sex and Parenthood Without Marriage. Washington: Brookings Institution Press.

Wang, Wendy and Kim Parker. 2014. "Record Share of Americans Have Never Married." Pew Research Center, September 24. http://www.pewsocialtrends.org/2014/09/24/record-share-of-americans-have-never-married/.

Wilson, William Julius. 1987. The Truly Disadvantaged: The Inner City, the Underclass, and Public Policy. Chicago: University of Chicago Press.

Wood, Robert G. 1995. "Marriage Rates and Marriageable Men: A Test of the Wilson Hypothesis." The Journal of Human Resources 30(1): 163–193.

Critical Thinking

1. What are the qualities you look for in a future partner? How much does their educational and job prospects matter to you?
2. How do men and women differ in the qualities they are looking for in a partner who may be "marriage material"?
3. Do you agree with the authors' assertion that there are fewer marriageable men? Why or why not? How compelling is the evidence they present to support their argument?

Internet References

Center for Children and Families at the Brookings Institution
https://www.brookings.edu/center/center-on-children-and-families/

Centers for Disease Control (CDC), National Center for Health Statistics: Marriage and Divorce Fast Facts
https://www.cdc.gov/nchs/fastats/marriage-divorce.htm

Pew Research Center: Marriage
http://www.pewresearch.org/data-trend/society-and-demographics/marriage/

Social Trends Institute
http://www.socialtrendsinstitute.org/

Isabel V. Sawhill is a senior fellow in the Center on Children and Families at the Brookings Institution.

Joanna Venator is a former senior research assistant in the Center on Children and Families at the Brookings Institution.

Article Prepared by: Patricia Hrusa Williams, *University of Maine at Farmington*

Not Wanting Kids Is Entirely Normal

Why the Ingrained Expectation that Women should Desire to Become Parents is Unhealthy.

Jessica Valenti

Learning Outcomes

After reading this article, you will be able to:

- Describe what "safe haven" laws are.
- Explain the challenges of motherhood.
- Recognize the negative effects of unintended pregnancies on families and children.

In 2008, Nebraska decriminalized child abandonment. The move was part of a "safe haven" law designed to address increased rates of infanticide in the state. Like other safe haven laws, parents in Nebraska who felt unprepared to care for their babies could drop them off at a designated location without fear of arrest and prosecution. But legislators made a major logistical error: They failed to implement an age limitation for dropped-off children.

Within just weeks of the law passing, parents started dropping off their kids. But here's the rub: None of them were infants. A couple of months in, 36 children had been left in state hospitals and police stations. Twenty-two of the children were over 13 years old. A 51-year-old grandmother dropped off a 12-year-old boy. One father dropped off his entire family—nine children from ages one to 17. Others drove from neighboring states to drop off their children once they heard that they could abandon them without repercussion.

The Nebraska state government, realizing the tremendous mistake it had made, held a special session of the legislature to rewrite the law in order to add an age limitation. Governor Dave Heineman said the change would "put the focus back on the original intent of these laws, which is saving newborn babies and exempting a parent from prosecution for child abandonment. It should also prevent those outside the state from bringing their children to Nebraska in an attempt to secure services."

On November 21, 2008, the last day that the safe haven law was in effect for children of all ages, a mother from Yolo County, California, drove over 1,200 miles to the Kimball County Hospital in Nebraska where she left her 14-year-old son.

What happened in Nebraska raises the question: If there were no consequences, how many of us would give up our kids? After all, child abandonment is nothing new and it's certainly not rare in the United States. Over 400,000 children are in the foster care system waiting to be placed in homes, thousands of parents relinquish their children every year. One woman even sent her adopted child back to his home country with an apology letter pinned like a grocery list to his chest. Whether it's because of hardship or not, many Americans are giving up on parenthood.

In February 2009, someone calling herself Ann logged onto the website Secret Confessions and wrote three sentences: "I am depressed. I hate being a mom. I also hate being a stay at home mom too!" Over three years later, the thread of comments is still going strong with thousands of responses—the site usually garners only 10 or so comments for every "confession." Our anonymous Ann had hit a nerve.

One woman who got pregnant at 42 wrote, "I hate being a mother too. Every day is the same. And to think I won't be free of it until I am like 60 and then my life will be over." Another, identifying herself only as k'smom, said, "I feel so trapped, anxious, and overwhelmed. I love my daughter and she's well taken care of but this is not the path I would have taken given a second chance."

Gianna wrote, "I love my son, but I hate being a mother. It has been a thankless, monotonous, exhausting, irritating and oppressive job. Motherhood feels like a prison sentence. I can't wait until I am paroled when my son turns 18 and hopefully goes far away to college." One D.C.-based mom even said that although she was against abortion before having her son, now she would "run to the abortion clinic" if she got pregnant again.

The responses—largely from women who identify themselves as financially stable—spell out something less explicit than well-worn reasons for parental unhappiness such as poverty and a lack of support. These women simply don't feel that motherhood is all it's cracked up to be, and if given a second chance, they wouldn't do it again.

Some cited the boredom of stay-at-home momism. Many complained of partners who didn't shoulder their share of child care responsibilities. "Like most men, my husband doesn't do much—if anything—for baby care. I have to do and plan for everything," one mother wrote. A few got pregnant accidentally and were pressured by their husbands and boyfriends to carry through with the pregnancy, or knew they never wanted children but felt it was something they "should" do.

The overwhelming sentiment, however, was the feeling of a loss of self, the terrifying reality that their lives had been subsumed into the needs of their child. DS wrote, "I feel like I have completely lost any thing that was me. I never imagined having children and putting myself aside would make me feel this bad." The expectation of total motherhood is bad enough, having to live it out every day is soul crushing. Everything that made us an individual, that made us unique, no longer matters. It's our role as a mother that defines us. Not much has changed.

"The feminine mystique permits, even encourages, women to ignore the question of their identity," wrote Betty Friedan. "The mystique says they can answer the question 'Who am I?' by saying 'Tom's wife . . . Mary's mother.' The truth is—and how long it's been true, I'm not sure, but it was true in my generation and it's true of girls growing up today—an American woman no longer has a private image to tell her who she is, or can be, or wants to be."

At the time she published *The Feminine Mystique,* Friedan argued that the public image of women was largely one of domesticity—"washing machines, cake mixes . . . detergents," all sold through commercials and magazines. Today, American women have more public images of themselves than that of a housewife. We see ourselves depicted in television, ads, movies, and magazines (not to mention relief!) as politicians, business owners, intellectuals, soldiers, and more. But that's what makes the public images of total motherhood so insidious. We see these diverse images of ourselves and believe that the oppressive standard Friedan wrote about is dead, when in fact it has simply shifted. Because no matter how many different kinds of public images women see of themselves, they're still limited. They're still largely white, straight upper-middle-class depictions, and they all still identify women as mothers or non-mothers.

American culture can't accept the reality of a woman who does not want to be a mother. It goes against everything we've been taught to think about women and how desperately they want babies. If we're to believe the media and pop culture, women—even teen girls—are forever desperate for a baby. It's our greatest desire.

The truth is, most women spend the majority of their lives trying *not* to get pregnant. According to the Guttmacher Institute, by the time a woman with two children is in her mid-40s she will have spent only five years trying to become pregnant, being pregnant, and not being at risk for getting pregnant following a birth. But to avoid getting pregnant before or after those two births, she would have had to refrain from sex or use contraception for an average of 25 years. Almost all American women (99 percent), ages 15–44, who have had sexual intercourse use some form of birth control. The second most popular form of birth control after the Pill? Sterilization. And now, more than ever, women are increasingly choosing forms of contraception that are for long-term use. Since 2005, for example, IUD use has increased by a whopping 161 percent. That's a long part of life and a lot of effort to avoid parenthood!

Now, it may be that these statistics simply indicate that modern women are just exerting more control over when and under what circumstances they become mothers. To a large degree that's true. But it doesn't jibe with an even more shocking reality: that half of pregnancies in the United States are unintended. Once you factor in the abortion rate and pregnancies that end in miscarriage, we're left with the rather surprising fact that one-third of babies born in the United States were unplanned. Not so surprising, however, is that the intention to have children definitively impacts how parents feel about their children, and how those children are treated—sometimes with terrifying results.

Jennifer Barber, a population researcher at the University of Michigan, studied more than 3,000 mothers and their close to 6,000 children from a range of socioeconomic backgrounds. Barber and her colleagues asked women who had recently given birth, "Just before you became pregnant, did you want to become pregnant when you did?" Those who answered yes were categorized as "intended"; those who answered no were then asked, "Did you want a baby but not at that time, or did you want none at all?" Depending on their answer, they were classified as "mistimed" or "unwanted." Over 60 percent of the children studied were reported as planned, almost 30 percent were unplanned ("mistimed"), and 10 percent were unequivocally "unwanted."

The results of Barber's research showed that the children who were unintended—both those who were mistimed and those who were unwanted—got fewer parental resources than those children who were intended. Basically, children who were unplanned didn't get as much emotional and cognitive support as children who were planned—as reported both by the researchers and the mothers themselves. Barber's research looked at things like the number of children's books in the home, and how often a parent read to a child or taught them skills like counting or the alphabet for the "cognitive" aspect. For the "emotional" support rating, they developed a scale measuring the "warmth" and "responsiveness" of the mother, how much time the family spent together, and how much time the father spent with the child. Across the board, children who were wanted got more from their parents than children who weren't. Children who were unplanned were also subject to harsher parenting and more punitive measures than a sibling who was intended.

Barber pointed out that this kind of pattern could be due to parental stress and a lack of patience that's "directed explicitly toward an unwanted child," and that a mistimed or unwanted birth could raise stress levels in the parents' interactions with their other children as well. She also says that in addition to benign emotional neglect, parenting unintended children is also associated with infant health problems and mortality, maternal depression, and sometimes child abuse.

[. . .]

When Torry Hansen of Shelbyville, Tennessee, sent her seven-year-old adopted son by himself on a plane back to his home country of Russia with nothing more than a note explaining she didn't want to parent him, she became one of the most reviled women in America. Russian officials were so incensed that they temporarily halted all adoption to the United States. We sometimes expect fathers to shirk their responsibility; but when mothers do it, it shakes the core of what we've been taught to believe about women and maternal instinct.

Anthropologist Sarah Blaffer Hrdy argued in a 2001 Utah lecture, for example, that being female is seen as synonymous with having and nurturing as many children as possible. So when mothers abandon their children, it's seen as unnatural. This simplistic, emotional response to parents—mothers, in particular—who give up their kids is part of the reason Americans have such a difficult time dealing with the issue. As Hrdy says, "No amount of legislation can ensure that mothers will love their babies."

That's why programs like safe haven laws—age limitations or not—will never truly get to the heart of the matter. As Mary Lee Allen, director of the Children's Defense Fund's child welfare and mental health division, has said, "These laws help women to drop their babies off but do nothing to provide support to women and children before this happens."

Unfortunately, discussing the structural issues has never been an American strong suit. Hrdy notes that legislators are too afraid to focus on sensible solutions. "Talking about the source of the problem would require policymakers to discuss sex education and contraception, not to mention abortion, and they view even nonsensical social policies as preferable to the prospect of political suicide."

If policymakers and people who care about children want to reduce the number of abandoned kids, they need to address the systemic issues: poverty, maternity leave, access to resources, and health care. We need to encourage women to demand more help from their partners, if they have them. In a way, that's the easier fix, because we know what we have to do there; the issues have been the same for years. The less-obvious hurdle is that of preparing parents emotionally and putting forward realistic images of parenthood and motherhood. There also needs to be some sort of acknowledgment that not everyone should parent—when parenting is a given, it's not fully considered or thought out, and it gives way too easily to parental ambivalence and unhappiness.

Take Trinity, one of the mothers who commented on the Secret Confessions board about hating parenthood. She wrote, "My pregnancy was totally planned and I thought it was a good idea at the time. Nobody tells you the negatives before you get pregnant—they convince you it's a wonderful idea and you will love it. I think it's a secret shared among parents . . . they're miserable so they want you to be too."

By having more honest conversations about parenting, we can avoid the kind of secret depressions so many mothers seem to be harboring. If what we want is deliberate, thought-out, planned, and expected parenthood—and parenting that is healthy and happy for children—then we have to speak out.

Critical Thinking

1. In Nebraska, why do you think parents were using the "safe haven law" to abandon older children rather than infants, as the law had originally intended?
2. In the article there is a quote by the author which states "American culture can't accept the reality of a woman who does not want to be a mother." Do you agree? Why or why not?
3. What are the challenges of being a mother in modern society? Given these challenges how can we better prepare and support those who become parents by choice or through unintended pregnancies?

Internet References

Administration for Children and Families: Infant Safe Haven Laws

https://www.childwelfare.gov/systemwide/laws_policies/statutes/safehaven.cfm

Planned Parenthood

http://www.plannedparenthood.org

The March of Dimes

www.marchofdimes.com

Article

Prepared by: Patricia Hrusa Williams, *University of Maine at Farmington*

Teen Moms Need Support, Not Shame

Alex Ronan

Learning Outcomes

After reading this article, you will be able to:

- Understand the experiences of teen moms using firsthand accounts.
- Consider stigma attached to teen pregnancy and their short- and long-term effects.
- Examine supports needed by teen parents and to prevent teen pregnancy.

When Gloria Malone and Natasha Vianna got pregnant as teens, they thought their lives were over. This is, after all, what many teen pregnancy campaigns suggest. "You think being in school sucks? You know what sucks a lot more? A baby—every two hours for feeding time," reads one ad from the Candie's Foundation. Another says, "You're supposed to be changing the world, not changing diapers."

Over the past 20 years, the teen birth rate has declined almost continuously, but the United States has the highest teen pregnancy rates in the developed world. Statistically, teen parents in the United States are less likely to finish high school, more likely to experience poverty as adults, and more likely to have kids with poorer behavioral, educational, and health outcomes. But many teens that become pregnant were already disadvantaged, and the stigma only makes things worse.

Giving birth at 15 and 17, respectively, inspired Malone and Vianna to improve the experiences of other teen moms. They founded #noteenshame with five other teen moms from across the country; and what started as a hashtag has become a larger effort to support teen moms, call out campaigns that traffic in stigma, and provide basic information and support to young parents. In addition to challenging shaming teen-pregnancy-prevention campaigns, founding members also consult with politicians around the country on improving outcomes for teen moms and how to create comprehensive sex ed. Vianna, now 27, gave a TedTalk in 2013, worked with Boston politicians to revise and implement a new policy for parenting students, and is the Digital Communications Manager at the Massachusetts Alliance on Teen Pregnancy. Malone, now 23, has written for the *New York Times*, taken on Bill O'Reilly, and created a website for teen moms in New York.

Over a three-way call one evening—"one of the perks of interviewing young parents is they're home on a Friday night," Malone quipped—they shared their experiences as pregnant and parenting teens, talked about the shame and stigma they've worked to overcome, and articulated what needs to change when it comes to teen pregnancy prevention.

I've noticed a lot of organizations that pose as supportive of teen pregnancy do so only because they're pro-life. How do you guys identify?

Natasha Vianna: I'm pro-choice and fully support abortion rights access.

Gloria Malone: Yeah, me too.

Vianna: With #noteenshame, we try to recognize that all young people deserve access to comprehensive and accurate information about their sexual and reproductive health as well as complete agency and autonomy over their own bodies.

What was it like becoming pregnant as a teen?

Vianna: Prior to pregnancy, I often heard that when you become a teen parent you lose all your friends. But actually, my friends became even more supportive than ever; it was the adults in my life that made things really hard.

Malone: Same for me. My academic adviser stopped talking to me completely. I had teachers not give me assignments; I had teachers who would change the seating arrangements and purposely put me in a tiny desk when I was super pregnant. When I decided to move to a table that was right behind me, they were like, "What do you think you're doing? You think you're an adult cause you're pregnant?" And I was like, "No, I just think I can't fit in my fucking desk."

Vianna: I remember going to my guidance counselor's office and asking, "Why am I removed from my honor's classes?" and my guidance counselor said, "Well, now that you're pregnant, you're not going to be able to do that kind of work anymore," as if getting pregnant meant losing my brain. Later, I came back to her office to ask if someone could help me apply for college and was told, "It's unlikely you'll even graduate, so let's just focus on finishing high school." When adults continue you tell you you're not capable, you start to believe it.

Statistically, teen moms are more likely to be black or Latina, face socioeconomic barriers, and lack access to comprehensive sex ed. Many are kicked out of their homes when they become pregnant. Do you feel like your experience mirrors that of most teen moms?

Vianna: Yeah. When I told my parents I was pregnant, they kicked me out of my house. I was just eight or nine weeks pregnant and I was forced to take whatever I could and move in with my boyfriend that same day. When I secretly shared my pregnancy with my school nurse and clarified that I wasn't sure if I would choose an abortion or carry to term, she violated privacy and told my teachers about my pregnancy and within a week, my whole school knew. I felt trapped and knew that if I chose an abortion, I couldn't hide it like I thought I had to, but if I carried to term, I also knew that the same people who would judge me for an abortion wouldn't have stuck around to support me.

After moving in with my boyfriend, my parents also stopped paying tuition for my high school (I was in a Catholic high school at the time) so I had to enroll myself in the local public high school where I would start my senior year as the new pregnant girl.

Malone: I'm a black Latina who grew up in deep poverty with my single mother and sibling. Thankfully, I didn't get kicked out. That said, my family struggled for a very long time with how to support me.

I returned to school maybe two weeks after having my daughter because I didn't want to be failed out of school on account of my pregnancy. My daily schedule was wake up, tend to my child, pack her and my bags for the day, drop her off at the sitter, illegally park my car to be able to go to school, go to school, pick up my daughter, go home, and get ready for work at the local Taco Bell until about 9 P.M. I didn't have much financial support from my family and my daughter's father worked out of town often so all of the child rearing was left up to me, alone.

Vianna: Yeah, I spent a lot of time alone with my daughter too. Not having love from my family made me feel like I was a burden. I wasn't asking anyone to support the reality that I got pregnant, but I wished there were people who cared that the isolation and stress I felt during my pregnancy wasn't healthy for me or for my baby. It took years (and I'm still trying) to unpack the ways in which I internalized a feeling of worthlessness.

How did that stigma and shaming impact your experience of giving birth and raising a newborn?

Malone: It was very, very isolating. I was in an abusive relationship, but that was the person that was "there for me" when everyone else was turning away.

Vianna: For my entire pregnancy people had been telling me, "this child is going to ruin your life," "you're never going to be able to accomplish your dreams." As I was giving birth I was thinking, Holy crap, I'm giving birth to this person whose life is going to end mine. I had a really hard time bonding with my daughter. I became really depressed, I didn't want to ask for help or ask those normal questions first-time parents have because I felt like asking would be a reflection of me as a teen parent and not just a first time parent.

Malone: I had no idea that your breast milk had to come in. I was too scared to ask anyone!

Vianna: Exactly. If I was struggling, I'd tell myself *I asked for this or it's my fault for getting pregnant.* When my daughter was younger, I would sometimes lay beside her while she slept and I would cry and apologize for not being the person she deserved. It was a horrible feeling to believe that I could never be what she needed, but I'm glad I overcame that. I have a strong relationship with her today.

It seems like part of the stigma surrounding teen parents is never allowing teen moms to express the positive aspects of their experiences. What were some of the best things about being a young parent?

Vianna: Oh, I love this question. In terms of parenting, it's great that I can look back at my relationship with my mom and I can remember so clearly what it feels like to be a kid and I can apply that to how I parent my child. Plus, I like the fact that she's going to be in college when I'm 35. That's exciting.

Malone: When my daughter is in college, I'm going to be a hot 30-year-old, [*laughs*], I'm going to have money in my account, I'm going to be traveling, and my friends are going to be calling me saying, "How do I breastfeed?" That's when I'll go, "Sorry, should've been a teen mom." [*Laughs*] But seriously, I love that we're learning together, that I feel comfortable saying, "I don't know, let me get back to you." I love that my daughter has seen me accomplish things. She's seen me graduate high school, she's seen me graduate college.

Vianna: Gloria and I were just talking about how our experiences being stigmatized have influenced how we're raising our daughters.

What do you mean?

Vianna: Maybe I can just give an example. When my daughter was in kindergarten, I picked her up one day and she was immediately like, "I have to tell you something. I got in trouble today." I asked what happened and she said, "There's a boy in my class who said girls can't burp. He kept saying it. So I burped. I got in trouble, but I had to show that girls can burp." On one hand I was like, hmm, she shouldn't be burping in class, but, also, high five. It was great to see my little feminist daughter challenging things.

But even on bigger issues she's really internalized our conversations. This one time, we were eating dinner and she was like, "I heard something at school today, one of the girls in my class told me that it's impossible for me to be here because you and my dad aren't married." I got really nervous, because I wasn't prepared to have that conversation. I was like, "Well, how does that make you feel?" She was like, "I'm not sure," got really quiet, and then was like, "Actually, y'know what? I'm fine because I'm the expert on my life and no one can tell me about my life but me."

Do you ever worry that in trying to counteract the narratives about teen moms you feel like you can't acknowledge the difficult aspects or that you feel like you're painting an overly rosy picture?

Malone: No, not really. Recently, I had a woman, 65 years old, email me and tell me that she's still terrified to say her age in relation to her daughters for fear that people will figure out she was a teen mom. That's a heavy-ass burden to carry around. Sometimes people think I'm glorifying my experience, but I think they're just uncomfortable hearing about a teen mom who's successful.

Motherhood was a very politicizing moment for both of you. How has your awareness and experience influenced what you want to see changed?

Malone: There's a whole system in place to prevent people from getting the help they need because there's this stereotype that they don't deserve it. For example, teen moms often get kicked out of their homes, but they're not allowed to stay in homeless shelters because it's "a child with a child."

Vianna: Instead of focusing on teen pregnancy prevention, we need to focus on positive youth development. My pregnancy was this lightning rod for people to blame all of my issues and all of my problems, but the reality is that preventing a pregnancy does not increase opportunities for young people. It does not improve their equitable access to quality education. It does not make their communities safer. As a society, we're so focused on making sure teens don't get pregnant before their 20th birthday that we miss out on conversations about consent, healthy relationships, and agency.

If we look at the communities, if we empower young people to make decisions for themselves and give them the tools to make those decisions, we will see a decrease in teen pregnancy because we know that 80 percent of teen pregnancies are unplanned.

You both embrace your position as teen moms. As you've grown older, does it still impact the way you're able to talk about motherhood?

Vianna: Yes. If society is going to stigmatize me and spend millions of dollars to label me and my child as a public health issue, I deserve at the very least, the basic right to share my truth. If we removed the teen aspect and I said, "I'm happy to be a mom," no one would say, "How dare you be happy to be a mom! You must be lying, and you're also setting a bad example."

Malone: Honestly, I would like to see the phrase teen *mom* disappear off the face of the earth. Why are we the only demographic of moms that are singled out by our age? Why are we teen moms? Why can't we just be moms?

Critical Thinking

1. What are some of the common perceptions of teen moms which exist in our society? What are the roots of these ideas?
2. Why do you think there is more backlash and stigma attached to being a teen mother versus a teen father? Do you think stigmatizing teen mothers serves as a true deterrent to teen pregnancy? Why or why not?
3. How can we better support teen mothers and prevent pregnancy? What do you think of positive youth development as an alternative to a focus on teen pregnancy prevention?

Internet References

Massachusetts Alliance on Teen Pregnancy
http://www.massteenpregnancy.org/

Natasha Vianna TedTalk
https://www.youtube.com/watch?v=MJUS4r_41fY

#Noteenshame
http://www.noteenshame.com/

The Candie's Foundation
http://candiesfoundation.org/

The National Campaign to Prevent Teen and Unplanned Pregnancy
https://thenationalcampaign.org

Article

Prepared by: Patricia Hrusa Williams, *University of Maine at Farmington*

What Happens to a Woman's Brain When She Becomes a Mother

ADRIENNE LAFRANCE

Learning Outcomes

After reading this article, you will be able to:

- Identity ways the brain changes during pregnancy and the early postpartum period.
- Understand the role of the amygdala and oxytocin for mother-infant bonding.
- Analyze how biology influences caregiving and early parenting behavior.

The artist Sarah Walker once told me that becoming a mother is like discovering the existence of a strange new room in the house where you already live. I always liked Walker's description because it's more precise than the shorthand most people use for life with a newborn: *Everything changes.*

Because a lot of things do change, of course, but for new mothers, some of the starkest differences are also the most intimate ones—the emotional changes. Which, it turns out, are also largely neurological.

Even before a woman gives birth, pregnancy tinkers with the very structure of her brain, several neurologists told me. After centuries of observing behavioral changes in new mothers, scientists are only recently beginning to definitively link the way a woman acts with what's happening in her prefrontal cortex, midbrain, parietal lobes, and elsewhere. Gray matter becomes more concentrated. Activity increases in regions that control empathy, anxiety, and social interaction. On the most basic level, these changes, prompted by a flood of hormones during pregnancy and in the postpartum period, help attract a new mother to her baby. In other words, those maternal feelings of overwhelming love, fierce protectiveness, and constant worry begin with reactions in the brain.

Mapping the maternal brain is also, many scientists believe, the key to understanding why so many new mothers experience serious anxiety and depression. An estimated one in six women suffers from postpartum depression, and many more develop behaviors like compulsively washing hands and obsessively checking whether the baby is breathing.

"This is what we call an aspect of almost the obsessive compulsive behaviors during the very first few months after the baby's arrival," maternal brain researcher Pilyoung Kim told me. "Mothers actually report very high levels of patterns of thinking about things that they cannot control. They're constantly thinking about baby. Is baby healthy? Sick? Full?"

"In new moms, there are changes in many of the brain areas," Kim continued. "Growth in brain regions involved in emotion regulation, empathy-related regions, but also what we call maternal motivation—and I think this region could be largely related to obsessive-compulsive behaviors. In animals and humans during the postpartum period, there's an enormous desire to take care of their own child."

There are several interconnected brain regions that help drive mothering behaviors and mood.

Of particular interest to researchers is the almond-shaped set of neurons known as the amygdala, which helps process memory and drives emotional reactions like fear, anxiety, and aggression. In a normal brain, activity in the amygdala grows in the weeks and months after giving birth. This growth, researchers believe, is correlated with how a new mother behaves—an enhanced amygdala makes her hypersensitive to her baby's needs—while a cocktail of hormones, which find more receptors in a larger amygdala, help create a positive feedback loop to motivate mothering behaviors. Just by staring at her baby, the reward centers of a mother's brain will light up, scientists have found in several studies. This maternal brain circuitry influences the syrupy way a mother speaks to her baby, how attentive she is, even the affection she feels for her baby. It's not surprising, then, that damage to the amygdala is associated with higher levels of depression in mothers.

Amygdala damage in babies could affect the mother-child bond as well. In a 2004 *Journal of Neuroscience* study, infant monkeys who had amygdala lesions were less likely to vocalize their distress, or pick their own mothers over other adults. A newborn's ability to distinguish between his mother and anybody else is linked to the amygdala.

Activity in the amygdala is also associated with a mother's strong feelings about her own baby versus babies in general. In a 2011 study of amygdala response in new mothers, women reported feeling more positive about photos depicting their own smiling babies compared with photos of unfamiliar smiling babies, and their brain activity reflected that discrepancy. Scientists recorded bolder brain response—in the amygdala, thalamus, and elsewhere—among mothers as they looked at photos of their own babies.

Greater amygdala response when viewing their own children was tied to lower maternal anxiety and fewer symptoms of depression, researchers found. In other words, a new mother's brain changes help motivate her to care for her baby but they may also help buffer her own emotional state. From the study:

> Thus, the greater amygdala response to one's own infant face observed in our study likely reflects more positive and pro-social aspects of maternal responsiveness, feelings, and experience. Mothers experiencing higher levels of anxiety and lower mood demonstrated less amygdala response to their own infant and reported more stressful and more negatively valenced parenting attitudes and experiences.

Much of what happens in a new mother's amygdala has to do with the hormones flowing to it. The region has a high concentration of receptors for hormones like oxytocin, which surge during pregnancy.

"We see changes at both the hormonal and brain levels," brain researcher Ruth Feldman told me in an e-mail. "Maternal oxytocin levels—the system responsible for maternal-infant bonding across all mammalian species—dramatically increase during pregnancy and the postpartum [period] and the more mother is involved in childcare, the greater the increase in oxytocin."

Oxytocin also increases as women look at their babies, or hear their babies' coos and cries, or snuggle with their babies. An increase in oxytocin during breastfeeding may help explain why researchers have found that breastfeeding mothers are more sensitive to the sound of their babies' cries than non-breastfeeding mothers. "Breastfeeding mothers show a greater level of [brain] responses to baby's cry compared with formula-feeding mothers in the first month postpartum," Kim said. "It's just really interesting. We don't know if it's the act of breastfeeding or the oxytocin or any other factor."

What scientists do know, Feldman says, is that becoming a parent looks—at least in the brain—a lot like falling in love. Which helps explain how many new parents describe feeling when they meet their newborns. At the brain level, the networks that become especially sensitized are those that involve vigilance and social salience—the amygdala—as well as dopamine networks that incentivize prioritizing the infant. "In our research, we find that periods of social bonding involve change in the same 'affiliative' circuits," Feldman said. "We showed that during the first months of 'falling in love' some similar changes occur between romantic partners." Incidentally, that same circuitry is what makes babies smell so good to their mothers, researchers found in a 2013 study.

The greatest brain changes occur with a mother's first child, though it's not clear whether a mother's brain ever goes back to what it was like before childbirth, several neurologists told me. And yet brain changes aren't limited to new moms.

Men show similar brain changes when they're deeply involved in caregiving. Oxytocin does not seem to drive nurturing behavior in men the way it does in women, Feldman and other researchers found in a study last year. Instead, a man's parental brain is supported by a socio-cognitive network that develops in the brain of both sexes later in life, whereas women appear to have evolved to have a "brain-hormone-behavior constellation" that's automatically primed for mothering. Another way to look at it: the blueprint for mothering behavior exists in the brain even before a woman has children.

Perhaps, then, motherhood really is like secret space in a woman's brain, waiting to be discovered. "Although only mothers experience pregnancy, birth, and lactation, and these provide powerful primers for the expression of maternal care via amygdala sensitization," researchers wrote, "evolution created other pathways for adaptation to the parental role in human fathers, and these alternative pathways come with practice, attunement, and day-by-day caregiving."

In other words, the act of simply caring for one's baby forges new neural pathways—undiscovered rooms in the parental brain.

Critical Thinking

1. What are some concerns and worries women may experience during pregnancy and during the early postpartum period?
2. In what ways does a woman's brain change as a result of pregnancy? What are some of the positive changes which result? Negative ones?
3. Given the dramatic changes women experience, especially after the birth of a first child, what policies and supports are needed to ensure the well-being of new mothers and their babies?

Internet References

The March of Dimes
www.marchofdimes.com

Babycenter: Pregnancy
http://www.babycenter.com/pregnancy

Zero to Three
www.zerotothree.org

Article

Prepared by: Patricia Hrusa Williams, *University of Maine at Farmington*

Sperm Donor, Life Partner

ALANA SEMUELS

Learning Outcomes

After reading this article, you will be able to:

- Identify reasons individuals may choose to develop partnerships only to have children.
- Understand the emotional, legal, and practical strengths and challenges of three-parent families and platonic/non-married parenting partnerships.

Dawn Pieke's relationship imploded just before she reached 40. Pieke had a miscarriage and shortly after, her boyfriend, whom she'd dated for almost a decade, met someone else on a business trip and had an affair. The two broke up and Pieke found herself in a tailspin: She knew she wanted a family, but she also knew her biological clock was ticking, and she wasn't sure, after two separate, decades-long relationships, that she could go through it all again.

A glass of wine in hand, she steeled herself for more dating, signed up for Match.com, and started going on dates in Omaha, Nebraska, where she lives.

"I thought, 'These guys look like jerks . . . I just want a kid, why can't I just have a baby and not worry about if it's *the* guy?'" she told me, in a phone interview. After eight months, she hadn't clicked with anyone.

Pieke, who works in sales, started diligently researching her options, but soon got discouraged. Adoption didn't seem like a good bet: She knew three separate couples trying to adopt, and it was taking forever for them to get approved—a potential single mother would have even more trouble, she figured. Pieke didn't love the idea of going to a sperm bank: She and her twin sister were raised by a single mom and they grew up always wanting to know more about their father. She wanted her child to know both parents, if possible.

"I always thought I would be married and have kids by the time I was 25, but it just didn't turn out that way," she said.

Then one day, she stumbled across something on the Internet that seemed like it might work: A website that connected people who wanted to have kids and raise them together, but without a romantic relationship. She paid a small fee and registered, and right away, a guy in Australia caught her eye. But she didn't contact him. Everyone she knew thought she was crazy to even consider having a child with a stranger.

"My family and friends thought I was nuts, they were like, 'chill out, you'll meet someone,'" she said. "But I thought, 'wow, this could maybe be something.'"

A few months later, Pieke was on the Facebook page of the co-parenting site and she got a message. It was from someone asking if she was looking for a co-parent, and it just happened to be from the very same man she'd seen on the website before, who was living in Australia.

He was gay, and from New York, and shared her beliefs about spirituality—she describes herself as spiritual, but not religious. The two struck up a correspondence. She liked that he was dark-haired, since she is blonde, and figured they might make a good-looking kid, and they agreed on lots of things. Most importantly, they had similar ideas about parenting: They would be gentle and nurturing, with no yelling or spanking, and would not use baby talk, but would instead speak to the child as a "person already full of intelligence," Pieke said.

"It felt like speaking to an old family member," said Fabian Blue, the man she met on the site. He made a documentary about his efforts to find a co-parent, called *The Baby Daddy Project* with the clever tagline, "No Sex, No Marriage, Just the Baby Carriage." Blue would set up his laptop with Pieke on Skype for dinner parties and special events, and the two would talk daily, sharing their hopes and fears for having a family, getting closer and closer to the conclusion that they might just want to make and raise a child together, though without any sort of romantic involvement.

They met in person for the first time in downtown Omaha on Thanksgiving 2011, when he pulled up in a horse-drawn

Cinderella carriage, handed her a bouquet of red roses, and asked, "Will you be my baby mama?" When she said yes, they gave each other high-fives and got into the carriage (you can see footage in this video Blue made about their meeting).

After that, he didn't go back to Australia. Instead, they started experimenting with an at-home insemination kit—basically a cup and a syringe (you can also see somewhat awkward footage of this—G-rated—in Blue's video). Two months and two tries later, Pieke got pregnant. Their daughter, Indigo, was born in October 2012 (yes, there's footage of that, too).

"Women my age hold out for romantic partnerships, if they don't find it, they say, 'well, I guess I'm not going to have kids,'" Pieke told me. "That's where I was when I turned 40, but I said, 'I'm going to make this happen, whether I find a guy or not. I'm not going to wait on guys anymore.'"

It's been decades since Louise Joy Brown, the first "test-tube" baby was born, allowing women to have biological children through in-vitro fertilization, and without a husband. Since then, millions of babies have been born to single women, through both natural conception and in-vitro, who couldn't find the right partner or want to go it on their own. In 2009, 19 percent of births to women aged 35–39 occurred outside of marriage, up from 5 percent in 1970, according to Child Trends, a Washington research group.

But that doesn't mean that women necessarily prefer to do it all themselves: Being a single-parent is financially and emotionally taxing. Studies show that single-parents are more likely to live in poverty, and that mothers earn and learn less, since they have to pay for child care and take more time off from work to care for a child.

That may be why more single women are trying to find a sperm donor who is also involved in a child's life. Sites like Modamily.com, PollenTree.com, and Familybydesign.com serve as places for people to meet potential co-parents: They're kind of like a Match.com for people who want to have kids without having sex.

"This could be a seismic shift in how people view what a family is," said Ivan Fatovic, the founder and CEO of Modamily, which launched in Feburary 2012. Fatovic started the site after talking with some girlfriends in a bar in New York: They were all approaching 40, and hadn't found a mate, and were worried about finding the right partner for them—and father for their children—in a few short years.

"We thought—we can introduce people who share the same vision and values. We're not saying it's better or worse, but we think it's an additional option."

It's not just single women looking for involved parenting partners, either. Increasingly, lesbian couples who want to have children are turning to men they know for genetic material, and are sometimes asking him to share some parenting responsibilities. It's possible that gay men who use a surrogate to have a child are involving the mother in the child's life too—at least if you believe the premise of the failed 2012 NBC comedy *The New Normal.*

"We are seeing a growing trend of a female, same-sex-couple parenting with the man who provides the genetic material but does not relinquish his rights as a sperm donor," said Diana Adams, a New York lawyer who advises families on issues like these.

To be sure, this new type of family can create a minefield of legal issues. A Florida judge last year allowed the names of three parents on a birth certificate after a sperm donor sued a lesbian couple, who had been his friends, after they asked him to cede parental rights. Last October, California amended its family code to provide that a child can have more than two parents. And the case of Jason Patric, who donated sperm to his ex-girlfriend on the condition he wouldn't be involved in the child's life, and then changed his mind and sued for custody, got widespread media attention in 2012 after Patric started lobbying for more rights for sperm donors.

"Three-parent families will be one of the next major legal issues for the LBGTQ community," Adams said.

Laws vary state-by-state regarding whose name goes on the birth certificate and who is responsible for child support. Generally speaking, in a sperm donor context, if a woman gets pregnant through at-home insemination, the biological father is responsible for child support if there is no donor-insemination contract in place, although the mother might not file for it.

Adams and other lawyers recommend that families decide whether a sperm donor will be a co-parent or just a donor, and sit down with a lawyer to draw up an agreement. If they are planning on co-parenting, there are a few other things they should iron out too: Whether the family is going to share a bank account and retirement accounts, who will cover the financial costs of raising a child, whether the parents want to commit to living in the same city or not. What will happen if one of the parents meets a romantic partner? What if someone gets a career opportunity in another city? What is the division of responsibilities for child care and decision making? What will they do about vaccinations, and medical interventions, and schooling?

Often, just having the conversation is just as important as putting the decisions into a legal document and submitting it to a family court, Adams said.

The legal issues can get even stickier when there are more than two people involved. Fatovic, of Modamily, said he helped a straight couple find a birth mother, because the woman in the couple couldn't have kids and the man wanted his own biological child. All three are involved in parenting. Usually gay couples want the donor or surrogate to cede all parental rights, but sometimes don't draw up any such agreement, Adams said.

New York State even bans paid surrogate pregnancies, part of a response to a 1980s court case in which a surrogate mother refused to give up custody of the baby (the parents who sued to be recognized as legal parents were straight, and eventually won parental rights in court).

Despite the legal issues, more parents can be better for a child's welfare, argues Rachel Hope, author of *Family By Choice: Platonic Partnered Parenting,* published in January. Hope might be one of the first people who tried platonic parenting in recent times—she had a son, who is now 24, with a colleague and best friend. Hope, who is 43, met her second platonic-parenting partner, Paul Wennaro, the creator of the Garden Burger, in Hawaii about 15 years ago. She asked him to be her parenting partner in 2007, and they have a 6-year old daughter, Grace. They all live together in Los Angeles.

But Wennaro is 67, and when Hope decided she wanted another child, he said he wanted to spend his time and energy on Grace. So Hope began an extensive search online, and after three years, found a 58-year-old ER doctor who already has a 13-year-old with a lesbian parenting partner he met on Craigslist. The two clicked, and are starting IVF in January. The three parents are hoping to live together, or at least close to one another, and be a new type of family with their children.

"Throughout history, the model that has worked for humankind was extended family—a village, a tribe," Hope told me. "It's only recently that we've started doing the nuclear family, with one mom and one dad, and it's really a failed experiment."

It's an especially good alternative to single parenthood, Hope said, since single parenting can be so fraught with stresses and challenges.

"The single parents I know are some of the most miserable people I've ever met," she said. "I've met quadriplegics who are happier than the single parents I know."

Of course, there are flaws to be found with this type of parenting. Although there isn't any research about the outcomes of children born into these non-traditional families, W. Bradford Wilcox, the director of the National Marriage Project, said that this type of family could create instability, which studies say is definitely bad for children.

"My concern about platonic parenting is that such an arrangement will not last," he wrote, in an e-mail. "In most cases, one or both of the parties will develop a non-platonic attraction to someone else and move on."

A healthy sexual relationship is what contributes to the emotional and physical bond that keeps many parents together over the long haul, he said. Platonic parents wouldn't have any such relationship.

It's not just the sexual bond: It's that children of platonic parents will miss out on the organic parts of living with a mother and a father who work together to raise them, said Glenn Stanton, director for Family Formation Studies at Focus on the Family.

"Parenting is not a time share," he said. "It's something you've got to own completely and full-time."

If women don't find a man they feel they want to marry and raise children with, he said, they should think about the child's welfare before deciding to have a child. After all, humans often desire a number of things that they sometimes can't have, he added.

It's true that sometimes people marry and have children with the best intentions and then split up, but they raise their children "doing the best they can in spite of the curveball life has thrown them," he said. "The idea of putting yourself intentionally in that situation is a whole other matter."

I asked Stanton whether he thought platonic parents were really any different than two people who marry without a strong romantic bond. You might remember "Marry Him!," an article from *The Atlantic* in 2008, in which single mom Lori Gottlieb caused a firestorm by advising women in their thirties who want children to marry someone without considering passion or an "intense connection."

"My advice is this: Settle!" she wrote. "Marriage isn't a passion-fest; it's more like a partnership formed to run a very small, mundane, and often boring nonprofit business."

Could a platonic-parenting relationship really be that different?, I asked Stanton Yes, Stanton said. Children learn from parents who have committed to sticking together, bumps and all, whether they're perfect life partners or not.

"That's what husbands and wives do, they say, 'I'm going to link up with you, for good and for bad, we're going to make it work.'" he said. "There's something wonderful about that that changes them and makes them better people, and the child learns from that."

But platonic parents commit to a lifetime commitment to raise a child in much the same way, Hope and Pieke argue. Before even trying to get pregnant, the parents nail down plans to make sure the emotional and financial support their child needs will be present from birth. Sometimes more effectively than married couples do, Hope said, since so many marriages end in unhappy divorces with a child torn between two feuding parents.

"We're releasing the expectation that building a family on the shifting sands of a romantic high is a smart thing to do," she said. "This is about building a family on common values, which really makes sense, has staying power, and is what's going to work for the kids."

For women in their thirties and forties, choosing someone to co-parent with can be a smarter decision than trying to find a mate because it takes the pressure off to marry or reproduce with someone you barely know, said Adams.

"A traditional model would have been a woman at 37 scrambling and trying to create a family with a romantic partner who she's known for two months," Adams said. "Wouldn't she be able to create a more stable family bond with her gay best friend of 20 years?"

There are alternatives to platonic parenting: Many single parents find that there are sufficient supports in things like cohousing, where families move into complexes with family dinners, shared living spaces and people in situations like theirs. Teri Hupfer moved into one such complex in the San Francisco area because she had two children, aged 15 months and seven years, and didn't know anyone else with kids.

"I wanted to move somewhere my kids would be able to run around outside and see other kids, but as a lesbian with biracial kids I couldn't see myself in a suburban home," she told me, in an e-mail. Cohousing did the trick. There were lots of families with young children, and they would take turns watching the kids while other parents cooked common meals, worked late, or even went out on dates. Some of the single moms in the complex turned out to be close friends, and their children grew up together too.

When she moved into the complex, 6 of the 32 families were single moms. Now, there are only two, she said, and some are lobbying for no more single mothers, because they are sometimes considered needy, she said. They ask for favors more—help babysitting, or picking up a child from daycare—and can only give back half as much time as couples can.

Dawn Pieke and Fabian Blue feel lucky that their daughter will know both of them, and have both of them involved in her life—they're so happy with their experience that they're trying to write a book about it. They also feel that they've vetted each other more extensively than married couples do. They performed extensive background checks on each other and shared tough moments that they might have tried to hide from a potential romantic partner, like when Pieke called Blue sobbing, nearly incoherent, because her dog died. They did testing to see what their fertility chances would be, and got various medical tests to make sure a potential child wouldn't have any genetic problems. Blue had come close to committing to other potential parenting partners, but something in his gut had told them that the other women weren't the right fit, but Pieke was.

The two felt so comfortable with each other that they didn't even create a co-parenting agreement—when couples get married, they don't sign a co-parenting agreement, Pieke points out. They're just trusting one another to stay involved. It's challenging at times—Pieke needs to stay in Omaha to care for her mother, who has Alzheimer's, and Blue needs to go where he can find a job. He works in high-end hotel management, and is currently based in Alabama. But he flies back frequently, and they're still on the same page about rearing Indigo. They split the costs 50-50.

They're still both looking for romantic partners who will accept their alternative lifestyle. If they don't find them, that's okay too. It's a totally different place than Pieke was in just a few years ago, after her relationship ended and she was left single and afraid that she'd never be able to have a family. She's even glad—in a weird way—about the breakups that led her to where she is now.

"I'm so thankful that everything did happen, because Indigo wouldn't be who she is without her dad," Pieke said. "She's amazing and funny and she's just awesome. Now that she's here, its hard to look back and say I wish this or that would have happened. She's here because of all of that."

Critical Thinking

1. Do you need to be in love and romantically linked to decide to have a child and parent together? Why or why not?
2. What might be some advantages of platonic parenting? Challenges or concerns?
3. What are legal and policy-related issues associated with three-parent families and platonic/non-married parenting partnerships?

Internet References

Path 2 Parenthood, The America Fertility Association
http://www.path2parenthood.org/

Partnered Parenting Magazine
http://www.partneredparenting.com/

Single Mothers by Choice
http://www.singlemothersbychoice.org/

Unit 3

UNIT

Prepared by: Patricia Hrusa Williams, *University of Maine at Farmington*

Family Relationships

And they lived happily ever after. . . . The romantic image conjured up by this well-known final line from fairy tales is not reflective of the reality of family life and relationship maintenance. The belief that somehow love alone should carry us through is pervasive. In reality, maintaining a relationship takes dedication, hard work, and commitment.

We come into relationships, regardless of their nature, with fantasies about how things ought to be. Partners, spouses, parents, children, siblings, and others—all family members, have at least some unrealistic expectations about each other and what their relationships should look and feel like. It is through the negotiation during the course of our lives together that we work through these expectations and hopefully, replace them with other more realistic ones. By recognizing and making their own contributions to the family, members can set and attain realistic family goals. Tolerance, acceptance of differences, and effective communication skills can facilitate this process. Along the way, family members need to learn new skills and develop new habits of relating to each other. This will not be easy, and not everything will be controllable. Patterns of interaction and communication can be hard to change. Factors both inside and outside the family may impede their progress.

Even before we enter a marriage or other committed relationships, attitudes, standards, and beliefs influence our choices. Increasingly, choices include whether we should commit to such a relationship in the first place. From the start of a committed relationship, the expectations both partners have and patterns they have learned during the course of other relationships have an impact. The need to reassess needs, patterns, and negotiate differences is a constant in the development of important relationships.

Adding a child to the family affects the lives of parents in ways that they could previously only imagine. Parenting is a complicated and often confusing process for which most of us have very little training or support. What's the "right" way to rear a child? How does the job of parents change as children grow and have different needs? There are a variety of different philosophies or approaches to parenting, many advocated through the popular media. We also have our own experiences of "being parented" which may influence our goals, choices, and ideals. These factors can all combine to make child-rearing more difficult than it might otherwise have been. Other family relationships also evolve, and in our nuclear-family-focused culture, it is possible to forget that family relationships extend beyond those between spouses, parents, and children.

This unit explores marital, parent–child, sibling, and intergenerational relationships within families. Among the topics explored include the characteristics of family communication, successful marriages and same-sex relationships, child-rearing philosophies, sibling relationships, and changes in parent–child relationships across the life span. A goal is to explore the diversity of structures and contexts in which couples, parents, children, and families develop and evolve.

Article Prepared by: Patricia Hrusa Williams, *University of Maine at Farmington*

Can Attachment Theory Explain All Our Relationships?

The Most Important Parenting You'll Ever Do Happens Before Your Child Turns One—and May Affect her for the Rest of her Life. One Mother's Journey through the Science of Attachment.

Bethany Saltman

Learning Outcomes

After reading this article, you will be able to:

- Explain attachment theory, attachment behaviors, and patterns of attachment.
- Understand ways attachments can be studied and assessed across the life span.
- Discuss the implications of attachment security/insecurity and later functioning.

The stage is set: a room with two chairs and some toys on the floor. A mother and her 1-year-old baby enter and begin the Strange Situation, a 20-min, eight-episode laboratory experiment to measure "attachment" between infants and their caregivers.

Through a one-way mirror, researchers observe the pair, cataloging every action and reaction. It doesn't take long to determine the baby's baseline temperament: physical, running to every corner of the room; inquisitive, intently exploring and mouthing every block; or reserved, wistfully holding a wind-up toy. The mother is told to sit down and read a magazine so the baby can do whatever she is naturally drawn to do. Then a stranger comes in, and the baby's reaction is observed—is she afraid of the stranger, nonchalant, or drawn to her? This indicates the style of relating to people in general and to the mother by comparison.

The mother is instructed to leave the room, leaving her purse on the chair, a sign that she will return. Here, we see how the baby responds to the experience of being left—does she howl and run to the door? Or does she stay put, on the floor, in a mountain of toys? The stranger tries to soothe the baby if she is upset. Otherwise, she leaves her to keep exploring.

After a few minutes, cut short if the baby is truly under duress (but that happens rarely), the mother returns for Reunion No. 1. The theory of attachment holds that a behavioral system has evolved to keep infants close to their caregivers and safe from harm. The presumption is that all babies will be under stress when left alone (and in fact, heart rate and cortisol levels indicate that even babies who don't appear distressed still are). So when the mother returns to the room, researchers are watching to see whether the relationship works as it should. Does the reunion do its job of bringing the baby from a state of relative anxiety into a state of relative ease? In other words, is the child soothed by the presence of the mother?

If the baby was upset during separation but sits still as a stone when her mother returns, it's likely a sign of an insecure attachment. If the baby was relaxed when left alone and is nonplussed by reunion, that's less significant. If the baby hightails it to her mother, then screeches mid approach, indicating a change of heart, that's a worrisome sign too.

But the most important moment is Reunion No. 2, after the mother leaves again and returns again. If a baby who was upset during separation *still* does nothing to acknowledge her mother's return, it's a sign that the baby, at only a year old, has already come to expect her advances to be rebuffed. If the baby reaches out for love but isn't able to settle down enough to receive it (or it's not offered), that may reflect a relationship filled with mixed messages. And if the baby is wild with sadness then jumps like a monkey into the mother's arms and immediately stops crying, the baby is categorized as secure, coming from a relationship in which she expects her needs to be met. The same goes for a mellow baby whose cues are more subtle, who simply looks sad during separation, then moves closer to Mother upon reunion. In both cases, the relationship works. (And just to be clear, a "working" relationship has nothing to do with the baby-wearing and co-sleeping and round-the-clock care popularized by Dr. William Sears's attachment-parenting movement; plenty of secure attachments are formed without following any particular parenting philosophy.)

Separate, connect. Separate, connect. It's the primal dance of finding ourselves in another, and another in ourselves. Researchers believe this pattern of attachment, assessed as early as one year, is more important than temperament, IQ, social class, and parenting style to a person's development. A boom in attachment research now links adult attachment insecurity with a host of problems, from sleep disturbances, depression, and anxiety to a decreased concern with moral injustice and less likelihood of being seen as a "natural leader." But the biggest subfield of attachment research is concerned, not surprisingly, with adult attachment in romantic relationships (yes, there's a quiz). Can we express our needs? Will they be met? If our needs are met, can we be soothed? Adults with high attachment security are more likely to be satisfied in marriage, experience less conflict, and be more resistant to divorce.

The trouble is that only around 60 percent of people are considered "secure." Which, of course, means that a good lot of us have some issues with attachment, which gets passed from generation to generation. Because if you had an insecure attachment with your parents, it is likely that you will have a more difficult time creating secure attachments for your own children.

The poet Philip Larkin was not the first or the last to notice that parents, "they fuck you up."

When my daughter Azalea was born, I was flooded with feelings of love. But it wasn't long before I returned to a more familiar sense of myself, and that love was mixed with ambivalence, internal conflict, impatience, and sometimes anger. Yes, I adored my baby, the way she nose-breathed on me as she nursed, her milky smell, her beautiful face, her charming smiles, her bright energy. *Her*. I loved *her*. But I was exhausted and overwhelmed, and what might be expressed as irritability in some parents felt more like rage to me. I knew better than to express anger at a baby, but my control dials felt out of reach. I never hit or shook my daughter, but I did yell at her, in real and frightening fury. One time, when she was 6 months old, she was supposed to be taking a nap, but instead she was pulling herself up in her crib, over and over again, nonstop crying. I was over it, done, nothing left. I sat on the floor in her darkened room, and made my ugliest, angriest, face at her, seething, yelling at her to just . . . go . . . to . . . SLEEP.

If this had been a one-off, I could have rationalized that every parent loses it at some point. But this kind of heat was all too available to me. I would occasionally confess my behavior to my husband, a psychotherapist, but he rarely saw it up close. So as much as he, my own therapist, and my friends tried to support us both, I was largely alone in my shame. And my daughter was alone with a warm and loving and sometimes scary mom.

I had read Dr. Sears and his attachment-parenting ideas before Azalea was born, but I was deeply suspicious that a checklist of behaviors could teach anyone how to raise a human being. I would read things like "Respond to your baby's cues," and think, *Right. As if.* Her cues were often inscrutable and always exhausting. Sears's cavalier oversimplification annoyed me to no end and added to the weight of expectations and disappointment.

As Azalea grew, some things got easier. Language helped. Her ever-increasing cuteness and sweetness helped. Our connection developed, and I loved doing things together—reading books, going to Target, cooking, cuddling, walking, and hanging out with friends. Things were good. Except when they weren't. Like the time in the grocery store as I was checking out with Thanksgiving groceries while struggling to manage Azalea's unwieldy 10-month-old body in front of a line of blankly staring, silently huffing adults. I remember the jaw-setting, skin-tingling, adrenaline-pumping feeling of anger overtake me. While I don't remember exactly what I said to my squirming baby, I will never forget the disgusted look on the checkout lady's face, confirming that whatever outburst I settled on was definitely not okay.

In my dark moments, I felt like something inside me was missing, that thing that functions deep down that keeps us from hurting the people we love. But I also tried to remind myself that the cult of perfect parenthood is a myth, that there is no way to avoid making a mess of our kids one way or another. That gave me some peace. Then, when Azalea was four, I interviewed Jon Kabat-Zinn, the mindfulness and meditation expert who has written many books, including *Everyday Blessings: The Inner Work of the Mindful Parent*. I think I was hoping he might encourage me to set down my burden of guilt and shame, maybe even offer a God-like *let it go*. But that wasn't what happened.

Kabat-Zinn: The meaning of being a parent is that you take responsibility for your child's life until they can take responsibility for their own life.

That's it!

Me: That's a lot.

Kabat-Zinn: True, and it doesn't mean you can't get help. Turns out how you are as a parent makes a huge difference in the neural development of your child for the first four or five years.

Me: That is so frightening.

Kabat-Zinn: All that's required, though, is connection. That's all.

Me: But I want to be separate from my child; I don't want to be connected all the time.

Kabat-Zinn: I see. Well, everything has consequences. How old is your child?

Me: Four and a half.

Kabat-Zinn: Well, I gotta say, I have very strong feelings about that kind of thing. She didn't ask to be born.

I knew then that I needed to figure out why I am the kind of mother I am, and what effect it was having on my daughter.

What began as a quiet inkling that studying attachment might help me understand my vast and varied shortcomings as a mother unfolded into a bona fide obsession with the entire field of attachment research, inspiring me to write a book and to sign up for training in the Strange Situation. So last August I traveled to Minneapolis where, for the past 30 years, professor Alan Sroufe, co-creator of what has become known as the Minnesota Study, a seminal, 30-year longitudinal study of attachment, has trained researchers, grad students, clinicians, and intrigued writers to become reliable coders of the Strange Situation. I knew that only through training could I learn to discern the bedrock of an infant's most important relationship. I wanted to become that trained eye.

From our seats in a big classroom, students from around the world—Italy, Peru, New Zealand, Mexico, Israel, Japan, and Zambia—watched several videotaped Strange Situations a day, spanning the history and breadth of the field itself, from early, grainy footage with American moms wearing Gloria Vanderbilts and wedge sandals to HD-quality contemporary Swedish pairs. The action is so simple—alone, together, alone, together—it's almost lyrical. Though the Strange Situation has been done with fathers and other primary caregivers (and monkeys!), the structure is always the same and always points to one thing: the crazy, difficult, beautiful, mysterious nature of trying to love someone.

At the beginning, I was lost. I couldn't track the action, let alone what mattered, and I got distracted by the wrong details, or hung up on my own reactions. Is it the whiny babies who are insecure and the robust, easygoing ones who are secure? Not necessarily. Attachment is not about temperament. If a big crier is soothed by his mother's return, he is securely attached. If an anxious kid knows how to scramble for safety and feel felt, it's another good sign. This is why the Strange Situation works so well—it highlights the relationship while controlling for almost everything else.

Eventually, I learned how to read the cues, and I began to notice the quickest glance and connect it with the rest of the baby's behavior. I began to notice the difference between a full-on wrap-around-the-legs greeting and a limp request for contact, and the significance of each. I started to wonder about the baby who reached up to be held and kicked at the same time. And I began to worry about all those "good" babies who just sat there, moving shapes around the floor, unaffected by their lifeline's comings and goings.

While attachment behaviors look different across cultures, the attachment system itself is universal. All babies fall into one of the patterns: Secure (B), Insecure/Avoidant (A), and Insecure/Resistant (C). (There are also eight subgroups and a whole other strain within these categories called disorganization.) In the case of Avoidant babies, there is often little or no acknowledgment of the mother's return. The chill in the air is unnerving. The marker of the avoidant baby, as opposed to the secure one who simply doesn't need as much contact, is either a subtle averting of their gaze, or an overt change of direction en route to connection. You can see babies literally change their mind as they make a beeline for comfort. Resistant babies, meanwhile, are pissed—kicking, arching, and hitting. They make a big show of wanting contact, but they are unable to settle even after the one they desire has returned.

B-4 is a subgroup of secure babies who express a lot, need a lot, can be a bit feisty, but who know where their bread is buttered. My favorite Strange Situation starred a little B-4 girl in a lavender dress who reminded me of Azalea. Sitting in the darkened classroom, I watched the baby toddle around in her little sneakers, bawling her head off when her mother, a thin, sad-seeming young woman with '80s hair and Reeboks, left. But when the mother returned, the baby ran to her and was immediately picked up. The crying stopped. This was not one of those moms with tons of affect and big expressions of *there, there*. She just picked her up, and the baby molded right to her, put her head on her shoulder, and then (and this is the best thing ever) the mother and daughter patted each other's shoulders simultaneously. Co-regulation, a mirror. Then the baby got back on the floor to play.

I thought back to when my daughter Azalea was that age, wearing dresses with giant bows, walking on stiff legs, flyaway curls in pig tails—an adorable, willful, comfort-seeking missile. Then there was me, self-concerned, kind of unavailable, moody, and angry. I looked around at all the mothers and daughters and fathers and sons in the classroom, staring up at the big screen, as this sad-looking mother and her big-feeling daughter showed us all how it's supposed to be done, each of us probably wondering the same thing: *What about me? What about her? What about us?*

Before attachment theory came into view in the 1950s, the field of developmental psychology was very much focused on the interior drives of each individual, not their relationships. Then a British psychoanalyst named John Bowlby came along and made the case that relationships mattered more than anyone had previously suspected. His theory, influenced by the study of animal behavior, was that primates require a primary caregiver for survival, not as a means to receive food (as the behaviorists believed), but in order to be and *feel* close to a protective adult. According to Bowlby, it was in service to this goal of real and felt security that certain so-called "attachment behaviors" had evolved to elicit a caregiver's response—crying, following, smiling, sucking, clinging. In other words, babies had evolved to send signals to their caregivers when vulnerable (afraid, sick, hurt, etcetera) that required a response (picking up, cuddling, tending to, etcetera) that kept them safe from danger. At the heart of the attachment system is a primitive kind of call and response that keeps the species alive.

While Bowlby is known as the father of attachment, a prodigiously smart psychologist who worked briefly as his researcher, Mary Salter Ainsworth, is the one who brought his theory to life. In 1954, Ainsworth's husband got a job in Uganda and she accompanied him, determined to set up a research project testing her and Bowlby's budding theory with real people. After a year of observing Ganda mothers and babies, she noticed that the babies who cried the least had the most attentive mothers. And she saw how "maternal attunement" to babies' cues seemed to determine these patterns.

While previous studies had noted of a mother's "warmth," or a child's smiles or cries, what made Ainsworth's observations original was that she noticed *relational* sensitivity, the actual relationship between two beings. The sensitive caregiver, she writes, "picks [the baby] up when he seems to wish it, and puts him down when he wants to explore . . . On the other hand, the [caregiver] who responds inappropriately tries to socialize with the infant when he is hungry, play with him when he is tired, or feed him when he is trying to initiate social interaction." She also noticed that the babies who were most comfortable exploring were the ones whose mothers made it clear they weren't going anywhere.

Ainsworth followed up her work in Uganda with her famous "Baltimore Study," the first to methodically observe mothers and babies in relationship, in the home, and then with the laboratory procedure designed to replicate what she saw in the home, the Strange Situation.

Bowlby's theory was that babies can't handle their own fear, sadness, wet-diaper-ness, hunger, etcetera and need someone to handle it for them. This process begins with "co-regulation" with the caregiver and ends, ideally, with "the establishment of the self as the main executive agency of security-based strategies." In other words, children who are effectively soothed by their caregivers eventually learn how to do it for themselves. And what of those for whom this doesn't happen?

It was with no small amount of trepidation that I began to wonder what happened to Azalea's tears when I wasn't able to absorb them. Where does a baby's unshared heartbreak *go*? I thought back to so many times when I turned away from her anguish, and how simple it would have been for me to turn toward her instead. I began to see her toddling along in the world, following the hot, human trail of seeking connection—checking back, exploring, moving away, and returning. And I saw how difficult it was for me to tolerate that much needy attention.

Was that because I had an insecure attachment myself? Pictures of myself as infant—actual 1969 Polaroids, as well as mental images—began coming into my mind. I know my mother nursed me, which was unusual at the time (I also know she smoked *while* nursing, as in at the same time). I know she was thrilled that I turned out to be a girl after two boys that she always knew she would name her daughter Bethany. I started to wonder how my mother and I would have done in the Strange Situation. When Azalea was born and I struggled with keeping her little body occupied, my mom recalled, *Gosh, I used to just put you kids on the blanket with some toys.*

As a writer who has been in and out of therapy pretty much my whole life, it's not like I had never thought about my childhood, or worked with difficult feelings before. But learning about Bowlby's and Ainsworth's work made me wonder if at least some of my troubles—all manner of adolescent acting out, complicated personal relationships, low self-esteem—were an expression of an insecure attachment. I was a poster child, really, for insecurity. As Sroufe and his colleagues write, "Attachment history itself, while related to a range of teenage outcomes, was most strongly related to outcomes tapping intimacy and trust issues."

And if I had an insecure attachment, was it affecting me even now, as an adult? One of the most profound modern advances in attachment theory came from a longitudinal study by Ainsworth's former student Mary Main. Main was trying to unravel the relationship between a child's attachment security and their caregiver's internal working model of attachment. So, in what became known as the "Berkeley Study," children were assessed in the Strange Situation as usual, but in addition their parents were asked a series of questions about their early attachment relationships, questions designed to "surprise the unconscious" and reveal the person's true state of mind. The first big news was just how closely correlated a child's attachment classification was to their parents' adult attachment representation. The correlation was so striking that Main decided to check back in with the children at age 19, to ask them the same series of questions about their early-childhood relationships. What she discovered was that most had the same attachment classification as when they were in the Strange Situation at a year old. Later, other researchers found that what came to be known as the Adult Attachment Interview actually predicted how someone's baby might do in the Strange Situation. Attachment, it seems, is remarkably consistent throughout a life (though can also be changed by positive and negative forces) and even from one generation to the next.

While generally a research tool, the AAI is sometimes used in clinical settings, with therapists administering the interview to patients. It's a highly specialized procedure, expensive and time-consuming, but so full of potential insight I couldn't get it out of my head. I knew that taking the AAI wouldn't change history—mine or Azalea's—but I might be able to get some answers.

I had met Dr. Howard Steele, the expert in attachment who agreed to administer my AAI, two summers before, when, after I told him about the research I was doing, he invited me to observe a Strange Situation in his lab. Still, taking the train to the *New School's Center for Attachment Research*, I was incredibly nervous.

The AAI contains 20 open-ended, slightly startling questions about one's relationships in early childhood, along with prompts to reflect about it all, designed to elicit and reveal the speaker's internal working model of attachment. The questions "require a rapid succession of speech acts, giving speakers little time to prepare a response." They begin with general inquiries about the nature of one's relationship with parents, then drill down a bit, asking for five adjectives that describe that relationship, with supporting memories and details. Then come questions about how your parents responded to you in times of early separation, times of illness or loss, feelings of rejection, "setbacks"—all with requests like "You mentioned that you felt your mother was tender when you were ill. Can you think of a time when this was so?"

Next, the AAI is transcribed verbatim, then carefully coded for adult attachment security. This is done through a two-pronged approach—assessing both the "probable experience," as in what the primary relationships were probably like, and the "state of mind," which investigates things like idealization, preoccupied anger, and disorganized responses as well as vague speech and insistence on lack of memory.

Secure adults tend to value attachment relationships and are able to describe experiences coherently, whether negative (e.g., parental rejection or overinvolvement) or positive, says Main. Dismissing adults tend either to devalue the importance of attachment relationships or to idealize their parents without being able to illustrate their positive evaluations with concrete events demonstrating secure interaction. Preoccupied adults are still very much involved and preoccupied with their past attachment experiences and are therefore not able to describe them coherently. Dismissing and preoccupied adults are both considered insecure.

The AAI has been found to be reliable independent of intelligence, or verbal fluency, or interviewer. The most articulate, detail-oriented trial lawyer, ordinarily linguistically unflappable, may report that her mother was kind, loving, warm, and fun but have an inability to recall any details to support that. In fact, she might repeat herself, or give irrelevant details. This would indicate a possibly insecure/dismissive state of mind, indicating the lawyer may well raise an avoidant baby. It's not a good relationship per se but the subject's state of mind in relation *to* their relationships that determines their children's attachment security, which provides a foundation for those children's socio-emotional health and happiness, which develops into their adult state of mind, which affects their own children's security, and so on.

Suddenly, there I was sitting in a little room with a professional listener, trying to come up with five adjectives to describe my mother and scrambling to find relevant memories to support my choices. I remembered my mother taking me into the bathroom at the end of the hall to talk about some drama that had happened at school. I described the sofa bed she used to make when I was sick, and the story of my dad blowing me off when I got a giant splinter in the backyard. I tried to explain my feelings of disconnection even in the presence of a mother who really did seem to try, and how that disconnection turned into anger and more distance. When Steele asked me about why I thought my parents raised me the way they did, it was easy to look at their parents and understand why my dad was shut down and my mom a little hard to access. And I didn't feel the least bit angry, not even for the thing that had plagued me my entire life—a pervasive feeling of shame for having been neglected, not cared for, not protected from danger.

I feared that if my results came back "preoccupied" (I knew I wasn't dismissive), I would feel humiliated, as if my entire interest in attachment was merely a manifestation of my neuroses. But when I returned to the office later that afternoon to receive my score, what I felt was relief. My score, Steele said, was secure/autonomous. I asked him if he would be so bold as to predict, were I pregnant today, what kind of baby I would have. A B4, he said—secure, with an edge. Like the girl in the lavender dress. I was the mom with the mullet and Azalea was the girl with the big, fat, soothable tears.

I didn't need a test to tell me that Azalea, who is now 10, does seem happy, well-regulated, and comfortable in the world. The other day, as I drove her and her five-year-old friend Leroi to violin, I watched them talk about their respective field trips in the rearview mirror. I was so proud of the way Azalea cut short her story of climbing the fire tower so that Leroi could tell his kindergarten tale. I could feel her softening her voice when she talked to him and watched her face turn gentle as she offered to help him with the seat belt.

Beyond all the research linking secure attachments to everything good, attachment is connected to something so profound it's hard to describe. The literature calls it "mentalization"; UCLA psychiatrist Dan Siegel refers to it as "mindsight." Basically, it's the experience of knowing you have a mind and that everyone else has one, too. Then it's one small step to see that others have feelings, too.

Was Azalea's behavior with Leroi a result of her capacity to mentalize and therefore take care of her friends? I hope so. Did she learn that from me? Maybe. If so, does this mean our work is done? Hardly. But it's comforting to see that, despite all my very real, very unsettling shortcomings, something so important is functioning well. After all, it's the attachment-inspired capacity to feel that makes us care for and attune to others. And apparently the process is much more forgiving than I imagined.

My AAI subgroup was F3B, a category for a small percentage of the population who have, Steele told me, "suffered adversity" but are still able to have some coherence of mind in relation to attachment. In my confidential feedback, Steele wrote: "Overall, there is a sense that this speaker knows her own mind and the mind of others she cares about. Probable past experiences are mixed . . . She learned to turn to herself and to her inner world, which became richly developed (as appears to be the case for her daughter too in the next generation) . . . an adaptive strategy!"

This was a revolutionary way for me to think about my childhood. Yes, I wish some things had been different, but what if my self-reliance and sense of reflection—two things I value greatly—developed not in spite of my upbringing but *because* of it? What if I was taught from a young age how to see myself, from parents who—research suggests—had a knack for the same thing.

I had spent a lifetime worrying that there was something wrong with me. Then with my kid. Then with my family. But, as Sroufe pointed out in Minneapolis while we watched some ultimately secure but hardly perfect mother–baby duos in the Strange Situation, *something was working*.

Attachment is a simple, elegant articulation of the fact that, yes, we really do need each other, and, yes, what we do in relation to each other matters. And yet we don't have to get it right all the time or even most of the time. As Steele and his wife Miriam write in an essay in the book *What Is Parenthood?*, "Even sensitive caregivers get it right only about 50 percent of the time. There are times when parents feel tired or distracted. The telephone rings or there is breakfast to prepare. In other words, attuned interactions rupture quite frequently. But the hallmark of a sensitive caregiver is that the ruptures are managed and repaired."

Maybe all this room for error means we're wired for forgiveness.

Or maybe, as Steele gently suggested at the end of our interview, even though I experienced my early life as very painful, maybe, in fact, it wasn't that bad. Technically speaking.

Critical Thinking

1. What kind of relationship do you have with your parents? How has your connection with them influenced how you relate to others?
2. What does it mean to be securely attached? What types of behaviors for both parent and child are associated with being securely attached?
3. Does experiencing adversity in parent–child relationships result in insecure attachment relationships? How can resilience and adaptive functioning come from challenging circumstances? Is there such a thing as a perfect parent? What's really needed to promote positive parent–child relationships and adaptive functioning as an adult?

Internet References

Attachment Parenting International
http://www.attachmentparenting.org/

Attachment Theory and Research at SUNY Stony Brook
http://www.psychology.sunysb.edu/attachment/

International Association for the Study of Attachment
http://www.iasa-dmm.org/

Mindful (Mindfulness and Mindful Parenting Resource)
https://www.mindful.org/

Minnesota Study of Risk and Adaptation
http://www.cehd.umn.edu/ICD/research/Parent-Child/

Article Prepared by: Patricia Hrusa Williams, *University of Maine at Farmington*

The Marriage Mindset

Lasting Love isn't Just a Matter of the Heart But Also Getting in the Right Frame of Mind.

Annemarie Scobey

Learning Outcomes

After reading this article, you will be able to:

- Describe communication practices of couples in healthy, long-term marriages and relationships.
- Understand daily challenges and hassles experienced by married couples with children.
- Consider how mind-sets or perspectives influence behavior and interactions with others.

When our kids were eight, four, and one, my husband Bill talked me into agreeing he could do worm composting in our basement. He sold me on the environmental benefits of the process and said it would also be educational for the kids to bring our table waste to the basement and see what an important job worms do creating rich soil. On the day, he came home with five-foot-long trays filled with dirt and hundreds of small, red, round worms, I was less than enthusiastic and deeply wished I had not agreed to this!

"This was not in the vows," I said. "Hey, I wasn't the one who married me," Bill said. He was right. One of the things I loved about Bill when we were dating was his commitment to the environment. He had Ansel Adams photos of national parks all over his apartment; he rode his bike to work; he toted a reusable lunch container to work when others brown-bagged it. While we were dating, I might not have been able to see worm composting as part of our future together, but I had certainly known that a commitment to the environment was a core part of who Bill was.

"I wasn't the one who married me" has become a recurring line in our marriage. We use it to gently remind whichever spouse is struggling with a habit or behavior of the other that we both chose each other—idiosyncrasies and all. The line reminds me of how I've heard friendship defined: Friendship is knowing fully the good and the bad of another person, and moving forward with the relationship anyway, accepting both.

For Bill and me, and many couples I know, one of the keys to a long-lasting and healthy marriage has less to do with date nights or weekends away, and more to do with the mind-set each partner brings into each day of the marriage.

Holding on to Gratitude—Especially When Life Gets Crazy

Couples in strong marriages make a conscious effort to be thankful for their spouses. Miguel, married almost 20 years to Juanita, comments, "We can't seem to find date-night time. We are working to meet the needs of our kids and to care for our aging parents; we are bad at putting our marriage ahead of all that. Nevertheless, when I feel like I am grinding it out day after day, I remind myself that I am so grateful to be sharing all of this with someone who cares as deeply about our kids and parents. Basically, there's no one I'd rather do this with. I appreciate the teamwork we forge together."

Patty, married to John for 26 years and mother to five young adult daughters, agrees on the importance of spouses being grateful. "We thank each other a lot. Sometimes one of us will respond 'you don't have to thank me for that,' but we're each genuinely grateful for the other and the thank-yous come naturally," she says. "One of our girls noted this recently when I thanked John for switching the wash. 'I just really appreciate your dad doing even the little things for us,' I explained."

Consciously Look for the Good

The socks in the middle of the floor, dishes piled on the counter, and the forgotten appointment can move a spouse in one of two directions. The daily annoyances of life with another person can either serve as proof points as to why a marriage isn't working or can propel a spouse to look more deeply into the other person and into the marriage to find all that is worthwhile. Married couples who are happy and enjoy each other don't necessarily have fewer issues to work through, but they may take a different approach to their challenges than those with less satisfying marriages.

Nancy, married to Scott, knows of many unhappy marriages among her peers, and counts herself fortunate to have Scott. "I remind myself that even though I get frustrated with him sometimes (and of course I am not perfect either), I'm really lucky to have married someone who values family, my work, and me," she says. "I know my grass is greener than a lot of people's. Two key points that almost always prove to be helpful for our perspective are having a sense of humor and realizing tomorrow is a new opportunity."

For Jenny and Brian, parents of three children under 10, perspective is key. Jenny notes that intentionally remembering what attracted her to her husband brings positive feelings to mind. "I flash back to our time dating," she says. Jenny also mentions how important it is for spouses to get out of their day-to-day environment and interact with others to bring freshness to the relationship. "If I'm frustrated with him, my attitude always changes as we are out with friends or family; I see him interacting with others and I easily remember how awesome he is and why I married him."

Amy, married 23 years to Kevin, jokingly says that if she's in a difficult moment she allows herself to go morbid. "I think about life without Kevin and it really makes me appreciate him," she says. Like Jenny, Amy takes herself out of the present moment and into the past. "I think of when we dated and how much I wanted to marry him. I remember all the reasons why. When I do both those reflections, I am all in again."

Lean on Honesty, Humor, and Faith

Brigid, married 23 years to Bob, says she has found that looking for the underlying truth in a small-issue moment she might be tempted to quarrel over has worked tremendously well for the couple. "I personally committed from the beginning to be honest with myself rather than play games. If I felt vulnerable, I committed to stating that truth rather than pick a fight over something else to get the reassurance I needed," she says. Brigid's practice could likely help many marriages. Too often, couples find themselves in endless rounds of arguments that have little to do with the underlying issue: Do you love me? Brigid balances her serious, intentional approach with quick wit. "I go out of my way to tease my husband. You don't tease people you don't like," she says.

Andrea and Greg, married 23 years, see the early years of marriage as critical. They credit their Catholic upbringing and long, committed marriages on both sides of the family as helping them with the more challenging early years of marriage—when misunderstanding sometimes led to hurt and distance. "As we have grown together as a couple, the trust in all areas has grown," Andrea says. "We strive to be caring of each other and to put the other first. We operate from a place of deep compassion and respect. This has been the glue that binds us together."

Critical Thinking

1. What does the author mean by the term "marriage mind-set"?
2. Conflict and hassles occur in any relationship. Describe some ways which couples in long-term, healthy relationships communicate with each other to manage these challenges.
3. Can you think of any other practices that are important to sustaining long-term marriages? List at least three and describe how and why they are important.

Internet References

Love Is Respect
http://www.loveisrespect.org/

National Healthy Marriage Resource Center
http://www.healthymarriageinfo.org

National Resource Center for Healthy Marriage and Families
https://www.healthymarriageandfamilies.org/

Article

Prepared by: Patricia Hrusa Williams, *University of Maine at Farmington*

Masters of Love

EMILY ESFAHANI SMITH

Learning Outcomes

After reading this article, you will be able to:

- Identify practices couples associate with marital satisfaction and dissatisfaction.
- Recognize the impact of Gottman's work on relationships.
- Explain what kindness is and why it is important in marital relationships.

Every day in June, the most popular wedding month of the year, about 13,000 American couples will say "I do," committing to a lifelong relationship that will be full of friendship, joy, and love that will carry them forward to their final days on this earth.

Except, of course, it doesn't work out that way for most people. The majority of marriages fail, either ending in divorce and separation or devolving into bitterness and dysfunction. Of all the people who get married, only three in ten remain in healthy, happy marriages, as psychologist Ty Tashiro points out in his book *The Science of Happily Ever After,* which was published earlier this year.

Social scientists first started studying marriages by observing them in action in the 1970s in response to a crisis: Married couples were divorcing at unprecedented rates. Worried about the impact these divorces would have on the children of the broken marriages, psychologists decided to cast their scientific net on couples, bringing them into the lab to observe them and determine what the ingredients of a healthy, lasting relationship were. Was each unhappy family unhappy in its own way, as Tolstoy claimed, or did the miserable marriages all share something toxic in common?

Psychologist John Gottman was one of those researchers. For the past four decades, he has studied thousands of couples in a quest to figure out what makes relationships work. I recently had the chance to interview Gottman and his wife Julie, also a psychologist, in New York City. Together, the renowned experts on marital stability run The Gottman Institute, which is devoted to helping couples build and maintain loving, healthy relationships based on scientific studies.

John Gottman began gathering his most critical findings in 1986, when he set up "The Love Lab" with his colleague Robert Levenson at the University of Washington. Gottman and Levenson brought newlyweds into the lab and watched them interact with each other. With a team of researchers, they hooked the couples up to electrodes and asked the couples to speak about their relationship, like how they met, a major conflict they were facing together, and a positive memory they had. As they spoke, the electrodes measured the subjects' blood flow, heart rates, and how much they sweat they produced. Then the researchers sent the couples home and followed up with them six years later to see if they were still together.

From the data they gathered, Gottman separated the couples into two major groups: the *masters* and the *disasters.* The masters were still happily together after six years. The disasters had either broken up or were chronically unhappy in their marriages. When the researchers analyzed the data they gathered on the couples, they saw clear differences between the masters and disasters. The disasters looked calm during the interviews, but their physiology, measured by the electrodes, told a different story. Their heart rates were quick, their sweat glands were active, and their blood flow was fast. Following thousands of couples longitudinally, Gottman found that the more physiologically active the couples were in the lab, the quicker their relationships deteriorated over time.

But what does physiology have to do with anything? The problem was that the disasters showed all the signs of arousal—of being in fight-or-flight mode—in their relationships. Having a conversation sitting next to their spouse was, to their bodies, like facing off with a saber-toothed tiger. Even when they were talking about pleasant or mundane facets of their relationships, they were prepared to attack and be attacked. This sent their heart rates soaring and made them more aggressive toward each other. For example, each member of a couple could be talking about how their days had gone, and a highly aroused husband might say to his wife, "Why don't you start talking about your day. It won't take you very long."

The masters, by contrast, showed low physiological arousal. They felt calm and connected together, which translated into warm and affectionate behavior, even when they fought. It's not that the masters had, by default, a better physiological make-up than the disasters; it's that masters had created a climate of trust and intimacy that made both of them more emotionally and thus physically comfortable.

Gottman wanted to know more about how the masters created that culture of love and intimacy, and how the disasters squashed it. In a follow-up study in 1990, he designed a lab on the University of Washington campus to look like a beautiful bed and breakfast retreat. He invited 130 newlywed couples to spend the day at this retreat and watched them as they did what couples normally do on vacation: cook, clean, listen to music, eat, chat, and hang out. And Gottman made a critical discovery in this study—one that gets at the heart of why some relationships thrive while others languish.

Throughout the day, partners would make requests for connection, what Gottman calls "bids." For example, say that the husband is a bird enthusiast and notices a goldfinch fly across the yard. He might say to his wife, "Look at that beautiful bird outside!" He's not just commenting on the bird here: he's requesting a response from his wife—a sign of interest or support—hoping they'll connect, however momentarily, over the bird.

The wife now has a choice. She can respond by either "turning toward" or "turning away" from her husband, as Gottman puts it. Though the bird-bid might seem minor and silly, it can actually reveal a lot about the health of the relationship. The husband thought the bird was important enough to bring it up in conversation and the question is whether his wife recognizes and respects that.

People who turned toward their partners in the study responded by engaging the bidder, showing interest and support in the bid. Those who didn't—those who turned away—would not respond or respond minimally and continue doing whatever they were doing, like watching TV or reading the paper. Sometimes they would respond with overt hostility, saying something like, "Stop interrupting me, I'm reading."

These bidding interactions had profound effects on marital well-being. Couples who had divorced after a six-year follow up had "turn-toward bids" 33 percent of the time. Only three in ten of their bids for emotional connection were met with intimacy. The couples who were still together after six years had "turn-toward bids" 87 percent of the time. Nine times out of ten, they were meeting their partner's emotional needs.

* * *

By observing these types of interactions, Gottman can predict with up to 94 percent certainty whether couples—straight or gay, rich or poor, childless or not—will be broken up, together and unhappy, or together and happy several years later. Much of it comes down to the spirit couples bring to the relationship. Do they bring kindness and generosity; or contempt, criticism, and hostility?

"There's a habit of mind that the masters have," Gottman explained in an interview, "which is this: they are scanning social environment for things they can appreciate and say thank you for. They are building this culture of respect and appreciation very purposefully. Disasters are scanning the social environment for partners' mistakes."

"It's not just scanning environment," chimed in Julie Gottman. "It's scanning the *partner* for what the *partner* is doing right or scanning him for what he's doing wrong and criticizing versus respecting him and expressing appreciation."

Contempt, they have found, is the number one factor that tears couples apart. People who are focused on criticizing their partners miss a whopping 50 percent of positive things their partners are doing and they see negativity when it's not there. People who give their partner the cold shoulder—deliberately ignoring the partner or responding minimally—damage the relationship by making their partner feel worthless and invisible, as if they're not there, not valued. And people who treat their partners with contempt and criticize them not only kill the love in the relationship, but they also kill their partner's ability to fight off viruses and cancers. Being mean is the death knell of relationships.

Kindness, on the other hand, glues couples together. Research independent from theirs has shown that kindness (along with emotional stability) is the most important predictor of satisfaction and stability in a marriage. Kindness makes each partner feel cared for, understood, and validated—feel loved. "My bounty is as boundless as the sea," says Shakespeare's Juliet. "My love as deep; the more I give to thee, / The more I have, for both are infinite." That's how kindness works too: there's a great deal of evidence showing the more someone receives or witnesses kindness, the more they will be kind themselves, which leads to upward spirals of love and generosity in a relationship.

There are two ways to think about kindness. You can think about it as a fixed trait: either you have it or you don't. Or you could think of kindness as a muscle. In some people, that muscle is naturally stronger than in others, but it can grow stronger in everyone with exercise. Masters tend to think about kindness as a muscle. They know that they have to exercise it to keep it in shape. They know, in other words, that a good relationship requires sustained hard work.

"If your partner expresses a need," explained Julie Gottman, "and you are tired, stressed, or distracted, then the generous spirit comes in when a partner makes a bid, and you still turn toward your partner."

In that moment, the easy response may be to turn away from your partner and focus on your iPad or your book or the television, to mumble "Uh huh" and move on with your life, but neglecting small moments of emotional connection will slowly wear away at your relationship. Neglect creates distance between partners and breeds resentment in the one who is being ignored.

The hardest time to practice kindness is, of course, during a fight—but this is also the most important time to be kind. Letting contempt and aggression spiral out of control during a conflict can inflict irrevocable damage on a relationship.

"Kindness doesn't mean that we don't express our anger," Julie Gottman explained, "but the kindness informs how we choose to express the anger. You can throw spears at your partner. Or you can explain why you're hurt and angry, and that's the kinder path."

John Gottman elaborated on those spears: "Disasters will say things differently in a fight. Disasters will say 'You're late. What's wrong with you? You're just like your mom.' Masters will say 'I feel bad for picking on you about your lateness, and I know it's not your fault, but it's really annoying that you're late again.'"

* * *

For the hundreds of thousands of couples getting married this month—and for the millions of couples currently together, married or not—the lesson from the research is clear: If you want to have a stable, healthy relationship, exercise kindness early and often.

When people think about practicing kindness, they often think about small acts of generosity, like buying each other little gifts or giving one another back rubs every now and then. While those are great examples of generosity, kindness can also be built into the very backbone of a relationship through the way partners interact with each other on a day-to-day basis, whether or not there are back rubs and chocolates involved.

One way to practice kindness is by being generous about your partner's intentions. From the research of the Gottmans, we know that disasters see negativity in their relationship even when it is not there. An angry wife may assume, for example, that when her husband left the toilet seat up, he was deliberately trying to annoy her. But he may have just absent-mindedly forgotten to put the seat down.

Or say a wife is running late to dinner (again), and the husband assumes that she doesn't value him enough to show up to their date on time after he took the trouble to make a reservation and leave work early so that they could spend a romantic evening together. But it turns out that the wife was running late because she stopped by a store to pick him up a gift for their special night out. Imagine her joining him for dinner, excited to deliver her gift, only to realize that he's in a sour mood because he misinterpreted what was motivating her behavior. The ability to interpret your partner's actions and intentions charitably can soften the sharp edge of conflict.

"Even in relationships where people are frustrated, it's almost always the case that there are positive things going on and people trying to do the right thing," psychologist Ty Tashiro told me. "A lot of times, a partner is trying to do the right thing even if it's executed poorly. So appreciate the intent."

Another powerful kindness strategy revolves around shared joy. One of the telltale signs of the disaster couples Gottman studied was their inability to connect over each other's good news. When one person in the relationship shared the good news of, say, a promotion at work with excitement, the other would respond with wooden disinterest by checking his watch or shutting the conversation down with a comment like, "That's nice."

We've all heard that partners should be there for each other when the going gets rough. But research shows that being there for each other when things go *right* is actually more important for relationship quality. How someone responds to a partner's good news can have dramatic consequences for the relationship.

In one study from 2006, psychological researcher Shelly Gable and her colleagues brought young adult couples into the lab to discuss recent positive events from their lives. They psychologists wanted to know how partners would respond to each other's good news. They found that, in general, couples responded to each other's good news in four different ways that they called: *passive destructive, active destructive, passive constructive,* and *active constructive.*

Let's say that one partner had recently received the excellent news that she got into medical school. She would say something like "I got into my top choice med school!"

If her partner responded in a *passive destructive* manner, he would ignore the event. For example, he might say something like: "You wouldn't believe the great news I got yesterday! I won a free t-shirt!"

If her partner responded in a *passive constructive* way, he would acknowledge the good news, but in a half-hearted, understated way. A typical passive constructive response is saying "That's great, babe" as he texts his buddy on his phone.

In the third kind of response, *active destructive,* the partner would diminish the good news his partner just got: "Are you sure you can handle all the studying? And what about the cost? Med school is so expensive!"

Finally, there's *active constructive* responding. If her partner responded in this way, he stopped what he was doing and engaged wholeheartedly with her: "That's great! Congratulations! When did you find out? Did they call you? What classes will you take first semester?"

Among the four response styles, active constructive responding is the kindest. While the other response styles are joy-killers, active constructive responding allows the partner to savor her joy and gives the couple an opportunity to bond over the good news. In the parlance of the Gottmans, active constructive responding is a way of "turning toward" your partners bid (sharing the good news) rather than "turning away" from it.

Active constructive responding is critical for healthy relationships. In the 2006 study, Gable and her colleagues followed up with the couples two months later to see if they were still together. The psychologists found that the only difference between the couples who were together and those who broke up was active constructive responding. Those who showed genuine interest in their partner's joys were more likely to be together. In an earlier study, Gable found that active constructive responding was also associated with higher relationship quality and more intimacy between partners.

There are many reasons why relationships fail, but if you look at what drives the deterioration of many relationships, it's often a breakdown of kindness. As the normal stresses of a life together pile up—with children, career, friend, in-laws, and other distractions crowding out the time for romance and intimacy—couples may put less effort into their relationship and let the petty grievances they hold against one another tear them apart. In most marriages, levels of satisfaction drop dramatically within the first few years together. But among couples who not only endure, but live happily together for years and years, the spirit of kindness and generosity guides them forward.

Critical Thinking

1. In Gottman's research on marriage he identified two groups, the masters and the disasters. Briefly describe the characteristics of each group and how they look in interaction with their partners.
2. Which characteristics did Gottman identify that predicted whether couples would divorce or not? Why do you think these characteristics or practices are important to maintaining a satisfying marriage?
3. The research cited in the article discusses the value of practicing kindness in relationships. What does it mean to be kind? What does kindness look like in interactions between partnerrs?

Internet References

Love is Respect
www.loveisrespect.org

National Healthy Marriage Resource Center
www.healtymarriageinfo.org

The Gottman Institute
www.gottman.com

Article

Prepared by: Patricia Hrusa Williams, *University of Maine at Farmington*

The Divorce Lawyer's Guide to Staying Married Forever

JANET CLEGG AND HILARY BROWNE WILKINSON

Learning Outcomes

After reading this article, you will be able to:

- Identify factors associated with relationship breakdown and divorce.
- Describe skills important to healthy relationships.

Between them, Janet Clegg and Hilary Browne Wilkinson have spent decades as leading divorce lawyers refereeing the end of dozens of high-profile marriages worth millions of pounds.

Here, they draw on a wealth of practical and legal experience to offer expert advice on keeping your marriage alive.

As divorce lawyers, we have helped hundreds of people deal with the messy end of relationships—the deep emotional impact, the profound sense of loss, and the financial turmoil.

In many cases, divorce occurs not because of some great rift, but because relationships drift into bad habits, get taken for granted or become boring.

In the United Kingdom, an estimated 42 percent of marriages now end in divorce, with a greater recent rise in marital breakdown among those aged 50–64 than in younger age groups.

In 2012, 13 divorces an hour were granted in England and Wales. But there is nothing inevitable about so many marriages ending this way.

In many cases, divorce occurs not because of some great rift, but because relationships drift into bad habits, get taken for granted or become boring.

We could—and should—try harder to save them. The best divorce lawyers understand not only what can go wrong in a marriage but also how solid, happy relationships are able to last the distance.

You can't help but see the pitfalls and that means you can see how to avoid them, too.

Why Saying Sorry Is So Important

At our practice, we would marvel at how forgiving people could be. It was rare that one act of infidelity or cruelty would trigger a divorce, and it seemed to us that most people in love tended to overlook or forgive bad behavior more than they might in friendships or relationships at work.

But most people didn't forget, either, and when the relationship came to an end, it was amazing how many clients could recall so much detail of the hurt they had endured over many years.

In our experience, three little words—"I am sorry"—can clear away a great deal of resentment and hurt.

Be considerate. It may sound trite, but a simple "thank you" and a hug for doing the shopping, listening to work problems, or just bringing a cup of tea in bed, really does oil the creaking wheels of a long-term relationship.

TIP: No matter how deep our feelings are for each other, it's inevitable that we'll hurt our partners at some stage, whether deliberately or through thoughtlessness. Saying sorry can prevent that hurt from becoming corrosive resentment.

Keep an Eye Out for Danger Signs

Time and again, we saw the following seemingly mundane problems cause a high degree of tension in marriages:

Terrible Timekeeping

Whether chronic bad timekeeping is a lack of self-discipline, a conscious effort to control a person, or a symptom of just trying to fit too many things into the day, the effect on the punctual partner can be explosive.

At the start, we may be inclined to excuse it as endearingly ditzy, but as a relationship progresses and trains and planes are missed, the beginnings of films and plays are never seen and friends smile grimly as they wait to order food, bad timekeeping can be seen as highly disrespectful and very expensive.

Be in no doubt that infidelity will change the nature of most relationships—and is quite likely to cause its complete breakdown

TIP: Lateness needn't be a deal-breaker, but don't passively give in to it, either. Find practical ways to reduce the irritation. For example, leaving tickets at the box office or traveling separately to the airport or restaurant can relieve stress for the punctual partner.

Tiffs over Tidiness

We were amazed at how frequently this came up. To the tidy half of the marriage, dirty pots and pans around the kitchen or clothes strewn around the bedroom were, too often, a visible symbol of contempt and laziness.

Be considerate. It may sound trite, but a simple "thank you" and a hug for doing the shopping, listening to work problems or just bringing a cup of tea in bed, really does oil the creaking wheels of a long-term relationship.

On the other hand, the tidy partner's need to keep chaos at bay at all times could stretch the other's nerves to breaking point.

If you're not careful, this argument can become a permanent battleground, with the untidy partner becoming "the naughty child" and the tidy half the "nagging parent."

TIP: We heard of one couple who drew an invisible line down the middle of the bedroom—one half was perfectly ordered while, in the other, chaos reigned.

Both agreed not to comment on the other's side nor encroach on it. Extreme, perhaps, but co-operation is key.

Solo, not shared, hobbies

A shared love of travel, Civil War reconstructions, paintballing, and so on can strengthen and add joy to any relationship.

But what if the hobby is not shared and takes hours of a partner's spare time away from us and/or costs a lot of money?

What if they're spending all night playing video games while spending hundreds of pounds on their virtual pastime?

TIP: A willingness to tolerate each other's traits will help. But be grown-up about it. Don't expect a partner to give up a hobby, but do expect them to cut back if it's getting out of hand.

Learn to Deal with Conflict

In our practice, perhaps counterintuitively, it seemed to us that some anger and disagreement between couples was necessary in order to keep a relationship energized and moving forward.

By contrast, indifference between partners usually heralded the end of a marriage.

If we saw a client shrug their shoulders, sigh and say: "What can I do? There's no point in arguing," it was a sign someone had checked out of the relationship and had neither the will nor desire to maintain it.

Crucially, however, we also saw that it was how couples dealt with conflict, rather than what they argued about, that determined whether the relationship would necessarily end in divorce.

Dysfunctional conflict takes many forms, from screaming and smashing things to refusing to engage, emotional blackmail to childish sulking.

If you can argue without falling prey to any of these bad habits, then you stand a much better chance of working through problems.

TIP: Conflict isn't always a bad thing. But think about your style of resolving disagreements. Remember, openly humiliating a partner can be as painful and damaging as a physical blow.

Make Your Sex Life a Priority

A lack of sex might seem to signal the end of a marriage, but in our experience, it rarely did.

Only diminishing intimacy combined with other factors might eventually spell the end of a relationship.

We found on many occasions that conflict relating to money, lifestyle, or children far outweighed sexual problems.

But what's going on outside the bedroom has a huge effect on what's going on inside it.

If you aren't kind to your partner and you don't respect them, it's more than likely your sex life will suffer or even be nonexistent.

TIP: There is nothing like contempt or resentment to kill desire.

Don't Assume That Love Conquers All

Figures for people admitting to extramarital sex vary wildly, with some surveys claiming up to 70 percent of married men and half of married women have had an affair. Infidelity was certainly a common cause of divorce in our practice.

The betrayed spouse is very often at a loss to explain why his or her partner has been unfaithful, and it's by no means always the case that affairs are all about sex.

In fact, we think the reason why people have affairs is, in the main, irrelevant. It's how each individual in the couple views infidelity that will determine whether the relationship will collapse.

Some of us may forgive our partner's infidelity time and again. Others may call an end to the relationship after one incident.

None of us really knows what we might do until we're faced with the situation, but one thing is for sure: on learning that our partner has been unfaithful, most of us will question every aspect of our life; and trust will be hard to regain.

TIP: Be in no doubt that infidelity will change the nature of most relationships—and is quite likely to cause its complete breakdown.

Always Ask to See a New Partner's Bank Statements

Times are changing—and now 31 percent of British women are the main financial provider in their family.

Times are changing—and now 31 per cent of British women are the main financial provider in their family.

Women are increasingly building up and bringing into marriages substantial personal assets, while more men are taking time out of careers to take on child-caring roles.

Anecdotally, some of the most bitter relationship breakdowns nowadays are between high-earning career women and househusbands. Women are also having to consider practical financial arrangements if they decide to remarry after divorce.

If we've already had to deal with difficult money wrangles with our ex-partner, do we really want to automatically share money or property we have in our sole name with our new partner?

There is no room for dewy-eyed naivety in this situation. If we are the one bringing more money into a second marriage, we need to address it early on.

TIP: It sounds hardheaded, but there is nothing wrong with asking your new partner to show you bank statements, credit card bills, and relevant financial information.

If you suspect they have a dodgy financial history, it's possible to search for records of county court judgments.

If you're serious about taking the plunge into that second marriage, seek legal advice about a prenuptial agreement—particularly if you have children.

Adapted by Alison Roberts from Happily Ever After . . . ? An Essential Guide to Successful Relationships by Janet Clegg and Hilary Browne Wilkinson, Splendid Publications, £7.99.

Critical Thinking

1. The lawyers identify five different factors which in their experience, have been found to underlie most divorces. Do you agree with the factors they identified? Which ones? Why?
2. They state that "divorce occurs not because of some great rift." In divorces of family members and friends, what do you think led to the breakdown in the relationship? Is there any way the relationship could be saved?
3. If you were asked to identify three relationship/communication skills those considering marriage should work on, what would they be? Why these three skills?

Internet References

Divorce Magazine
http://www.divorcemag.com/

Love Is Respect
http://www.loveisrespect.org/

National Healthy Marriage Resource Center
http://www.healthymarriageinfo.org

National Resource Center for Healthy Marriage and Families
https://www.healthymarriageandfamilies.org/

Article

Prepared by: Patricia Hrusa Williams, *University of Maine at Farmington*

The Gay Guide to Wedded Bliss

Research finds that same-sex unions are happier than heterosexual marriages. What can gay and lesbian couples teach straight ones about living in harmony?

LIZA MUNDY

Learning Outcomes

After reading this article, you will be able to:

- Define the Defense of Marriage Act.
- Explain trends in marriage in the United States.
- Identify and discuss the role which gender plays in couple's relationships and marital unions.

It is more than a little ironic that gay marriage has emerged as the era's defining civil-rights struggle even as marriage itself seems more endangered every day. Americans are waiting longer to marry: according to the U.S. Census Bureau, the median age of first marriage is 28 for men and 26 for women, up from 23 and 20, respectively, in 1950. Rates of cohabitation have risen swiftly and sharply, and more people than ever are living single. Most Americans still marry at some point, but many of those marriages end in divorce. (Although the U.S. divorce rate has declined from its all-time high in the late '70s and early '80s, it has remained higher than those of most European countries.) All told, this has created an unstable system of what the UCLA sociologist Suzanne Bianchi calls "partnering and repartnering," a relentless emotional and domestic churn that sometimes results in people forgoing the institution altogether.

[. . .]

College graduates enjoy relatively stable unions, but for every other group, marriage is collapsing. Among "middle American" women (those with a high-school degree or some college), an astonishing 58 percent of first-time mothers are unmarried. The old Groucho Marx joke—"I don't care to belong to any club that will have me as a member"—applies a little differently in this context: you might well ask why gays and lesbians want to join an institution that keeps dithering about whether to admit them even as the repo men are coming for the furniture and the fire marshal is about to close down the clubhouse.

Against this backdrop, gay-marriage opponents have argued that allowing same-sex couples to wed will pretty much finish matrimony off. This point was advanced in briefs and oral arguments before the Supreme Court in March, in two major same-sex-marriage cases. One of these is a constitutional challenge to a key section of the Defense of Marriage Act, the 1996 law that defines marriage as a union between a man and a woman, and bars the federal government from recognizing same-sex marriages. The other involves California's Proposition 8, a same-sex-marriage ban passed by voters in 2008 but overturned by a federal judge in 2010. Appearing before the high court in March, Charles J. Cooper, the lawyer defending the California ban, predicted that same-sex marriage would undermine traditional marriage by eroding "marital norms."

The belief that gay marriage will harm marriage has roots in both religious beliefs about matrimony and secular conservative concerns about broader shifts in American life. One prominent line of thinking holds that men and women have distinct roles to play in family life; that children need both a mother and a father, preferably biologically related to them; and that a central purpose of marriage is abetting heterosexual procreation. During the Supreme Court arguments over Proposition 8, Justice Elena Kagan asked Cooper whether the essence of his argument against gay marriage was that opposite-sex couples can procreate while same-sex ones cannot. "That's the essential thrust of our position, yes," replied Cooper. He also warned that "redefining marriage as a genderless institution could well lead over time to harms to that institution."

Threaded through this thinking is a related conviction that mothers and fathers should treat their union as "permanent and exclusive," as the Princeton professor Robert P. George and his co-authors write in the new book *What Is Marriage? Man and Woman: A Defense*. Marriage, seen this way, is a rigid institution that exists primarily for the rearing of children and that powerfully constrains the behavior of adults (one is tempted to call this the "long slog 'til death" view of marriage), rather than an emotional union entered into for pleasure and companionship between adults. These critics of gay marriage are, quite validly, worried that too many American children are being raised in unstable homes, either by struggling single parents or by a transient succession of live-in adults. They fear that the spread of gay marriage could help finally sever the increasingly tenuous link between children and marriage, confirming that it's okay for dads, or moms, to be deleted from family life as hedonic fulfillment dictates.

In mounting their defense, advocates of same-sex marriage have argued that gays and lesbians who wish to marry are committed to family well-being; that concern for children's welfare is a chief reason many do want to marry; that gay people are being discriminated against, as a class, in being denied rights readily available to any heterosexual. And to the charge that same-sex marriage will change marriage, they tend to argue that it will not—that married gays and lesbians will blend seamlessly with the millions of married straight Americans. "The notion that this group can somehow fundamentally change the institution of marriage—I find it difficult to wrap my head around," says Gary Gates, a demographer with the Williams Institute, a research center affiliated with the UCLA School of Law.

But what if the critics are correct, just not in the way they suppose? What if same-sex marriage does change marriage, but primarily for the better? For one thing, there is reason to think that, rather than making marriage more fragile, the boom of publicity around same-sex weddings could awaken among heterosexuals a new interest in the institution, at least for a time. But the larger change might be this: by providing a new model of how two people can live together equitably, same-sex marriage could help haul matrimony more fully into the 21st century. Although marriage is in many ways fairer and more pleasurable for both men and women than it once was, it hasn't entirely thrown off old notions and habits. As a result, many men and women enter into it burdened with assumptions and stereotypes that create stress and resentment. Others, confronted with these increasingly anachronistic expectations—expectations at odds with the economic and practical realities of their own lives—don't enter into it at all.

Same-sex spouses, who cannot divide their labor based on preexisting gender norms, must approach marriage differently than their heterosexual peers. From sex to fighting, from child-rearing to chores, they must hammer out every last detail of domestic life without falling back on assumptions about who will do what. In this regard, they provide an example that can be enlightening to all couples. Critics warn of an institution rendered "genderless." But if a genderless marriage is a marriage in which the wife is not automatically expected to be responsible for school forms and child care and dinner preparation and birthday parties and midnight feedings and holiday shopping, I think it's fair to say that many heterosexual women would cry "Bring it on!"

Beyond that, gay marriage can function as a controlled experiment, helping us see which aspects of marital difficulty are truly rooted in gender and which are not. A growing body of social science has begun to compare straight and same-sex couples in an attempt to get at the question of what is female, what is male. Some of the findings are surprising. For instance: we know that heterosexual wives are more likely than husbands to initiate divorce. Social scientists have struggled to explain the discrepancy, variously attributing it to the sexual revolution; to women's financial independence; to men's failure to keep modern wives happy. Intriguingly, in Norway and Sweden, where registered partnerships for same-sex couples have been in place for about two decades (full-fledged marriage was introduced several years ago), research has found that lesbians are twice as likely as gay men to split up. If women become dissatisfied even when married to other women, maybe the problem with marriage isn't men. Maybe women are too particular. Maybe even women don't know what women want. These are the kinds of things that we will be able to tease out.

[. . .]

Whatever happens with the high court, it seems likely that gay marriage will continue its spread through the land. So what happens, then, to the institution of marriage? The impact is likely to be felt near and far, both fleetingly and more permanently, in ways confounding to partisans on both sides.

Rules for a More Perfect Union

Not all is broken within modern marriage, of course. On the contrary: the institution is far more flexible and forgiving than it used to be. In the wake of women's large-scale entry into the workplace, men are less likely than they once were to be saddled with being a family's sole breadwinner, and can carve out a life that includes the close companionship of their children. Meanwhile, women are less likely to be saddled with the sole responsibility for child care and housework, and can envision a life beyond the stove top and laundry basket.

And yet for many couples, as Bianchi, the UCLA sociologist, has pointed out, the modern ideal of egalitarianism has proved "quite difficult to realize." Though men are carrying more of a domestic workload than in the past, women still bear the brunt of the second shift. Among couples with children, when both spouses work full-time, women do 32 hours a week of housework, child care, shopping, and other family-related services, compared with the 21 hours men put in. Men do more paid work—45 hours, compared with 39 for women—but still have more free time: 31 hours, compared with 25 for women. Betsey Stevenson and Justin Wolfers, economists and professors of public policy at the University of Michigan, have shown that happiness rates among women have dropped even as women have acquired more life options. One possible cause is the lingering inequity in male-female marriage: women's at-home workload can become so burdensome that wives opt out of the paid workforce—or sit at the office making mental lists of the chores they do versus the chores their husbands do, and bang their heads on their desks in despair.

Not that everything is easy for fathers in dual-earner couples, who now feel afflicted by work-life conflict in even greater numbers than their wives (60 percent of men in such couples say they experience this conflict, versus 47 percent of women, according to a 2008 study by the Families and Work Institute). And men face a set of unfair expectations all their own: the Pew Research Center found in 2010 that 67 percent of Americans still believe it's "very important" that a man be ready to support a family before getting married, while only 33 percent believe the same about women.

This burden, exacerbated by the economic realities facing many men today, has undoubtedly contributed to marriage's recent decline. As our economy has transitioned away from manufacturing and industry, men with a high-school education can no longer expect the steady, well-paying union jobs that formerly enabled many to support their families. Outdated assumptions that men should bring something to the table, and that this something should be money, don't help. Surveying their prospects, many working-class mothers reject marriage altogether, perhaps reasoning that they can support a child, but don't want a dependent husband.

It's not that people don't want to marry. Most never-married Americans say they still aspire to marriage, but many of them see it as something grand and out of reach. Getting married is no longer something you do when you are young and foolish and starting out; prosperity is not something spouses build together. Rather, marriage has become a "marker of prestige," as the sociologist Andrew Cherlin puts it—a capstone of a successful life, rather than its cornerstone. But while many couples have concluded that they are not ready for marriage, they have things backwards. It's not that they aren't ready for marriage; it's that marriage isn't ready for the realities of 21st-century life. Particularly for less affluent, less educated Americans, changing economic and gender realities have dismantled the old institution, without constructing any sort of replacement.

As we attempt to come up with a more functional model, research on same-sex unions can provide what Gary Gates of the Williams Institute calls an "important counterfactual." Although gays and lesbians cannot solve all that ails marriage, they seem to be working certain things out in ways straight couples might do well to emulate, chief among them a back-to-the-drawing-board approach to divvying up marital duties. A growing body of scholarship on household division of labor shows that in many ways, same-sex couples do it better.

This scholarship got its start in the late 1960s, with a brilliant insight by the sociologist Pepper Schwartz. [. . .] Like many of her peers, she was keen to figure out what women were and what men were: which traits were biological and which social, and where there might be potential for transformational change. "It occurred to me," she says, that "a naturally occurring experiment" could shed light on these issues. Actually, two experiments: the rise of unmarried heterosexual cohabitation, and the growing visibility of gay and lesbian couples. If she surveyed people in three kinds of relationships—married; straight and cohabiting; and gay and cohabiting—and all showed similarity on some measures, maybe this would say something about both men and women. If the findings didn't line up, maybe this would say something about marriage.

After taking a teaching position at the University of Washington (where she remains a faculty member), Schwartz teamed up with a gay colleague, the late Philip Blumstein, to conduct just such a survey, zeroing in on the greater San Francisco, New York City, and Seattle metropolitan areas. It was a huge effort. Unmarried cohabiting couples were not yet easy to find, and gays and lesbians were so leery of being outed that when Schwartz asked a woman who belonged to a lesbian bridge group whether she could interview the other players about their relationships, the woman said, "We don't even talk about it ourselves." Schwartz and Blumstein collected responses to 12,000 questionnaires and conducted hundreds of interviews; at one point, they had 20 graduate students helping tabulate data. The project took about a decade, and resulted in a groundbreaking piece of sociology, the book *American Couples: Money, Work, Sex.*

What Schwartz and Blumstein found is that gay and lesbian couples were fairer in their dealings with one another than straight couples, both in intent and in practice. The lesbians in the study were almost painfully egalitarian—in some cases putting money in jars and splitting everything down to the penny in a way, Schwartz says, that "would have driven me crazy." Many unmarried heterosexual cohabitators were also careful about divvying things up, but lesbian couples seemed to take the practice to extremes: "It was almost like 'my kitty, your litter.'" Gay men, like lesbians, were more likely than straight couples to share cooking and chores. Many had been in heterosexual marriages, and when asked whether they had helped their wives with the housework in those prior unions, they usually said they had not. "You can imagine," Schwartz says, "how irritating I found this."

There were still some inequities: in all couples, the person with the higher income had more authority and decision-making power. This was least true for lesbians; truer for heterosexuals; and most true for gay men. Somehow, putting two men together seemed to intensify the sense that "money talks," as Schwartz and Blumstein put it. They could not hope to determine whether this tendency was innate or social—were men naturally inclined to equate resources with power, or had our culture ingrained that idea in them?—but one way or another, the finding suggested that money was a way men competed with other men, and not just a way for husbands to compete with their wives. Among lesbians, the contested terrain lay elsewhere: for instance, interacting more with the children could be, Schwartz says, a "power move."

Lesbians also tended to discuss things endlessly, achieving a degree of closeness unmatched by the other types of couples. Schwartz wondered whether this might account for another finding: over time, sex in lesbian relationships dwindled—a state of affairs she has described as "lesbian bed death." [. . .] She posits that lesbians may have had so much intimacy already that they didn't need sex to get it; by contrast, heterosexual women, whose spouses were less likely to be chatty, found that "sex is a highway to intimacy." As for men, she eventually concluded that whether they were straight or gay, they approached sex as they might a sandwich: good, bad, or mediocre, they were likely to grab it.

RULE 1: Negotiate in advance who will empty the trash and who will clean the bathroom. Other studies have since confirmed Schwartz and Blumstein's findings that same-sex couples are more egalitarian. In 2000, when Vermont became the first state to legalize same-sex civil unions, the psychologist Esther Rothblum saw an opportunity to explore how duties get sorted among a broad swath of the same-sex population. Rothblum, now at San Diego State University, is herself a lesbian and had long been interested in the relationships and mental health of lesbians. She also wanted to see how legal recognition affected couples.

As people from around the country flocked to Vermont to apply for civil-union licenses, Rothblum and two colleagues got their names and addresses from public records and asked them to complete a questionnaire. Then, they asked each of the civil-union couples to suggest friends in same-sex couples who were not in civil unions, and to identify a heterosexual sibling who was married, and wrote those people asking them to participate. This approach helped control for factors like background and upbringing among the subjects. The researchers asked people to rate, on a scale of one to nine, which partner was more likely to do the dishes, repair things around the house, buy groceries. They asked who was more likely to deal with the landlord, punish the children, call the plumber, drive the kids to appointments, give spontaneous hugs, pay compliments. They also asked who was more likely to appreciate the other person's point of view during an argument.

They found that, even in the new millennium, married heterosexual couples were very likely to divide duties along old-fashioned gender lines. Straight women were more likely than lesbians to report that their partner paid the mortgage or the rent and the utility bills, and bought groceries, household appliances, even the women's clothing. These wives were also more likely to say they did the bulk of the cooking, vacuuming, dishes, and laundry. Compared with their husbands, they were far, far more likely to clean the bathroom. They were also more likely than their husbands to perform "relationship maintenance" such as showing affection and initiating serious conversations. When Rothblum and her colleagues held the heterosexual husbands up against the gay men, they found the same pattern. The straight guys were more likely to take care of the lawn, empty the trash, and make household repairs than their partners. They were the ones to fix drinks for company and to drive when the couple went out. They cooked breakfast reasonably often, but not dinner. On all these measures and more, the same-sex couples were far more likely to divide responsibilities evenly. This is not to say that the same-sex couples split each duty half-and-half. One partner might do the same chore regularly, but because there was no default assignment based on gender, such patterns evolved organically, based on preferences and talents.

Rothblum's observations are borne out by the couples I interviewed for this piece. "I'm a better cook, so I take on most of that responsibility," said Seth Thayer, who lives in a small coastal town in Maine. His husband, Greg Tinder, "is a better handyman." Others spoke of the perils of lopsided relationships. Chris Kast, a Maine newlywed, told me that he and his husband, Byron Bartlett, had both been married to women. In Bartlett's first marriage, it was tacitly assumed that he would take out the garbage. Now the two men divide tasks by inclination. "I'm more of a Felix Ungar—I notice when something's dirty—but we both clean," Kast said. "With Chris and I," Bartlett added, "we have to get *everything* done." Isabelle Dikland, a Washington, D.C., business consultant who is married to Amy Clement, a teacher, told me about a dinner party she recently attended with a group of mostly straight parents. Dikland and Clement, who had just had a second daughter, were extolling the virtues of having two children. The straight mother they were talking with seemed dubious, "if we had a second kid, guess who would do all the work," she told them. "I'd have to give up my career; I'm already doing everything." The woman glanced surreptitiously at her husband, at which point Dikland "dropped the subject really quickly."

RULE 2: When it comes to parenting, a 50-50 split isn't necessarily best. Charlotte J. Patterson, a psychologist at the University of Virginia, has arresting visual evidence of the same egalitarianism at work in parenting: compared with husband-and-wife pairs, she has found, same-sex parents tend to be more cooperative and mutually hands-on. Patterson and a colleague, Rachel Farr, have conducted a study of more than 100 same-sex and heterosexual adoptive parents in 11 states and the District of Columbia; it is among the first such studies to include gay fathers. As reported in an article in a forthcoming issue of the journal *Child Development*, the researchers visited families in their homes, scattered some toys on a blanket, invited the subjects to play with them any way they chose, and videotaped the interactions. "What you see is what they did with that blank slate," Patterson says. "One thing that I found riveting: the same-sex couples are far more likely to be in there together, and the opposite-sex couples show the conventional pattern—the mom more involved, the dad playing with Tinkertoys by himself." When the opposite-sex couples did parent simultaneously, they were more likely to undermine each other by talking at cross-purposes or suggesting different toys. The lesbian mothers tended to be egalitarian and warm in their dealings with one another, and showed greater pleasure in parenting than the other groups did. Same-sex dads were also more egalitarian in their division of labor than straight couples, though not as warm or interactive as lesbian moms. (Patterson says she and her colleagues may need to refine their analysis to take into account male ways of expressing warmth.)

By and large, all of the families studied, gay and straight alike, were happy, high functioning, and financially secure. Each type of partner—gay, straight; man, woman—reported satisfaction with his or her family's parenting arrangement, though the heterosexual wife was less content than the others, invariably saying that she wanted more help from her husband. "Of all the parents we've studied, she's the least satisfied with the division of labor," says Patterson, who is in a same-sex partnership and says she knows from experience that deciding who will do what isn't always easy.

Even as they are more egalitarian in their parenting styles, same-sex parents resemble their heterosexual counterparts in one somewhat old-fashioned way: a surprising number establish a division of labor whereby one spouse becomes the primary earner and the other stays home. Lee Badgett, an economist at the University of Massachusetts at Amherst, told me that, "in terms of economics," same-sex couples with children resemble heterosexual couples with children much more than they resemble childless same-sex couples. You might say that gay parents are simultaneously departing from traditional family structures and leading the way back toward them.

In his seminal book *A Treatise on the Family*, published in 1981, the Nobel Prize–winning economist Gary Becker argued that "specialization," whereby one parent stays home and the other does the earning, is the most efficient way of running a household, because the at-home spouse enables the at-work spouse to earn more. Feminists, who had been fighting for domestic parity, not specialization, deplored this theory, rightly fearing that it could be harnessed to keep women at home. Now the example of gay and lesbian parents might give us all permission to relax a little: maybe sometimes it really is easier when one parent works and the other is the supplementary or nonearning partner, either because this is the natural order of things or because the American workplace is so greedy and unforgiving that something or somebody has to give. As Martha Ertman, a University of Maryland law professor, put it to me, many families just function better when the same person is consistently "in charge of making vaccinations happen, making sure the model of the World War II monument gets done, getting the Christmas tree home or the challah bought by 6 o'clock on Friday." The good news is that the decision about which parent plays this role need not have anything to do with gender.

More surprising still, guess who is most likely to specialize. Gay dads. Using the most recent Census Bureau data, Gary Gates found that 32 percent of married heterosexual couples with children have only one parent in the labor force, compared with 33 percent of gay-male couples with children. (Lesbians also specialize, but not at such high rates, perhaps because they are so devoted to equality, or perhaps because their earnings are lower—women's median wage is 81 percent that of men—and not working is an unaffordable luxury.) While the percentage point dividing gay men from straight couples is not statistically significant, it's intriguing that gay dads are as likely as straight women to be stay-at-home parents.

Gay men's decisions about breadwinning can nonetheless be fraught, as many associate employment with power. A study published in the *Journal of GLBT Family Studies* in 2005 by Stephanie Jill Schacher and two colleagues found that when gay men do specialize, they don't have an easy time deciding who will do what: some stay-at-home dads perceived that their choice carried with it a loss in prestige and stature. As a result, gay men tended to fight not over who got to stay home, but over who didn't have to. "It's probably the biggest problem in our relationship," said one man interviewed for that study. Perhaps what Betty Friedan called "the problem that has no name" is inherent in child-rearing, and will always be with us.

RULE 3: Don't want a divorce? Don't marry a woman. Three years after they first gathered information from the couples who received licenses in Vermont, Esther Rothblum and her colleagues checked back to evaluate the condition of their relationships. Overall, the researchers found that the quality of gay and lesbian relationships was higher on many measures than that of the straight control group (the married heterosexual siblings), with more compatibility and intimacy, and less conflict.

Which is not to say same-sex couples don't have conflict. When they fight, however, they fight fairer. They can even fight funny, as researchers from the University of Washington and the University of California at Berkeley showed in an article published in 2003, based on a study of couples who were navigating potentially tense interactions. Recruiting married straight couples as well as gays and lesbians in committed relationships, the researchers orchestrated a scenario in which one partner had to bring up an area of conflict to discuss with the other. In same-sex couples, the partner with the bone to pick was rated "less belligerent and less domineering" than the straight-couple counterpart, while the person on the receiving end was less aggressive and showed less fear or tension. The same-sex "initiator" also displayed less sadness and "whining," and more affection, joy, and humor. In trying to make sense of the disparity, the researchers noted that same-sex couples valued equality more, and posited that the greater negativity of straight couples "may have to do with the standard status hierarchy between men and women." Which perhaps boils down to something like this: straight women see themselves as being less powerful than men, and this breeds hostility.

When it comes to conflict, a crucial variable separates many gay and lesbian couples from their straight counterparts: children. As Rothblum points out, for married heterosexual parents, happiness tends to be U-shaped: high at the beginning of marriage, then dipping to a low, then high again. What happens in that low middle is child-rearing. Although the proportion of gay and lesbian couples with children is increasing, same-sex couples are still less likely than straight couples to be parents. Not all research comparing same-sex and married straight couples has done an adequate job of controlling for this important difference. One that did, a 2008 study in the *Journal of Family Psychology*, looked at couples during their first 10 years of cohabitation. It found that childless lesbians had a higher "relationship quality" than their child-free gay-male and heterosexual counterparts. And yet a 2010 study in the same journal found that gay-male, lesbian, and straight couples alike experienced a "modest decline in relationship quality" in the first year of adopting a child. As same-sex couples become parents in greater numbers, they could well endure some of the same strife as their straight peers. It remains to be seen whether the different parenting styles identified by Charlotte Patterson might blunt some of the ennui of child-rearing.

As for divorce, the data are still coming in. A 2006 study of Sweden and Norway found higher dissolution rates among same-sex couples in registered partnerships than among married straight people. Yet in the United States, a study by the Williams Institute has found that gay unions have lower dissolution rates than straight ones. It is simply too soon to tell with any certainty whether gay marriages will be more or less durable in the long run than straight ones. What the studies to date do (for the most part) suggest is this: despite—or maybe because of—their perfectionist approach to egalitarianism, lesbian couples seem to be more likely to break up than gay ones. Pepper Schwartz noted this in the early 1980s, as did the 2006 study of same-sex couples in Sweden and Norway, in which researchers speculated that women may have a "stronger general sensitivity to the quality of relationships." Meaning maybe women are just picky, and when you have two women, you have double the pickiness. So perhaps the real threat to marriage is: women.

The Contagion Effect

Whatever this string of studies may teach us about marriage and gender dynamics, the next logical question becomes this: Might such marriages do more than merely inform our understanding of straight marriage—might their attributes trickle over to straight marriage in some fashion?

In the course of my reporting this year in states that had newly legalized same-sex marriage, people in the know—wedding planners, officiants, fiancés and fiancées—told me time and again that nuptial fever had broken out around them, among gay and straight couples alike. Same-sex weddings seemed to be bestowing a new frisson on the idea of getting hitched, or maybe restoring an old one. At the Gay and Lesbian Wedding Expo in downtown Baltimore, just a few weeks after same-sex marriage became legal in Maryland, Drew Vanlandingham, who describes himself as a "wedding planner designer," was delighted at how business had picked up. Here it was, January, and many of his favorite venues were booked into late summer—much to the consternation, he said, of his straight brides. "They're like, 'I better get a move on!'" It was his view that in Maryland, both teams were now engaged in an amiable but spirited race to the altar.

Ministers told me of wedding booms in their congregations. In her years as the pastor of the Unitarian church in Rockville, Maryland, Lynn Strauss said she had grown accustomed to a thin wedding roster: some years she might perform one or two services; other years, none. But this year, "my calendar is full of weddings," she said. "Two in March, one in April, one in May, one in September, one in October—oh, and one in July." Three were same-sex weddings, but the rest were heterosexual. When I attended the church's first lesbian wedding, in early March, I spoke with Steve Greene and Ellen Rohan, who had recently been married by Strauss. It was Steve's third marriage, Ellen's second. Before he met Ellen, Steve had sworn he would never marry again. Ellen said the arrival of same-sex marriage had influenced their feelings. "Marriage," she said simply, "is on everyone's mind."

Robert M. Hardies, who is a pastor at the Unitarian All Souls Church in Washington, D.C., and who is engaged to be married to his longtime partner and co-parent, Chris Nealon, told me that he has seen "a re-enchantment of marriage" among those who attend same-sex ceremonies: "Straight folks come to [same-sex] weddings, and I watch it on their face—there's a feeling that this is really special. Suddenly marriage is sexy again." We could chalk these anecdotes up to the human desire to witness love that overcomes obstacles—the same desire behind all romantic comedies, whether Shakespeare's or Hollywood's. But could something a bit less romantic also be at work?

There is some reason to suppose that attitudes about marriage could, in fact, be catching. The phenomenon known as "social contagion" lies at the heart of an increasingly prominent line of research on how our behavior and emotions affect the people we know. One famous example dates from 2008, when James H. Fowler and Nicholas A. Christakis published a study showing that happiness "spreads" through social networks. They arrived at this conclusion via an ingenious crunching of data from a long-running medical study involving thousands of interconnected residents—and their children, and later their grandchildren—in Framingham, Massachusetts. "Emotional states can be transferred directly from one individual to another," they found, across three degrees of separation. Other studies have shown that obesity, smoking habits, and school performance may also be catching.

Most relevant, in a working paper that is under submission to a sociology journal, the Brown University political scientist Rose McDermott, along with her co-authors, Fowler and Christakis, has identified a contagion effect for divorce. Divorce, she found, can spread among friends. She told me that she also suspects that tending to the marriages of friends can help preserve your own. McDermott says she readily sees how marriage could itself be contagious. Intriguingly, some of the Scandinavian countries where same-sex unions have been legal for a decade or more have seen a rise, not a fall, in marriage rates. In response to conservative arguments that same-sex marriage had driven a stake through the heart of marriage in northern Europe, the Yale University law professor William N. Eskridge Jr. and Darren Spedale in 2006 published an analysis showing that in the decade since same-sex partnerships became legal, heterosexual marriage rates had increased 10.7 percent in Denmark, 12.7 percent in Norway, and 28.8 percent in Sweden. Divorce rates had dropped in all three countries. Although there was no way to prove cause and effect, the authors allowed, you could safely say that marriage had not been harmed.

So let's suppose for a moment that marital behavior is catching. How, exactly, might it spread? I found one possible vector of contagion inside the Washington National Cathedral, a neo-Gothic landmark that towers watchfully over the Washington, D.C., skyline. The seat of the bishop of an Episcopal diocese that includes D.C. and parts of Maryland, the cathedral is a symbol of American religious life, and strives to provide a spiritual home for the nation, frequently hosting interfaith events and programs. Presiding over it is the Very Reverend Gary Hall, an Episcopal priest and the cathedral's dean. Earlier this year, Hall announced that the cathedral would conduct same-sex weddings, a declaration that attracted more attention than he expected. Only people closely involved with the church and graduates of the private schools on its grounds can marry there. Even so, it is an influential venue, and Hall used the occasion to argue that same-sex couples offer an image of "radical" equality that straight couples can profitably emulate. He believes, moreover, that their example can be communicated through intermediaries like him: ministers and counselors gleaning insights from same-sex couples, and transmitting them, as it were, to straight ones. Hall says that counseling same-sex couples in preparation for their ceremonies has already altered the way he counsels men and women.

"I have a list of like 12 issues that people need to talk about that cause conflict," said Hall, who is lanky, with short gray hair and horn-rims, and who looks like he could be a dean of pretty much anything: American literature, political philosophy, East Asian studies. As we talked in his office one morning this spring, sunlight poured through a bank of arched windows onto an Oriental rug. Over the years, he has amassed a collection of cheesy 1970s paperbacks with names like *Open Marriage* and *Total Woman*, which he calls "books that got people into trouble." The dean grew up in Hollywood, and in the 1990s was a priest at a church in Pasadena where he did many same-sex blessings (a blessing being a ceremony that stops short of legal marriage). He is as comfortable talking about Camille Paglia and the LGBT critique of marriage as he is about Holy Week. He is also capable of saying things like "The problem with genital sex is that it involves us emotionally in a way that we're not in control of."

When Hall sees couples for premarital preparation, he gives them a list of hypothetical conflicts to take home, hash out, and report back on. Everybody fights, he tells them. The people who thrive in marriage are the ones who can handle disagreement and make their needs known. So he presents them with the prime sticking points: affection and lovemaking; how to deal with in-laws; where holidays will be spent; outside friendships. He talks to them about parenting roles, and chores, and money—who will earn it and who will make decisions about it.

Like Esther Rothblum, he has found that heterosexual couples persist in approaching these topics with stereotypical assumptions. "You start throwing out questions for men and women: 'Who's going to take care of the money?' And the guy says, 'That's me.' And you ask: 'Who's responsible for birth control?' And the guy says, 'That's her department.'" By contrast, he reports, same-sex couples "have thought really hard about how they're going to share the property, the responsibilities, the obligations in a mutual way. They've had to devote much more thought to that than straight couples, because the straight couples pretty much still fall back on old modes."

Now when Hall counsels heterosexuals, "I'm really pushing back on their patriarchal assumptions: that the woman's got to give up her career for the guy; that the guy is going to take care of the money." Every now and then, he says, he has a breakthrough, and a straight groom realizes that, say, contraception is his concern too. Hall says the same thing is happening in the offices of any number of pastors, rabbis, and therapists. "You're not going to be able to talk to heterosexual couples where there's a power imbalance and talk to a homosexual couple where there is a power mutuality," and not have the conversations impact one another. As a result, he believes there will be changes to marriage, changes that some people will find scary. "When [conservatives] say that gay marriage threatens my marriage, I used to say, 'That's ridiculous.' Now I say, 'Yeah, it does. It's asking you a crucial question about your marriage that you may not want to answer: If I'm a man, am I actually sharing the duties and responsibilities of married life equally with my wife?' Same-sex marriage gives us another image of what marriage can be."

Hall argues that same-sex marriage stands to change even the wedding service itself. For a good 1,000 years, he notes, the Christian Church stayed out of matrimony, which was primarily a way for society to regulate things like inheritance. But ever since the Church did get involved, the wedding ceremony has tended to reflect the gender mores of the time. For example, the Book of Common Prayer for years stated that a wife must love, honor, and obey her husband, treating him as her master and lord. That language is long gone, but vestiges persist: the tradition of the father giving away the bride dates from an era when marriage was a property transfer and the woman was the property. In response to the push for same-sex marriage, Hall says, the General Convention, the governing council of the entire Episcopal Church, has devised a liturgy for same-sex ceremonies (in most dioceses, these are blessings) that honors but alters this tradition so that both spouses are presented by sponsors.

"The new service does not ground marriage in a doctrine of creation and procreation," Hall says. "It grounds marriage in a kind of free coming-together of two people to live out their lives." A study group has convened to look at the Church's teachings on marriage, and in the next couple of years, Hall expects, the General Convention will adopt a new service for all Episcopal weddings. He is hopeful that the current same-sex service will serve as its basis.

The legalization of same-sex marriage is likely to affect even members of churches that have not performed such ceremonies. Delman Coates, the pastor of Mt. Ennon Baptist, a predominantly African American mega-church in southern Maryland, was active in his state's fight for marriage equality, presenting it to his parishioners as a civil-rights issue. The topic has also led to some productive, if difficult, conversations about "what the Scriptures are condemning and what they're confirming." In particular, he has challenged his flock over what he calls the "typical clobber passages": certain verses in Leviticus, Romans, and elsewhere that many people interpret as condemnations of homosexuality. These discussions are part of a long-standing effort to challenge people's thinking about other passages having to do with divorce and premarital sex—issues many parishioners have struggled with at home. Coates preaches that what the Bible is condemning is not modern divorce, but a practice, common in biblical times, whereby men cast out their wives for no good reason. Similarly, he tells them that the "fornication" invoked is something extreme—rape, incest, prostitution. He does not condone illicit behavior or familial dissolution, but he wants the members of his congregation to feel better about their own lives. In exchanges like these, he is making gay marriage part of a much larger conversation about the way we live and love now.

Gay marriage's ripples are also starting to be felt beyond churches, in schools and neighborhoods and playgroups. Which raises another question: Will gay and lesbian couples be peacemakers or combatants in the "mommy wars"—the long-simmering struggle between moms who stay at home and moms who work outside it? If you doubt that straight households are paying attention to same-sex ones, consider Danie, a woman who lives with her husband and two children in Bethesda, Maryland. (Danie asked me not to use her last name out of concern for her family's privacy.) Not long after she completed a master's degree in Spanish linguistics at Georgetown University, her first baby was born. Because her husband, Jesse, works long hours as a litigator, she decided to become a full-time parent—not an easy decision in work-obsessed Washington, D.C. For a while, she ran a photography business out of their home, partly because she loves photography but partly so she could assure people at dinner parties that she had paying work. Whenever people venture that women who work outside the home don't judge stay-at-home moms, Danie thinks: *Are you freaking kidding me?*

She takes some comfort, however, in the example of a lesbian couple with whom she is friendly. Both women are attorneys, and one stays home with their child. "Their life is exactly the same as ours," Danie told me, with a hint of vindication. If being a stay-at-home mother is "good enough for her, then what's my issue? She's a huge women's-rights activist." But while comparing herself with a lesbian couple is liberating in some ways, it also exacerbates the competitive anxiety that afflicts so many modern mothers. The other thing about these two mothers, Danie said, is that they are so relaxed, so happy, so present. Even the working spouse manages to be a super-involved parent, to a much greater extent than most of the working fathers she knows. "I'm a little bit obsessed with them," she says.

Related to this is the question of how gay fatherhood might impact heterosexual fatherhood—by, for example, encouraging the idea that men can be emotionally accessible, logistically capable parents. Will the growing presence of gay dads in some communities mean that men are more often included in the endless e-mail chains that go to parents of preschoolers and birthday-party invitees? As radically as fatherhood has changed in recent decades, a number of antiquated attitudes about dads have proved strangely enduring: Rob Hardies, the pastor at All Souls, reports that when his partner, Chris, successfully folded a stroller before getting on an airplane with their son, Nico, he was roundly congratulated by passersby, as if he had solved a difficult mathematical equation in public. So low are expectations for fathers, even now, that in Stephanie Schacher's study of gay fathers and their feelings about care-giving, her subjects reported that people would see them walking on the street with their children and say things like "Giving Mom a break?" Hardies thinks that every time he and Chris take their son to the playground or to story hour, they help disrupt this sort of thinking. He imagines moms seeing a man doing this and gently—or maybe not so gently—pointing it out to their husbands. "Two guys somehow manage to get their act together and have a household and cook dinner and raise a child, without a woman doing all the work," he says. Rather than setting an example that fathers don't matter, gay men are setting an example that fathers do matter, and that marriage matters, too.

The Sex Problem

When, in the 1970s and early 1980s, Pepper Schwartz asked couples about their sex lives, she arrived at perhaps her most explosive finding: non-monogamy was rampant among gay men, a whopping 82 percent of whom reported having had sex outside their relationship. Slightly more than one-third of gay-male couples felt that monogamy was important; the other two-thirds said that monogamy was unimportant or that they were neutral on the topic. In a funny way, Schwartz says, her findings suggested that same-sex unions (like straight ones) aren't necessarily about sex. Some gay men made a point of telling her they loved their partners but weren't physically attracted to them. Others said they wanted to be monogamous but were unsupported in that wish, by their partner, gay culture, or both.

Schwartz believes that a move toward greater monogamy was emerging among gay men even before the AIDS crisis. Decades later, gay-male couples are more monogamous than they used to be, but not nearly to the same degree as other kinds of couples. In her Vermont research, Esther Rothblum found that 15 percent of straight husbands said they'd had sex outside their relationship, compared with 58 percent of gay men in civil unions and 61 percent of gay men who were partnered but not in civil unions. When asked whether a couple had arrived at an explicit agreement about extra-relational sex, a minuscule 4 percent of straight husbands said they'd discussed it with their partner and determined that it was okay, compared with 40 percent of gay men in civil unions and 49 percent of gay men in partnerships that were not legally recognized. Straight women and lesbians, meanwhile, were united in their commitment to monogamy, lesbians more so than straight women: 14 percent of straight wives said they had had sex outside their marriage, compared with 9 percent of lesbians in civil unions and 7 percent of lesbians who were partnered but not in civil unions.

The question of whether gays and lesbians will change marriage, or vice versa, is at its thorniest around sex and monogamy. Private behavior could well stay private: when she studied marriage in the Netherlands, Lee Badgett, the University of Massachusetts economist, found that while many same-sex couples proselytize about the egalitarianism of their relationships, they don't tend to promote non-monogamy, even if they practice it. Then again, some gay-rights advocates, like the writer and sex columnist Dan Savage, argue very publicly that insisting on monogamy can do a couple more harm than good. Savage, who questions whether most humans are cut out for decades of sex with only one person, told me that "monogamy in marriage has been a disaster for straight couples" because it has set unrealistic expectations. "Gay-male couples are much more likely to be realistic about what men are," he said. Savage's own marriage started out monogamous; the agreement was that if either partner cheated, this would be grounds for ending the relationship. But when he and his husband decided to adopt a child, Savage suggested that they relax their zero-tolerance policy on infidelity. He felt that risking family dissolution over such an incident no longer made sense. His husband later suggested they explicitly allow each other occasional dalliances, a policy Savage sees as providing a safety valve for the relationship. If society wants marriage to be more resilient, he argues, we must make it more "monagamish."

This is, to be sure, a difficult argument to win: a husband proposing non-monogamy to his wife on the grounds that it is in the best interest of a new baby would have a tough time prevailing in the court of public opinion. But while most gay-marriage advocates stop short of championing Savage's "wiggle room," some experts say that gay men are better at talking more openly about sex. Naveen Jonathan, a family therapist and a professor at Chapman University, in California, says he sees many gay partners hammer out an elaborate who-can-do-what-when sexual contract, one that says, "These are the times and the situations where it's okay to be non-monogamous, and these are the times and the situations where it is not." While some straight couples have deals of their own, he finds that for the most part, they simply presume monogamy. A possible downside of this assumption: straight couples are far less likely than gay men to frankly and routinely discuss sex, desire, and the challenges of sexual commitment.

Other experts question the idea that most gay males share a preference for non-monogamous relationships, or will in the long term. Savage's argument that non-monogamy is a safety valve is "very interesting, but it really is no more than a claim," says Justin Garcia, an evolutionary biologist at the Kinsey Institute for Research in Sex, Gender, and Reproduction. Garcia points out that not all men are relentlessly sexual beings, and not all men want an open relationship, "in some ways, same-sex couples are healthier—they tend to have these negotiations more," he says. But negotiating can be stressful: in many cases, Garcia notes, one gay partner would prefer to be monogamous, but gives in to the other partner.

So which version will prevail: non-monogamous marriage, or marriage as we conventionally understand it? It's worth pointing out that in the U.S., same-sex unions are slightly more likely between women, and non-monogamy is not a cause women tend to champion. And some evidence suggests that getting married changes behavior: William Eskridge and Darren Spedale found that in the years after Norway, Sweden, and Denmark instituted registered partnerships, many same-sex couples reported placing a greater emphasis on monogamy, while national rates of HIV infections declined.

Sex, then, may be one area where the institution of marriage pushes back against norms that have been embraced by many gay couples. Gary Hall of the National Cathedral allows that in many ways, gay relationships offer a salutary "critique" of marriage, but argues that the marriage establishment will do some critiquing back. He says he would not marry two people who intended to be non-monogamous, and believes that monogamy will be a "critical issue" in the dialogue between the gay community and the Church. Up until now, he says, progressive churches have embraced "the part of gay behavior that looks like straight behavior," but at some point, churches also have to engage gay couples whose behavior doesn't conform to monogamous ideals. He hopes that, in the course of this give-and-take, the church ends up reckoning with other ongoing cultural changes, from unmarried cohabitation to the increasing number of adults who choose to live as singles. "How do we speak credibly to people about their sexuality and their sexual relationships?" he asks. "We really need to rethink this."

So yes, marriage will change. Or rather, it will change again. The fact is, there is no such thing as traditional marriage. In various places and at various points in human history, marriage has been a means by which young children were betrothed, uniting royal houses and sealing alliances between nations. In the Bible, it was a union that sometimes took place between a man and his dead brother's widow, or between one man and several wives. It has been a vehicle for the orderly transfer of property from one generation of males to the next; the test by which children were deemed legitimate or bastard; a privilege not available to black Americans; something parents arranged for their adult children; a contract under which women, legally, ceased to exist. Well into the 19th century, the British common-law concept of "unity of person" meant a woman *became* her husband when she married, giving up her legal standing and the right to own property or control her own wages.

Many of these strictures have already loosened. Child marriage is today seen by most people as the human-rights violation that it is. The Married Women's Property Acts guaranteed that a woman could get married and remain a legally recognized human being. The Supreme Court's decision in *Loving v. Virginia* did away with state bans on interracial marriage. By making it easier to dissolve marriage, no-fault divorce helped ensure that unions need not be lifelong. The recent surge in single parenthood, combined with an aging population, has unyoked marriage and child-rearing. History shows that marriage evolves over time. We have every reason to believe that same-sex marriage will contribute to its continued evolution.

The argument that gays and lesbians are social pioneers and bellwethers has been made before. Back in 1992, the British sociologist Anthony Giddens suggested that gays and lesbians were a harbinger of a new kind of union, one subject to constant renegotiation and expected to last only as long as both partners were happy with it. Now that these so-called harbingers are looking to commit to more-binding relationships, we will have the "counterfactual" that Gary Gates talks about: we will be better able to tell which marital stresses and pleasures are due to gender, and which are not.

In the end, it could turn out that same-sex marriage isn't all that different from straight marriage. If gay and lesbian marriages are in the long run as quarrelsome, tedious, and unbearable; as satisfying, joyous, and loving as other marriages, we'll know that a certain amount of strife is not the fault of the alleged war between men and women, but just an inevitable thing that happens when two human beings are doing the best they can to find a way to live together.

Critical Thinking

1. How do you think the legalization of same-sex marriage may change what it means to be married in the United States?

2. What are some of the differences in the gender roles, division of labor, and decision-making practices in same-sex and heterosexual couples?
3. Given the insights noted in this article, what are three ways marriage in the United States may change in the next 30 years? Why do you think these changes will occur? Do you think these changes will strengthen or weaken the institution of marriage?

Internet References

Coalition for Marriage, Family, and Couples Education
www.smartmarriages.com

Council on Contemporary Families
www.contemporaryfamilies.org

National Council of State Legislatures, Defining Marriage
www.ncsl.org/issues-research/human-services/same-sex-marriage-overview.aspx

The Pew Forum on Religion and Public Life: Gay Marriage and Homosexuality
www.pewforum.org/Topics/Issues/Gay-Marriage-and-Homosexuality

Article Prepared by: Patricia Hrusa Williams, *University of Maine at Farmington*

Parenting Wars

JANE SHILLING

Learning Outcomes

After reading this article, you will be able to:

- Recognize familial, societal, cultural, historical, and media influences on parenting.
- Understand child traits such as character and identity that are associated with positive developmental outcomes.

Recently I embarked on a long-overdue purge of my bookshelves. In the several dozen bin bags that made their way to the Oxfam bookshop (where the expressions of the staff slowly morphed from pleased gratitude, on my first visit, to unconcealed dread by the fifth) were two copies of the Communist Manifesto (*two?*); a formidable collection of works by Foucault, Sarraute, Perec and Queneau (I suppose I must once have read them—bookmarking postcards fell out of some of them—but if I did, no trace of the experience has remained); and all my parenting books. Penelope Leach's *Baby and Child,* Steve Biddulph's *Raising Boys* and *The Secret of Happy Children,* Kate Figes on *The Terrible Teens*—none of them, I realised, had been purchased by me: all had been acquired for some exercise in journalism—reviewing or interviewing, but never for private reading.

I don't know what made me think I could raise a child without an instruction manual, especially as I was the single mother of a boy, with no partner or brothers to consult about the mysteries of maleness. Sheer wilfulness, I suppose (and a certain bruised desire to avoid books that wrote of families as consisting of a child with two parents who were, in the days when I was doing my child-rearing, invariably assumed to be a mummy and a daddy). No doubt I should have made a better fist of it if I had been able to embrace Leach and Biddulph as my mentors, but my son is 21 now, and we are far into the territory for which no self-help books on parent/child relationships exist (unless you count D H Lawrence's *Sons and Lovers,* as a handy guide on what not to do).

As I began to inhabit my new identity as a mother and a lone parent, bringing up my child felt like an experience too personal and intimate to be trimmed to a template provided by experts. I was keen on babies and small children, and imagined that maternal instinct would cover the basics adequately. In this, I was faithfully replicating my own upbringing. My mother owned a copy of Dr Spock's *Baby and Child Care,* but it hadn't the air of a book that had been consulted frequently (though oddly enough I read it avidly as a child—so perhaps my son was, by default, a Spock baby).

My mother's maternal style must in turn have been modelled on her childhood, though my maternal grandmother was the youngest of a family of 13, so there would have been lots of people to offer advice on teething and potty training, a resource that my mother, an only child, and I, the first of my close friends to have a baby, both lacked.

I don't think that any of the women in my family took a conceptual or political view of child-rearing or parenthood. We were too absorbed by the day-to-day business of reading stories and wiping bottoms to find time to analyse what we were about. (I was the only one of us to combine work with motherhood throughout my son's childhood, and that wasn't a considered decision: as a lone parent, I had no choice.)

In my childhood—and, I think, my mother's—the visionary thinking came from my grandfather, who had spent his infancy and early childhood in the St Pancras workhouse and had, not coincidentally, strong views about the necessity for setting life goals and working towards them, preferably by getting an excellent education.

Even 20 years ago, my unprofessional attitude to bringing up a child was anachronistic; these days I suspect it would be regarded as borderline negligent. Mine was certainly the last generation in which one could allow oneself to muddle along without the assistance of the experts, treating parenthood as though it were analogous to friendship—a relationship that would grow and flourish of its own accord.

I might have done my best to ignore the fact, but as a single parent I was a fragmentary factor in what has grown into an urgent social crisis around the issues of childhood and family. If ever there was a time when one could raise children unselfconsciously, it is long past. Now every aspect of parenthood, from conception and birth to the forming of intellect and character, is the subject of anxious and often agonised scrutiny.

The crisis is both personal and political. On the one hand, as engaged parents, we feel that we are in some sense our children: their successes and failures represent us almost more vividly than our own achievements. And as the condition of youth becomes ever more extended, lasting in attenuated form until middle age and beyond, our children can help to feed our vision of ourselves as perennially young. (Whenever I hear a parent say that they are "more of a friend than a parent" to their son or daughter, I wonder what privately the child might think about that.)

The inevitable consequence of seeing our children as our alter egos and friends is the sense of dread that fills us when they become opaque to us. Children and adolescents need to have parenting from somewhere, and if it isn't offered by their parents they will seek it among their peers—a group that once might have included mainly the people in their year at school, but which now, thanks to social media and the internet, comprises a global community of "friends" and acquaintances, a world in which the most adhesive parent can find it difficult to stick with its offspring.

Beyond the family, there lies society—a construct composed, alarmingly enough, of other people and their children, many of them not as conscientiously raised as one's own. The media reports are dismaying; this is a generation disaffected and resentful, alienated from education, or unable to obtain the jobs that were promised them in return for their hard-won examination results, debarred by the lack of an income from buying their own home, the dependency of childhood uneasily protracted by having to return to living in the family home as adults after a taste of freedom at college. Despite our excellent intentions and our strenuous efforts, is this the world we have made for our children?

The confusion of western attitudes to parenting is reflected in a cacophony of contradictory images. Last year the cover of *Time* magazine featured a photograph of the 26-year-old attachment parenting advocate Jamie Lynne Grumet breastfeeding her son Aram, aged nearly four, who was dressed in military-style camouflage pants and standing on a small chair to reach the magnificently tanned breast protruding from her sexy black camisole top.

While Aram suckles in his miniature army fatigues, the infant literacy movement encourages parents to believe that it is never too early to begin learning to read, with initiatives such as Reading Bear, a free online programme for tinies whose editor-in-chief is Larry Sanger, the co-founder of Wikipedia. Not that a Tiger Mother-ish enthusiasm for prodigies of infant learning is an exclusively 21st-century phenomenon. Dr Johnson's friend Hester Thrale recorded in her Family Book of 1766 the achievements of her two-year-old daughter, Queeney, who later became the disaffected protagonist of Beryl Bainbridge's splendid novel *According to Queeney:*

> *She repeats the Pater Noster, the three Christian virtues, and the signs of the Zodiac in Watts' verses; she likewise knows them on the globe perfectly well. . . . She knows her nine figures and the simplest combinations of them; but none beyond a hundred; she knows all the Heathen Deities by their Attributes and counts to 20 without missing one.*

Eat your heart out, Amy Chua.

It is true that there has probably never been a time when parenting was regarded as the exclusive preserve of parents. In *Dream Babies,* her 1983 study of child-rearing advice to parents from Locke to Spock, Christina Hardyment notes that the history of childcare manuals is almost as old as that of mass publication. The original manuals were booklets written by doctors for use by nurses in foundling hospitals. "It is with great Pleasure I see at last the Preservation of Children become the Care of Men of Sense," wrote William Cadogan in his *Essay on Nursing* (1748). "In my opinion this Business has been too long fatally left to the management of Women who cannot be supposed to have a proper Knowledge to fit them for the Task, notwithstanding they look upon it to be their own Province."

The sentiment, if not the language, is curiously familiar from the plethora of modern parenting books which, even as they reassure anxious parents, cannot help but undermine their confidence with categorical but contradictory claims to know what is best for their offspring. Baby not sleeping? Gina Ford will fix that in no time. What a relief. Unless, that is, you happen to pick up Penelope Leach's most recent tome, *The Essential First Year: What Babies Need Parents to Know* (2010), from which you learn that leaving a distressed baby to cry can produce levels of the stress hormone cortisol (in the baby, that is, rather than the parent) that are toxic to its developing brain and may have long-term emotional consequences, as the anxiety of being left to weep unanswered pursues the beleaguered infant throughout childhood and adult life.

In short, you have a choice between inflicting brain damage and emotional distress if you leave little Magenta to cry herself to sleep; or an identical result if you rush to comfort her every time she wakes in the small hours and then—in an unforgivable, if perhaps understandable, episode of insomnia-induced rage—hurl her into her cot and lie on the floor beside it sobbing inconsolably and screaming, "I wish I'd never had a baby."

Still, let's not catastrophise. Somehow you and your child have both survived the essential first year, and even the essential first decade. Now you are entering the difficult hinterland of adolescence, and there are yet more things to worry about.

If you've got sons, there is the academic underperformance of boys in the overly feminised school environment, not to mention peer pressure to engage in all kinds of highly hazardous, not to say illegal, behaviour, and the long hours they spend closeted with their computer in their dark and malodorous rooms. For the parents of girls, there are problems of early sexualisation and their fragile relationship with their body image; nor is there any room for complacency about their examination results, which are likely to be affected by their desire not to be regarded as a nerd, neek, or anything other than one of the "popular girls".

For both sexes there is, besides the universal hazards of bullying and being mugged in the park for your cool stuff, the horrible complication of the way in which emergent adolescent sexuality is formed (or deformed) by online pornography.

Here, happily, Steve Biddulph the no-nonsense Australian family therapist and childcare guru can help, with his best-selling books *Raising Boys* and (most recently) *Raising Girls.* When it comes to bringing up daughters, a mother's place is invariably in the wrong, and Biddulph's warmth and wisdom will doubtless console many. Nevertheless, there is something about the spectacle of a middle-aged male expert issuing advice on raising girls that conjures a faint echo of Cadogan's conviction that the raising of children is best left to men of sense.

The happiness of children (as opposed to their moral education, which predominated in child-rearing manuals before the mid-20th century) is something to which a prodigious amount of expertise has been devoted over the past couple of generations.

Almost two decades ago, in 1994, Penelope Leach published a premonitory tract about the treatment of children in affluent western society. *Children First,* subtitled *What Our Society Must Do—and Is Not Doing—for Our Children Today,* was a scathing anatomy of the societal approach to child-rearing which saw parenting as "a universal hobby that is awkward because it cannot be shelved during the working week, interrupts important adult business and is hard on soft furnishings".

Some of Leach's most urgent priorities for a child-friendly society have been addressed in the intervening years. Yet her sunlit vision of a world in which children's needs have equal weight with those of adults remains dismayingly far from reality. In 2007, a Unicef study that assessed the well-being of children in six categories—material; health and safety; education; peer relationships; behaviours and risks; and young people's own perceptions of their happiness—placed the US second-to-last and the UK last in a league of 21 economically advanced nations.

In the introduction to his book *The Beast in the Nursery* (1998), the psychoanalyst Adam Phillips writes, "As children take for granted, lives are only liveable if they give pleasure." Yet the Unicef study suggests that despite our obsession with raising happy, successful children, many of them are trapped in lives that are, by Phillips's measure, unliveable.

So, what has gone wrong? In *Kith,* her strange, poetic book on the relationship between childhood and the natural world (to be published in May), the writer Jay Griffiths asks the intractable question: "Why are so many children in Euro-American cultures unhappy?" and concludes that, in the affluent west, childhood has become a lost realm.

Children's books are written by grownups, so it is unwise to call them in evidence when discussing styles of parenting. Nevertheless, it is striking that the fiction best loved by children—from Captain Marryat and Mark Twain, E Nesbit and Richmal Crompton to Jacqueline Wilson and J K Rowling—describes childhood as a state unencumbered by parental interference, in which children confront all kinds of challenges and dangers and survive by their own resourcefulness.

In modern America and Europe, Griffiths notes, children may read about the adventures of Huck Finn or William Brown but they are unlikely to share their experiences: "Many kids today are effectively under house arrest. . . . If there is one word which sums up the treatment of children today, it is 'enclosure'. Today's children are enclosed in school and home . . . and rigid schedules of time". Society, she adds, "has historically contrived a school system that is half factory, half prison, and too easily ignores the very education which children crave".

In *How Children Succeed,* the Canadian-American writer Paul Tough addresses the question of childhood unhappiness from a perspective that is the precise opposite of Griffiths's: her approach is lyrical, emotional and elegiac; his is logical, analytical and didactic. Nonetheless their theories converge on a single point—that, as a preparation for life, education is failing huge numbers of children.

Tough's book, as he writes, "is about an idea that is . . . gathering momentum in classrooms and clinics and labs and lecture halls across the country and around the world. According to this new way of thinking, the conventional wisdom about child development over the past few decades has been misguided. We have been focusing on the wrong skills and abilities in our children, and using the wrong strategies to nurture and teach those skills. . . ."

There is something very satisfying about an educational theory that denounces all previous theories. It seems to offer the possibility of a miraculous redemption of past errors and the hope of a certain path to a better future. The main mistake of recent years, Tough argues, has been to focus on measurable academic attainment by our children, to the exclusion of the more nebulous personal qualities (or "character") necessary to translate examination results into the kind of stable success that makes young people good citizens.

"Character" is a term with curiously Victorian overtones; the more formidable early child-rearing volumes that Christina Hardyment discusses in *Dream Babies* are keen on this quality. Yet the interdisciplinary school of thought that Tough describes, which is based on the theories of Martin Seligman, a professor of psychology at the University of Pennsylvania, and the late Christopher Peterson of the University of Michigan, factorises the success trait into seven separate elements: grit, self-control, zest, social intelligence, gratitude, optimism and curiosity.

Gurus of the Nursery

For 52 years after it was first published in 1946, **Benjamin McLane Spock**'s *Baby and Child Care* was the second-bestselling book after the Bible. A physician by training, Spock turned to psychoanalysis to examine child-rearing. His ideas were highly influential and encouraged parents to see their children as individuals.

The psychologist **Penelope Leach**'s *Baby and Child: from Birth to Age Five,* was published in 1977 and has sold more than two million copies. Much of her writing has focused on the drawbacks of childcare, a position that has attracted significant criticism.

Gina Ford, the author of *The Contented Little Baby Book* (1999), has long divided opinion, in part because she has no children (she bases her writing and advice on having looked after "over 300" babies as a maternity nurse). Some swear by her philosophy of strict routines, whereas others deplore the rigidity of her approach.

When *Battle Hymn of the Tiger Mother* was published in 2011, readers and critics were stunned at **Amy Chua**'s candid account of raising her two daughters. Chua, a Yale law professor, writes that "this was supposed to be a story of how Chinese parents are better at raising kids than western ones. But instead, it's about a bitter clash of cultures, a fleeting taste of glory, and how I was humbled by a 13-year-old. . . ."

Paul Tough is a journalist and former editor at *The New York Times* Magazine. In *How Children Succeed* (newly published by Random House), he analyses the character traits that help a child have a secure and happy future.

An endorsement by Bill Clinton gives some indication of the praise that has greeted **Andrew Solomon**'s latest book, *Far From the Tree,* in the United States. Solomon—who is also an activist and lecturer—spent years researching the work by interviewing families with diverse and challenging experiences of child-rearing.

Gurus of the Nursery

For 52 years after it was first published in 1946, **Benjamin McLane Spock**'s *Baby and Child Care* was the second-bestselling book after the Bible. A physician by training, Spock turned to psychoanalysis to examine child-rearing. His ideas were highly influential and encouraged parents to see their children as individuals.

The psychologist **Penelope Leach**'s *Baby and Child: from Birth to Age Five,* was published in 1977 and has sold more than two million copies. Much of her writing has focused on the drawbacks of childcare, a position that has attracted significant criticism.

Gina Ford, the author of *The Contented Little Baby Book* (1999), has long divided opinion, in part because she has no children (she bases her writing and advice on having looked after "over 300" babies as a maternity nurse). Some swear by her philosophy of strict routines, whereas others deplore the rigidity of her approach.

When *Battle Hymn of the Tiger Mother* was published in 2011, readers and critics were stunned at **Amy Chua**'s candid account of raising her two daughters. Chua, a Yale law professor, writes that "this was supposed to be a story of how Chinese parents are better at raising kids than western ones. But instead, it's about a bitter clash of cultures, a fleeting taste of glory, and how I was humbled by a 13-year-old. . . ."

Paul Tough is a journalist and former editor at *The New York Times* Magazine. In *How Children Succeed* (newly published by Random House), he analyses the character traits that help a child have a secure and happy future.

An endorsement by Bill Clinton gives some indication of the praise that has greeted **Andrew Solomon**'s latest book, *Far From the Tree,* in the United States. Solomon—who is also an activist and lecturer—spent years researching the work by interviewing families with diverse and challenging experiences of child-rearing.

Armed with these attributes, the theory goes that children from all kinds of unpromising backgrounds, from the vastly affluent with no experience of character-forming misfortune to the underprivileged with a discouraging excess of "deep and pervasive adversity at home", can achieve both the academic qualifications that are the golden ticket to the security of regular employment and the qualities that will make them useful members of society.

On this side of the Atlantic, the case for character development as an element of education has been vigorously promoted by Anthony Seldon, the Master of Wellington College. In May last year, the University of Birmingham's Jubilee Centre for Character and Values was launched, with funding from the John Templeton Foundation, established by the American philanthropist.

Tough describes how the principle of teaching—and assessing—character as well as academic attainment was initially taken up by two schools, KIPP Academy Middle School in the South Bronx, whose students are mostly from low-income families, and Riverdale Country School, situated in one of the most affluent neighbourhoods of New York City, and where pre-kindergarten fees start at $40,750 a year.

KIPP was already something of a model institution after a programme of immersive schooling produced a startling improvement in its academic results. But the instigator of that programme, David Levin, a Yale graduate, was dismayed by how many of his high-achieving students subsequently dropped out of college. Meanwhile, the headmaster of Riverdale, Dominic Randolph, had begun to feel that "the push on tests" at high-achieving schools such as his was "missing out on some serious parts of what it means to be human".

For the students, the problems at both ends of the socio-economic spectrum were oddly similar: low levels of maternal attachment, high levels of parental criticism, minimal after-school adult supervision, emotional and physical isolation from parents and—in the case of the rich children—excessive pressure to succeed, resulting in anxiety, depression and chronic academic problems.

The evolution of the character development programme diverged sharply at the two schools during the course of the trial. At KIPP it leaned towards the practical and prescriptive; at Riverdale the emphasis was more moral and philosophical, on leading a good life rather than wearing the uniform correctly and paying attention in class.

As the programme has continued, the statistics on college dropout rates among KIPP students have seemed modestly encouraging. It is harder to measure the success of the experiment among Riverdale students, as their path towards academic success was always much clearer. Tough acknowledges that what he calls the "new science of adversity . . . presents a real challenge to some deeply held political beliefs on both the left and the right". In the UK, Seldon concedes that "character" might be seen as a synonym for "middle-class" or "public-school" values. Yet both men appear convinced that it is the only means of enabling young people to alter what might otherwise appear to be a fixed destiny of failure and unhappiness.

While Tough proposes the formal exercise of grit and optimism as the key to personal success, Andrew Solomon's new book, *Far From the Tree,* is a study of families whose ideas about what constitutes "success" for their child have had to be recalibrated, sometimes very sharply. Solomon interviewed 200 families for his epic survey of identity and difference, which was a decade in the writing. Each chapter is devoted to the experiences of children and parents living with one of a dozen forms of "otherness"—deafness, dwarfism, Down's syndrome, autism, schizophrenia, prodigies, criminal children and those born of rape.

Solomon's theme is the development of identity. He argues that children acquire identity both "vertically", in the form of inherited traits such as language and ethnicity, and "horizontally", from a peer group. The greater the differences between the child and his or her parents, the more powerful the tensions between the horizontal and vertical identities.

The germ of the book sprang from an article on deaf culture that Solomon wrote in 1993 for *The New York Times.* He found that most deaf children are born to hearing parents, who often feel compelled to help their children "succeed" in a hearing world by focusing on the ability to communicate orally, often to the detriment of other aspects of their development. For such children, the discovery of a culture that celebrates deafness, regarding it as a state of being as vibrant and creative as the hearing world, often appears a liberation, a portal to an identity that does not have to be lived out against a contrasting "normality".

But within that experience of liberation lies the seed of a painful truth: that, for all children marked by difference, whatever its nature (Solomon is gay, and writes movingly about his experience of growing up in a straight family), their first experience of their otherness is almost invariably provided by their own family. He explores the complicated nexus of "normalities" which exists within the family of a child who is in some way different, and between the family and the outside world, with a dogged forensic elegance.

Solomon's account, like Tough's, is laden with anecdote, but while Tough uses his case histories to personalise his theories, Solomon's purpose in writing is narrative and exploratory, rather than ideological or didactic. Like Griffiths, he seeks the key to a universe of familial complexity, and finds it in the most obvious place of all. Love, he concludes, is all you need.

That was pretty much my guiding principle when I began my own experience of parenthood. And on the whole I'm not persuaded that the outcome would have been very different if I had spent more time consulting the experts. Which is not the same thing as feeling that I have been a success as a parent. Raising a child involves a circuitous journey of many branching routes that may lead, if parents and children are lucky, loving and tolerant, to a destination that everyone involved finds bearable.

Twenty years ago, or ten, or even five, if you had asked me whether I thought I was a good mother, I would have answered "good enough" with a degree of self-satisfaction. I had, after all, raised a kind, sane, personable grown-up with a decent clutch of exam results, an entrenched reading habit and an unusual ability to discuss with enthusiasm both West Ham's position in the League table and the nuances of female fashion; and I felt that I had done it largely contra mundum.

More recently, as my son and I have settled into our roles as adult equals and our accounts of the past have diverged, I have begun to understand that he has grown into the person he is as much despite me as because of me. My main aim as a mother had been to try to avoid the aspects of my own upbringing that had caused me pain. I thought that would be easy, but it was not.

Sometimes my son's narratives of his childhood (still so recent and fresh in his mind) make me think that almost everything I did was wrong. It is a melancholy reflection, to put it mildly. But it makes me think that perhaps the real work of parenthood is to learn to accommodate the stories that your children tell you about their upbringing.

Critical Thinking

1. Shilling's article discusses and reviews several different philosophies of rearing children. Which is closest to the style of parenting your parents used? Which style or attributes do you want to adopt as a parent? Why?
2. Why are modern parents believed to be more fearful and protective than past generations?
3. What is the single most important thing parents can do to help promote the healthy development of their children?
4. The article suggests that parents have over-emphasized academic success in children and under-emphasized character development. Do you agree or disagree? Why?

Internet Reference

Health and Parenting Center
www.webmd.com/parenting

Tufts University Child and Family Webguide
www.cfw.tufts.edu

Positive Parenting
www.positiveparenting.com

The National Association for Child Development
www.nacd.org

Child Trends
www.childtrends.org

Jane Shilling is the author of *The Stranger in the Mirror.*

Article Prepared by: Patricia Hrusa Williams, *University of Maine at Farmington*

Raising a Moral Child

Adam Grant

Learning Outcomes

After reading this article, you will be able to:

- Define moral behavior.
- Compare and contrast the terms guilt and shame.
- Identify parenting strategies associated with moral behavior in children.

What does it take to be a good parent? We know some of the tricks for teaching kids to become high achievers. For example, research suggests that when parents praise effort rather than ability, children develop a stronger work ethic and become more motivated.

Yet although some parents live vicariously through their children's accomplishments, success is not the No. 1 priority for most parents. We're much more concerned about our children becoming kind, compassionate and helpful. Surveys reveal that in the United States, parents from European, Asian, Hispanic, and African ethnic groups all place far greater importance on caring than achievement. These patterns hold around the world: When people in 50 countries were asked to report their guiding principles in life, the value that mattered most was not achievement, but caring.

Despite the significance that it holds in our lives, teaching children to care about others is no simple task. In an Israeli study of nearly 600 families, parents who valued kindness and compassion frequently failed to raise children who shared those values.

Are some children simply good-natured—or not? For the past decade, I've been studying the surprising success of people who frequently help others without any strings attached. As the father of two daughters and a son, I've become increasingly curious about how these generous tendencies develop.

Genetic twin studies suggest that anywhere from a quarter to more than half of our propensity to be giving and caring is inherited. That leaves a lot of room for nurture, and the evidence on how parents raise kind and compassionate children flies in the face of what many of even the most well-intentioned parents do in praising good behavior, responding to bad behavior, and communicating their values.

By age 2, children experience some moral emotions—feelings triggered by right and wrong. To reinforce caring as the right behavior, research indicates, praise is more effective than rewards. Rewards run the risk of leading children to be kind only when a carrot is offered, whereas praise communicates that sharing is intrinsically worthwhile for its own sake. But what kind of praise should we give when our children show early signs of generosity?

Many parents believe it's important to compliment the behavior, not the child—that way, the child learns to repeat the behavior. Indeed, I know one couple who are careful to say, "That was such a helpful thing to do," instead of, "You're a helpful person."

But is that the right approach? In a clever experiment, the researchers Joan E. Grusec and Erica Redler set out to investigate what happens when we commend generous behavior versus generous character. After 7- and 8-year-olds won marbles and donated some to poor children, the experimenter remarked, "Gee, you shared quite a bit."

The researchers randomly assigned the children to receive different types of praise. For some of the children, they praised the action: "It was good that you gave some of your marbles to those poor children. Yes, that was a nice and helpful thing to do." For others, they praised the character behind the action: "I guess you're the kind of person who likes to help others whenever you can. Yes, you are a very nice and helpful person."

A couple of weeks later, when faced with more opportunities to give and share, the children were much more generous after their character had been praised than after their actions had been. Praising their character helped them internalize it as part of their identities. The children learned who they were from observing their own actions: I am a helpful person. This dovetails with new research led by the psychologist Christopher J. Bryan, who finds that for moral behaviors, nouns work better than verbs. To get 3- to 6-year-olds to help with a task, rather than inviting them "to help," it was 22 to 29 percent more effective to encourage them to "be a helper." Cheating was cut in half when instead of, "Please don't cheat," participants were told, "Please don't be a cheater." When our actions become a reflection of our character, we lean more heavily toward the moral and generous choices. Over time it can become part of us.

Praise appears to be particularly influential in the critical periods when children develop a stronger sense of identity. When the researchers Joan E. Grusec and Erica Redler praised the character of 5-year-olds, any benefits that may have emerged didn't have a lasting impact: They may have been too young to internalize moral character as part of a stable sense of self. And by the time children turned 10, the differences between praising character and praising actions vanished: Both were effective. Tying generosity to character appears to matter most around age 8, when children may be starting to crystallize notions of identity.

Praise in response to good behavior may be half the battle, but our responses to bad behavior have consequences, too. When children cause harm, they typically feel one of two moral emotions: shame or guilt. Despite the common belief that these emotions are interchangeable, research led by the psychologist June Price Tangney reveals that they have very different causes and consequences.

Shame is the feeling that I am a bad person, whereas guilt is the feeling that I have done a bad thing. Shame is a negative judgment about the core self, which is devastating: Shame makes children feel small and worthless, and they respond either by lashing out at the target or escaping the situation altogether. In contrast, guilt is a negative judgment about an action, which can be repaired by good behavior. When children feel guilt, they tend to experience remorse and regret, empathize with the person they have harmed, and aim to make it right.

In one study spearheaded by the psychologist Karen Caplovitz Barrett, parents rated their toddlers' tendencies to experience shame and guilt at home. The toddlers received a rag doll, and the leg fell off while they were playing with it alone. The shame-prone toddlers avoided the researcher and did not volunteer that they broke the doll. The guilt-prone toddlers were more likely to fix the doll, approach the experimenter, and explain what happened. The ashamed toddlers were avoiders; the guilty toddlers were amenders.

If we want our children to care about others, we need to teach them to feel guilt rather than shame when they misbehave. In a review of research on emotions and moral development, the psychologist Nancy Eisenberg suggests that shame emerges when parents express anger, withdraw their love, or try to assert their power through threats of punishment: Children may begin to believe that they are bad people. Fearing this effect, some parents fail to exercise discipline at all, which can hinder the development of strong moral standards.

The most effective response to bad behavior is to express disappointment. According to independent reviews by Professor Eisenberg and David R. Shaffer, parents raise caring children by expressing disappointment and explaining why the behavior was wrong, how it affected others, and how they can rectify the situation. This enables children to develop standards for judging their actions, feelings of empathy and responsibility for others, and a sense of moral identity, which are conducive to becoming a helpful person. The beauty of expressing disappointment is that it communicates disapproval of the bad behavior, coupled with high expectations and the potential for improvement: "You're a good person, even if you did a bad thing, and I know you can do better."

As powerful as it is to criticize bad behavior and praise good character, raising a generous child involves more than waiting for opportunities to react to the actions of our children. As parents, we want to be proactive in communicating our values to our children. Yet many of us do this the wrong way.

In a classic experiment, the psychologist J. Philippe Rushton gave 140 elementary- and middle-school-age children tokens for winning a game, which they could keep entirely or donate some to a child in poverty. They first watched a teacher figure play the game either selfishly or generously, and then preach to them the value of taking, giving or neither. The adult's influence was significant: Actions spoke louder than words. When the adult behaved selfishly, children followed suit. The words didn't make much difference—children gave fewer tokens after observing the adult's selfish actions, regardless of whether the adult verbally advocated selfishness or generosity. When the adult acted generously, students gave the same amount whether generosity was preached or not—they donated 85 percent more than the norm in both cases. When the adult preached selfishness, even after the adult acted generously, the students still gave 49 percent more than the norm. Children learn generosity not by listening to what their role models say, but by observing what they do.

To test whether these role-modeling effects persisted over time, two months later researchers observed the children playing the game again. Would the modeling or the preaching influence whether the children gave—and would they even remember it from two months earlier?

The most generous children were those who watched the teacher give but not say anything. Two months later, these children were 31 percent more generous than those who observed the same behavior but also heard it preached. The message from this research is loud and clear: If you don't model generosity, preaching it may not help in the short run, and in the long run, preaching is less effective than giving while saying nothing at all.

People often believe that character causes action, but when it comes to producing moral children, we need to remember that action also shapes character. As the psychologist Karl Weick is fond of asking, "How can I know who I am until I see what I do? How can I know what I value until I see where I walk?"

Critical Thinking

1. What does it mean to be a moral child?
2. How much and what aspects of being moral are due to nature? Nurture?
3. In the article the author states "If we want our children to care about others, we need to teach them guilt rather than shame when they misbehave." Explain what they mean by this.

Internet References

Health and Parenting Center
www.webmd.com/parenting

Positive Parenting
www.positiveparenting.com

Raising a Moral Child: Ask Dr. Sears
http://www.askdrsears.com/topics/parenting/discipline-behavior/morals-manners/moral-child

Adam Grant is a professor of management and psychology at the Wharton School of the University of Pennsylvania and the author of *Give and Take: Why Helping Others Drives Our Success.*

Article

Prepared by: Patricia Hrusa Williams, *University of Maine at Farmington*

The Collapse of Parenting: Why It's Time for Parents to Grow Up

If Anyone can be Called the Boss in Modern, Anti-hierarchical Parenthood, it's the Children.

CATHY GULLI

Learning Outcomes

After reading this article, you will be able to:

- Define terms such as parent–child dynamics, nurturance, parental authority, role confusion, power imbalance, hierarchy, and authoritative parenting.
- Compare and contrast different hierarchical structures in families, their function, and how they influence parent–child dynamics.
- Understand the potential motives which underline parenting behavior and the challenges facing modern parents.

For modern families, the adage "food is love" might well be more true put another way: food is power. Not long ago, Dr. Leonard Sax was at a restaurant and overheard a father say to his daughter, "Honey, could you please do me a favor? Could you please just try one bite of your green peas?" To many people, this would have sounded like decent or maybe even sophisticated parenting—gentle coaxing formed as a question to get the child to co-operate without threatening her autonomy or creating a scene.

To Sax, a Pennsylvania family physician and psychologist famous for writing about children's development, the situation epitomized something much worse: the recent collapse of parenting, which he says is at least partly to blame for kids becoming overweight, overmedicated, anxious, and disrespectful of themselves and those around them.

The restaurant scene is a prime example of how all too often adults defer to kids because they have relinquished parental authority and lost confidence in themselves. They're motivated by a desire to raise their children thoughtfully and respectfully. In theory, their intentions are good and their efforts impressive—moms and dads today are trying to build up their kids by giving them influence; they also want to please them and avoid conflict. In reality, parents are at risk of losing primacy over their children.

The dinner table is ground zero. "When parents begin to cede control to their kids, food choices are often the first thing to slide," Sax writes in his new book, *The Collapse of Parenting: How We Hurt Our Kids When We Treat Them Like Grown-Ups*. A rule such as "No dessert until you eat your broccoli" has recently morphed into "How about three bites of broccoli, and then you can have dessert?" The command has become a question capped with a bribe, as Sax puts it. Dinner at home requires polling kids on what they're willing to eat; the options might include roast chicken and potatoes or chicken fingers and fries. You can bet which they choose. So parents renegotiate: *How about sweet potato fries?*

Parents in North America have become prone to asking their children rather than telling them. "It's natural," says Gordon Neufeld, a prominent Vancouver psychologist cited in Sax's book. "Intuitively, we know that if we're coercive, we're going to get resistance." For trivial choices such as which color of pants to wear, this approach is fine, he says. But "when we consult our children about issues that symbolize nurturance like food, we put them in the lead." That triggers an innate psychological response, and their survival instincts activate: "They don't feel taken care of and they start taking the alpha role."

So if the girl served green peas does eat one bite as her dad asked, Sax says, "she is likely to believe that she has done her father a favor and that now he owes her a favor in return." Food may be the first manifestation of the collapse of parenting, but many of the problems within families are a result of this type of role confusion. In this way, what happens over a meal is a metaphor for how uncomfortable parents have become in their position as the "alpha" or "pack leader" or "decider" of the family—the boss, the person in charge. The grown-up.

That discomfort comes from a loving place, of course. Many parents strive to raise their kids differently from how they grew up. They say, "I can't do the stuff I was raised with, it doesn't feel right. I don't want to yell, I don't want to spank," says Andrea Nair, a psychotherapist and parenting educator in London, Ontario. "There's a massive parenting shift between our generation and the one before. We've come a long way from when you called your dad 'sir' and when he walked in the house you would jump out of 'his' chair."

The evolution hasn't been easy, though. "We're trying to pull off the emotion coaching but we haven't received the training," says Nair. "It's like teaching your kids to speak French while you're learning it in the textbook." Parents have made it a top priority that their kids feel heard and respected from a young age. They want to be emotionally available to them, and for their children to be able to express their own emotions. "Kids have permission to have tantrums now because [they're] learning how to manage feelings," says Nair. "Someone said to me, 'Are we seeing more tantrums now than we used to?' And I wonder."

Parents also want a democratic household where each family member has a say about what happens—*Should we go outside now? Are we ready to have a bath? Would you like to have the party here?*—and they cultivate independence and freedom of thought in their children. Strict obedience used to be praised; now, it is seen as outdated and potentially dangerous. Compliance might mean your kid is a pushover, which no parent wants, especially as bullying has spread from the schoolyard to cyberspace.

There are broader influences shifting the parent–child dynamic as well. Over the past half-century or more, the public has come to scorn power imbalances based on gender, race, religion, and sexual orientation, and historic gains have been achieved in the pursuit of equality. Even corporations are now replacing pyramidal management with "flat organization." In Western society, where equality for everyone has become a cultural objective and a constitutional right, children are treated like they are one more minority group to honor and empower. "Empower has come to seem virtuous," Sax says. "Empower everyone, why not?"

But many kids are actually overpowering their parents. That's the problem, say those working in child development. A functional family unit hinges on the one social construct that contemporary society has been working hard to dismantle: hierarchy. "You need a strong alpha presentation to inspire a child to trust you and depend upon you," says Neufeld of parents. "If we don't have enough natural power then we're hard-pressed to [make] the demand or [set] the limit" for children. "The parent always has to be honored as the ultimate person," he continues. "We need to put parents back in the driver's seat."

If not, the consequences can be far-reaching, starting with children's eating habits, which might contribute to them becoming overweight and obese. Like the father in the restaurant, many parents can't convince their kids to eat well. It doesn't help that junk food is sometimes a reward for acing a test or scoring a goal. The message: healthy food is for losers. On-demand snacking—in the car, at the mall, while out for a walk—appears to disrupt metabolism and circadian rhythms, as well as hormonal balance. That many parents carry with them a canteen of water and a stash of goodies wherever their kids go is further proof of how much they want to satisfy their children, literally and figuratively. "I don't want them to get hypoglycemic," one mom told Sax while lugging a cooler of snacks to her car for a 30-min drive.

Contributing to the extraordinary weight gain among North American children in recent years is a dramatic decline in fitness. There is even a medical term for it, "deconditioning," which is described in the *Collapse of Parenting* as a euphemism for "out of shape." It has landed kids as young as 11 and 12 in the cardiologist's office complaining of heart disease symptoms including chest tightness and shortness of breath. In fact, some hospitals in the United States have even opened pediatric preventive cardiology clinics.

While children are less active than ever, they do not, ironically, get enough rest. A common question Sax asks students is, "What's your favorite thing to do in your spare time, when you are by yourself with no one watching?" The most common answer in recent years: sleep. That's because children are too busy with school assignments and extracurricular activities to go to bed at a good hour, or because when they get to bed, they are on their cellphone or computer, or playing video games.

This chronic fatigue may be associated with the rise of attention-deficit hyperactivity disorder and prescription drug use among children. "Sleep deprivation mimics ADHD almost perfectly," writes Sax. In his experience as a doctor, insufficient sleep is one reason why kids are more likely to be diagnosed with the disorder. In general, "It is now easier to administer a pill prescribed by a board-certified physician, than to firmly instruct a child and impose consequences for bad behavior." Stephen Camarata, a professor of hearing and speech sciences and psychiatry at Vanderbilt University in Nashville echoes that point: "Parents say, 'My child can't do this particular exercise, they're not paying attention,' therefore I have to identify them as having a clinical condition." A medical diagnosis might negate parental shortcomings or a child's misbehavior. "It displaces that failure," he says.

Camarata worries that parents are asking too much of kids too soon, as he outlines in his latest book, *The Intuitive Parent: Why the Best Thing For Your Child Is You*. He points to the surge of books, toys, and software marketed to parents of young children promising to accelerate learning. The ubiquitous metaphor that kids are information sponges has parents saturating them with educational exercises. "We're treating them like little hard drives," says Camarata, but "this idea of pushing children to the absolute max of their developmental norm doesn't give them time to reason and problem-solve. It actually undermines both self-confidence and fluid reasoning, or the ability to think."

Schools, too, have been focusing more on academic achievement than socialization. Sax documents how, 30 years ago, American students in kindergarten and Grade 1 learned "Fulghum's rules," which include tenets such as "Don't take things that aren't yours" and "Clean up your own mess" as well as "Share everything" and "Don't hit people." But since the 1980s, as other nations pulled ahead of the United States in scholastic performance, the primary objective of educators has become literacy and numeracy. In Canada too, says Neufeld, "we have lost our culture. Our society is far more concerned that you perform. Schools will always drift to outcome-based things."

That's partly why a "culture of disrespect" has sprouted in North America. As kids have become less attached to and influenced by the adults in their lives, same-age peers have come to matter more to them. It's a theme in Neufeld's book, *Hold On to Your Kids: Why Parents Need to Matter More Than Peers*, co-authored by Dr. Gabor Maté. Young children "are not rational beings," says Neufeld. Part of growing up is testing boundaries; little ones, by their very nature, can't be relied on to hold each other accountable—nor should they.

"Kids are not born knowing right from wrong," says Sax, pointing to longitudinal studies showing that children who are left to discover right from wrong on their own are more likely to have negative outcomes in the future: "That child in their late 20s is much more likely to be anxious, depressed, less likely to be gainfully employed, less likely to be healthy, more likely to be addicted to drugs or alcohol. We now know this," he says. "Parents who are authoritative have better outcomes, and it's a larger effect than the effect of race, ethnicity, household income, or IQ."

With stakes so high, authoritative parenting would seem imperative. But there is a psychological hurdle that people will have to overcome first, says Nair: "How to respect their child but also be the decider" of the family. Part of the challenge lies in the fact that parents don't want to fail—at nurturing and governing *simultaneously*—and they certainly don't want their children to fail in their personal development, in school and at social networking. These worries feed off each other in the minds of parents; that's why parents second-guess the way they speak to their kids, what they feed them, how they discipline them, and what activities they permit.

This is all the more true for the growing number of parents who delayed having children until they were "ready" with a secure job, a good home, and a dependable partner. "People purposely wait so they can nail it," says Bria Shantz, a 35-year-old mother of two in Vancouver. "That creates even more pressure. They want to get this perfect." Shantz is, in fact, the daughter of Neufeld, and she has called upon him for advice or reassurance. That Shantz, who has a leading child psychologist in her family, one who helped raise her, can still occasionally succumb to parental insecurity, says everything about its potency: "There's this slight panic. You want to do everything right," she says. "Nothing prepares you for how much you want it to go well."

So as soon as parents conceive, they begin amassing a library of books on how to deal with the fantastic chaos about to enter their lives in the form of a baby; the collection grows with each developmental stage. They subscribe to online newsletters and smartphone apps that alert them on milestones their children should reach by a certain age. From the outset, parents are tracking how quickly their child is growing, how much they are achieving. For every expert, a parent consults by phone or in person, they're also checking in with the virtual wise man, Google. That almost never helps.

There is no parental concern too obscure not to have an online group devoted to it. Shantz is part of one focused on "babywearing" because she's trying to decide whether a "wrap" or a "ring sling" would be better for her nine-month-old. "It's the weirdest site to be on. You see posts and you feel guilty because [parents] are carrying their babies everywhere, doing all these things, having this connection." And yet Shantz hasn't been able to delete herself from the group, even though she keeps meaning to; nor has she been able to pick between a wrap or sling.

That pull and push moms and dads feel—between caring about how other parents are raising their kids while rejecting the constant comparisons—defines this generation of parents for better and worse. Katie Hurley, a psychotherapist in Los Angeles and author of *The Happy Kid Handbook: How to Raise Joyful Children in a Stressful World*, says, "We've been conditioned to question ourselves—to constantly look for information to make sure we're doing it right. Because of that, parents are in a state of learned helplessness."

So what are people supposed to do? The answer is so basic that at first it might seem unsatisfying: For starters, says Hurley, realize that "nobody knows what they're doing when they leave the hospital with an infant. Every parent learns by trial and error"—every year of their child's life, and with every child they raise. That's as true today as it ever was, and parents who recognize this will shed some guilt and anxiety. Building on this idea, Nair says that parents must "have a higher tolerance for things not going well." How they recover from their own occasional mistake, outburst, loss of patience, or bad call may say more to a child than how they are in happy times. "We're missing that opportunity, which is how learning works," she says. "That's how we become more confident."

A significant portion of Sax's book is devoted to the importance of parents modelling traits they want to encourage in their children. Chief among them, he says, should be humility and conscientiousness—which run counter to inflating a child's self-esteem and sense of entitlement. To that end, he encourages parents to fortify their adult relationships so they are not overly concerned with pleasing their kids as a way of satisfying their own need for affection. Neufeld also urges parents, including his own adult children, to establish a network of surrogate caregivers—relatives, neighbors, and daycare workers—who will not undermine their authority but back them up when they need help.

And invariably, they will. "Parenting is awfully frustrating and often a lonely place," says Neufeld, especially when a child misbehaves. In those moments, he recommends parents reassure kids that their relationship isn't broken. "When parents realize that they are their children's best bet, it challenges them to their own maturity." It gives them the confidence that they know what's good for their kids, and that they should stand up to them—this is, in fact, an act of love required of parents. They become, in effect, the grown-ups their children need.

Critical Thinking

1. Sax suggests that there has been a collapse in parenting, as parents relinquish authority to their children. Do you agree with his perspective and argument? Why or why not?
2. Does a functional family system, as the authors' suggest, need a hierarchy with the parent at the topic? What happens when children receive too much power or control too soon? What does it mean to be an authoritative parent? What are challenges to implementing this parenting style in modern society?
3. Several of the authors quoted within the article attribute a variety of societal ills including high rates of obesity, chronic fatigue, high rates of ADHD, and a "culture of disrespect" to overindulgent parenting. What are strengths of their argument? What are issues or problems with their reasoning and assumptions? Are we quick to blame parents for problems without considering other factors which may contribute?

Internet References

Center for Disease Control: Parenting
https://www.cdc.gov/parents/

Dr. Leonard Sax, MD, PhD
http://www.leonardsax.com/

National Parent Helpline
http://www.nationalparenthelpline.org

Neufeld Institute
http://neufeldinstitute.org/

Parents Magazine
http://www.parents.com/parenting/

Article Prepared by: Patricia Hrusa Williams, *University of Maine at Farmington*

The Science of Siblings

Francine Russo

Learning Outcomes

After reading this article, you will be able to:

- Analyze ways siblings influence personality and development at different points of the lifespan.
- Understand the research basis behind common beliefs about the influence of siblings on behavior and personality.

Growing up in North Miami Beach, Tobi Cohen Kosanke, now 48, adored her brother Keith. Seven years older, he was a "laid-back surfer dude," while she was a "chubby, nerdy" little girl. Tobi knew she could never live up to Keith's cool persona, so while he was quitting school, experimenting with drugs, and focusing on riding the next wave, Tobi threw herself into school, with her brother's encouragement. The hard work paid off: She went on to earn her PhD and become a geologist. "I hung out with the geeky kids, the good kids, the smart kids, because of my brother," she says. "I loved Keith, and I know he was proud of me, but I owe my success to taking the road that he didn't take."

Tobi's story is not unusual. Of all the factors that shape your personality—your genes, your parents, your peers—siblings are at the top, according to one major theory of human development. If you think about it, the relationships with your sisters and brothers will likely last longer than any others in your lifetime. Research shows that even in adolescence, you spend 10 to 17 hours a week with them—and experts are finding that their impact continues long after you've left the nest. Study after study has shown that the ways you interact with each other growing up can affect your relationships, your happiness, even the way you see yourself throughout the rest of your life.

"I'm First!" "I'm the Baby!"

Some of the earliest studies of siblings focused on how birth order influences personality and fate. You're familiar with the basic types: Firstborns are said to be responsible and high-achieving, youngest siblings charmers and free spirits, and middle children lost in the mix.

It's easy to dismiss these as mere stereotypes, and indeed there are researchers who do, but others have found statistical evidence that bears them out. A Norwegian study found that firstborns had slightly higher IQs than their sibs. Other research has shown they're also more successful: According to Sandra Black, PhD, professor of economics at the University of Texas at Austin, "Firstborns earn more than secondborns, who earn more than thirdborns."

On the other hand, research has found that youngest siblings really do tend to be risk-takers. Frank Sulloway, PhD, of the Institute of Personality and Social Research at UC Berkeley, studied baseball-playing brothers—like Joe, Dom, and Vince DiMaggio—and found that the younger ones tried to steal base more often than their older brothers. Meanwhile, middle children grow up to be more peer-oriented, says Sulloway. First- and last-borns turn to parents in an emotional crisis; middle kids, to their friends. Still, birth order is hardly destiny, says Sulloway. What's more important, researchers say, is the quality and dynamics of your relationships with your siblings.

"I'm Nothing like Him!"

Within a family, children devise all sorts of strategies to increase their status and feeling of belonging, and one of the most important is what experts call "sibling de-identification." To reduce competition with brothers and sisters who may be cuter or smarter (not to mention bigger and stronger), we each carve out our own niche.

Much like Tobi Kosanke, younger siblings typically start out adoring their older brothers or sisters, says Laurie Kramer, PhD, professor of applied family studies at the University of Illinois at Urbana. "They want to mimic their strengths and talents, but over time, they realize they can't succeed at the same level. That leads them to develop their own attributes."

"You can be the smartest kid in your class or the fastest on the track team," says Susan McHale, PhD, professor of human development at Penn State University. "But if you have a brother or sister who's smarter or more athletic, it doesn't matter." In other words, your self-image is shaped at least in part by how you compare to your siblings.

And it's not just that younger kids de-identify from more capable older siblings, says McHale. In early adolescence, when we're trying to figure out who we are, it's often older siblings who emphasize their differences. For example, a boy with a feminist younger sister might adopt a more macho stance. Even among tight-knit sibs, "you want to be close but also to be your own person," says Victoria Hilkevitch Bedford, PhD, professor emerita of psychology at the University of Indianapolis.

And experts speculate that our tendency to compare ourselves to our siblings continues well into adulthood. For example, the sibling dynamic could affect what we try to achieve, says Kramer. "Asked to give a speech or do a challenging job, a less accomplished younger sibling might decline, thinking, 'If they knew my older brother, they wouldn't think I was so great.'"

"Oh, Her? She's Just One of the Guys."

When it comes to learning about the opposite sex, researchers say, there's nothing better than having an older member at home. "If you are a girl with an older brother or a boy with an older sister, you should thank them for whatever romantic success you've had," jokes William Ickes, PhD, professor of psychology at the University of Texas at Arlington.

In Ickes's now classic 1983 study, he instructed unacquainted male-female pairs to talk to each other. Girls with older brothers and boys with older sisters broke the ice more easily and were more likely to rate each other favorably.

Because the genders don't mix much in middle childhood, "kids who see opposite-sex siblings and their friends in everyday settings may come to know more about how the other sex behaves and connects," says McHale.

Melissa Payne, a 29-year-old medical industry account manager in Orlando, says her relationship with her 33-year-old brother, Dave Payne, a publicist in Tarpon Springs, Fla., not only helped pave the way for romantic connections but allowed the two to share dating advice. A few years ago, when both siblings were seeing people who did not treat them well, each reminded the other that not all women—or men—were such shabby partners. Within a year, they had broken off the relationships. "When you're dating someone, you can make excuses, but it was different hearing a guy's perspective from my brother," says Melissa.

"Hey, that's Mine!"

Young siblings fight up to eight times an *hour,* research shows. While all that squabbling may drive parents crazy, it's also how some kids learn to negotiate conflict—training ground for dealing with neighbors, bosses, and spouses down the line.

When it comes to arguing and expressing our opinions, we can take risks with our siblings because they're stuck with us, says Corinna Jenkins Tucker, PhD, associate professor of family studies at the University of New Hampshire. "Children can test which conflict resolution strategies work and which don't," she says. (Refuse to share? Just watch your brother's reaction.) And what we learn during childhood can have far-reaching effects.

Kids who learn coercive or hostile approaches to handling conflict are more likely in adolescence to join risky peer groups and engage in negative social behaviors (like smoking, drinking, or skipping school), according to McHale. But siblings can be taught to compromise—that's why parental involvement is so crucial. Reluctant referees who consider sibling aggression normal and don't help resolve clashes are making a mistake, says McHale. Their kids may end up with poorer social skills and more conflict compared with kids whose parents help them work out their disagreements.

And what about as you grow older? Some experts say that kids who learn hostile patterns of interaction with sibs may repeat those patterns with friends or coworkers. Others, however, suggest that kids who never develop close relationships with their brothers or sisters may be more likely to go out of their way to form strong connections outside the family.

"Of Course We Love You Both the Same."

It's not possible to talk about the sibling relationship without considering Mom and Dad, the central pole on the family merry-go-round. Siblings may receive a lot of things from their parents, including cues on how to treat someone in a close relationship. Good marriages tend to make for kids who get along better, says Katherine Jewsbury Conger, PhD, associate professor of human development at UC Davis.

Yet there's one parental behavior that can really make or break the sibling relationship. As every kid knows almost from his or her first breath, if Mommy or Daddy gives me less than my sister, then it's game over. Social scientists call this "differential treatment." Kids call it favoritism, and if we think Susie is Mommy's favorite, we don't like it, and sometimes maybe don't like Susie, either.

Children of different ages and abilities are bound to be treated differently, says Conger, but for kids, the real question is fairness. And if children see differential treatment as unfair, those negative feelings can last—even into the next generation, with an adult sibling resenting that Grandma gives Susie's kids better Christmas gifts.

Paige D. feels that favoritism came between her and her older brother, with whom she no longer speaks (she says their parents skipped both her college graduation and her wedding but attended her brother's graduation). "As a child, I loved my brother more than the moon and the stars," says Paige. "But I think the overt favoritism made him feel so uncomfortable that it was easier for him to block me out as a way to justify our parents' eccentricity."

Interestingly, though, while some children are highly attuned to variations in their parents' attentions, they are often mistaken about favoritism. When Deborah T. Gold, PhD, associate professor of medical sociology at Duke University, studied pairs of adult siblings, she found that in many cases each thought the *other* was their parents' favorite.

"What are We Going to do About Mom?"

How siblings get along in adulthood also depends greatly on how they manage one of the most volatile family passages—the aging and death of their parents. As grown-up sibs see their time with Mom or Dad running out, it stirs up deep childhood desires for love and approval. Research shows that in 90 percent of families, one person does most of the caregiving, and Bedford notes that if siblings grew up with a sense of unfairness, those feelings can reignite over how sisters and brothers perceive elder care. On the other hand, this passage also brings enormous opportunities to strengthen and renew sibling relationships. Putting your heads together during stressful times can help you and your siblings get to know each other as adults. Hey, my brother's not that incompetent little kid! Where did my sister acquire so much patience?

And even if things are tense (or worse), it's not impossible to repair the relationship. As young adults, Wendy Beckman and her older sister, Bonnie Nielson, were little more than cordial. Wendy, now 55 and a writer in Cincinnati, still thought of her older sister as annoyingly overprotective. But in her 30s, she made efforts to connect with Bonnie, whose marriage was unraveling.

"Bit by bit," Wendy recalls, "we started talking honestly about things in our adult lives, not just 'You took my socks when I was 12.' She actually started asking me for advice!"

Confronting their father's Alzheimer's and their mother's death from cancer, they grew even closer. "We still come at the world completely differently," says Bonnie, now 61, of Augusta, Maine. "But when you see your siblings as fully formed adults, the relationship is so much more fulfilling."

Experts say this pattern of sibling drift, followed by reconnection, is common. When siblings move away and start their own careers and families, they often have little contact except through their parents. But in middle age and beyond, as other loved ones pass away, surviving siblings can be important sources of support. In fact, research shows the healthiest, happiest, and least lonely people have warm sibling relationships.

As time passes, Patti Wood's relationship with her two older sisters has become more precious. Patti, 53, an author and speaker in Decatur, Ga., always adored her sisters, now 62 and 66. The three "military brats" stayed close during their many moves, and have bonded even more tightly after caring for their 92-year-old mother.

Despite their differences—single, long-married with grandkids, divorced with a grown child—they talk to each other nearly every day, travel together, and call each other first in a crisis. And they share a unique history. Patti's oldest sister, Robin, speaks for them all when she says, "We know we'll always be there for each other. I can't imagine not having my sisters there to count on."

Only the Lonely?

Pity the poor only child—no one to play with. (Or maybe you envied onlies, with no bratty little brother trashing their stuff.) Regardless, "there's a big misconception in American popular culture that singletons are selfish, lonely, or maladjusted," says Toni Falbo, PhD, a professor of educational psychology at the University of Texas at Austin and an only child herself. But in fact, only children have one major advantage, says Falbo: They don't have siblings competing for their parents' resources, including college funds. As a result, onlies tend to achieve high levels of education and occupational prestige.

As little kids, Falbo acknowledges, single children may be more comfortable with adults. "But peer sociability grows with experience," she says, and by high school, onlies are on par with kids who have sisters and brothers. "Every day, my mother shoved me out the door and insisted I play with other children, which forced me to develop social skills," says Falbo. "And it also helped me learn to appreciate my family, which was just the right size for me."

Critical Thinking

1. The article suggests that sibling relationships shape personality development more than other factors including genetics, parenting, or peer relationships. Do you agree or disagree and why?
2. The article presents several different stereotypes about sibling relationships and dynamics. Are there any which you feel apply to your own life and family? If so, which ones? Are there any which you do not feel are valid or based on research and why?

3. What about the outcomes of individuals who are only children, lose a sibling, or have a sibling with special needs—how might the absence, loss, or difference in their sibling connection shape their personality and development?

Internet References

Dr. Frank J. Sulloway, PhD., Birth Order Researcher
www.sulloway.org

Sibling Issues: Center for Parent Information and Resources
www.parentcenterhub.org/repository/siblings

Sibling Support Project
www.siblingsupport.org

Sibs
www.sibs.org.uk

Tufts University Child and Family Webguide
www.cfw.tufts.edu

FRANCINE RUSSO is the author of *They're Your Parents, Too! How Siblings Can Survive Their Parents' Aging Without Driving Each Other Crazy,* and frequently speaks about sibling relationships.

Francine Russo, "The Science of Siblings," from *Parade Magazine*, June 22, 2013.

Article

Prepared by: Patricia Hrusa Williams, *University of Maine at Farmington*

How to Make Peace With Your Sibling

EVAN IMBER-BLACK

Learning Outcomes

After reading this article, you will be able to:

- Define terms: Family dynamics and family roles.
- Identify factors which influence the relationship between siblings.
- Understand strategies for identifying and changing patterns in relationships.

You've just sat down to eat, and the phone rings. When you answer, your dining companion doesn't have to ask who it is. The expression on your face gives away the fact that it's your quarrelsome brother. You roll your eyes and think, *Here we go again.*

The topics may change—money, caring for parents, holiday plans, children—but the tension between you two is on an endless loop. You know that within two minutes you'll be having the same old fight. And the answer to the question "What can I do differently to create a different outcome?" is nowhere to be found.

It's Not the Person, It's the Pattern

Changing your sibling relationship starts with recognizing that the problem isn't one person's fault. It takes two people to create the clash—though often there are others lurking in the shadows.

Once you decide you genuinely want to improve a relationship that is distant, contentious, agitated or empty, the first step is figuring out the underlying emotional and behavioral pattern. Some examples: Your brother provokes, you seek harmony. Your sister demands, you placate. One of you is a giver, the other a taker. One aggressively confronts, the other meekly submits.

These patterns are less linear than circular in nature: Each action elicits the same response. By the time you've reached midlife, trying to figure out "who started it" is fruitless. More important are these realizations: Blame is pointless, we're in this together, and the work it takes to change is worth it.

When your sibling relationship becomes less bound by old patterns, more real and open to allowing the differences between you to peacefully exist, your lives will become richer and more meaningful. Authentic connections with people who share your history and mythologies, who speak your special family language and can laugh at common foibles, are worth their weight in gold.

The Sources of Sibling Patterns

Many believe that altering a long-standing sibling relationship requires initial agreement from both parties. But in my 35 years of practice I have found that one determined person can *initiate* a process of change. The ideas I offer in this article are derived from a well-established practice called Family Therapy With One Person, and with mindful thought and careful action, you can implement them on your own.

This work begins with *your* deliberations and reflections, proceeds to taking action and ends with having conversations with your sibling(s). Conventional wisdom suggests that communication is required, but with this approach, it comes at the *end* of the process, not the beginning.

The second step to transforming your sibling relationship is acknowledging that you are stuck in a repetitive pattern. To gain insight, assume the role of "anthropologist." However sibling dynamics are playing out today, they're usually traceable to our families as a whole, so you need to review the intergenerational "culture" of brothers and sisters in the household in which you grew up.

Many factors influence how siblings will interact. And until we question them, these become our model of relationships. Often, without realizing it, parents assign certain roles to their children: the smart one, the funny one, the beautiful one, the ditzy one. Although the roles likely contain some elements of truth, nobody is that one-dimensional. Furthermore, these roles "imprint" us, and unconsciously we all start to manifest more and more of those qualities and interact with our siblings from these "childish" starting points.

As you dig deeper, you may discover, for example, that your mother and her younger sister had a relationship characterized by one demanding and the other appeasing—and that that's exactly what happens between you and your sister. Or maybe your father and uncle were in business together and one was a methodical thinker and the other a dreamer, just like you and your brother today.

Birth Order and What to Do About It Now

Most family therapists acknowledge that birth order plays a role in sibling dynamics. The first-born is often the most responsible and the custodian of family traditions. Middle children usually need to figure out for themselves where and how they fit in. The youngest may have had more freedom and been encouraged to be carefree.

A last-born, for instance, may grow up feeling her parents trusted an older sibling with information and responsibilities, while viewing her as irresponsible. We "grow into" expected roles, and this can set up a state of permanent tension and conflict.

Changing these roles and the patterns they engender allows us to experiment with new behavior—parts of ourselves that have been submerged or sublimated in larger family expectations. As you begin to do so, your sibling will likely discover there is more room in the relationship for aspects he or she has kept hidden from you.

9 Steps to Changing Sibling Dynamics

Once you've discerned your repetitious patterns, you can begin to act differently to break a vicious cycle and inaugurate a "virtuous" cycle. As in all our important relationships, siblings often get stuck waiting for the other person to change. It's helpful to think about this as a nine-step process.

1. **Determine your repetitive sibling pattern.** Pursuing-distancing? Demanding-placating? Achieving-failing? Caretaking-care receiving? Awareness of rigid patterns is the first step to deliberate change.
2. **Identify *your* place in the pattern.** What do you do over and over again in response to your sibling? We're all good at noting what other people do, but what's *your* role in the interaction? This non-blaming recognition will help you to decide what you might change in your own behavior. Relationships improve when we stop trying to change others and take responsibility for our own actions and own a new role.
3. **Plan one small and manageable change.** If your usual dynamic with your sister is that she always needs support and you always provide it, try sharing a struggle *you're* having and ask for her help. Be specific about what she can do. Relationships are not transformed all at once, but rather with thoughtful steps.
4. **Anticipate "openings," or moments in family life when change is more likely.** These include times when other shifts are occurring, like the death of a parent, children leaving home, retirement, divorce or the birth of grandchildren. At such moments, people are more emotionally available and the dynamics more fluid.
5. **Consider who else will be impacted.** Whenever we change a pattern with one person, other relatives are often affected. If you and your mother are especially close and you begin to confide in your brother for the first time, how might your mom respond? If you and your partner have long discussed your brother's unavailability and he starts to show up, expect some changes in your primary relationship. Also, because we tend to play out these same roles in other situations (at work, with friends), you could experience some changes there too.
6. **Be prepared for positive and negative reactions.** Moving out of a familiar pattern can be highly disconcerting to others. Don't be surprised if your sibling's initial response is to try to pull you back to the tried and true. If you have always been the helper in the relationship and now you are asking for assistance, watch out for a new call for help.
7. **Maintain your new position.** Pay attention to the pull to familiar old anger and defensiveness—and resist. Think about ways to repeat your new place in the pattern, and implement them. If your older brother has always been demanding and you have always placated, your refusal of a demand will likely not be met with applause initially. Calmly let your brother know how he might help you—or himself.
8. **Watch for your sibling's new responses.** When you take a new and unexpected action in the relationship, observe what she begins to do differently. There will be more room for flexibility.
9. **Initiate a deeper conversation with your sibling.** What would each really like going forward?

Once you've demonstrated that you're genuinely committed to something new between the two of you, your sibling will be more likely to participate in the process. This may be a time to engage in some short-term family therapy.

Critical Thinking

1. The article suggests that while the topic of sibling disputes change, the tension between siblings are a consistent part of the dynamic between siblings. Do you agree? Why/why not?
2. In your own family, what are some of the patterns in relationships between siblings you have noted? Do children in your family assume different roles? How has this influenced interactions between family members? Are relationships between siblings in your family improving or do they remain the same as everyone has grown older?
3. Why is it so difficult to change patterns in relationships? What are strengths and weaknesses of the suggestions made in the article for altering these patterns and changing the dynamics of relationships?

Internet References

Family Dynamics
https://www.healthychildren.org/English/family-life/family-dynamics/Pages/default.aspx

One Person Family Therapy
https://www.ncjrs.gov/html/ojjdp/jjbul2000_04_3/pag7.html

Sibling Issues: Center for Parent Information and Resources
www.parentcenterhub.org/repository/siblings/

Sibs
www.sibs.org.uk

Tufts University Child and Family Webguide
www.cfw.tufts.edu

Evan Imber-Black is the program director of the marriage and family therapy master's degree program at Mercy College and the director of the Center for Families and Health at the Ackerman Institute for the Family. This article has been edited for style and republished with the permission of our content partner Next Avenue.

Article Prepared by: Patricia Hrusa Williams, *University of Maine at Farmington*

The Sandwich Generation Juggling Act

How to Avoid Dropping the Caring-for-Yourself Ball.

SHERRI SNELLING

Learning Outcomes

After reading this article, you will be able to:

- Define terms and concepts such as sandwich generation, Family and Medical Leave Act (FMLA).
- Identify sources of stress and potential resources for caregivers juggling children, careers, and caring for an older parent.
- Understand how the FMLA may assist members of the sandwich generation and the limitations of the law.

For anyone who has learned to juggle, you start with one ball and slowly add another. Eventually, most people can learn to juggle three balls as hand–eye coordination becomes accustomed to the rhythm. It is adding the fourth ball that separates the amateurs from the serious jugglers. The best juggler in the world could juggle four balls for only a couple of hours.

In America today, there is a societal juggling act occurring within the Sandwich Generation of caregivers—the group defined as 24 million Americans who are juggling children, careers, and caring for an older parent—and it is a juggling act that lasts for much longer than two hours. While many Americans can handle three balls (me, children, and career), once the caregiving ball is added, inevitably the ball getting dropped is "me."

A Growing Number

According to a 2013 Pew Research study, more Americans—47 percent of the nation's 40- and 50-year-olds—are joining the Sandwich Generation and attempting this challenging juggling act. How does this at-risk group avoid the common pitfall of ignoring self-care in order to care for everyone else around them? The answer may just lie in the mental focus and rhythm of . . . juggling.

Jennifer Slaw, a professional juggler, said in an interview last year with The Huffington Post that juggling offers a unique form of stress relief. The focus of having just one ball in the air at a time but keeping the synchronicity of movement flowing with the other balls takes intense concentration and may offer some clues for our Sandwich Generation caregivers.

Caregivers can take each ball of responsibility and focus on ways to keep that ball moving in a fluid motion.

If we take the premise that juggling only requires getting one ball into the air at a time, caregivers can take each ball of responsibility and focus on ways to keep that ball moving in a fluid motion. Here is how:

Ball 1: Children

Whether children are younger, in their teens or early 20s, they can become an essential ingredient in the care of an older grandparent. Consider that most children, even as young as four or six, are tech-savvy unlike any generation before them. Having a grandchild connect with a grandparent, whether via video chats, playing multiple-player online games, or singing along with a therapeutic music app, both young and old benefit from the intergenerational connection—in person or across the miles.

This "play time" also gives caregivers a needed break even for a few minutes to attend to other tasks, sit down and read a few pages of a magazine or book, phone a friend, or simply rest the eyes and mind to rejuvenate with a quick 15- to 20-min cat nap. A quick afternoon nap has been proven to aid recuperative sleep time, increase alertness, and improve mood, according to Dr. Gregory Belenky, research professor and director of The Sleep and Performance Research Center at Washington State University. In fact, afternoon naps were secret energizers for illustrious individuals such as Winston Churchill, Albert Einstein, Leonardo da Vinci, and President John F. Kennedy.

Ball 2: Career

Many working caregivers do not realize their employer may have elder care or caregiving services that can help them juggle work and caring for an aging parent. Some employers offer elder care research and referral services, employee flex time, back-up care, or telecommuting options, acknowledging the challenges of the Sandwich Generation. Checking with an employer's human resources department may even uncover a special benefit offered by thousands of employers—access to a professional geriatric care manager who can assess the older adult's needs and create a care plan for the family that can include help coordinating needed home and community-based services.

In addition, many working caregivers forget that the Family and Medical Leave Act (FMLA) was created for just the type of caregiving situations 15 percent of the workforce faces today: the dilemma of caring for older parents. According to the 2014 National Study of Employers released earlier this year from the Society of Human Resources Management (SHRM), 99 percent of all U.S. employers offer some unpaid leave to full-time employees. FMLA calls for eligible employees to receive 12 weeks of unpaid leave (26 weeks if caring for a covered service member or veteran). Some states, including California, Rhode Island, New Jersey, and the District of Columbia, actually offer some level of *paid* leave.

While FMLA provides job-protected leave, legal same-sex spousal caregiving eligibility, and continuation of group health insurance coverage, it also has limitations. Only 60 percent of all employers offer the full FMLA benefits (private employers with less than 50 employees are exempt), and the SHRM report found there has been a decline since 2012 of employers fulfilling the full 12-week leave provision under FMLA. In addition, FMLA does not require leave for the caregiving of a grandparent, in-law, or sibling, leaving that to each state's definition of care recipient. Of the states offering paid leave, only Rhode Island and the District of Columbia include these additional loved ones in their eligibility definition.

Ball 3: Caring for an Aging or Ailing Parent

Adding this third ball to the juggling act is challenging but achievable. Many valuable resources are available to assist caregivers. The most crucial caregiving decisions focus on senior living options or in-home care and the financial aspect of caregiving that can include long-term care plan benefits, legal documents, medical billing, and insurance coverage.

For senior living, online sites such as Caring.com and A Place for Mom offer excellent, comprehensive listings of various communities such as assisted living, memory care, and nursing home, all with ratings, photos, and facility details. Both also offer telephonic support from an expert adviser who can answer questions and help guide families to the best choices, avoiding what I call the "Goldilocks Syndrome."

For in-home care, traditional agencies with national services such as Home Instead, Visiting Angels, and Right At Home, or the nation's largest online caregiver marketplace CareLinx (full disclosure: I serve on the advisory board for CareLinx) provide various personal care, nonmedical services for caregivers helping their older loved one age in place.

For the review and verification or dispute of insurance claims and medical billing, hiring a patient navigator can take this time-consuming task off a caregiver's plate. And, perhaps the best adviser who can help caregivers save both their piggy banks and maximize a parent's fixed income, long-term care insurance and retirement savings is an elder law attorney—typically estate attorneys who have special credentials in elder care and senior issues.

Ball 4: Me

In baseball, "Ball Four" means the player gets a "walk"—an easy jog to first base. As caregivers focus on each ball and achieve a solution for each, the most important ball becomes the fourth ball that says "me."

According to a health risk study conducted by the National Alliance for Caregiving, stress is a caregiver's No. 1 enemy. Stress relief can be found in finding caregiver support groups in person or online.

There are also online communities where caregivers create private groups inviting family and friends to volunteer to help out. Whether it's delivering a meal to the family while the caregiver is at the hospital with a parent, offering to carpool children to school and events, or be a companion to the older person while the caregiver attends to other activities or gets a little respite, online sites such as Lotsa Helping Hands and CaringBridge are great resources for caregivers to ask for and accept help from those that care about the caregiver.

Caregivers also have to acknowledge that finding "me time" is essential to maintaining the stamina and energy required to juggle the other balls. Whether it's a weekly luxurious bath, finding time for a yoga class, or taking that "Ball Four walk" around the neighborhood, self-care is the most important ball caregivers need to get up in the air and never drop.

Critical Thinking

1. Do you know a family member or friend who is a part of the sandwich generation? If so, describe some of the challenges they have experienced. If you do not know someone personally trying to juggle children, career, and caring for an older parent, what do you see as the greatest challenge they might experience?
2. What are strengths of the Family and Medical Leave Act (FMLA)? What are challenges and limitations of the law for those caring for an elderly or sick family member?
3. This article mentions many different resources available to help caregivers locate care for an aging or ailing parent. Imagine you needed for find care for one of your parents. Explore the resources mentioned in the article for your local area. What kinds of supports did you find? What surprised you most in your search?

Internet References

Alzheimer's Association
https://www.alz.org/

Caregiver Action Network
https://caregiveraction.org/

Caring.com
https://www.caring.com/

National Alliance for Caregiving
http://www.caregiving.org/

Article

Prepared by: Patricia Hrusa Williams, *University of Maine at Farmington*

More Grandparents Become Caregivers for Grandkids. Is That Good?

Modes of Thought: The trend reflects growing pressures, both financial and social, that many parents in the US face. The question is: Who should help?

Jessica Mendoza

Learning Outcomes

After reading this article, you will be able to:

- Discuss the prevalence of family caregiving by grandparents in the United States.
- Identify factors which underlie the increase in the number of grandparents caring for their grandchildren.
- Consider the benefits and challenges of family caregiving.

More grandparents are becoming caregivers to their grandchildren—an ongoing trend that underscores how America's approach to childcare is putting increasing stress on families dealing with a variety of trends, from substance abuse to two-parent working families, experts say.

Census data show that about 2.7 million grandparents in the United States are the primary caregiver for children in their household, up 7 percent from 2009. The figures are part of a new Associated Press report.

While grandparents and other relatives have long played the role of caregiver in many American families, that role has grown more pronounced among the working and middle classes since the Great Recession. Long, irregular working hours for young parents, coupled with the rising costs of professional childcare, also transformed grandparents from occasional baby-sitters into a critical safety net for parents with young children.

The situation is characteristic of America's approach to childcare—leaving the responsibilities of raising children to parents. But as those responsibilities become more complicated, it is inevitable that many parents will need to turn to the only reliable and cost-effective they can find—their families.

"We don't have a culture that thinks about children as a national responsibility," says Kathy Simons, an early childhood specialist and senior program manager at the Massachusetts Institute of Technology's Work-Life Center. "I do think people still think of kids as the responsibility of their direct relations."

To some, that is as it should be.

"A strong case can be made that parents deserve tax relief to ease the financial strain associated with raising the next generation," writes Carrie Lukas, managing director of the Independent Women's Forum, in an opinion article for The Federalist. "But focusing that support solely on those who use formal daycare programs would be unfair to the millions of parents who have different preferences for their families."

For her part, Dr. Simons worries about the effect that is having on American families.

"We're expecting families to do too much," she says. "Childcare is a really complicated thing. You don't solve it once, you solve it six times a month—you have a regular arrangement, a backup arrangement, you have sick days, you have something for trips. You need a bunch of different kinds of arrangements.

Grandparents have increasingly filled many of those roles. In 2008, about 40 percent of grandparents who had grandchildren under age 13 and lived within an hour from them reported providing childcare while parents were at work or school, according to the National Association of Child Care Resource & Referral Agencies. Of those, nearly ⅔ said they had grandchildren under six years old.

"Childcare is expensive, and it's often not available, especially for lower-income families," says Elizabeth Peters, director of the Center on Labor, Human Services, and Population at the Urban Institute in Washington. "Often the mother, father, both parents, are working nonstandard hours. That's the advantage of having a grandparent who may be able to provide care during hours when a more formal system is not available."

There's also a growing contingent of grandparents who—due to a host of issues, including the growing number of parents struggling with substance abuse or parents away on military deployment—not only provide part-time childcare, but are actively raising their grandchildren.

That's "a whole different ball game," says Amy Goyer, a family and caregiving expert with the AARP, a national nonprofit that focuses on improving the quality of life of people age 50 and older. "This usually happens when there's a crisis or chronic problem in the family. There are usually grief and loss issues, [or] the kids have some kind of instability in their life."

Such situations could have long-term negative impacts on children, families, and society at large, Dr. Peters says. A lack of affordable childcare disproportionately affects women's participation in the labor force—especially among women living at or below the poverty line, she notes.

Research also shows stable environments are critical in early childhood.

"The kind of care we provide our kids can help them develop the early skills and learning that can put them on the right track," Peters says. "That's very important, especially for kids coming from disadvantaged backgrounds."

Initiatives do exist at the state and federal levels, she says. The Department of Health and Human Service's Head Start program has for decades sought to foster stable family environments for children from low-income homes. Childcare subsidies and tax credits also work toward the same goal, Peters says.

Still, some industry experts and advocates say more needs to be done. Simons at MIT, for instance, says enlisting seniors in childcare beyond their own grandchildren might be helpful as a way of providing supplementary care that could also be fulfilling for the elderly.

"If we could develop new models for engaging seniors in early education and care; and if the work also got them learning, and kept them mentally active and engaged with other people, that would be fabulous," she says.

But she and others also would like to see childcare made a national priority.

"There are lots of good reasons why family are the best caregivers, but parents should not be forced to rely on grandparents and relatives because they can't afford any other options," says Vivien Labaton, co-founder and co-executive director of the Make It Work campaign, a three-year initiative that seeks to improve conditions for working families. "We need to value caregiving in this country."

Adds Simon: "Grandparents have a really important place to fill in that. But a reliable system of nationally supported childcare has to be a big part of the solution, and we're a long way from that."

Critical Thinking

1. In the United States, why are grandparents assuming more caregiving responsibility for their grandchildren?
2. A quote within the article states "We don't have a culture that thinks about children as a national responsibility"? What is meant by this quote? Do you agree or disagree?
3. What may be some of the benefits and challenges of grandparents providing care for their grandchildren?

Internet References

Alliance for Family, Friend, and Neighbor Child Care
http://www.familyfriendandneighbor.org/

Families and Work Institute
http://www.familiesandwork.org

Make It Work Campaign
http://www.makeitworkcampaign.org/

Unit 4

UNIT

Prepared by: Patricia Hrusa Williams, *University of Maine at Farmington*

Challenges and Opportunities

Life is stressful. However, stress can be a powerful force in moving us forward, propelling us to face and try to master new challenges and situations we encounter during our life course. When a stressful event occurs in families, many processes occur simultaneously as families and their members try to cope with the stressor and its effects. Sometimes, there is a reduction in family members' ability to act as resources for each other. Indeed, a stressor can overwhelm the family system, and family members may be among the least effective people in coping with each other's behavior. Families can also develop new skills and ways of working together, growing as individuals and as a unit in the face of adversity. In this unit, we consider a wide variety of stressful life events and crises families may experience. Some are normative, stressful life events which occur as families evolve and change. Families add and lose family members. Family members' age and one's health can fail. Individuals experience changes in employment and the need to balance work–family concerns as families develop and change.

There are also other nonnormative, stressful life events and crises which many families experience. Marital partners may stray and grow apart. Marriages can fail and breakup. Divorced spouses remarry and create new families. A family member may be called on to serve their country or be separated from their family for a period of time. Children and adults in the family can be diagnosed with chronic illnesses or health problems. Personal, economic, relationship, and social strains can result in maladaptive coping strategies such as drug and alcohol use, mental health crises, violence, and infidelity. However, many individuals and families find a new equilibrium and way of looking at the world through these experiences, learning from both the good and bad of life.

The articles in this unit explore a variety of family crises, stresses, and strains. Among them are the impact of child maltreatment, family violence, substance abuse, infidelity, and economic concerns. The nature of stress resulting from a life-threatening and chronic illness, disability, and loss is also considered. Family challenges and adaption for single parent, divorced, and stepfamilies are also considered. Throughout this unit, the focus is not only on understanding the challenges these events and circumstances can present. An important goal is to also consider how individuals and families can best manage these crises and access supports as they navigate the stresses of life.

Article

Prepared by: Patricia Hrusa Williams, *University of Maine at Farmington*

Anguish of the Abandoned Child

CHARLES A. NELSON III, NATHAN A. FOX, AND CHARLES H. ZEANAH, JR.

The plight of orphaned Romanian children reveals the psychic and physical scars from first years spent without a loving, responsive caregiver.

Learning Outcomes

After reading this article, you will be able to:

- Understand the political, social, and economic reasons behind the "orphan problem" in Romania.
- Explain reasons why children become orphans worldwide.
- Identify how early experiences of deprivation impact child development and later outcomes.
- Define and explain the term "sensitive period."

In a misguided effort to enhance economic productivity, Nicolae Ceauşescu decreed in 1966 that Romania would develop its "human capital" via a government-enforced mandate to increase the country's population. Ceauşescu, Romania's leader from 1965 to 1989, banned contraception and abortions and imposed a "celibacy tax" on families that had fewer than five children. State doctors—the menstrual police—conducted gynecologic examinations in the workplace of women of child-bearing age to see whether they were producing sufficient offspring. The birth rate initially skyrocketed. Yet because families were too poor to keep their children, they abandoned many of them to large state-run institutions. By 1989 this social experiment led to more than 170,000 children living in these facilities.

The Romanian revolution of 1989 deposed Ceauşescu, and over the next 10 years his successors made a series of halting attempts to undo the damage. The "orphan problem" Ceauşescu left behind was enormous and did not disappear for many years. The country remained impoverished, and the rate of child abandonment did not change appreciably at least through 2005. A decade after Ceauşescu had been removed from power, some government officials could still be heard saying that the state did a better job than families in bringing up abandoned children and that those confined in institutions were, by definition, "defective"—a view grounded in the Soviet-inspired system of educating the disabled, dubbed "defectology."

Even after the 1989 revolution, families still felt free to abandon an unwanted infant to a state-run institution. Social scientists had long suspected that early life in an orphanage could have adverse consequences. A number of mostly small, descriptive studies that lacked control groups were conducted from the 1940s to the 1960s in the West that compared children in orphanages with those in foster care and showed that life in an institution did not come close to matching the care of a parent—even if that parent was not the natural mother or father. One issue with these studies was the possibility of "selection bias": children removed from institutions and placed into adoptive or foster homes might be less impaired, whereas the ones who remained in the institution were more disabled. The only way to counter any bias would require the unprecedented step of randomly placing a group of abandoned children into either an institution or a foster home.

Understanding the effects of life in an institution on children's early development is important because of the immensity of the orphan problem worldwide (an orphan is defined here as an abandoned child or one whose parents have died). War, disease, poverty and sometimes government policies have stranded at least eight million children worldwide in state-run facilities. Often these children live in highly structured but hopelessly bleak environments, where typically one adult oversees 12 to 15 children. Research is still lacking to gain a full understanding of what happens to children who spend their first years in such deprived circumstances.

In 1999, when we approached Cristian Tabacaru, then secretary of state for Romania's National Authority for Child Protection, he encouraged us to conduct a study on institutionalized children because he wanted data to address the question of whether to develop alternative forms of care for the 100,000 Romanian children then living in state institutions. Yet Tabacaru faced stiff resistance from some government officials, who believed for decades that children received a better upbringing in institutions than in foster care. The problem was exacerbated because some government agencies' budgets were funded, in part, by their role in making institutional care arrangements. Faced with these challenges, Tabacaru thought that scientific evidence about putative advantages of foster care for young children over state institutions would make a convincing case for reform, and so he invited us to go ahead with a study.

Infancy in an Institution

With the assistance of some officials within the Romanian government and especially with help from others who worked for SERA Romania (a nongovernmental organization), we implemented a study to ascertain the effects on a child's brain and behavior of living in a state institution and whether foster care could ameliorate the effects of being reared in conditions that run counter to what we know about the needs of young children. The Bucharest Early Intervention Project was launched in 2000, in cooperation with the Romanian government, in part to provide answers that might rectify the aftereffects of previous policies. The unfortunate legacy of Ceauşescu's tenure provided a chance to examine, with greater scientific rigor than any previous study, the effects of institutionalized care on the neurological and emotional development of infants and young children. The study was the first-ever randomized controlled study that compared a group of infants placed in foster care with another raised in institutions, providing a level of experimental precision that had been hitherto unavailable.

We recruited, from all six institutions for infants and young children in Bucharest, a group of 136 whom we considered to be free of neurological, genetic and other birth defects based on pediatric exams conducted by a member of the study team. All had been abandoned to institutions in the first weeks or months of life. When the study began, they were, on average, 22 months old—the range of ages was from six to 31 months.

Immediately after a series of baseline physical and psychological assessments, half the children were randomly assigned to a foster care intervention our team developed, maintained and financed. The other half remained in an institution—what we called the "care as usual" group. We also recruited a third group of typically developing children who lived with their families in Bucharest and had never been institutionalized. These three groups of children have been studied for more than 10 years. Because the children were randomly assigned to foster care or to remain in an institution, unlike previous studies, it was possible to show that any differences in development or behavior between the two groups could be attributed to where they were reared.

Because there was virtually no foster care available for abandoned children in Bucharest when we started, we were in the unique position of having to build our own network. After extensive advertising and background checks, we eventually recruited 53 families to foster 68 children (we kept siblings together).

Of course, many ethical issues were involved in conducting a controlled scientific study of young children, a trial in which only half the participants were initially removed from institutions. The design compared the standard intervention for abandoned children—institutional rearing—with foster care, an intervention that had never been available to these children. Ethical protections put in place included oversight by multiple Romanian- and U.S.-based institutions, implementation of "minimal risk" measures (all used routinely with young children), and noninterference with government decisions about changes in placement when children were adopted, returned to biological parents or later placed in government-sponsored foster care that at the outset did not exist.

No child was moved back from foster care to an institution at the end of the study. As soon as the early results became available, we communicated our findings to the Romanian government at a news conference.

To ensure high-quality foster care, we designed the program to incorporate regular involvement of a social work team and provided modest subsidies to families for child-related expenses. All foster parents had to be licensed, and they were paid a salary as well as a subsidy. They received training and were encouraged to make a full psychological commitment to their foster children.

Sensitive Periods

The study set about to explore the premise that early experience often exerts a particularly strong influence in shaping the immature brain. For some behaviors, neural connections form in early years in response to environmental influences during windows of time, called sensitive periods. A child who listens to spoken language or simply looks around receives aural and visual inputs that shape neural connections during specific periods of development. The results of the study supported this initial premise of a sensitive period: the difference between an early life spent in an institution compared with foster care was dramatic. At 30, 40 and 52 months, the average IQ of the institutionalized group was in the low to middle 70s, whereas it was about 10 points higher for children in foster care. Not surprisingly, IQ was about 100, the standard average, for the group that had never been institutionalized. We also discovered a sensitive period when a child was able to achieve a maximum gain in IQ: a boy or girl placed in a home before roughly two years of age had a significantly higher IQ than one put there after that age.

The findings clearly demonstrate the devastating impact on mind and brain of spending the first two years of life within the impersonal confines of an institution. The Romanian children living in institutions provide the best evidence to date that the initial two years of life constitute a sensitive period in which a child must receive intimate emotional and physical contact or else find personal development stymied.

Infants learn from experience to seek comfort, support and protection from their significant caregivers, whether those individuals are natural or foster parents—and so we decided to measure attachment. Only extreme conditions that limit opportunities for a child to form attachments can interfere with a process that is a foundation for normal social development. When we measured this variable in the institutionalized children, we found that the overwhelming majority displayed incompletely formed and aberrant relationships with their caregivers.

When the children were 42 months of age, we made another assessment and found that the children placed in foster care displayed dramatic improvements in making emotional attachments. Almost half had established secure relationships with another person, whereas only 18 percent of the institutionalized children had done so. In the community children, those never institutionalized, 65 percent were securely attached. Children placed into foster care before the end of the 24-month sensitive period were more likely to form secure attachments compared with children placed there after that threshold.

These numbers are more than just statistical disparities that separate the institutionalized and foster groups. They translate into very real experiences of both anguish and hope. Sebastian (none of the children's names in this article are real), now 12, has spent virtually his entire life in an orphanage and has seen his IQ drop 20 points to a subpar 64 since he was tested during his fifth year. A youth who may have never formed an attachment with anyone, Sebastian drinks alcohol and displays other risk-prone behaviors. During an interview with us, he became irritable and erupted with flashes of anger.

Bogdan, also 12, illustrates the difference that receiving individualized attention from an adult makes. He was abandoned at birth and lived in a maternity ward until two months of age, after which he lived in an institution for nine months. He was then recruited into the project and randomized to the foster care group, where he was placed in the family of a single mother and her adolescent daughter. Bogdan started to catch up quickly and managed to overcome mild developmental delays within months. Although he had some behavioral problems, project staff members worked with the family, and by his fifth birthday the foster mother had decided to adopt him. At age 12, Bogdan's IQ continues to score at an above-average level. He attends one of the best public schools in Bucharest and has the highest grades in his class.

Because children raised in institutions did not appear to receive much personal attention, we were interested in whether a paucity of language exposure would have any effect on them. We observed delays in language development, and if children arrived in foster care before they reached approximately 15 or 16 months, their language was normal, but the later children were placed, the further behind they fell.

We also compared the prevalence of mental health problems among any children who had ever been institutionalized with those who had not. We found that 53 percent of the children who had ever lived in an institution had received a psychiatric diagnosis by the age of four and a half, compared with 20 percent of the group who had never been institutionalized. In fact, 62 percent of the institutionalized children approaching the age of five had diagnoses, ranging from anxiety disorders—44 percent—to attention-deficit hyperactivity disorder (ADHD)—23 percent.

Foster care had a major influence on the level of anxiety and depression—reducing their incidence by half—but did not affect behavioral diagnoses (ADHD and conduct disorder). We could not detect any sensitive period for mental health. Yet relationships were important for assuring good mental health. When we explored the mechanism to explain reduced emotional disorders such as depression, we found that the more secure the attachment between a child and foster parent, the greater probability that the child's symptoms would diminish.

We also wanted to know whether first years in a foster home affected brain development differently than living in an institution. An assessment of brain activity using electroencephalography (EEG)—which records electrical signals—showed that infants living in institutions had significant reductions in one component of EEG activity and a heightened level in another (lower alpha and higher theta waves), a pattern that may reflect delayed brain maturation. When we assessed the children at the eight-year mark, we again recorded EEG scans. We could then see that the pattern of electrical activity in children placed in foster care before two years of age could not be distinguished from that of those who had never passed time in an institution. Children taken out of an orphanage after two years and those who never left showed a less mature pattern of brain activity.

The noticeable decrease in EEG activity among the institutionalized children was perplexing. To interpret this observation, we turned to data from magnetic resonance imaging, which can visualize brain structures. Here we observed that the institutionalized children showed a large reduction in the volume of both gray matter (neurons and other brain cells) and white matter (the insulating substance covering neurons' wire-like extensions).

On the whole, all the children who were institutionalized had smaller brain volumes. Placing children in foster care at any age had no effect on increasing the amount of gray matter—the foster care group showed levels of gray matter comparable to those of the institutionalized children. Yet the foster care children showed more white matter volume than the institutionalized group, which may account for the changes in EEG activity.

To further examine the biological toll of early institutionalization, we focused attention on a crucial area of the genome. Telomeres, regions at the ends of chromosomes that provide protection from the stresses of cell division, are shorter in adults who undergo extreme psychological stresses than those who escape this duress. Shorter telomeres may even be a mark of accelerated cellular aging. When we examined telomere length in the children in our study, we observed that, on the whole, those who had spent any time in an institution had shorter telomeres than those who had not.

Lessons for All

The Bucharest Early Intervention Project has demonstrated the profound effects early experience has on brain development. Foster care did not completely remedy the profound developmental abnormalities linked to institutional rearing, but it did mostly shift a child's development toward a healthier trajectory.

The identification of sensitive periods—in which recovery from deprivation occurs the earlier the child begins to experience a more favorable living environment—may be one of the most significant findings from our project. This observation has implications beyond the millions of children living in institutions, extending to additional millions of maltreated children whose care is being overseen by child-protection authorities. We caution readers, however, not to make unwarranted assumptions that two years can be rigidly defined as a sensitive period for development. Yet the evidence suggests that the earlier children are cared for by stable, emotionally invested parents, the better their chances for a more normal development trajectory.

We are continuing to follow these children into adolescence to see if there are "sleeper effects"—that is, significant behavioral or neurological differences that appear only later in youth or even adulthood. Further, we will determine whether the effects of a sensitive period we observed at younger ages will still be observed as children enter adolescence. If they are, they will reinforce a growing body of literature that speaks to the role of early life experiences in shaping development across one's life span. This insight, in turn, may exert pressure on governments throughout the world to pay more attention to the toll that early adversity and institutionalization take on the capacity of a maturing child to traverse the emotional hazards of adolescence and acquire the needed resiliency to cope with the travails of adult life.

More to Explore

Cognitive Recovery in Socially Deprived Young Children: The Bucharest Early Intervention Project. Charles A. Nelson III et al. in Science, vol. 318, pages 1937–1940; December 21, 2007.

Effects of Early Intervention and the Moderating Effects of Brain Activity on Institutionalized Children's Social Skills at Age 8. Alisa N. Almas et al. in Proceedings of the National Academy of Sciences USA, vol. 109, Supplement no. 2, pages 17, 228–17,231; October 16, 2012.

Scientific American Online

For a video that details more about the importance of early-life caregiving, visit http://ScientificAmerican.com/apr2013/orphans.

Critical Thinking

1. Why did Romania experience an "orphan problem?"
2. Is it possible that children could receive a better upbringing in a state-run institution than they could in foster care or the care of their parents? Why or why not?
3. What do you see as ethical issues in randomly placing children to be cared for either in state-run institutions or foster families?

4. Describe some of the issues experienced by children who spent their early years in a state institution.
5. What is the best strategy to use to provide care for orphans? What should we do in situations when there are not enough foster families available to care for orphans or abused/maltreated children?

Internet References

Scientific American

http://www.scientificamerican.com/article.cfm?id=orphans-how-adversity-affects-young-children

Child Rights Information Network

www.crin.org

Child Welfare Information Gateway

www.childwelfare.gov

Charles A. Nelson III is professor of pediatrics and neuroscience and professor of psychology in psychiatry at Harvard Medical School. He has an honorary doctorate from the University of Bucharest in Romania.

Nathan A. Fox is Distinguished University Professor in the Department of Human Development and Quantitative Methodology at the University of Maryland, College Park.

Charles H. Zeanah, Jr. is professor of psychiatry and clinical pediatrics at Tulane University and executive director of the university's Institute of Infant and Early Childhood Mental Health.

Article

Prepared by: Patricia Hrusa Williams, *University of Maine at Farmington*

An Epidemic of Children Dying in Hot Cars

A Tragedy that can be Prevented

DAVID DIAMOND

Learning Outcomes

After reading this article, you will be able to:

- Understand the prevalence of and factors that contribute to hot car deaths.
- Describe how processes related to the brain and memory are related to forgetting a child in a car.
- Consider factors important to consider in making the decision to hold parents criminally responsible to hurting or contributing to the death of their child.

I have been studying the brain and memory since 1980, but I was baffled when a news reporter asked me in 2004 how parents can forget that their children are in the car with them. It seemed incomprehensible that parents could leave a child in a car and then go about their daily activities, as their child dies of hyperthermia in a car that reaches scorching temperatures.

My first inclination was to assume negligent parenting. Then, I learned from a children's advocacy group that more than 100 children had died as a result of being mistakenly left in cars since the 1990s. None of those cases had evidence of prior abuse or neglect by their parents.

I then spoke with many of these parents. I heard the gut-wrenching 911 calls they made after their child was found dead. I have realized that, in the vast majority of cases, this was not the act of uncaring or negligent parents.

Since I began studying forgotten children in cars in 2004, more than 300 additional children have died or suffered brain damage as a result of being left in hot cars.

Three times as many children have died this year over last year after being left inside cars that overheat, the National Safety Council reported in early June. The first day of summer is a good time to remind ourselves about the dangers of children being left in parked cars—and also to examine what causes and what can possibly prevent these tragedies.

As a neuroscientist, I have studied this phenomenon from neurobiological and cognitive perspectives. I have interviewed parents, studied police reports, served as an expert witness in civil and criminal cases, and contributed to media segments and documentaries on the topic.

Based on my research and my expertise, I have developed a hypothesis as to how this tragedy occurs. This type of memory failure is the result of a competition between the brain's "habit memory" system and its "prospective memory" system—and the habit memory system prevails.

Prospective memory refers to the planning and execution of an action in the future, such as planning to take a child to day care. Habit memory refers to tasks that involve repetitive actions that are performed automatically, as in routinely driving from one location to another, such as from home to work.

Prospective memory is processed by two brain structures, the hippocampus, which stores all new information, and the prefrontal cortex, which is essential to making plans for the future. The hippocampus provides access to one's awareness that a child is in the car. The prefrontal cortex enables a parent to plan a route, including the plan to bring their child to the day care, rather than to drive straight to work.

The habit brain memory system is centered on the basal ganglia, which enables people to perform repetitive tasks automatically. Examples of habit memory abound in our daily lives, including tasks such as riding a bike or tying shoelaces. It also applies in regard to children unknowingly left in cars. When we repeatedly drive along a fixed route, as between home (or other typical start locations) and work, habit memory can supersede plans stored in our prospective memory.

A suppression of prospective memory caused by the dominance of the brain's habit memory system is an almost daily occurrence. It happens, for example, when we forget to interrupt a drive home to stop at the store for groceries. In this case, the habit memory system takes us directly home, suppressing our awareness (prospective memory) that we had planned to stop at the store.

The magnitude of prospective memory failures, however, is not always so benign as forgetting to buy groceries. There are documented examples of memory-related tragedies: pilot memory failures are a significant threat to flight safety, police officers forget their loaded guns in public restrooms, and service dogs have died of hyperthermia after they were forgotten in cars.

Therefore, our flawed prospective memory puts those we love at risk. This is especially true when we assume that precautions are not necessary because such tragedies happen only to negligent parents. The evidence is clear that this assumption is wrong.

Change in Routine, Stress Contribute to Lapses

Although each case is different, the cases tend to share factors in common that contribute to children being left in cars: a change in the parent's routine that leads him or her to follow an alternate, but well-traveled, route; a change in how the parent interacted with the child during the drive, such as when a child might have fallen asleep en route; and a lack of a cue, such as a sound or an object associated with the child—for example, a diaper bag in plain view.

Typically, there was a choice point during the drive where the parent could go to day care or to another a destination (usually work or home). At that choice point, the parents report having lost awareness that the child was in the car.

Parents who have forgotten their children in cars often report stressful or distracting experiences before or during the drive. Many also report sleep deprivation.

The stress and sleep deprivation factors are important, as they are known to bias brain memory systems toward habit-based activity and to impair prospective memory processing. Ultimately, all or a subset of these factors have caused parents to follow a well-traveled route, controlled by their brain habit memory system, that did not include stopping at the day care.

In theory, therefore, activation of the habit memory system suppressed their prospective memory system. This caused them to lose awareness of the presence of their child in the car.

A universal observation I have made is that each parent's brain appears to have created the false memory that he or she had brought the child to day care. This scientific anomaly explains why these parents went about their routine activities, which even included telling others that they needed to leave work on time to retrieve their child from day care. Having this "false memory" caused them to be oblivious to the fact that their child had remained in the car all day.

Many of these parents have been charged with manslaughter or even murder. I do not think that incarcerating parents for the deaths of their children in these cases is appropriate. The hijacking of prospective memory by habit memory, and the parent's loss of awareness of a child's presence in the car, is a tragic way for us to learn how the brain can malfunction when it is in "memory multitasking mode." There is no indication in the cases I have studied that these parents demonstrated an act of willful recklessness or gross negligence for the child's welfare.

Finally, how do we stop this tragedy? The first step is to accept that human memory is faulty and that loving and attentive parents can unintentionally leave their children in cars. Many strategies have been suggested, such as using a phone app linked to an occupied car seat, but most people refuse to take any precautionary measures because they believe this could never happen to them, a potentially fatal mistake.

Some progress has been made by General Motors (GMs), which has developed a child reminder system for its cars. Although I applaud GM's efforts, they have chosen to apply this lifesaving technology to only one of their models. To ensure that no more children will die in hot cars, it is urgent that legislation mandates that a child reminder system be standard equipment in all cars.

Critical Thinking

1. How are the brain and memory processes related to hot car deaths? What are common characteristics of cases in which children are left in hot cars?
2. Should parents involved in hot car injuries or deaths be held criminally responsible?
3. How can we prevent hot car deaths?

Internet References

ChildHelp: Preventing Hot Car Deaths
https://www.childhelp.org/preventing-hot-car-deaths/

Child Welfare Information Gateway
https://www.childwelfare.gov/

Kids and Cars.Org
http://www.kidsandcars.org/

No Heat Stroke.Org
http://noheatstroke.org/

David Diamond is a professor of psychology, molecular pharmacology, and physiology and the director of Neuroscience Collaborative Program and Center for Preclinical and Clinical Research on PTSD, University of South Florida.

Article

Prepared by: Patricia Hrusa Williams, *University of Maine at Farmington*

Gluten-free Baby: When Parents Ignore Science

Inside the Troubling and Dangerous Rise of Alternative Medicine for Kids.

AARON HUTCHINS

Learning Outcomes

After reading this article, you will be able to:

- List factors which influence parents' diet and health-care decisions for their children.
- Compare and contrast differences in parents' philosophies, values, and choices for their children.
- Discuss factors important to determining whether a parent is being neglectful or abusive.

The first time Daniel Bissonnette saw Goldfish crackers, Fruit Loops, and blue Jell-O, his mother recalls, he mistook them for art supplies. He was three-years-old and his preschool teacher had just served the kids snacks. Daniel began smearing the Jell-O on a piece of paper as if he were painting the ocean. The Fruit Loops were going to represent bubbles and the bright orange crackers, obviously, fish. But he was really confused when the teacher handed him a spoon. Then, Daniel looked around the room and saw the other kids eating their materials.

"He'd only seen food in its unrefined raw form," says Ilana Bissonnette from their home near Coquitlam, BC. "Then he saw that things out there in the world were very different."

That story may seem incredible, but for the first six years of his life, she says, Daniel was raised on a raw, vegan, non-GMO, unprocessed diet, which means he only ate uncooked, unprocessed foods, and no meat or products of animal origin. The diet stemmed from Ilana's experience trying to get pregnant. When she went off birth control, her menstrual cycle wasn't getting back to normal. She and her husband sought out solutions through conventional medicine, without success. Then, a year later, she switched to a vegan, mostly raw diet. She says her cycle resumed and she got pregnant with Daniel. So when it came time for him to start eating solid foods, she decided it was best to start him off on the same diet—despite objections from both doctors and relatives.

"My parents thought I was insane for going vegan, for going raw, and for breastfeeding as long as I did," Ilana says—three years for Daniel and four years for her second son, Adam. It wasn't just the extended breastfeeding. "It was pretty much exclusive breastfeeding for the first two years. My approach was to put the best nutrition in me so I could produce the best breast milk and feed it to my children."

Bissonnette didn't stop with her own sons; she created "Raising Raw Babies," a three-hour audio program for interested parents (cost: US$75), which covers topics such as conception, pregnancy, breastfeeding, and feeding children. Bissonnette acknowledges she's not a nutritionist or a doctor. "I found the experts that I knew would have the answers and I did the research," she says.

Bissonnette is among the growing number of parents discounting conventional nutrition—and in many cases, conventional medicine, too—to carve their own path in raising their children. It's difficult to know just how many parents are raising their children sugar-free, gluten-free, or on raw food or Paleolithic diets. But browse your local bookstore, or Amazon, and you'll find an abundance of literature on the subjects, from *Well Adjusted Babies: A Chiropractic Guide for Holistic Parenting from Pregnancy Through to Early Childhood*, written by

Australian chiropractor Jennifer Barham-Floreani, to *Eat Like a Dinosaur*, which offers tips and recipes to raise kids on a Paleo diet. Online there is a plethora of blogs, such as *The Raw Food Mum*, *The Vegan Momma*, *Fruit-Powered* and *The Paleo Mom*, whose author, Sarah Ballantyne, has published a book, *The Paleo Approach*, and claims the diet can help manage and even reverse autoimmune diseases like rheumatoid arthritis and psoriasis.

Ballantyne discovered the benefits of going Paleo firsthand. A Canadian expat who got her doctorate in medical biophysics at Western University in London, Ontario, but who now calls Georgia home, she was seeking help for her psoriasis and eczema five years ago, so she did what comes naturally to her: research. Ballantyne found her answer in "the caveman diet," as it is often dubbed, which gives the green light to fruits, vegetables, meats, seafood, nuts, and seeds and shuns all dairy, grains, legumes, and vegetable oils as well as refined or processed foods.

"I thought it sounded really extreme," she admits. But she gave it a shot, and not only did her skin soon clear up, her migraines disappeared and her irritable bowel syndrome was gone. She felt so good she followed through on the diet with her kids—first making the shift to cut out gluten and then transition them to the Paleo diet.

Ballantyne insists she relies only on reputable research, but many of the alt-parenting books and blogs draw from a wealth of popular yet contested work in alternative nutrition and health.

In their day-to-day lives, the Bissonnettes' primary online health resource is the website of Joseph Mercola, an antivaccine, alternative health physician who often counsels against trusting medical professionals, scientific researchers, and government agencies. While Mercola has been a guest on Dr. Oz's TV show, he was presented as "the man your doctor doesn't want you to listen to."

These are arguably boom times for people who fit that description. Alternative therapies are a growing business, while celebrities and bloggers are emerging as authorities on lifestyle and nutrition, advocating for everything from the latest dieting trends to homeopathic remedies. Now, we are witnessing the phenomenon filter down to society's most vulnerable members—children. The parenting choices of Kourtney Kardashian are broadcast to her more than 50 million Instagram followers and become fodder for tabloid news outlets, like her decision to raise her kids on a gluten-free, dairy-free diet. Meanwhile, Rainbeau Mars, a Hollywood yogi and former global ambassador for Adidas, encourages families to go vegan.

But when does out-of-the-box parenting end up going too far? A recent article on *Gizmodo*, the popular tech website, argued, "If you feed your baby the Paleo diet you should be in prison." Last summer, an Italian parliamentarian put forward the idea of jailing parents who raise their kids on a vegan diet, after a spate of high-profile cases of vegan toddlers needing emergency hospital care.

Those are extreme reactions, but dieticians agree that diets can be risky for children. "Once you start restricting food groups or large chunks of food groups, you start running into problems like vitamin and mineral deficiency," says Karen Kuperberg, a registered dietician who works with the Failure to Thrive program at the Hospital for Sick Children in Toronto. "In general, any diets for kids aren't recommended. You want kids to eat a variety of foods from all food groups."

Should parents be left to decide what diet is best for their children, even against the advice of medical professionals? Should they be allowed to impose alternative remedies on their children like chiropractic care or homeopathy? Parents only want what's best for their own children, after all. And yet parents following dubious authorities can go astray despite their best of intentions. As Bissonnette puts it, coming from another perspective: "It's not something you want to play around with. It's your kid's life."

The phenomenon of kids on fad diets is not merely the reflection of recent fashions in dieting, but may rather be the product of a number of broader cultural tendencies. For one, there is the trend toward vilifying or fetishizing components of food, be it sugar, fat, gluten, salt, or protein. Consider the gluten-free boom: despite the fact that only an estimated 1 percent of Americans lives with celiac disease, an autoimmune disorder that would require a gluten-free diet, a 2015 survey found about one of every five Americans actively choose to eat gluten-free foods. Meanwhile the spike in protein consumption is so far-reaching that General Mills created a "Cheerios Protein."

Couple all the nutritional tips and dietary hand-wringing with the influx of parenting advice—via books and blogs on topics ranging from attachment parenting to helicopter parenting to "tiger" parenting—and it's not surprising that what kids eat has become an area of serious focus in North America. A 2013 survey from an independent American advertising agency found that 52 percent of Millennial parents closely monitor their children's diet, while food-tracking apps like Kurbo allow parents and their children to monitor eating habits via a traffic light system (red: foods to avoid; yellow: eat in moderation; and green: help yourself).

Another factor in the rise of the phenomenon is a broader data illiteracy in our culture. "Stories and narratives always win out over the data," says Timothy Caulfield, a professor in law and public health at the University of Alberta and the Canada Research Chair in Health Law and Policy. "One good cover story in *People* magazine about Kourtney Kardashian is always going to win out over a whole body of evidence."

With cherry-picked scientific evidence, it's possible to find support for almost any argument, and medical professionals and scientists—no matter their qualifications—now compete on the Internet with alternative health proponents or bloggers who have little more than a personal success story. A claim on Mercola's website about certain kinds of brassieres potentially causing cancer, for example, cited leaders in the alternative medical field and a 1995 study from an anthropologist. Even though cancer researchers have found no such linkage, the theory circulated far and wide—even ending up on the popular (albeit equally controversial) lifestyle website *Goop*, curated by Oscar-winning health authority Gwyneth Paltrow.

One frequently cited source for going raw (he pops up on Bissonnette's website) is Gabriel Cousens, a holistic nutritionist who claims to have a cure for diabetes through a 21-day program where insulin is no longer needed after as little as four days. Another popular figure is Brian Clement, a nutritionist who boasted that his alternative therapy health spa in Florida has cured everything from leukemia to multiple sclerosis. (He was ordered by the Florida Department of Health to stop calling himself a medical doctor after treating leukemia-stricken Ontario First Nations girls with vitamin C injections, laser therapy, and a raw food diet.)

In a more mainstream vein, the Paleo diet has come under plenty of criticism from experts. An evidence-based review of the diet for the Dieticians of Canada led by Tanis Fenton, a dietician and epidemiologist at the University of Calgary, concluded that "several of the premises of the Paleo diet are not supported by evidence." Harvard's medical school came to the same conclusion in a 2015 article: "There is no strong scientific evidence at this time for claims that a Paleo diet helps prevent or treat many medical conditions." Yet interest shows no signs of ebbing.

For children, following a strict Paleo diet does offer some benefits: it means eating whole foods as opposed to the prepackaged kind, long relied upon by hurried parents. But it can also potentially lead to serious dietary deficiencies. "A child would have to consume five cups of cooked spinach to get the same amount of calcium as in two cups of milk," says Fenton. "A couple of cups of milk is possible in a day. I've never met a child that would eat five cups of cooked spinach a day." Fenton adds that shunning grains and legumes isn't recommended either because those foods can be rich in important vitamins, minerals, and nutrients.

It's not that restrictive diets—such as raw, vegan or Paleo—can't be followed; it's just easy to get them wrong. They're also often unnecessary for parents looking for ways to raise healthier kids.

Kuperberg, the nutritionist at Sick Kids hospital in Toronto, has seen children in her clinic with everything from cognitive delays to rickets, a softening of the bones due to lack of vitamin D or calcium. One family, she remembers, had a diet that encompassed basically fruit, nuts, seeds, and homemade almond milk—and the child came in with vitamin D deficiency, vitamin B12 deficiency, and, well, "the list was endless," Kuperberg says. Some families dutifully follow Kuperberg's advice to get their child's diet back on track. For parents who fail to provide their kids a healthy diet, under worst-case scenarios, she says, Children's Aid has had to step in.

Professionals like Kuperberg, of course, can only help the kids who end up at a hospital or clinic in the first place. Families with nutritionally starved children can easily fly under the radar. "When the kids are at home, there's no way of knowing—especially infants or toddlers who aren't even at school," Kuperberg says. In which case, parents are at risk of their own misinformation hurting the ones they love.

"It's an interesting question: when does it cross over from reasonable parenting to almost abuse?" says Caulfield. "When is that line crossed? When you're compromising the health of a child in some way, I think that's when it becomes an issue."

Caulfield thinks more science is the answer. "We need better information about what basic nutrition is," he says. "We need to have a science-literate society and a food-literate society. The best we can do is work with the best evidence available."

Consider the popular gluten-free diet. "It's a restrictive diet that's totally unnecessary," says Peter Green, director of the Celiac Disease Center at Columbia University. "A gluten-free diet is a lifesaving diet for those with celiac disease. But if you don't have celiac disease, we don't think it's a healthy diet." Green says that, for children, a gluten-free diet can often be low in both vitamins and fiber, and there is the worry of companies adding unhealthy ingredients so that gluten-free products still maintain their taste. "If parents buy a lot of products labeled as gluten-free, often when they take gluten out of the product, they add more salt," Green adds.

A commentary published last year in the *Journal of Pediatrics* likewise stated that gluten-free packaged foods often have more fat and sugar than the equivalent foods containing gluten. Other studies have found that a gluten-free diet coincided with increases in obesity, caloric intake, and new-onset insulin resistance. As for the claims that gluten is toxic or that a gluten-free diet is a good idea for infants at risk of developing celiac disease—all these were labeled as "fiction" by the commentary's author, gastroenterologist Norelle Reilly, director of the Celiac Disease Center's pediatric program.

Green is all in favor of going gluten-free if it's medically required. But therein lies another problem: parents who incorrectly self-diagnose themselves or their children. A 2013 study of people who self-reported as having nonceliac gluten sensitivity found that "gluten-specific effects were observed in only

8 percent of participants." "If children are having problems, they should be evaluated rather than [for parents to] assume that it's gluten," Green says.

But no matter how many decades of research Green has published about why gluten isn't evil, or how many talks Fenton gives on reasons to avoid going Paleo, or how many times Kuperberg recommends parents avoid any kind of diet but a balanced one, none of them can compete with the reach of the rich and famous like Kardashian or Paltrow or the market appeals of a celebrity chef like Australian Pete Evans.

Evans's Paleo cookbook, *Bubba Yum Yum: The Paleo Way for New Mums, Babies and Toddlers*, was delayed when the Public Health Association of Australia brought up major concerns—namely that his liver-based do-it-yourself baby formula recipe would have 10 times the daily maximum amount of vitamin A considered safe for babies. "There's a very real possibility that a baby may die if this book goes ahead," Heather Yeatman, president of the Public Health Association of Australia, told local media. The publisher pulled the plug on the book, but Evans opted to self-publish with minor modifications. The Dieticians Association of Australia said the reworked recipe could still seriously harm babies, though Evans did give the formula a new name: "Happy Tummy Brew."

It seems unfair to take parents to task for feeding their kids too many beets. Part of the appeal of these new diets is the damage that more conventional eating patterns can do. A gluten-free or dairy-free diet is counter to most nutritionists' recommendations, but so too is taking a child regularly to fast food restaurants or allowing them to fill up on pop or sugary treats at home, as millions of North American parents do routinely. In Canada, 13 percent of children between the ages of five and 17 are obese, according to a 2016 Senate report, nearly tripling the percentage from 1980. Another 20 percent are considered overweight, and the health consequences of the excess pounds range from Type 2 diabetes to poor emotional health.

But the failures of the mainstream are not a direct path to alternative nutrition or medicine, notes Caulfield. For alternative medicine proponents who argue some practices in conventional medicine lack scientific evidence, "that's an argument for better science," Caulfield says, as opposed to "alternative medicine saying, 'We want our turn to provide useless therapies too'."

Parents who are committed to newfangled diets do have an advantage: they are paying close attention to what their children eat; they may also be more vigilant about other health factors, like ensuring their kids get enough exercise. With good science, their dedication would be commendable. With dubious science, though, the results can be disastrous.

That's a lesson Katya Nova learned the hard way. Originally from Edmonton, Nova had plans to her raise her son Zion on a vegan diet—and she had thousands of Instagram followers giving her plenty of love throughout her journey. But trouble struck when Zion's teeth started to come in. One tooth, she recalls, had started to crumble apart by his first birthday. "It happened so fast," Nova says. "His teeth are just really weak."

She decided to introduce some animal products into Zion's diet, such as cod liver oil and grass-fed dairy. When she announced her decision on social media, she says, "My Instagram followers dropped by 2,000 in 48 hr. There were a lot of angry vegans who said, 'How dare you use your huge platform to say that a vegan diet may not be suitable to all children?' "

Nevertheless, Nova says her family has dropped the labels and won't get neurotic if their child has cake at a birthday party. "I can understand the danger of a plant-based mama who is passionate about the ethical part of veganism but does not know how to come up with a really balanced diet," she says. "That can be dangerous."

Indeed, the headlines point to the tragic consequences when overzealous ideas about "all-natural" food or medicine—for children, especially, the two are very closely tied—go way too far. In Mississauga, Ontario, in 2011, two-year-old Matinah Hosannah died of complications from asthma and severe malnutrition stemming from a vegan diet lacking in vitamin D and B12. A similar tragic outcome occurred in 2012 with 19-month-old Ezekiel Stephan of Cardston County, Alta. His parents diagnosed their toddler's meningitis as croup and treated it with natural remedies like olive leaf extract, garlic, hot peppers, and horseradish. When his condition worsened—his tiny body was too stiff to settle into a car seat—the parents consulted a naturopath (not a pediatrician) and were given an echinacea treatment. After Ezekiel arrived at the Alberta Children's Hospital in Calgary with abnormal breathing, he was quickly put on life support but died within two days. David and Collet Stephan were sentenced last summer to four months in jail and house arrest, respectively, for failing to provide the necessaries of life.

If anyone wants to see what living on natural medicine looks like, Michael Rieder suggests, they should go to Afghanistan. "Afghanistan is about as natural as you're going to get in terms of accessibility to 21st-century health care," says the clinical pharmacologist and professor of pediatrics at Western University. For every 10 children born in Afghanistan today, odds are one of them won't see their fifth birthday. "Most of them die before they turn one and most of them die from infection," Rieder says. "That's what happens when you don't have vaccination or antibiotics."

"We're slipping into this 'all knowledge is relative' dark age," says Caulfield. "You don't see this in other areas of science. We don't have alternative physics or people who believe there's a natural healing force that can be utilized to build bridges. But in health, we have this huge tolerance for this alternative, nonscientific perspective."

Imposing adult lifestyle choices on infants and children often extends beyond diet and into the realm of alternative medicine. At the Thrive Natural Family Health clinic in Toronto, Jennifer Wise tries to dispel all the preconceived notions of her job as a pediatric chiropractor, where she's treated newborns as young as a day old on their way home from the hospital. "There's a common perception that a chiropractor is going to crack your bones. It doesn't work in that kung fu style," she says. "With little ones, we're certainly not doing those gross manipulations. It's very gentle contact. Usually it's just holding the area, light touch, light force." She equates the amount of force to what someone might do to a tomato at the grocery to check its ripeness.

But other chiropractors might not be as gentle, as seen in a video posted by Australian chiropractor Ian Rossborough (and subsequently watched over a million times), who loudly cracked the back of a four-day-old as an attempt to treat her colic. The newborn immediately screamed. Amid swift online backlash, the Australian Health Practitioner Regulation Agency quickly banned Rossborough from working on the spines of anyone under six years of age or any kind of chiropractic work on children under the age of two.

Wise says patients come to her for various reasons: maybe the baby is having trouble latching during breastfeeding or consistently sleeps with the head facing one direction. "Sometimes I'll find jaw misalignments so I'll do some cranial work, and within a few adjustments babies start nursing more effectively," Wise says.

In some instances, Wise adds, the results of her work can't be seen for decades, if at all. "So you have a baby that's born in a traumatic situation and as a result maybe the top two bones in their spine are slightly twisted," she offers as an example. "As an infant or child, they don't get any chiropractic care. They end up 35-years-old in the workplace and have chronic migraines, sinus issues, and allergies."

Of course, there are no longitudinal scientific studies to back up a claim that pediatric chiropractic care prevents hypothetical migraines decades later; even short-term, double-blind, placebo-controlled studies on infants, Wise will readily admit, aren't abundant in her field. And the studies that do exist have mixed results. A clinical trial of 86 infants from 2001—one of the few studies coauthored by both pediatric researchers and a private practice chiropractor—found that chiropractic spinal manipulation therapy was no more effective in treating colic than a placebo. A 2008 study from the Anglo-European College of Chiropractic, of 43 infants younger than eight weeks old who typically cried more than three hours a day, did find two weeks of spinal manipulation and occipital-sacral decompression "appear to offer significant benefits to infants with colic." But in this study, there was no control group, which is often a requisite for researchers to eliminate potential variables or bias that can influence results.

Reliable studies can be especially hard to conduct when infants are concerned, according to Brian Gleberzon, a Toronto-based chiropractor who conducted a review of the scientific literature regarding the use of spinal manipulative therapy for pediatric health conditions. "It could just be that over time, the [baby's] teeth erupted or they just grew up a little bit," he says. "You try to control for these variables but sometimes you can't. And they're babies, so they can't really fill out a form. The only outcome is what the parent perceives in how much crying time is related to what they thought as colic."

And yet, Gleberzon still believes chiropractors should be allowed to treat for colic, though parents should know it's no sure-fire solution to their sleepless nights. "It's the same principle with your dentist or your chiropractor or psychotherapist," he says. "There's no guarantee they can help you. You pay your money and take your chances."

Others aren't so sure. "I don't think any amount of spinal manipulation cures colic," says Rieder, the Western University professor. "I think it's insane. It's a bad idea. As a pediatrician, you don't want my advice on building bridges. I stick to my domain. Chiropractors shouldn't be going into areas like colic."

Britt Marie Hermes is even more critical of alternative medicine than Rieder. That is because she has seen the issue from the other side. She has no idea how many serious diagnoses she missed in her three-year career as a naturopath, but she can think of a few. Hermes does not have an MD; after an almost lifelong interest in natural medicine, she completed the doctoral program in naturopathic medicine from Bastyr University—an accredited American university specializing in alternative medicine—which allowed her to use the "doctor" designation in a few states, including Washington, where she later worked as a naturopathic pediatrician.

But Hermes has since emerged as a fierce critic of naturopathic medicine, via her blog and as a regular contributor to *Forbes* covering medical pseudoscience; she is now pursuing a master of science in biomedicine at the University of Kiel in Germany.

Her four years at Bastyr University, Hermes says, included more of a focus on homeopathy than pharmacology. She was confident when it came to taking blood pressure and drawing blood, but when it came to managing prescriptions, for example, she had no clue. "I never learned how to prescribe insulin, which was a major problem when I saw patients with diabetes," she says. "I became friends with a pharmacist. So what I would do is step out of the room, look up the information on a physician database and then I'd call the pharmacist and run it past her to see if I calculated the dosage wrong. I depended on her a lot."

So why would any parent take their child to a pediatrician who is so unprepared? Hermes said there were two groups of patients: the first sought her out specifically because she was as a "naturopathic pediatrician" and thus they believed she would have a different philosophy toward vaccines or antibiotics compared to most pediatricians. The second group blindly trusted Hermes when she said she was trained as a medical doctor. After all, "doctor" and "pediatrician" were in her title.

One missed diagnosis that stands out was a little girl just over a year old, who Hermes had been seeing since birth as her "primary care doctor." The child started to get persistent diarrhea and rashes. "I was seeing her in the office a lot and I was getting the impression the mom was hyper-concerned about her daughter's health," Hermes remembers. "Mom seemed to be panicked all the time and I brushed it off as new-mom nerves. I spent most of my time in those visits trying to reassure mom, but not doing so much physical examination of the child because I thought she was healthy." Food allergy testing didn't resolve anything, nor did the dairy-free or gluten-free diets the young girl was asked to try. Hermes prescribed supplements like probiotics and L-glutamine to help with the girl's gut inflammation.

"I think I diagnosed her with something like tummy aches or diarrhea," Hermes explains. Turns out the girl had cancer, something Hermes found out later—indirectly, through social media; she never learned what type.

"Sadly, there are probably other cases," Hermes says. "Maybe not missing cancer, but I think about it all the time: maybe I missed childhood diabetes or maybe I missed some tumor. Maybe I missed growth or developmental problems because I was doing my best to play doctor."

When it comes to kids, Hermes now argues there should be an outright ban on naturopaths treating minors. "I think adults can make whatever decision they want regarding their health, but I don't think parents should be allowed to voluntarily take their children out of the medical system."

If gluten-free and raw-food diets have something to teach the rest of us, alternative medicine does have some lessons for doctors. One reason Hermes says she had such a good rapport with her patients is because she took the time to listen to them. A visit with each patient could last upward of 90 min, where she asked about their family life, their diet, what time they were waking up. The minutiae may not have pertained in any way to what health concern they came in with, but "it just feels good to know that someone is listening to you."

Engaging more with parents is a way to actually serve their health needs better. It's also one way to ferret out families trying out restrictive diets—or those feeding the kids fast food three times a week, often because of socioeconomic factors.

"It would be lovely if pediatricians questioned a little bit more about what the child's diet is like at home," says Kuperberg, the nutritionist. "That'd be a perfect place to start screening these families." If a doctor learned a family is instilling a gluten-free or vegan diet, for example, Kuperberg says that would be an opportunity to do some nutritional blood work to ensure the child is getting all the required vitamins and nutrients.

Back in BC, Daniel Bissonnette is now 12-years-old and appears to be a healthy, energetic, and well-spoken boy. His mother says he gets tested to make sure he isn't missing any vitamins or minerals from his diet. He has his own breakfast book, speaks at anti-GMO rallies, and has a weekly "Ask Daniel" segment on his YouTube channel, offering tips on topics like cold therapy and dieting choices. The Bissonnette family has also since relaxed from being strict raw vegans; Daniel's diet is now described as being whole foods, organic, non-GMO, unprocessed, and primarily vegan, and his mom says it's extremely important to do one's homework to make sure children stay healthy.

"It's okay if you're an adult and go on a diet. If it doesn't work, you switch," says Daniel's mom, Ilana. "But you cannot afford to make any mistakes when it comes to your children."

Critical Thinking

1. Making diet and health-care decisions for your family today involves a complex set of choices. How do you think parents make these decisions—what factors influence their choices?
2. What would you consider "out of the box parenting"? What are your concerns around using alternative therapies and diets with very young children?
3. Should parents be able to choose to use diets and alternative therapies with their children that go against the advice of medical professionals? When do their choices enter into the realm of where they should be charged with child abuse or neglect?

Internet References

Celiac Disease Center at Columbia University
https://celiacdiseasecenter.columbia.edu/

Nutrition.gov for Children
https://www.nutrition.gov/life-stages/children

Women, Infants, and Children (WIC) of the USDA
https://www.fns.usda.gov/wic/women-infants-and-children-wic

Article Prepared by: Patricia Hrusa Williams, *University of Maine at Farmington*

Family Privilege

A resilience researcher and former youth in care describes the pains of family loss and provides a roadmap for restoring the powerful benefits that result from healthy families.

John R. Seita

Learning Outcomes

After reading this article, you will be able to:

- Define family privilege.
- Compare and contrast terms: virtual parents, alloparenting, and monoparenting.
- Explain the Circle of Courage Model.

For much of my life until well into my adult years, I found the idea of families to be a mysterious, wondrous, and elusive thing. Spending my first eight years in an abusive home and then being shuttled through a long string of foster homes and other residential settings, I longed for but really did not understand what I imagined to be the magic of family. My lack of real experience in a loving family caused me to wonder about how families worked, or if most were places of pain as I had experienced.

On the rare occasions I visited with friends in their homes, this social unit was a mystery to me, and it felt foreign and out of place. When sent to live with the next in a line of social worker prescribed families, I was emotionally paralyzed. I had no idea what, if anything, they expected of me, or what I expected out of them. If my own family had failed me, why would I trust these phony replacements? Yet in spite of my ambivalence, I wanted a family and instinctively understood the importance of these bonds. I felt lost and discarded, believing that my own family had abandoned me.

The strong pull for family is almost primeval. The loss of family is profoundly sad and enduring as shown in decades of research on attachment and loss. Psychologist Rosalyn Folman (2009) recalls her own childhood growing up in an orphanage:

> The desire to be part of a family always tugged at me, even though I never consciously thought about it. It was just there, deep down in that dark place, as were all my feelings, hopes and dreams, and sometimes I could not hold it back. (p. 150)

Folman's words reflect a deep sense of pain, of loss, and of longing. Her sorrow rings true because that was once my journey as well. Now that my own wife and daughter have taught me the ropes, family is no longer foreign or fearful. But in some ways for me, and perhaps for others, family is still quite a mystery. How do families impact the well-being and development of children and young people? Moreover, if a child or adolescent lacks a stable family, is there any mechanism to compensate for this loss?

In seeking to understand family, important questions emerge. We know it is possible to articulate the tangible benefits of having a well-functioning family. Bill Buford (1955) notes that family is the essential presence—the thing that never leaves a person even if one has to leave it. An equally important quest is to explore the disadvantages of not having a well-functioning family, or any family at all.

In *Kids Who Outwit Adults* (Seita & Brendtro, 2005), the concept of *family privilege* was introduced to articulate the roles and dynamics that family plays in development of children and young people. The inspiration for family privilege was Peggy McIntosh (1990) who wrote of white privilege. Persons who have unearned advantages from either type of privilege are usually unaware of the profound assets they have gained. Few contemplate how many benefits, both hidden and seen, exist for those with solid family connections. While families have been around since the dawn of time, for most of human history they operated with backup mechanisms of intergenerational support. The phenomenon of a two-parent nuclear family—or in my case a struggling single mother—had no counterpoint in cultures where all shared in rearing the young.

Like the air we breathe, we take family for granted and do not recognize how important it is until its absence is felt.

Defining family seems straightforward enough to be easily understood by just about anyone. We presume that everyone knows what a family is and does. Yet like an onion, the more it is peeled back, the more layers are revealed, and the more potent family privilege really becomes. Like the air we breathe, we take family for granted and do not recognize how important it is until its absence is felt. This points to our obligation to cultivate family privilege, especially when no family is available.

Family Privilege

Family privilege is defined as *strengths and supports gained through primary caring relationships.* A generation ago, the typical family included two parents and a bevy of kids living under one roof. Now, every variation of blended caregiving qualifies as family. But over the long arc of human history, a real family was a multigenerational tribal community who shared responsibility for nurturing the young.

Whatever the configuration, in an increasingly fractured society, the challenge is to reclaim the spirit of family.

In our earlier resilience research (Seita, Mitchell, & Tobin, 1996), we focused on four dimensions called CCDO—Connections, Continuity, Dignity, and Opportunity. These are foundations of family privilege:

Connections underscore the need to live in relationships. Urie Bronfenbrenner distilled this to its basics, namely that every child needs at least one adult who is irrationally crazy about him or her (Bronfenbrenner, 2005).

Continuity highlights the developmental pathways that provide stability and permanence. Long-term relationships and cultural and spiritual roots give a sense of purpose and direction to life.

Dignity is grounded in the value and worth of each individual who is entitled to be treated with respect. Children deprived of *dignity* become *indignant* or descend into worthlessness.

Opportunity results as young people are able to achieve their potential, notably by meeting universal growth needs for belonging, mastery, independence, and generosity (Brendtro, Brokenleg, & Van Bockern, 2002).

The family is a child's first and principal source of these strengths and supports. However, when primary caregivers cannot deliver family privilege, others in the broader community must step forward if the child is to grow and thrive.

Virtual Family Privilege

In every culture that has ever existed, there were always some parents who were too young, immature, troubled, or clueless to properly parent their offspring. But even in supposedly primitive hunter-gatherer cultures, there was an inbuilt solution with a network of *virtual* parents in the extended family or clan. This process of sharing child rearing and backing up inadequate or overly stressed parents is called *alloparenting* (Lamb & Hewlett, 2005). Too often we are stuck with *monoparenting.*

"All kids are our kids," said Peter Benson (1997) of the Search Institute. As long as any children are at risk, then all our children reside in *at-risk communities.* Ironically, those who most need virtual family privilege from the school and community are the first to be expelled, rejected, and relegated to subsubstandard services.

Beyond the immediate family, young people live in a network of ecosystems including school, peer group, workplace, teams, youth centers, places of worship, neighborhoods, and communities. These complement family privilege when they are welcoming, safe, fair, and enriching. Young people without stability at home need support from other healthy ecosystems. Our challenge is to create caring community, organizational, and school cultures that promote virtual family privilege.

Practicing Family Privilege

How do we put family privilege into practice? The Circle of Courage model highlights four growth needs: belonging, mastery, independence, and generosity. Specific strategies are needed to build strengths in each of these areas.

Belonging: Building Trust

Belonging is the most basic biosocial need of humans. It begins with healthy parenting but can be provided by other relatives, or by adults and peers who are not biologically related. In Native American and First Nations cultures, children were reared in communities of belonging. Lakota anthropologist Ella Deloria (1998) described the core value of belonging as being related, somehow, to everyone we know. Treating others as kin forges powerful social bonds that draw all into relationships of respect.

The book *Growing Up in the Care of Strangers* (Brown & Seita, 2009) documents the gripping reflections of 11 professionals in our field who as youth were removed from their homes and placed in foster care, residential group care, or juvenile corrections. A common thread is the powerful, raw, and shameless desire to belong in a loving family. Even as adults, the confusion about family and the longing to belong remains. Social worker Claudette Braxton (2009) describes the impact of this experience of being torn from family which she and a sibling shared:

> The fact that we both grew up in placement meant that we had little personal experience with family permanence, parental role models, or unconditional love that we could include in our own philosophy of family. (p. 136)

Psychologist Rosalind Folman (2009) recalls how removal from her parents left her clueless about what a normal family provided to children:

> To this day, I have no sense of family. I cannot even imagine it. I wish that I had even vague images of my mother or father hugging or kissing me or glimpses of mundane things such as sitting at the dinner table or riding in a car with them, but I do not. The sense of family, of loving parents, is so alien to my thinking that as an adult when I walked into my neighbor's apartment and she was hugging her seven-year-old son, I asked her, "Is he sick?" When she said "No," I asked, "Is he going away on a long trip?" She said, "No." She was as puzzled by my questions as I was by her behavior. I later asked my therapist to explain it to me. He said she was hugging him because he is her son and she loves him. I sat there shocked. I said, "Parents really do that?" I just could not believe it. (p. 145)

The sense of loss of family is tangible, more real than real. Growing up without family has lifelong impact. But there are strategies to provide a sense of belonging through creating virtual family privilege. For example, schools and organizations like Big Brothers-Big Sisters enlist adults to serve as mentors for students at risk of failure. The goal is to ensure that no student is lost but has at least one advocate throughout the school year. Some schools have formed "connections committees" to reattach the most marginal students to the community bond.

Mastery: Cultivating Talent

In kinship cultures, children were reared by the village which guaranteed abundant opportunities for mastery. The young were taught to carefully observe and listen to elders and peers with more experience. Vygotsky (1978) considered the mentoring process as the foundation for competence: *the zone of proximal development* is the difference between what a person can achieve with skillful instruction versus what can be learned in isolation. In the quest for mastery, families provide modeling, practice, shared history of family lessons learned, wisdom, and pathways to competence. In short, a well-functioning family is a pathway for success.

In my own experience, I was not able to bathe in the fountain of family learning; still, many caring adults took on the role of mentor for mastery. Even though I felt inadequate, they were constantly on talent hunts to identify and nurture my untapped potentials. Mr. Wilson was an athletic instructor at my residential school who provided great encouragement. He had high expectations and constantly inspired me to strive for excellence on the basketball court. He never let me give up, no matter what the odds seemed to be. Failure was not an option.

One afternoon, we were playing one-on-one on the outdoor basketball court. As usual, the game was intense and neither Mr. Wilson nor I was giving an inch. I was playing what he called "tenacious defence" by forcing him further and further from the basket. I hounded him to the edge of the court, far beyond shooting range. In my mind's eye, I had a vision of him falling out of bounds far from the basket. But just as he was about to fulfill my fantasy and land on the grass, he turned, spun in mid-air and launched the ball toward the basket. The high, arching shot seemed to float in the air for an eternity. I stood by in astonishment as it floated through the hoop as effortlessly as a feather on the wind. "See?" he said to me with a smile on his face and a glow in his eyes, "never give up." No doubt Mr. Wilson did not view this as mastery in action, but in the end, the persistence to see a meaningful task through to its completion leads to mastery. He was teaching me a lesson for life.

Independence: Fostering Responsibility

Competence is not enough without confidence and the power to control one's destiny. Albert Bandura (1995) calls this *self-efficacy,* which is the belief in one's own ability to complete tasks and reach goals. This sense of personal power is grounded in self-control rather than the use of power to dominate others. Authentic independence is always rooted in a secure sense of belonging. In contrast, the myth of individualism ignores the interdependence of all humans. Stated succinctly by child care pioneer Henry Maier (1982), healthy development involves being both attached and free.

Young people cannot develop responsible independence through obedience models of discipline. Moral development psychologist Martin Hoffman (2001) observes that there are three types of discipline used by families: power assertion, love withdrawal, and inductive reasoning.

- *Power assertion* is part of the parental role, particularly with younger children who have not yet developed the values and capacities for self-regulation. But when force becomes the focus of discipline, it fuels powerlessness or rebellion. Such was my experience in many foster placements which were long on coercion and low on concern.
- *Love withdrawal* has no legitimate role in child rearing or teaching as it violates the principle of dignity. Feeling unloved unleashes the destructive emotion of shame, eroding the sense of self-worth. This was my story of serial rejection as my angry and defiant pain-based behavior led foster parents and so-called child care professionals to give up on me.
- *Inductive reasoning* entails using discipline problems as opportunities for learning and growth. Rather than reacting to pain-based behavior with pain-based punishment, adults treat misbehavior as a lag in learning. From the time I was removed from my mother at age eight, it took four years and 15 placements until I finally found permanency in a relationship-based residential group care center. In that setting, the more problems I presented, the more opportunities for learning ensued. The most powerful consequences were conversations with caring staff and peers who helped me see how my behavior hurt myself and others.

As I gained in self-control and responsibility, I moved from the structured residential program to a group home where I attended public school in the community. I had brief glimpses of what a real family might be on occasions when I visited in homes of fellow students, one of whom was the son of the college coach. Most of my peers from the group home and public school were college bound, and so my own progress in academics and athletics led to a college scholarship. But in spite of this success, I had spent over half of my life without family privilege. My transition to independence following a decade in foster care was treacherous. Easing into college life and its responsibilities is difficult for many young adults, but my situation was especially so because I lost my most important connections.

Without a family, I expected no phone calls from home, because there was no home. There were no requests for "care packages," for who would prepare and send them? There was no one to bail me out when I was broke, and there was no one to help me navigate the confusing and Byzantine world of academia. I had no one to cheer me on, or if needed, to kick me in the rear as I faced the challenges of college.

While the "sink or swim" approach to independence eventually worked for me, in the short term, the pain, loss of belonging, and confusion was almost unbearable. We know enough about the science of youth development to not rely on chance. Instead, all young people need supports on the challenging pathway to independence. Given the lack of a traditional family for many youth who are at risk, constructing family privilege becomes a priority.

Generosity: Finding a Purpose

While caring for others is at the core of all ethical systems, this value was largely neglected in Western approaches to education and psychology. In contrast, most indigenous cultures are more rooted in spiritual than materialistic values; children are reared to be generous and treat all others with respect. Now modern research has begun to validate the importance of generosity. Notable is the title of brain scientist Bruce Perry's book *Born for Love: Why Empathy is Essential—and Endangered* (Perry & Szalavitz, 2011). Without concern for others, human existence has little meaning; it is in helping others that we create our own proof of worthiness.

Without experiencing love for oneself, there would appear to be little reason to care for others. Yet, it is no accident that a large number of persons who themselves had painful childhoods are committing themselves to careers in service to children with similar backgrounds. In my experience, those who heal from a love-deprived life have been blessed by the unconditional acceptance of another caring human being. Such it was with me when I first encountered Mr. Leffert, a young group worker who refused to be driven away by my insolence and adult-avoidant behavior.

He stood observing from afar my solo pursuit of basketball perfection on a hot and breezeless summer day. The cement basketball court was lonely and barren, a metaphor for much of my life. I wondered why he was watching me and what he wanted. His name was Mr. Leffert but that was all I knew. So I pretended to ignore him and finished my practice. I walked away from the courts with not even a polite nod toward my spectator—it was my coping strategy to keep my distance from all adults.

A couple days later, he showed up again, this time carrying a bag of something. As usual, I focused on basketball and on being aloof. Upon finishing my workout, I once again started to walk away without acknowledging his presence. "John," he called, "do you have a minute?" "No," I replied feeling both wary and belligerent. "Here, I have something that might improve your game. They're ankle weights and chest weights. They might help you jump higher and become quicker." I cautiously inched toward him, like a hungry stray dog might toward a stranger with scraps of food but then pulled back. Suspicious as ever, I snapped, "Why would I want these and what do you want from me?" "I've seen you working hard," he replied, "and I don't want anything except for you to have a chance to be as good a basketball player as you seem to want to be. Besides," he went on, "they're not new, I got them at a garage sale, but they are barely used, and I think they'll help you."

I was suddenly speechless, and my heart was pounding. No one had ever given me much of anything. "So," I replied sarcastically, "you're giving me someone else's used junk?" I accused. He didn't look hurt. "They're yours, John, if you want them I'll just leave them here on the side of the court." He walked away, and so did I, without his weights. But I thought about them for the next few hours and retrieved them after dark. It turns out that my goals were bigger than my anger. I decided to use his weights.

I later became both all-conference and all-state in basketball. I think Mr. Leffert's weights and his generosity both played a role in my basketball success and eventually in life. His thoughtful act and selfless generosity made a deep and long-lasting impact upon me—this happened 40 years ago. It took me a while, but that single act of generosity set the tone for a profound understanding of the power of giving which drew me into the helping profession.

Beyond Understanding to Practice

Those lacking family privilege are those most in need of it. All of us have the potential to impact the lives of these young people, often in what seem to be small ways. We help them take tentative steps toward trust. We search to discover and develop their talents and strengths. We provide coaching rather than criticism on their sometimes halting journey toward responsibility. And we model generosity so that they can pay it forward and find purpose in caring for others. Family privilege might be defined as putting the Circle of Courage into action.

My own journey from neglect, abuse, and homelessness to being a husband, father, and professional is largely a case of "luck and pluck." In other words, I was lucky to find myself in a series of serendipitous developmental opportunities. Moreover, my strong-willed and stubborn nature presented both problems and pathways to success. Using terms from resilience science, I benefited from both external and internal protective factors. It is clear what children need to grow and thrive is more than "luck and pluck." As members of the human community, it is our responsibility to ensure that all young people experience the rich benefits of family privilege.

References

Bandura, A. (Ed.). (1995). *Self-efficacy in changing societies.* New York, NY: Cambridge University Press.

Benson, P. (1997). *All kids are our kids: What communities must do to raise caring and responsible children and adolescents.* San Francisco, CA: Jossey-Bass.

Braxton, C. (2009). Pay me now or pay me later. In W. Brown & J. Seita (Eds.), *Growing up in the care of strangers: The experiences, insights and recommendations of eleven former foster kids* (pp. 127–140). Tallahassee, FL: William Gladden Foundation.

Brendtro, L., Brokenleg, M., & Van Bockern, S. (2002). *Reclaiming youth at risk.* Bloomington, IN: Solution Tree.

Bronfenbrenner, U. (2005). *Making human beings human: Bioecological perspectives on human development.* Thousand Oaks, CA: Sage Publications.

Brown, W., & Seita, J. (2009). *Growing up in the care of strangers: The experiences, insights and recommendations of eleven former foster kids.* Tallahassee, FL: William Gladden Foundation.

Buford, B. (Ed.). (1955). *The family.* New York, NY: Granta Books.

Deloria, E. (1998). *Speaking of Indians.* Lincoln, NE: University of Nebraska Press.

Folman, R. (2009). It is how children live that matters, not where children live. In W. Brown & J. Seita (Eds.), *Growing up in the care of strangers: The experiences, insights and recommendations of eleven former foster kids* (pp. 141–158). Tallahassee, FL: William Gladden Foundation.

Hoffman, M. (2001). *Empathy and moral development: Implications for caring and justice.* New York, NY: Cambridge University Press.

Lamb, M., & Hewlett, B. (2005). *Hunter-gatherer childhoods: Evolutionary, developmental, and cultural perspectives.* Piscataway, NJ: Aldine Transaction.

Maier, H. (1982). To be attached and free: The challenge of child development. *Child Welfare,* 61(2), 67–76.

McIntosh, P. (1990). White privilege: Unpacking the invisible knapsack. *Independent School,* 49, 31–35.

Perry, B., & Szalavitz, M. (2011). *Born for love: Why empathy is essential—and endangered.* New York, NY: William Morrow.

Seita, J., & Brendtro, L. (2005). *Kids who outwit adults.* Bloomington, IN: Solution Tree.

Seita, J., Mitchell, M., & Tobin, C. (1996). *In whose best interest. One child's odyssey, a nation's responsibility.* Elizabethtown, PA: Continental Press.

Vygotsky, L. (1978). *Mind in society: The development of higher psychological processes.* Cambridge, MA: Harvard University Press.

Critical Thinking

1. What is family privilege? Explain what the author views as the foundations of family privilege and why they are important to children.
2. Why in our society do we engage in "monoparenting" instead of "virtual" parenting? What supports and systems do we have in place for "alloparenting"?
3. What are some ways we can practice family privilege and the Circle of Courage Model in our work with vulnerable children and families? All children and families?

Internet References

Child Welfare Information Gateway
www.childwelfare.gov/

Reclaiming Child and Youth Journal
www.reclaimingjournal.com

Search Institute
www.search-institute.org

John R. Seita is associate professor of social work at Michigan State University, East Lansing, Michigan, and the author of numerous publications on resilience with youth who are at risk. He may be contacted at john.seita@scc.msu.edu.

Article

Prepared by: Patricia Hrusa Williams, *University of Maine at Farmington*

Terrorism in the Home

Eleven myths and facts about domestic violence

VICTOR M. PARACHIN

Learning Outcomes

After reading this article, you will be able to:

- Identify the signs of domestic violence.
- Understand several causes or factors associated with the occurrence of domestic violence.
- Explain strategies which may be effective in reaching out to and assisting victims.

If anything is truly equal opportunity, it is battering. Domestic violence crosses all socioeconomic, ethnic, racial, educational, age, and religious lines.

— K. J. Wilson, *When Violence Begins At Home*

Sadly, a U.S. Department of Justice study indicates that approximately one million violent crimes are committed by former spouses, boyfriends, or girlfriends each year, with 85 percent of the victims being women. For domestic violence to be defeated, it must begin with information. Here are 11 myths and facts about domestic violence.

Myth 1: Domestic violence is only physical.

Fact: Abusive actions against another person can be verbal, emotional, sexual, and physical.

There are four basic types of domestic violence:

- Physical (shoving, slapping, punching, pushing, hitting, kicking, and restraining)
- Sexual (when one partner forces unwanted, unwelcome, uninvited sexual acts upon another)
- Psychological (verbal and emotional abuse, threats, intimidations, stalking, swearing, insulting, isolation from family and friends, forced financial dependence)
- Attacks against property and pets (breaking household objects, hitting walls, abusing or killing beloved pets)

Myth 2: Domestic violence is not common.

Fact: While precise statistics are difficult to determine, all signs indicate that domestic violence is more common than most people believe or want to believe. Here's one example: due to lack of space, shelters for battered women are able to admit only 10 to 40 percent of women who request admission. Another example is from divorced women. Though they make up less than 8 percent of the U.S. population, they account for 75 percent of all battered women and report being assaulted 14 times more often than women still living with a partner. Whatever statistics are available are believed to be low because domestic violence is often not reported.

Myth 3: Domestic violence affects only women.

Fact: Abuse can happen to anyone! It can be directed at women, men, children, the elderly. It takes place among all social classes and all ethnic groups. However, women are the most targeted victims of domestic violence. Here are some statistics:

- One in four American women report being physically assaulted and/or raped by a current or former spouse, cohabiting partner, or date at some time in their life.
- According to the FBI, a woman is beaten every 15 seconds.

- In 1996, 30 percent of all female murder victims in the United States were slain by their husbands or boyfriends.
- Around the world, at least one in every three women has been beaten, coerced into sex, or otherwise abused in her lifetime.
- While men are victims of domestic abuse, 92 percent of those subjected to violence are women.

Myth 4: Domestic violence occurs only among lower class or minority or rural communities.

Fact: Domestic violence crosses all race and class lines. Similar rates of abuse are reported in cities, suburbs, and rural areas, according to the Bureau of Justice. Abusers can be found living in mansions as well as in mobile homes. Susan Weitzman, Ph.D., is author of the book *Not to People Like Us: Hidden Abuse in Upscale Marriages.* In her book, Dr. Weitzman presents case-by-case studies of domestic violence in families with higher than average incomes and levels of education.

Myth 5: Battered women can just leave.

Fact: A combination of factors makes it very difficult for the abused to leave. These include: family and social pressure, shame, financial barriers, children, religious beliefs. Up to 50 percent of women with children fleeing domestic violence become homeless because they leave the abuser. Also, many who are abused face psychological ambivalence about leaving. One woman recalls: "My body still ached from being beaten by my husband a day earlier. But he kept pleading through the door. 'I'm sorry. I'll never do that to you again. I know I need help.' I had a 2-week-old baby. I wanted to believe him. I opened the door." Her abuse continued for two more years before she gained the courage to leave.

Myth 6: Abuse takes place because of alcohol or drugs.

Fact: Substance abuse does not cause domestic violence. However, drugs and alcohol do lower inhibitions while increasing the level of violence, often to more dangerous levels. The U.S. Department of Health and Human Services estimates that one-quarter to one-half of abusers have substance abuse issues.

Myth 7: They can just fight back or walk away.

Fact: Dealing with domestic violence is never as simple as fighting back or walking out the door. "Most domestic abusers are men who are physically stronger than the women they abuse," notes Joyce Zoldak in her book *When Danger Hits Home: Survivors of Domestic Violence.* "In the case of elder abuse, the victims' frail condition may limit their being able to defend themselves. When a child is being abused, the adult guardian is far more imposing—both physically and psychologically—than the victim."

Myth 8: The victim provoked the violence.

Fact: The abuser is completely responsible for the abuse. No one can say or do anything which warrants being beaten and battered. Abusers often try to deflect their responsibility by blaming the victim via comments such as: "You made me angry." "You made me jealous." "This would never have happened if you hadn't done that." "I didn't mean to do that, but you were out of control." Victims need to be assured that the abuse is not their fault.

Myth 9: Domestic abuse is a private matter and it's none of my business.

Fact: We all have a responsibility to care for one another. Officials at the National Domestic Violence Hotline offer this advice to people who see or suspect domestic violence: "Yes, it is your business. Maybe he's your friend, your brother-in-law, your cousin, co-worker, gym partner, or fishing buddy. You've noticed that he interrupts her, criticizes her family, yells at her, or scares her. You hope that when they're alone, it isn't worse. The way he treats her makes you uncomfortable, but you don't want to make him mad or lose his friendship. You surely don't want to see him wreck his marriage or have to call the police. What can you do? Say something. If you don't, your silence is the same as saying abuse is OK. He could hurt someone, or end up in jail. Because you care, you need to do something—before it is too late."

Myth 10: Partners need couples counseling.

Fact: It is the abuser alone who needs counseling in order to change behavior. Social Worker Susan Schechter says couples counseling is "an inappropriate intervention that further endangers the woman." Schechter explains her position: "It encourages the abuser to blame the victim by examining her 'role' in his problem. By seeing the couple together, the therapist erroneously suggests that the partner, too, is responsible for the abuser's behavior. Many women have been brutally beaten following couples counseling sessions in which they disclosed violence or coercion. The abuser alone must take responsibility for assaults and understand that family reunification is not his treatment goal: the goal is to stop the violence."

Myth 11: Abusers are evil people.

Fact: "Anyone can find himself or herself in an abusive situation, and most of us could also find ourselves tempted to be abusive to others, no matter how wrong we know it to be," notes Joyce Zoldak. Abusers are people who may be strong and stable in some areas of their lives but weak, unreasonable and out of control in other ways. This does not excuse their behavior, because abuse is always wrong. Abusers need to be held accountable for their actions and encouraged to seek help promptly by meeting with a psychologist, psychiatrist, therapist, or spiritual leader. Abusers can also receive help from The National Domestic Violence Hotline 1-800-799-7233 or via their website: http://www.thehotline.org.

With an informed community, and with the help of family and friends, the cycle of abuse can be broken.

Critical Thinking

1. What are some impediments or reasons why women do not report domestic violence?
2. What are some reasons why domestic violence occurs in couple relationships and in families?
3. Explain why it can be difficult to identify and assist victims.
4. Why do you think some of these myths about domestic violence persist?
5. Given the information in the article, what do you think may be effective strategies which can be used to reach out to and assist victims of domestic violence?

Internet References

Futures Without Violence
www.futureswithoutviolence.org

National Coalition Against Domestic Violence
www.ncadv.org

National Network to End Domestic Violence
www.nnedv.org

National Resource Center on Domestic Violence
www.nrcdv.org

Victor M. Parachin writes from Tulsa, Oklahoma.

Article

Prepared by: Patricia Hrusa Williams, *University of Maine at Farmington*

When Your Parents Are Heroin Addicts

A mother is dead and a father jailed after they overdosed at a children's hospital. Their story may seem extreme, but it isn't unique.

TRACEY HELTON

Learning Outcomes

After reading this article, you will be able to:

- Understand the prevalence, causes, and stigma of opioid addiction in the United States.
- Describe the lived experience of parenting opioid addicts and what it means to be a good parent.
- Consider the complex legal issues around prosecution for opioid addiction and the removal of children from their addicted parents.

Last week, it was hard to escape headlines that read, "Mom Dead, Dad Revived at Cincinnati Children's Hospital." The story of two young parents who traveled from Alabama for their 7-month-old daughter's reconstructive windpipe surgery was a heartrending one, one with a tragic ending.

While his child recovers from a successful surgery, Wesley Landers, 32, sits in jail. His wife, 31-year-old Mary Ann Landers, is dead from a reported heroin overdose. As a recovering heroin addict with children of my own, I wondered: How could this have happened? The facts are shocking, even to a seasoned veteran of addiction like myself: the mother found dead, the father extracted from the bathroom, a gun in his pocket, and a needle still in his arm, fatefully revived with naloxone.

The Landers' family photos on Facebook and GoFundMe reveal little of a battle with heroin.

But parents who abuse opioids lead a shadowy existence where any knowledge of their substance abuse could lead to loss of their children. Exposure of children to illegal drug activity is also addressed in 33 states' criminal statutes.

As a former heroin user, I am continually grateful my children were born long after my active addiction. In my search for parents with dependence on opioids, I was shocked when close to 20 individuals contacted me in less than 24 hr. They're addicts with children, children of addicts, "functional users," and those who recovered along the way to parenthood. All wished to remain anonymous, and names have been changed throughout.

"I've really wanted to talk about this for quite a long time," one told me. He repeatedly mentioned that he had never spoken about addiction with anyone else.

Another was a father who lost his children due to heroin use. "It's awful," he wrote. "They are my whole world. In fact, they are probably the only reason I'm still alive because I want to be in their life.

"I can relate to the [Cincinnati] story," he said. "When my daughter was born I had to stay well [by using heroin] for the two days we were in the hospital after she was born, and I was on methadone when my son was born." He said he recently "made the decision to tell my parents everything . . . [and] hopefully gain full custody for the time being until I can get my life together."

There was a common thread among the parents I talked to. A man who used the alias John Batt summed it up to me by writing, "We have a problem, that doesn't mean we love our children any less. We want the best for our children and we want them to be better than we are. We teach them right and wrong. We're just like you, imperfect."

Addict parents are not unique in their struggle. The National Institute of Health estimates that over 2.5 million Americans currently abuse opioids, and the National Survey on Drug Use and Health reported 2.2 million children live with a parent who is dependent on or abuses illicit drugs. In cases where help is requested, systems are frequently unprepared to meet the needs of family systems where substance abuse is an issue. Many families, like the Landers, fly under the radar.

Autumn Lee is a single mother raising a toddler and a 7-year-old. "I've been familiar with opiates for almost five years now, from occasional use for the first year or so to . . . now, IV heroin," she told me. "[I stopped] for about a year, and now I'm back to using anywhere from three to seven days a week."

After an incident in which Autumn's child ended up in the hospital for a spiking fever, "Her father had come for us with [drugs] for me. When we got home, I went ahead and did some. I felt lousy for doing it. Even though [my daughter] was deemed healthy, it made me feel guilty and pretty selfish that I was willingly detaching myself from the situation. Nothing bad came from my dose, and my stressful night/morning had come to an end. I'm not telling you this because the situation was caused by my using, but that I chose it to cope."

In asking what she feels makes her different from other parents, Autumn said, "along with the normal parental struggles, I need to make it possible to be well. While I probably should be spending that money on the kids, it's spent on myself—though my girls never go without, so to speak. They always come first. Just like I would go without food for them to eat, I would never place them behind my own wellness or well-being. They're happy, healthy, smart little ladies, and that will always be my primary concern—just like any other parent."

Autumn told me that she "gets up at 6:30 A.M. to get my oldest ready for school. Some of the time she will get a ride, but for the most part I walk her to (and from) school. After that we do homework, dinner, movies/entertainment, bath, and bed. I know that all sounds redundant, but that's my day."

John Batt wrote, "My wife had been in pain management for some serious issues with her back. When she started it was legitimate and abusing the prescriptions really wasn't a thought to us, but that soon changed." Things escalated for the couple over time.

"As with most pain management I assume, the prescriptions were low," he said. "However, over time the quantities and dosage increased. For about the last year, she was prescribed 360 30-mg Oxycodones along with fentanyl patches and some other medications. We thought we hit the lottery and that there was no way we would ever run out again. But as is the story, what would last us a month became three weeks, then two, and by the end we somehow managed to go through that in a week. During this time, we would supplement with heroin. Eventually, the prescriptions stopped altogether and we were solely using heroin. We've been using heroin via IV for about two years now. . . . We didn't even realize we were addicted until it was too late."

John's story echoed Autumn's: "We are like any other parents. We help our children with their homework, we play and color. We hug and dance. We teach and discipline. As addicts, we have as much love in hearts for our children as a clean parent."

The difference comes with the lack of the drug. "Once we're well again, everything goes back to normal," John wrote.

Child welfare experts would disagree. According to a report on child welfare and substance abuse, being raised by a drug-dependent parent leads to poor cognitive, delayed social and emotional development, depression, anxiety, and other mental health symptoms, physical health issues, and substance-use problems for the child.

Users argue that the stigma surrounding their use creates many of these problems. Unable to reach out for support for fear of losing their children, parents with opioid dependence are frequently pushed into isolation where they cannot access resources that are widely available for parents. "I think the stigma associated with abuse is abhorrent in general," Autumn told me. "Yes, there are some very sad cases, but a drug doesn't necessarily dictate your parenting. Just because someone has vices doesn't make them a bad person or parent—just like being clean won't guarantee a good one."

There has been much speculation as to why the young parents overdosed in the bathroom at the hospital in Cincinnati. The consensus seems to be that as users from out of state, they would have been unfamiliar with potency of the drugs available in Cincinnati. In addition, the area surrounding Cincinnati has been plagued by heroin tainted with fentanyl. Whatever the case, using in unfamiliar surroundings could have exacerbated their problems, leading to the fatal overdose. Wesley Lander remains in jail on numerous charges, and only time will tell if he will be given the opportunity to rehabilitate himself.

Cincinnati, like many of the towns the couple would have passed as they drove along route 75, has been transformed by heroin. There are now so many children in foster care, Ohio had to expand to 20 family courts peppered throughout the state. It has used the expansion of Medicaid to increase treatment services to address burgeoning demand.

For those lucky enough to get services, BL (his alias) provides some hope. "I've been, in the past, 100 percent physically dependent on IV opioids, homeless, living literally on the streets. [Now I'm] a registered nurse working in psychiatry, with a substance abuse certificate, working with mostly homeless folks with co-occurring disorders.

"Opioids are still fun to me," BL told me, "but I don't seek them out, and I don't use IV anymore. I probably do [prescription opiates] a couple times a year."

When asked how BL's history with drugs impacts his relationship with his son, he said, "I affirm and validate [my son] and his choices and actions. I explain why things are okay and not okay. And he loves me and tells me I am the greatest dad in the universe. What a triumph. This is the greatest success in my life."

Critical Thinking

1. What starts parents down the path to opioid addiction? Why do they continue on this path in spite of the challenges addiction brings to their lives?
2. Can you still be good parent and addicted, as some of the parents in the story purport? Should addicts' children always be removed from their care? Why?
3. In the past year, there have been several pictures of overdosed parents with their child in close proximity which have been published by media outlets. What do you think of this practice? Do you think it is a deterrent to addiction or only services to shame the victims?

Internet References

American Society for Addiction Medicine
https://www.asam.org/

Child Welfare Information Gateway
https://www.childwelfare.gov/

National Center on Addiction and Substance Abuse
https://www.centeronaddiction.org/

National Institute on Drug Abuse
https://www.drugabuse.gov/

Article

Prepared by: Patricia Hrusa Williams, *University of Maine at Farmington*

"We Never Talked About It": As Opioid Deaths Rise, Families of Color Stay Silent

LEAH SAMUEL

Learning Outcomes

After reading this article, you will be able to:

- Describe racial stigmas of drug addiction.
- Compare and contrast differences in coping with death by addiction in different racial and cultural groups.
- Develop ideas regarding needed services and supports for families impacted by addiction.

Detroit—When Ria Noriega's cousin Manuel died of a heroin overdose six years ago, his obituary mentioned his quick wit and his model-car collection. But it made no mention of the overdose that killed him.

"We never really talked about it," Noriega said, standing near the banks of the Detroit River at a rally against heroin earlier this month, where about 30 people were gathered on a chilly afternoon.

"It was kind of a Mexican pride thing, I guess. I mean, people already don't want us here, so being a drug addict kind of makes it worse."

There's a new honesty these days about drug abuse. In obituaries, media interviews, and letters to lawmakers, families that have lost loved ones to overdoses are naming the drugs that killed them.

As more and more people emerge from the shadows to put a face on the nation's opioid epidemic, however, faces of color are notably absent.

In part that reflects the makeup of the epidemic itself: While deaths among white Americans have soared, those among blacks and Latinos have stayed relatively steady.

But interviews here and around the country by STAT found that the invisibility of blacks, Latinos, Asians, and Native Americans in the opioid crisis also reflects a cultural divide that comes both from outside and within minority communities.

Nationally, deaths from opioids—primarily fentanyl, prescription painkillers, and heroin—continue to climb. From 8,400 opioid overdose deaths in 2000, the fatalities now surpass 33,000. White Americans made up 82 percent of those deaths in 2014; blacks and Latinos comprised just 8 and 7 percent, respectively.

But those thousands of deaths are rarely publicly discussed.

The stigma of addiction is one factor. Contending with shame and the real or imagined judgment of others is hard for any family. Addiction also brings with it the baggage of long association with criminality, unemployment, and violence—characteristics that have been stereotypically attributed to blacks, Latinos, and immigrants.

"I'm a black person," said Dr. Helena Hansen, a New York University psychiatrist and anthropologist who researches addiction and race. "And if I were to die of an opioid overdose, my mother would not say anything about my overdose death, because she is working against stereotypes of black women as addicts and sex workers."

"As Mexicans, we get called enough names," Noriega said. "And then to be called a junkie, too? No. We'd just rather take care of our own and keep it quiet."

Instead, said Devin Reaves, a social worker and drug counselor in Philadelphia, "there are code words. So [the obituary] might say, 'Johnny died suddenly in his sleep.' But if Johnny is 25 and not 70, and he didn't have a heart condition, he probably overdosed. And nobody knows he died of an overdose until we see it on Facebook."

That's if there is an obituary at all, said Albert Gilbert, an addiction counselor in Detroit.

"[Black families] don't have funerals for those people," he said. "We cremate those people. You're kicked out of the family for that behavior, and the family is often glad when [the addict dies] and it's finally over."

Hansen, who works at a public hospital, sees this often.

"Sometimes I have to go and identify the body of a client who has overdosed," she said, "because they're estranged or have lost touch with their families."

A similar silence often surrounds overdose deaths among immigrant families. Iman Numan, an Iraqi-American who owns a funeral home in the Detroit suburb of Hazel Park, lost her 26-year-old nephew Peter Alraihani to heroin in 2014.

Recalling his years-long struggle with addiction, she said, "there was always a question in his eyes, and it was there when he died."

His obituary didn't mention his drug use, nor have his immediate family spoken publicly about it.

Since then Numan, who is also a social worker, has started a support group at her church for families struggling with addiction.

"We first had a good turnout," she said. "Some people would just come and sit and listen and never talk about their own families. And then they would stop coming. For most of the families we know, there is still some denial and closed-mindedness, still some shame."

But she admits her own family members have wrestled with similar feelings. "We left Iraq for a better life. We are very loyal to this land and we feel very bad when our children fail in this society that has welcomed us."

Hansen sees the racial stigma on drug use as a vestige of the war on drugs that began in the 1970s. As heroin (and later, crack cocaine) ravaged black and Latino communities, policies designed to fight the epidemic were largely punitive, with many addicts getting jail time rather than treatment.

Now, she says, with more white deaths, that approach to addiction has gotten more scrutiny. "When the victims are coming from white, suburban and rural areas where people are better organized and feel that they deserve better, we no longer blame addicted people because it's no longer politically supportable," she said. "Instead, we're taking a harm reduction approach and expanding access to naloxone kits. And we have Good Samaritan laws to maximize the reporting of overdoses and save lives. It's the image of the epidemic that drives policies."

Numan pointed out those policies as reason for families like hers to acknowledge addiction in their community.

"They have all these ways of getting help, and we don't know about them because we don't want to accept that our kids are using," she said. "But we need to come up with a way to voice this or more of them are going to overdose."

Noriega agrees. A recovering addict herself, she said that being open and honest is more helpful than secrecy.

"I'm done being quiet about it," she said before heading off to join the march. "That doesn't keep anybody sober and it damn sure doesn't keep anybody alive."

Critical Thinking

1. Why don't many families, particularly those of color and immigrants, not talk about addiction?
2. What does the article mean by the term "racial stigma of drug use"?
3. What types of supports are needed by families who lose a member to drug addiction? How might the needs of families of color and immigrant families be different than those of other families?

Internet References

American Society for Addiction Medicine
https://www.asam.org/

National Center on Addiction and Substance Abuse
https://www.centeronaddiction.org/

National Institute on Drug Abuse
https://www.drugabuse.gov/

Article Prepared by: Patricia Hrusa Williams, *University of Maine at Farmington*

Growing Pains: Are Perfect Families a Recipe for Stress?

Vanessa Thorpe speaks to three couples about the exhaustion of being modern parents—and expert Tony Crabbe offers his suggestions.

VANESSA THORPE

Learning Outcomes

After reading this article, you will be able to:

- Identify sources of stress and challenges to work–life balance in family.
- Explore the notion of what it means to be a "perfect parent" or "perfect family."
- Discuss strategies parents and families can employ to cope with and manage stress.

It was tough finding time to write this piece, what with the children, the e-mails, the laundry, the meetings, and the phone calls. Want to know more about my struggle? No, I bet you don't. We have all listened to frenzied itineraries from parents who also hold down a job and who evidently hope to impress and inspire sympathy in equal measure. The truth is that many of Britain's families are in the same beleaguered state. More mothers and fathers than ever are tired out yet believe that's just how it is.

The findings of January's Modern Families Index show that almost a third (29 percent) of the nation's parents are complaining of burnout, not just from long hours at work but from toiling at home. Domestic chores and the logistics of children's aspirational hobbies mean more than a third (35 percent) of those asked by the charity Working Families believe they are chasing their tails in a race they do not remember entering. Annual leave is regarded as a coping mechanism, many said, and 28 percent of parents admitted faking sickness to deal with hectic lives.

So while joyful images of orthodox family life—the so-called "quality time" made up of country walks and fond joshing around the dinner table—still dominate advertising, that time is rapidly diminishing, even as it is being labelled and sold to us.

Tony Crabbe, a business psychologist who last year wrote *Busy: How to Thrive in a World of Too Much*, believes working parents in Britain now bear the brunt of an obsession with cramming the day, particularly those educated, professional parents who work longer hours. "The quality of the attention we are supposed to give is exhausting, with the jumping backwards and forwards from work and home," he argues. "And what creates a perfect storm is this pressure to be a perfect parent. There is a kind of arms race at the school gates as to how many after-school activities kids are doing."

The Index study, conducted with the care provider Bright Horizons, spoke to 1,000 British mothers and fathers across a range of ages and from varied income brackets, and it shows that almost half of working families now have both parents in full-time jobs. Men no longer have that time-honored right to come in, sit down and kick their shoes off, although according to the findings, mothers are nearly twice as likely as fathers to pick up domestic tasks as soon as they walk in the door. Flexible working, if it is possible, does not reduce stress levels either. Far from it being a panacea, an occupational health study earlier this year reported a growing danger that employees feel "on duty" all the time.

"There has never been a generation that has less time alone with its brain than ours," says Crabbe. "Yet the skills workers will need in the future are creative ones. Creativity is a muscle, and it doesn't work without some dead time in our diaries, time to let things settle and sediment."

A good test of a stressed-out family is when the suggestion of something fun and new to do simply sounds like another burden. But what has driven so many households into this ceaseless battle with the clock? Is it a fear of wasting time? Most parents believe it is the high cost of living and a wish to secure a good life for their children that urges them on. Yet if the cost is surrendering "a good life" now, is it worth it? We asked three busy families to explain how they cope—and why.

"It's about How Much We Want for Our Children"

Carrie and Matt James have Erin, 16, Patrick, 14, Catherine, 11, and Orla, 7

Carrie and Matt James live in a cul-de-sac not far from the front in Leigh-on-Sea, Essex, and have four children, Erin, Patrick, Catherine, and Orla. Their daughters have a consuming interest in Irish dance, which takes up two hours every evening, with occasional three-hour weekend workshops, and Patrick, who loves both rugby and football, plays a couple of evenings in the week, with regular matches at the weekend. On one average weekday evening their kitchen table is covered with fairy cakes to decorate for a school sale.

Carrie, 46, works across the county as an immunization nurse three days a week and also does a spot of cleaning. The extra money goes on expensive Irish dancing outfits. "There are times I look at my life and think: well, I haven't actually got time to breathe. I go into overdrive, and then feel I could go under tomorrow," she admits. Her girls go to the sought-after grammar school nearby. Some childcare comes courtesy of Matt's mother, with Carrie's mother stepping in, too.

"Patrick and the girls walk home and let themselves in, or Granny picks them up. Most nights everyone goes off in different directions. Patrick has sports. Orla has running club and gymnastics, as well as the dance practice in Raleigh, though some nights we have to drive further. If we are in traffic, I just tell myself I can only do what I can. I don't want to have a heart attack."

What keeps Carrie going, she says, is a faith that being active is good and will help her children. "Although if you speak to my mother she would say you only need to make sure you feed your children and get them to Mass. My brain is always thinking about the next thing. When it all pushes down on me I have a good cry."

Erin is tackling A-levels, Irish dance and a Duke of Edinburgh Award. "We are usually all together for a Sunday roast," she says. "We have enough time together, I think, although Dad doesn't enjoy going up to town." In the morning, Matt, 44, who works at a bank, makes a packed lunch for the girls before he leaves at 7.30 a.m., and in the evening, he comes in at 8 p.m. to change his clothes for rugby with Patrick or to drive his dancing girls to and fro. "A lot of what we do is based around how much we want for our children. There is a push for them to have better things and do better things, but we do have to pinch ourselves sometimes because of how lucky we know we are."

Tony Crabbe's Expert Opinion

When Carrie describes moments when she has "no time to breathe," she's describing a lack of control. We plan a busy day, but when real life intervenes, and there's no slack, we're in trouble. Even in a traffic jam, however, you can take a few seconds to breathe and stop your mind racing. An involving hobby, like dance, is great, but unstructured family time is also good. My wife Dulcie and I have ritualized the idea of having three cups of tea together, to talk in a freer way.

"I'm Not Sure I'd Be a Good Mother If I Didn't Work"

Katy and Simon Daniels have Luca, 4, and Scarlett, 2

At 8.30 p.m. in a three-bedroom townhouse in Greenhithe, Kent, Katy, a 34-year-old IT training officer in a financial firm, and Simon Daniels, a 44-year-old foreign exchange trader, have a little stretch of evening ahead now that their young children are asleep.

For Katy, who commutes to Canary Wharf three days a week, leaving the house with both children at 7 a.m. and returning with them just before 6 p.m., the hardest thing is an unwelcome feeling of "living from one day to the next. If one of the kids looks ill on a Tuesday I have to think: will they be worse tomorrow? I went back to work so we would have money to do nice things and then, of course, it had to be the kind of job that allowed me to afford 20 hours of childcare each week for both of them. I like working—I don't know if I would be a good mother if I didn't."

Eight months into her first maternity leave Katy remembers wondering: "Is that it? What purpose do I have now?" and realizing she wanted to talk about more than her children. "I do have that guilt factor though. If I could change one thing it would be that my husband was able to take up more of the responsibility. But because he earns more, if one of us needs the day off then it will be me."

Simon, who is ironing after putting Luca to bed, sees his own routine—getting up for work at 5.30 a.m. and returning home at 6.45 p.m.—as a natural development. "We don't talk about what we are doing it for. We don't know if we are doing parenting right, but it is always busy: dancing, swimming, football. My elder child from my previous marriage has netball on Saturday and the other one has athletics. When we need to relax we go for a walk."

Simon believes it is to do with social conditioning. "We are programmed in a particular way, and unless something is put in front of you that changes that, like being made redundant, you just do what others are doing."

Tony Crabbe's Opinion

Katy feels "ambushed" by each day, but actually this is not a bad strategy. We often feel burdened by the anticipation of the stuff that lies ahead of us, so one of the best things we can do is to decide to deal with something later. Simon is concerned about simply conforming. He could build some variety into his routine for just one week, which makes it easier to imagine changes if you need to make them later. "Dead time"—such as the walks Simon enjoys—is crucial for mental health; TV doesn't cut it, as your mind should wander.

"I Want Good Schools to Give Them the Edge"

Afua and Emmanuel Okoye have Mary, 7, and Marise, 16 months

Afua and Emmanuel Okoye both work full-time and have two young daughters. Afua is head of marketing for a health-care company with a head office in London, so sometimes she has a two-hour commute from her home in Kent. On other days, she works in a local office but leaves home at 6.45 a.m. to be at her desk early so she can set off in the afternoon in time to reach her baby's nursery before it closes at 6 p.m.

"It is a demanding job, and when you put two kids on top, it is challenging. The system doesn't reward working mums—you feel more punished. If you leave on time, they ask why you are in such a hurry." Mary goes to a breakfast club at school, which she says she loves, and she is picked up later by Afua from an after-school club. "She is awake before 7 a.m., and so it is a long day for her. And it is worse for the baby, because she has to be up by 6.30 a.m."

On Saturdays, there are ballet and swimming lessons, followed by gymnastics. "There's no time for the games I'd like to play with Mary, so I feel like I've failed anyway. I wonder if I am missing the time to talk to her and find out if things are going right and if she is happy. I worry about it all: in the morning, when my husband takes Mary to school, I constantly ring him to check has she got this or done that. I only sleep well on a Friday night when I am at home the next day."

Yet Afua values her working life and says that if Emmanuel earned twice as much, she'd still like to work, just shorter hours. "You do question what you are doing. You know you'll blink and your daughter will be 15 and you won't get that time back. But society looks down on people who don't seem busy. It is a status thing, perhaps."

For Emmanuel, 35, there is no choice in his mind. He is the head of retail for a company based in London and he leaves at 7 a.m. each weekday to drop off Mary, often returning at 8 p.m. after she is in bed.

"The only time I have to myself is on the train, when I listen to music," he says, "apart perhaps from Sunday afternoon, although that is full of homework. There are times it is very stressful, but I suppose this is what we wanted when we got married. I am doing it to give the children the best. Mary says she is bored when there is nothing to do, so it is those extra things that keep her occupied that I am working to pay for. I want to get both of them into good schools, so that they have qualifications that will give them the edge."

Tony Crabbe's Opinion

Afua recognizes things are stacked against her. She is keen to do the right thing, so not having time for games is a cause of guilt. But pausing if your child randomly asks you to do something is not as hard as we think—often they just want two minutes. I call them butterfly moments, they don't last long but they shouldn't be put off. Emmanuel wants to give his children what they need. But boredom is a gift we might forget to give them. Children need time off and they perform better if they learn how to think for themselves.

Since this final interview was conducted, Afua has changed jobs and has asked for the names of her family to be changed.

Critical Thinking

1. What does it mean to be a "perfect parent" or "perfect family"? Where do families get their ideas and models regarding the choices they make for themselves and their children?
2. How and why are the British families profiled in this piece stressed out?
3. Identify some ways the families profiled could better manage their stress. What individual decisions, programs, supports, and family policies might assist them in finding better work–life balance?

Internet References

American Psychological Association: Stress
http://www.apa.org/topics/stress/index.aspx

Families and Work Institute
http://www.familiesandwork.org/

The American Institute of Stress
https://www.stress.org/

Article Prepared by: Patricia Hrusa Williams, *University of Maine at Farmington*

Your Kid Goes to Jail, You Get the Bill

For 40 years, many parents have had to pay for their children's incarceration, but that may be changing.

ELI HAGER

Learning Outcomes

After reading this article, you will be able to:

- Identify reasons why some states require that parents are held financially responsible for their children's transgression and incarceration.
- Identify sources of stress for families with children involved in the juvenile justice system.
- Compare and contrast different strategies to keep families engaged with their children who are involved in the juvenile justice system.

In dozens of one-on-one meetings every week, a lawyer retained by the city of Philadelphia summons parents whose children have just been jailed, pulls out his calculator, and hands them more bad news: a bill for their kids' incarceration.

Even if a child is later proved innocent, the parents still must pay a nightly rate for the detention. Bills run up to $1,000 a month, and many of the parents of Philadelphia's roughly 730 detained children are so poor they can afford monthly installments of only $5.

The lawyer, Steven Kaplan—who according to his city contract is paid up to $316,000 a year in salary and bonuses, more than any city employee, including the mayor—is one agent of a deeply entrenched social policy that took root across the country in the 1970s and 1980s. The guiding principle was simple: states, counties, and cities believed that parents were shedding responsibility for their delinquent children and expecting the government to pick up the tab.

If parents shared the financial cost of incarceration, this thinking went, they would be more involved in keeping their children out of trouble.

"I mean, do we think the taxpayers should be supporting these bad kids?" Kaplan said in an interview.

Today, mothers and fathers are billed for their children's incarceration—in jails, detention centers, court-ordered treatment facilities, training schools or disciplinary camps—by 19 state juvenile justice agencies, while in at least 28 other states, individual counties can legally do the same, a survey by The Marshall Project shows.

Charging Parents for kids' Incarceration

Of the nation's 50 state-level juvenile justice systems, 19 regularly or sometimes bill parents for their children's detention. California, Pennsylvania, and several other states have highly decentralized juvenile justice systems; their state agencies do not bill parents—but most of their counties do.

Groups of law students, juvenile defense lawyers and others have begun to challenge this payment system, arguing that it is akin to taxing parents for their child's loss of liberty—and punishing them with debt. In Philadelphia, the City Council is meeting Friday to consider abolishing the practice. In California—which incarcerates more children than any other state, at a typical cost to parents of $30 a night—activists have succeeded in getting the practice banned in three counties. Two senators have introduced a bill to ban it statewide.

"Aside from all the emotional stuff—holding my son together, holding myself together—now they're going to say,

'By the way, you owe us cash for this?'" said Tamisha Walker, one of the mothers who fought, successfully, for a moratorium in California's Contra Costa County.

Because these parents are so often from poor communities, even the most aggressive efforts to bill them seldom bring in meaningful revenue. Philadelphia netted $551,261 from parents of delinquent children in fiscal 2016, a small fraction of the $81,148,521 the city spent on all delinquent placements, according to city records.

A similar pattern emerges in financial data gathered from all 50 states—significant operating budgets for collections officers and mailing out invoices but low amounts of money actually collected from the families.

Many juvenile-corrections administrators say the payment system is a way of keeping parents engaged with their children, whose food, clothing, and medical expenses they would be paying for anyway.

"It increases buy-in. It keeps the parents' skin in the game," said James Bueche, who heads Louisiana's Office of Juvenile Justice, adding that in a state with severe budget problems, his department needs all the funding it can get.

Bueche and others also said the agencies are constrained by state laws, frequently outdated, that hold parents financially responsible for their children's transgressions, ranging from truancy and curfew violations to shoplifting to murder.

"It was a very different time, when too many parents frequently wanted to essentially 'dump' their adolescent children on juvenile courts when they found them unruly, ungovernable, uncontrollable," Linda O'Neal, executive director of the Tennessee Commission on Children and Youth, said of the era decades ago when the laws were implemented.

"This was put into the statute so courts could say . . . 'OK, but you will have to pay the costs of detention,'" O'Neal said. "The experience was then parents would suddenly decide, maybe they could manage their children after all rather than pay."

Until recently, that logic had gone mostly unexamined, in part because juvenile defenders advocate for children, not parents, whose separate problems often go overlooked when a child is accused of a crime.

But family advocates have increasingly taken the position that detention payments introduce new obstacles for young people already struggling to succeed—and run counter to the juvenile justice system's century-old mission to improve children's outcomes by helping them learn from their mistakes.

"Here's a family that needs support, and what we're going to do instead is put a whole lot of economic pressure on them?" said Jessica Feierman, associate director of Juvenile Law Center, a national advocacy group based in Philadelphia. "Parents don't choose for their kids to go to jail. They just don't."

States' Practices Vary

How juvenile justice agencies go about charging mothers and fathers for their children's incarceration varies widely by state, but the basics are the same: a monthly bill, frequently in the low hundreds of dollars, that covers some but not all of the actual costs of the child's imprisonment.

Florida's brochure on its "Cost of Care" program depicts the intertwined hands of an adult and a child, with a caption reading: "A joint effort between the parents and the State improves the quality of life for our children. Together we can reduce juvenile crime."

To calculate the amounts owed, at least a dozen states make use of an existing metric: standard child-support guidelines.

Other states operate a "parental reimbursement unit" that charges the parents a flat sum. The ones that detain youths in privately operated facilities tend to charge the highest rates.

When parents fail to pay on time, the state can send collection agencies after them, tack on interest, garnish 50 percent of their wages, seize their bank accounts, intercept their tax refunds, suspend their driver's licenses, or charge them with contempt of court. Virginia, for instance, uses several of those methods to try to collect from parents, state officials and parents told the Marshall Project.

An ability-to-pay process, by which parents can provide pay stubs and documentation of their expenses to get the charges lowered, is usually offered. But it often entails navigating a maze of paperwork and rarely takes place before a judge or neutral third party. In many cases, it is no more than a correspondence or meeting between the parent and a representative of the state agency, like Kaplan.

Not all states take action to be reimbursed. Maryland seeks child support from parents only in certain circumstances, such as to defray costs from placement in a for-profit medical facility. The District does not collect any fees.

Anders Jacobson, director of the Colorado Division of Youth Corrections, which does not bill parents, said that any well-functioning juvenile justice system depends on youths returning home to a stable environment. Thrusting parents into debt, he said, undercuts their ability to keep the lights on and the refrigerator stocked. Such households already are dealing with additional costs from the juvenile's crime, parents point out, including steep rates for phone calls, gas for long-distance visits, and thousands of dollars in restitution and public-defender fees.

As significantly, parents and advocates say, the goal of incarceration is not to address problems in the family the way a child-support order can do. They argue that detention facilities should exist for the larger societal purpose of public safety and getting young offenders back on the right track, for which all taxpayers ought to be responsible.

"I pay taxes every single year—isn't that supposed to be what pays for the justice system?" said Alison Devine, the parent of a formerly delinquent child in Philadelphia.

"Little Financial Gain"

When Mariana Cuevas's son was released from a California jail, after being locked up in a juvenile hall for more than 300 days for a homicide he did not commit, the boy's public defender, Jeffrey Landau, thought his work was done. The case had been dismissed; his client was free.

But at a celebratory dinner afterward, Cuevas, a Bay Area home cleaner, pulled out a plastic bag full of bills and showed Landau that the state had tried to collect nearly $10,000 for her child's imprisonment. She had been able to pay back only about $50 a month.

"Sure, your son was stolen from you for a year," said Landau, stunned, "but here's what it cost." Animated by stories such as Cuevas's, juvenile defenders at the East Bay Community Law Center in Berkeley teamed up with students at the University of California at Berkeley School of Law to begin gathering county-level data to determine whether the payment requirement, so long ignored, was cost-effective.

It hardly was, they found. In fiscal 2014 to 2015, Alameda County, which contains Oakland, spent $250,938 collecting $419,830 from parents. An internal county report called that "little financial gain." By last March, in the wake of the group's findings, county officials had placed a moratorium on the practice. They later banned it outright, forgiving the debt of almost 3,000 families.

"From a macro level we weren't even aware this existed, but it hurt so many vulnerable people," said Richard Valle, a member of the Alameda County Board of Supervisors. "The parents deserve the credit—they came to the podium and spoke up." Valle also said there has been zero loss of services for children in juvenile hall, despite the lost revenue.

Then, in October, the Berkeley-based campaign won another moratorium in neighboring Contra Costa County, and later Cuevas's debt was frozen. Officials there are considering reparations for some of the parents who had already paid the detention fees.

In August, Judge Stephen Reinhardt of the U.S. Court of Appeals for the 9th Circuit weighed in forcefully on the side of Maria Rivera, a parent who sold her house and went bankrupt in order to pay Orange County more than $9,500 for her son's incarceration.

"Not only does such a policy unfairly conscript the poorest members of society to bear the costs of public institutions, operating 'as a regressive tax,'" Reinhardt wrote, "but it takes advantage of people when they are at their most vulnerable, essentially imposing 'a tax upon distress'."

In Philadelphia last year, juvenile defenders learned about the city's collection practices from the parents of clients. They alerted a group of law students at Temple University, who then brought the issue to the attention of aides in the office of Democratic Mayor Jim Kenney.

Heather Keafer, a spokeswoman for Philadelphia's Department of Human Services, said that the students made a "compelling argument" and that the department has asked the state of Pennsylvania for a legal review as to whether abandoning the practice would be allowable under existing state and federal regulations. "This has just been the way it works for so long that it has kind of proceeded as a matter of course," Keafer said.

Kathaleen Gillis, a spokeswoman for the state's Department of Human Services, said the matter is still under review, in part because a decision must be made not just for Philadelphia but for all counties, and practices vary widely.

Since the state's decision may take months, Philadelphia City Councilman Kenyatta Johnson called for Friday's hearing. "This whole thing reminded me of Ferguson," said Johnson, drawing a straight line between the parental-billing practices and the debate around allegedly predatory fines and fees in the larger criminal-justice system—a controversial issue in Ferguson, MO, even before the killing of an unarmed African American teen by a white officer there in 2014 brought tensions between police and the community to a head.

"What Did I Just Pay for?"

Steve Kaplan, who is 62 and has lived in Philadelphia for his entire life, calls himself the "most experienced child-support attorney in America." He began collecting from the mothers and fathers of incarcerated children in 1998, when a friend of his—then-Philadelphia mayor and future Democratic Pennsylvania governor Ed Rendell—instructed him to do so. Rendell did not respond to multiple requests for comment on the practice.

Kaplan is likely to be replaced by a collection agency when his contract expires March 31, Keafer said via e-mail Thursday. The lawyer, who currently gets bonuses of up to $160,000 based on the amounts he can collect from the parents, would not comment late Thursday.

One of those parents was Jonelle Mills, a single mother and janitor whose teenage daughter has been in and out of juvenile facilities for over two years. Mills said Kaplan billed her nearly $3,000 for those stays and now the city is garnishing her paycheck. She also said her child returned home "institutionalized" and physically aggressive.

"What did I just pay for exactly?" she said. "It clearly didn't buy any kind of rehabilitation."

To Kaplan, that was still the wrong question. For 18 years, he said in the earlier interview, parents are obligated to pay for whatever housing their children are in—even if it's a jail.

"Child support is child support is child support," he said. "It really doesn't matter if the kid lives with Mom, Dad, Aunt Betsy, or with me—Uncle Steve—in detention."

Critical Thinking

1. Should parents be held accountable for the behavior of their children? Should that accountability include financial responsibility for their incarceration?
2. Do you think being financially responsible for their child's actions and incarceration promotes parental responsibility or involvement or further victimizes a vulnerable child and their family?
3. What are the needs of families with children involved in the juvenile justice system? What strategies can be used to effectively support them and their children?

Internet References

Coalition for Juvenile Justice
http://www.juvjustice.org/

Office of Juvenile Justice and Delinquency Prevention (OJJDP)
https://www.ojjdp.gov/

The Marshall Project
https://www.themarshallproject.org

Article

Prepared by: Patricia Hrusa Williams, *University of Maine at Farmington*

Separation Anxiety: How Deportation Divides Immigrant Families

HANK KALET

Learning Outcomes

After reading this article, you will be able to:

- Understand the asylum seeking and deportation process for immigrants in the United States.
- Identify the challenges experienced by "mixed immigrant families."
- Explore the impact of immigration policies on family health and well-being.

Unauthorized immigrants live in fear that a husband or wife will be deported and then blocked from legal reentry, even if there are children living in the United States.

Clemente Pacaja is a naturalized citizen. He is married but has been forced to act as a single father, raising his teenage daughter by himself because his wife has been caught in the web of bureaucracy that is the American immigration system. It is a story that is becoming all too familiar for many immigrant families and is sure to become the norm if President-elect Donald Trump follows through on his campaign pledges.

Pacaja, who lives in Trenton with his 13-year-old daughter Keyle, works two jobs. He wakes at 5:00, gets breakfast ready for his daughter, goes to work on a cleaning crew at Quaker bridge Mall in Lawrence, stops home to prepare lunch for Keyle, and then heads to his full-time job as a cook at the Trenton Country Club.

His wife Zonia Ruiz Perez is in Quetzaltenango, Guatemala. Zonia entered the United States illegally during the late 1990s, fleeing the violence in her home country. She returned to Guatemala earlier this year as the first step toward legalizing her immigration status.

The U.S. immigration law requires the undocumented, regardless of marital status, to return to their home countries to apply for an adjustment of status and green card, but bars most from returning for at least three years—10 years if the immigrant had been in the United States for more than a year. Immigrants can appeal for a waiver of these "time bars" if they can demonstrate family hardship. The U.S. Citizenship and Immigration Services says that it received 38,274 applications for waivers during the first three quarters of the fiscal year (October 2015 to June 2016) and approved 21,590 applications. There are 27,317 applications still pending.

Zonia Perez was granted hardship status because she suffers from a seizure disorder that is aggravated by stress. Being forced to live in Guatemala, which has been designated by the U.S. State Department as one of the world's most dangerous nations, exacerbates her condition and limits access to needed medications.

Her application for legal entry into the United States was denied, however, because the American Embassy in Guatemala determined that she helped her half brother enter the United States illegally by providing money, which she denies. The money in question was sent to her stepparents in Mexico to take care of her children from an earlier marriage, she says, adding that she should be allowed to return to her family in Trenton.

Immigration advocates say that American diplomatic personnel responsible for reviewing applications like Zonia's have been overly aggressive in seeking reasons to deny green-card petitions for those seeking reentry. They say it is part of a broader focus on enforcement and deportation, noting that immigrants who attempt to regularize their status by following the rules and returning to their home country sometimes find themselves unable to return.

Johanna Calle, program coordinator for the New Jersey Alliance for Immigrant Justice, a coalition of about two-dozen organizations, says that breaking up families has been a real problem in the immigrant community and can be addressed if the federal government were to provide real options for immigrants who want to come to the United States and stay here legally. The effect of current law is to punish those who are trying to make a life for themselves, she says.

"We have a legal system that is broken," Calle says. "When folks talk about enforcement first, that really is just delaying the process, not fixing the process. There is no way to come legally—the law is very limited."

Plus, coming legally is costly. A petition for a family member costs close to $2,000, plus thousands in legal fees, Calle says. That does not take into account the wages lost because of forfeited work hours or the reality that most immigrants here without authorization will be sent to their home countries before even being interviewed by federal authorities.

That's what happened to Zonia Ruiz Perez. Pacaja says he has spent $30,000 so far and still has no resolution.

Calle says family separation and deportation are directly linked.

"Some of the folks being deported are just not threats to public safety," she says. "They are not planning terrorist attacks. The federal government is sitting and doing nothing as innocent people are being deported."

After a decade of partisan gridlock in Washington on the immigration issue, President Barack Obama signed two executive orders that created temporary protections for the so-called childhood arrivals and their families but also expanded enforcement efforts.

Deferred Action for Childhood Arrivals (DACAs) was created by a 2012 order and allowed immigrants between the ages of 16 and 30 who entered the United States before their 16th birthday to apply for work authorization and a two-year delay of potential deportation by the federal Department of Homeland Security. The 2014 order, called Deferred Action for Parents of Americans and Lawful Permanent Residents (DAPAs), would have allowed immigrants who were in the United States continuously since January 1, 2010, and are the parent of a child who is a citizen or "lawful permanent resident" to petition to avoid deportation and potentially be granted legal work status for three years.

The 2014 program was never enacted, because a federal court in Texas ruled it an unconstitutional overreach by the executive branch.

Trump ran on a hard-line immigration platform, promising to reverse Obama's immigration orders and immediately deport criminal aliens. He estimates that 3 million of the 11 million undocumented immigrants in the United States would be deported under his plans, though immigration authorities have placed the number of undocumented immigrants who have criminal histories at well under a million.

According to an analysis by the Migration Policy and Urban institutes in Washington, DC, about 53,000 unauthorized immigrants in New Jersey were eligible under the original DACA program. Another 12,000 would have been eligible under the expanded DACA called for in the 2014 executive order, and 133,000 would have been eligible for DAPA. There are about 498,000 undocumented immigrants in the state, which is the fourth highest total in the nation.

The New Jersey Alliance for Immigrant Justice signed onto a friend-of-the-court brief in March asking the U.S. Supreme Court to lift the injunction and let DAPA stand. The brief says DAPA will allow families to "be more secure, without the looming threat that loved ones will be deported at a moment's notice" and give immigrants "access to better jobs and the ability to improve their lives, the lives of their families, and their communities."

DAPA and DACA are important, Calle says, but limited solutions. They will help in the short term, but something more broad-based needs to be done for immigrants—including eliminating the time bars.

"We have all of these policies in place that make it difficult for people to adjust their status," she says. "If you are not married to a U.S. citizen or are not related in a direct way, there is no way to adjust your status."

The time bar, she says, "limits it more" and ultimately is "holding people hostage in the country without getting legal status." Immigrants know that they will not be able to return to the United States if they return to their native countries, so they stay here and remain in the shadows, she says.

DAPA and DACA are supposed to help address this—and they will help some—but they "are not permanent." Immigrants' status will remain "up in the air."

"It is a temporary (thing) that allows them to get a license, to work, but it is not permanent status," she says.

The current system damages mixed immigrant families because it leaves some members—usually a parent—vulnerable to deportation. Spouses and children who either have legal status or citizenship, are then left behind.

Clemente Pacaja serves as both parents, though his daughter Keyle acts as "the woman of the house," her father says. She does the cleaning and tends to her mother's vegetable garden in their small backyard. She is finishing seventh grade at Grace Middle School and will move to Trenton High School West in the fall. She talks to her mother daily on the phone and via Skype, but "it's not the same."

During these conversations they discuss the same things they would if Zonia were in the United States—"how's your day, how's your grades, what are you doing all day"—but the phone calls cannot bridge the distance, Keyle says.

"She wanted to see me graduate seventh grade but she won't be there," Keyle says. "It's stuff like that. I really want her to be there in those moments."

"I've been depressed lately," she says. "I really miss my mom."

Jeannette Kouame misses her husband—and her two American children miss their father. Her husband, Njuessan, was deported to the Ivory Coast about nine years ago, after he had been in the United States for some 14 years.

The Kouames were married in 1990 in the Ivory Coast. Njuessan immigrated to Newark in 1993. Jeannette followed about five years later. They had two children—a daughter in 2000 and a boy in 2006, both of whom are U.S citizens—and had hoped to stay and become permanent residents, possibly citizens. Kouame attempted to regularize his status and filed for asylum, which was denied in 2000. A deportation order was issued and he was detained in 2006. He was deported a year later.

"We came here because there was no future for me and my children in the Ivory Coast," Jeannette says. "I wanted my children to have a better future, a better life than I had as a child."

The Ivory Coast has been mired in political conflict, including a civil war and ethnic strife, for more than two decades. Nearly half its population lives in poverty and about a million people are considered to be internally displaced persons or refugees.

"Most of the time when I was there, there was strikes," Jeannette says. "When there are strikes they burn and riot—it depends on the parties. There is violence in the street."

Her husband worked numerous jobs when he was in the United States, the last of which, as a bus driver, provided health benefits. She was able to go to school and they could provide for their children.

Since his detention and eventual deportation, however, money has become an issue, she says, as is the extra effort that she is forced to put in as a single mother.

"It was easier with two incomes," Jeannette notes. "When he left, I had to do everything on my own. I had to get them to school, pick them up, feed them, go to work."

She cannot apply for public assistance because she does not have her own green card—though she has been allowed to remain in the country on a "cancelation of removal" for humanitarian reasons.

Kouame, who still lives in Newark, says her daughter suffers from depression brought on by her husband's absence. She locks herself in her room and sometimes struggles in school because she has trouble focusing.

"She used to be active, but now she is always in her bedroom," Kouame says. "Other children, they go through the same struggle. It is not fair for the children."

Kadi Cisse who lives in East Orange, says she and her sisters were forced to grow up quickly when her mother was sent back to the Ivory Coast 14 years ago. Her parents had come to New Jersey in the late 1980s, had three children, and worked hard to make a life for the family. Her mother worked at Newark Liberty International Airport until her visa expired and she was detained and eventually deported.

That made her father a single parent, though he was unable to be around very much because he worked double shifts to earn enough to support his family and send money to his wife. The girls spent a lot of time alone, though friends of the family would check in and bring them food.

"As a kid I wasn't able to do a lot of things," Kadi says. "We couldn't have new clothes. When mom was here we had new clothes every season. After she left, my sisters couldn't go to the prom. Every summer I worked, even when I was 11, even to make $25 a week, so I could save money for clothes."

Their hardships, however, were relatively minor when compared with what her mom had to endure in the Ivory Coast. Her mother had been in the United States for more than a decade, so she had little connection to the country where she was being returned.

"She faced a lot of hardships," Kadi says. "The war was going on when she was there. My sisters and I would send her money. She didn't have a place to stay. It was a rural area, and she couldn't go out."

In the end, her mother was able to come back to the United States—but Kadi calls it a bittersweet victory.

"My dad and my sisters, we always dreamed of being able to reconnect. We kept faith for 15 years. It was one of my dad's greatest dreams," she says. But he was diagnosed with congestive heart failure and died just a few months before his wife returned.

"I know that when they come up with these laws and stuff it is always America's best interests that they say are at heart, but there are so many American citizens with immigrant parents. They have to take the children into consideration."

Kouame agreed.

"Because of the children, they should allow them to say," she says. "It's not fair to have them separated. They need both a father and mother to bring them up. They need to leave the family united."

Critical Thinking

1. Immigration is a controversial topic in the United States as in other countries. Why?
2. Why don't some asylum seekers who face deportation just move their families back to their home country?
3. What does it mean to be a "mixed immigrant family"? What are the challenges these families experience? What policies might be put in place to help families stay together?

Internet References

Migration Policy Institute

http://www.migrationpolicy.org/

Urban Institute" Program on Immigrants and Immigration

http://www.urban.org/policy-centers/cross-center-initiatives/program-immigrants-and-immigration

U.S. Immigration and Customs Enforcement

https://www.ice.gov/

Article

Prepared by: Patricia Hrusa Williams, *University of Maine at Farmington*

Myths about Military Families

JENNIFER WOODWORTH

Learning Outcomes

After reading this article, you will be able to:

- Identify common myths about military families.
- Understand the special support needs and resources available to military personnel and their families.

Many stereotypes about the military and their families exist. Each person's experience is unique and cannot be put into any one category stereotypes about military families are presented in movies, books, reality television shows, and biases of civilians; however, military families struggle with many of the same things civilian families do. Presented here are some myths about military families and the facts that dispute them.

MYTH: Military families don't pay taxes and receive a lot of benefits.

FACT: Many military families receive tax breaks due to their low annual income (depending on state of residence and family size), and they might qualify for food stamps or Women Infant Children vouchers based on family size and income. Over 35 percent of families reported that they have difficulty making ends meet, at least occasionally (2014 Military Spouse Employment Report), however, for the majority of military families income covers their needs. Yes, many companies and organizations offer discounts for active duty or veterans of the military and there are perks to being a military family (Blue Star Families offers free entrance to some museums around the country from Memorial Day through Labor Day for active duty military and their families.)

MYTH: Military spouses do not have career aspirations.

FACT: Even though moving often can create challenges to completing a degree or certification, transferring credits and online learning have been an asset to military spouses. According to the 2014 Military Spouse Employment Report, 38 percent of military spouses have earned a Bachelor's degree, 21 percent a Master's degree, 8 percent a professional degree, and almost 3 percent, a Doctoral degree. Officer's spouses do tend to have higher percentage of degrees than active duty spouses. The 2014 Demographics Report of the Military reports that 65 percent of spouses work in a civilian job, are part of the Armed Forces themselves, or are seeking employment.

Also, the cost of childcare might deter spouses from seeking employment, especially if the family consists of more than one child that has not reached school age.

MYTH: All military spouses are women.

FACT: Approximately 93 percent of the armed forces are male, 7 percent female. According to the 2014 Demographics Report of the Military half of those 7 percent are married to another active duty military member.

MYTH: Children from military families are misbehaved or "brats."

FACT: Children from military families have many of the same issues as their civilian family counterparts (mental health, physical health, moving due to jobs, family issues, etc.). Adjustment to change can be difficult for many children (a move, time away from a parent, addition of a sibling), and usually time is all that is needed to adjust. Support from the community, school, and family are the most effective tools for adjustment to new situations.

MYTH: Base housing is free.

FACT: Most base housing is paid for by a housing allowance from the military. The amount is determined by rank, marital status, dependents, and location.

MYTH: Military members marry and have families at a young age.

FACT: According to 2014 Demographics Report of the Military, 42 percent of military families include children. Granted 49 percent of the active duty component are under the age of 25 which does make the chances of having a young family higher than their civilian counterparts, especially when 55 percent of the active duty military were married or are currently married.

MYTH: Shopping at the commissary or exchange on base is cheaper than shopping "out in town."

FACT: This is not necessarily true. Shopping sales and couponing can save families money whether they shop on base or out in town. Often prices at commissaries fluctuate based on military paydays; however the exchanges on base now offer price matches with "in town" prices.

MYTH: Military families get free health care.

FACT: Payments are taken from the military member's paycheck to cover the medical bill. Depending on the plan chosen, there can be additional copays and catastrophic caps that need to be met. Also, there are often long waits to see specialists or other professionals that take TriCare insurance. Sometimes, there are limited resources where the family is located or there might be long travel times to see specialists.

Also, reserve families only receive TriCare health benefits if the reservist is activated for more than 30 days, otherwise they have to pay for health insurance out of pocket.

MYTH: All military families move every two to three years.

FACT: Each family's experience is unique and moving depends on a variety of factors including how much time is left on contract, main job/responsibility, where personnel are needed, and the family's needs (a family typically will not be moved to a location that does not have the services needed for a family member with special needs). The 2014 Military Spouse Employment Report found that in the previous five years 79 percent of families had made at least one Permanent Change of Station move, which left 21 percent being stationed at the same base for the past five years.

MYTH: Families like deployments because it means extra money.

FACT: While there may be a financial benefit to multiple deployments (various types of pay for being in a danger zone and extra pay for time away from family), stress on the family at home increases with the spouse taking on all of the duties that he/she might have shared. Couples are at increased risk for relationship issues as the months of cumulative deployment increase. The deployed service member misses birthdays, anniversaries, holidays, births, and milestones of their own children every time they are away. Do military families like deployments? Some do and some don't but they all come with costs and benefits. Deployments are part of the current military environment and cannot be avoided, therefore "bracing for impact" and finding resources during the deployment are helpful strategies.

MYTH: "You should have known what you were getting into."

FACT: As mentioned before, each family has their own military experience, so what exactly were you supposed to know about military life before marrying into the lifestyle? Military life rarely meets up with expectations because it is so rapidly changing.

MYTH: Military members are only away during deployments.

FACT: Inconsistent schedules, long hours, being "on duty" 24/7, and training at other bases are all examples of how families are separated from loved ones. These separations could last for days or months at a time and usually do not include extra pay or time off.

MYTH: Active duty military members leave the military without a skill set or education.

FACT: According to the 2014 Demographics Report of the Military, 20 percent of the active duty military force have a bachelor's degree or higher. Characteristics of flexible thinking, quick decision-making, ability to prioritize information, organize tasks, take directions from superiors, and lead junior personnel, make military members coveted by employers.

MYTH: "You went to war, you must have PTSD." or "you can't have PTSD, you didn't go to war."

FACT: According to the National Center on PTSD "about 7 or 8 of every 100 people (or 7–8 percent of the population) will have PTSD at some point in their lives." This compares to about 11 to 20 of every 100 veterans of Operations Iraqi Freedom and Enduring Freedom in a given year. Some military members or veterans meet criteria for other mental health issues, including depression, anxiety, and substance use disorders, which may have resulted from their experience in the military. Examples of traumatic experiences include an overseas frontline deployment, witnessing a tragic accident during training, or a sexual assault.

References

2014 Demographics Report of the Military: http://download.militaryonesource.mil/12038/MOS/Reports/2014-Demographics-Report.pdf

2014 Military Spouse Employment Report: Vets.syr.edu.

Critical Thinking

1. What did you know about military families prior to reading this article? What myths were dispelled for you? What new questions do you have about military families and their experiences?
2. Given what you have read in this article, identify three support needs of military families.
3. After visiting the websites listed below describe two to three programs or supports developed to meet the needs of military families in the United States.

Internet References

Military Families Learning Network
https://militaryfamilies.extension.org/

Military OneSource
http://www.militaryonesource.mil/

National Military Family Association
http://www.militaryfamily.org

Jennifer Woodworth is a licensed clinical psychologist in private practice in Vista, CA. She has worked in the mental health field for seven years. Her husband is retired from the Marine Corps and she has three children ages 6, 8, and 10.

Article

Prepared by: Patricia Hrusa Williams, *University of Maine at Farmington*

A Whole-family Approach to Workforce Engagement

KERRY DESJARDINS

Learning Outcomes

After reading this article, you will be able to:

- Explain the tenets or components of a whole-family, two-generation approach to human services.
- Describe strengths and weakness of existing safety-net programs for low-income families such as Temporary Assistance for Needy Families (TANF) and noncustodial parent child support requirements.
- Discuss how existing safety-net programs for low-income families could be modified, so they are whole-family approaches to promoting the self-sufficiency and well-being of low-income families.

Human service programs and social policies frequently focus only on adults or only on children. This is true of many programs and policies explicitly aimed at families. A two-generation approach to human services is one that focuses on the needs of parents and the needs of children together, out of recognition that children do better when their parents are healthy and stable, and that parents do better when their children are healthy and stable.

While the terms two-generation or multigeneration approach are commonly used, APHSA's Center for Employment and Economic Well-Being prefers the whole-family label to accurately describe the most productive approach to human services and workforce engagement; this term is more inclusive and considers the extended family context, including challenges and resources of family members outside of the assistance unit, including nonresident or noncustodial parents (NCPs), adult siblings, extended family members, and kin. The whole-family approach recognizes the importance of the roles these individuals often play in supporting family stability and well-being.

Many of the safety-net programs for low-income families include work requirements, in some instances, or opportunities for family members to voluntarily engage in various programs aimed at increasing their employment and earnings. These work-oriented efforts are critical components to moving them to a path of self-sufficiency, well-being, social integration, and greater opportunity. However, being a working caregiver presents a number of challenges, and the nature and circumstances of the work can have significant impacts, positive or negative, on a child's well-being and future. Studies show that stress and dissatisfaction at work negatively impact relationships and parenting style. At the same time, stress and concerns at home can negatively impact work performance. Both need to be addressed by attaching families to necessary work supports, including transportation, childcare, and ongoing job counseling and case management.

The Argument for a Whole-family Approach to Workforce Engagement

A whole-family approach to workforce engagement not only reviews the parent or caregivers needs, but also considers the needs, challenges, and resources of family members outside of the traditional assistance unit. NCPs, adult siblings, and other working age family members besides parents often contribute to household income. In fact, most low-income families, including single-parent families, do have more than one potential wage earner. Addressing the employment needs of the entire family is important because low-income families often need more than one wage earner to secure an adequate household income.

By utilizing a whole-family approach to workforce engagement, we can encourage and support the gainful employment of all potential wage earners in a family, which increases the likelihood that they will successfully increase their income and self-sufficiency.

Unfortunately, many current policies and practices fail to consider and address the whole family. Workforce programs are typically funded based on individual eligibility and individual outcomes and are not rewarded for their work with families. Therefore, there is little incentive for programs to address the employment needs of the entire family, or the impact of a participant's employment on their household. For example, the Temporary Assistance for Needy Families (TANF) program places strong emphasis on work activities that count toward work participation rates rather than those which lead to meaningful outcomes that strengthen each unique family. As a result, parents may feel pressure to accept jobs or work assignments even when the working conditions create instability or another situation where they cannot adequately meet their children's physical or psychosocial needs for healthy development. In order to preserve and promote healthy families, while simultaneously ending needy parents' dependence on public assistance to support their children, the TANF program must have the flexibility to meet the varying needs of individual families, by conducting individual assessments of their unique barriers to sustainable, gainful employment opportunities, and strengthening their capacity to balance work and family responsibilities.

Engaging NCPs—A Key Element of the Whole-family Approach

While a whole-family approach can have many dimensions, one of its key elements is engaging absent NCPs both economically and socially, where possible, in their children's lives. When child support policies and practices lack a whole-family approach, the resources and needs of NCPs can be overlooked. Noncustodial parental employment has significant implications for low-income families with children. On average, child support payments from the absent parent represent 40 percent of additional income for poor families. New family-first payment rules provide this income to those who have established paternity, have a child support order in place, and receive collections, usually through the Title IV-D child support program. Child support payments represent one of the largest wage supplements for low-income working families and a critical add-on to families receiving cash assistance.

Unfortunately, many NCPs, including a disproportionate share of those whose children are living in poverty, have low incomes themselves. They are often unable to pay child support orders that constitute a large percentage of their already limited income. Efforts to enforce child support without offering low-income NCPs supports and incentives can drive them underground or to informal work arrangements and job-hopping when wage-withholding orders cause their disposable income to fall below their living expenses.

Some states and localities have established programs for NCPs (most often fathers) to improve their parenting skills, increase their earnings and employment, and encourage them to pay child support. More than half of states have work programs with active child support agency involvement that serve NCPs; however, these programs tend to be local. Maryland is a notable exception. Maryland's statewide NCP Employment Program, funded using TANF dollars, links NCPs who cannot afford to pay child support to job training, educational opportunities, and work experiences. Between 2007 and 2014, the program enrolled more than 17,500 NCPs in job training and job readiness programs to help them find and retain employment. Collectively, those parents made $97 million in child support payments, much of which was disbursed to former recipients of TANF cash assistance.

Another state that is proving to be a leader in engaging low-income NCPs is Texas. Texas' NCP Choices program targets low-income unemployed or underemployed NCPs who are behind on their child support payments and whose children are current or former recipients of public assistance. The NCP Choices program is not statewide, but is operated by 17 of the state's Workforce Development Boards. Like Maryland, Texas' NCP Choices program is funded with TANF dollars. The results of the program have been outstanding; 71 percent of participating parents entered employment, and 77 percent of participating parents retained employment for at least six months. Between 2005 and 2015, program participants paid more than $202 million in child support.

Direct-service programs for NCPs can be an effective method of engagement, but New York has proven that policy changes can be as well. For years, New York has offered an Earned Income Tax Credit to NCPs who stay current on their child support payments. The NCP New York State Earned Income Tax Credit is just one of a number of state initiatives to address the needs of low-income NCPs in an effort to help them be more involved in the economic and social well-being of their children. It has proven to be one of the nation's most effective tools for increasing labor force participation of low-skilled workers and an efficient means of supplementing the income of low-wage workers.

Conclusion

Employment is one of the surest and most long-lasting means for working-age individuals and their families to achieve self-sufficiency and economic well-being. Human service agencies, along with their workforce development partners, the economic development community, the education and training system, and other stakeholders, play a critical role in supporting our customers' success in the workforce. The implementation of the Workforce Innovation and Opportunity Act and impending reauthorizations, such as the Carl D. Perkins Career and Technical Education Act and the TANF program, hold the potential to enable workforce programs to better serve the employment needs of the entire family. In the meantime, implementing a whole-family approach to workforce engagement requires deliberate collaboration and creativity in utilizing multiple funding sources. Human service agencies must lead their partners in utilizing a whole-family approach to workforce engagement efforts in order, most effectively, to support the success of low-income working families, and to empower them to achieve self-sufficiency, economic mobility, and broader family well-being. Learn more about a whole-family approach to workforce engagement by visiting APHSA's Center for Employment and Economic Well-Being website.[1]

Note

1. http://www.aphsa.org/content/APHSA/en/pathways/center-for-workforceengagement.html.

Critical Thinking

1. What are the problems with existing safety-net programs for low-income families? What are obstacles which impede their effectiveness?
2. What does it mean to use a whole-family, two-generation approach to human services?
3. How can we make existing safety-net programs such as work requirements and child support enforcement efforts more effective in promoting both family self-sufficiency and family well-being?

Internet References

Center for the Study of Social Policy
http://www.cssp.org/

Office of Family Assistance of the Administration for Children and Families
https://www.acf.hhs.gov/ofa

Stanford Center on Poverty and Inequality
http://inequality.stanford.edu/

Kerry Desjardins is a policy associate with APHSA's Center for Employment and Economic Well-Being.

Article Prepared by: Patricia Hrusa Williams, *University of Maine at Farmington*

Working Hard, Hardly Working

Our obsession with putting in long hours on the job doesn't mean we're actually getting much done.

CHRIS SORENSEN

Learning Outcomes

After reading this article, you will be able to:

- Identify trends in modern workplaces, including factors associated with our workaholic tendencies.
- Discuss threats to workplace productivity and work–family balance.
- Consider the pros and policies of programs and policies instituted to restore work–life and work–family balance.

Canadians see themselves as a hardworking bunch. We spend long hours at the office, eat at our desks, and guzzle as many Tim Hortons "double-doubles" as needed to get through a workday that, thanks to smartphones, no longer really begins or ends. Even when it comes time to take a hard-earned vacation, we're reluctant to go idle: a TD study last year discovered that less than half of Canadian workers use all their paid days off, while a more recent study by human resources consulting firm Randstad found that 40 percent of Canadians didn't mind working while on holidays.

It would be an impressive and industrious, if slightly dull, approach to life were it not for one nagging detail: we don't get much done. Canada's productivity—the total amount of economic output divided by the total amount of hours worked–lags most other developed countries, according to figures from the Organisation for Economic Co-operation and Development (OECD). That includes those nations we enjoy making fun of for their famously carefree approach—namely France.

And yet, when faced with a persistent productivity gap, Canadian politicians have mostly ignored the issue or implied, as Prime Minister Stephen Harper did in a preelection campaign ad, that the country's myriad woes can be solved by staying at the office long after the sun goes down. But study after study has shown that, after a certain point (around 50 hr a week), there's little benefit to spending more time at work, and it may in fact be counterproductive, a reality recognized nearly a century ago by Henry Ford when he slashed his employees' workweek to 40 hr in a bid to build more Model Ts.

So why do we persist in trying to work longer hours to less effect? Researchers call the trend "perceived productivity" and blame it on everything from the nature of work in a modern economy to the increasingly precarious nature of jobs themselves. The current obsession with technology companies like Apple, Google, and Facebook also plays a role, helping to popularize the idea that work and play can comfortably coexist in a 24-7 office equipped with Ping-Pong tables, nap rooms, and free gourmet meals.

But the downsides are potentially huge, ranging from bleary-eyed workers who make frequent mistakes, to a persistent pay gap for women in the workplace. Breaking out of the cycle isn't easy, or straightforward. But Canada, for one, may ultimately find it has little choice. The economy, having slipped into recession earlier this year, remains precarious. Getting back on track means figuring out ways to squeeze more actual work out of each hour, which, in addition to the usual calls for more corporate investment in labor-saving technology and equipment, may ironically mean devoting fewer hours to your job.

Like most hungry entrepreneurs, Katie Fang didn't realize that her grinding work schedule was holding her back. The recent graduate of the University of British Columbia's Sauder School of Business spent a year-and-a-half struggling to get SchooLinks, an online platform to connect students with foreign schools and recruiters, off the ground. Fang found herself working six or seven days a week and pulling frequent all-nighters–anything to improve the Austin, TX-based company's chances of making money. A low point came during a recent 2 A.M. taco run with her six-member team of sleep-deprived coders. "I backed my car into a pole," Fang says.

The warning signs had been there all along, of course. Fang, 24, and her colleagues had been nodding off at work while their coffee consumption spiked. More importantly, she noticed her employees were getting less work done. "I saw that we were burning out, including myself," she says. "Our productivity had dropped. You can see where things are slowing down because [in software development] everything can be tracked."

Fang's realization shouldn't have come as a surprise. There's plenty of research demonstrating the limits of human endurance when it comes to work. British economist John Hicks reasoned back in the 1930s that longer hours would negatively impact productivity as employees become tired and lose focus. Stanford University economics professor John Pencavel retested the theory in a paper last year that looked at data originally collected on munitions factory workers in England during the First World War. Now, as then, the conclusion was the same: workers' productivity begins to decline after 49 hr a week, and that working more than 70 hr a week is essentially a waste of time.

Other studies have found that the most productive employees frequently work less than eight hours a day, taking frequent breaks, and that the best musicians practice less than their peers and take extended rest periods. "There's strong evidence that disengagement, breaking away, can help recharge people cognitively," says University of Toronto sociology professor Scott Schieman. Schieman is studying the relationship between work, health, and stress among Canadians. "This is anecdotal, but if I've gone on vacation and I come back, the ideas flow and things really move along. By contrast, if I'm sitting at my desk trying to squeeze out the last bit of idea, it just doesn't work."

The notion that the most productive employees aren't necessarily the ones who work all the time helps explain France's surprisingly efficient workforce, which, despite enjoying an average of 30 vacation days a year, still manages to produce about $63 (U.S.) worth of national GDP per capita, per hour, well above the OECD average. Canadian workers, by contrast, devote among the least number of hours per week in the OECD to leisure activities, but only manage to produce about $51 worth of GDP per hour worked. Even Italy fares better. . . .

It's not just a Canadian problem. Employees in the notoriously workaholic U.S., where there's no mandated paid vacation, sick days, or maternity leave, are also seeing their famous productivity slip, threatening to hold back the country's economic recovery. While Americans work some of the longest hours in the developed world, productivity is up by just 1.3 percent over the past eight years, less than half the rate of the past half-century. What the numbers don't capture is just how miserable some American workers have become, with eight out of 10 saying they feel stressed about some aspect of their job, according to a 2014 poll by Nielsen. No wonder critics jumped on Republican U.S. presidential hopeful Jeb Bush when he suggested Americans "need to work longer hours" to power the country's economic recovery.

The potential human cost of overwork recently made headlines when *the New York Times* wrote about Amazon's "bruising" workplace culture. The newspaper suggested the online retailer was on the vanguard of figuring out new ways to drive its 154,000 employees harder and longer, leaving many of them sobbing in the conference rooms of its Seattle headquarters. Among the complaints: e-mails that arrive past midnight with the expectation of a prompt response, internal systems that can be used to rat out employees who aren't pulling their weight, and an annual culling of staff that was described as "purposeful Darwinism." While CEO Jeff Bezos said the "soulless, dystopian workplace" described by the Times didn't sound like the Amazon he knows, it's hardly the first time the company has been singled out for its workplace practices. Amazon fought and won a U.S. Supreme Court case over its policy not to pay employees for time spent waiting in security screening lines (to make sure they haven't stolen anything from Amazon's warehouses) following their shifts. During a heat wave in Pennsylvania several years ago, Amazon hired ambulances to be stationed outside its warehouses to whisk away workers who succumbed to heat exhaustion instead of simply sending them home, according to a local newspaper.

How we got into this mess is anything but clear. Some blame the lingering impact of the Great Recession, which prompted employers across North America to cut to the bone and made employees everywhere fear for their jobs. "When there's economic downturns, and job security decreases, people want to be seen as the ideal worker," Schieman says. "Anything that signals to employers that you're not fully on board could maybe get you into trouble when times are tight." At the same time, technological advances like e-mail-equipped BlackBerrys and iPhones have provided both hard-driving employers and eager-to-please employees with the necessary tools to realize something approximating a perpetual workday.

But if tough economic times exacerbated North America's culture of overwork, they did not create it. The underlying issue, experts say, is the slow march toward a "knowledge economy," where designers and consultants replace laborers and factory workers. Put another way: while it was relatively straightforward for British officials to see the relationship between employee hours worked and the number of bombs that rolled off the assembly line, it's not nearly as easy to measure how many positive vibes a director of public relations produces for a big insurance firm. The same goes, to varying degrees, for architects, software engineers, and financiers. And so, at many companies, "work hours get used as a proxy measure for productivity," says Youngjoo Cha, an assistant professor of sociology at Indiana University, who has studied the overwork phenomenon. "But research suggests that time is not a good predictor of how productive workers are. A lot of people spend a lot of hours at work but aren't necessarily working a lot of hours."

This will come as no surprise to anyone who has worked in a modern office. Most employees begin the day by responding to a flood of e-mails before heading off to a series of meetings that must be prepared for and followed up on later. Next, it's lunch, more meetings and a few unannounced visits from coworkers who stop by to chat. "You walk into the front door and it's like a Cuisinart," Jason Fried, a cofounder of Basecamp, which makes web-based workplace collaboration tools, said during a 2010 TED talk that's received nearly four million online views. "Your day is just shredded to bits." The constant stream of interruptions makes it difficult to accomplish relatively simple tasks—never mind employing the sort of unbroken concentration needed to solve complex problems. Some liken the experience to having one's sleep constantly interrupted before they reach the all-important REM stage, leaving them feeling fatigued and frazzled with little to show for their efforts.

E-mail, in particular, is a source of frustration. While normally seen as an efficient communication tool, Schieman says in reality many managers' e-mails are loaded with layered sets of demands, unclear expectations, and passive-aggressive tone. That, in turn, forces workers to waste time deciphering them and crafting suitable responses—even late at night. Says Schieman, "I've had instances where people send e-mail at 10:45 P.M. and if I don't respond until the next morning, sometimes I get a little bit of flak for it."

And yet, despite the mounting evidence that the office is a poor place to get actual work done, racking up long hours under fluorescent lights has emerged as a badge of honor in North American business culture. A recent study by Erin Reid, an assistant professor at Boston University's business school, found that one large U.S. consulting firm rewarded employees who worked 80-hr weeks and travelled at the drop of a hat with higher salaries and promotions, whereas employees who asked for more manageable, part-time schedules were marginalized. While that might sound reasonable on the face of it—employees who work more, deserve more—the same study also showed that workers who merely pretended to be among the firm's "superheroes" received the professional and compensation benefits despite putting in far fewer hours. A Seinfeld episode comes to mind: the one where George leaves his car parked at the New York Yankees' head office overnight, creating the impression he's the first in and last to leave, and is put in line for a promotion.

Cha calls the phenomenon "perceived productivity," or the notion that "so-and-so must be fantastic because he's working all the time, and is always on call." Her research found that people who fall into that category by working more than 50 hr a week are paid up to seven percent more than people who don't, with the gap even wider among professionals and managers. She argues it's a major reason why women continue to be disadvantaged in the workplace when it comes to pay and promotions, despite having closed the gap in other areas likes education. "If you think about who workers are, these people who can actually work all the time, as if they have no other life"—or can at least pretend like that's the case—"they're male workers in a traditional family arrangement with a stay-at-home wife who can take care of the children and other family members."

Nor does it help that many of America's corporate heroes—mostly male and mainly in tech—are proud workaholics. The late Apple cofounder Steve Jobs would call people at all hours, take business meetings at home and, by all accounts, worked right up until the day he died of complications from cancer in 2011. His successor, Tim Cook, isn't much better. He reportedly begins sending e-mails at 4:30 A.M. and held staff meetings on Sunday nights to get a jump on the workweek. Similarly, billionaire Dallas Mavericks owner Mark Cuban has boasted about how he didn't take a vacation for seven years while starting his first software company.

Back in Austin, Fang says she, too, got caught up in Silicon Valley's mantra of "all work, no play." But after recognizing that her startup was suffering, she limited her staff to a four-day workweek. The results were unexpected, but shouldn't have been surprising. "So far, I would say the results have been great," she says. "I've seen a boost in productivity." An added bonus: Many of her young team members are using the extra day off to read about programming or work on side projects, which inevitably helps build skills and, indirectly, benefits the company.

Other firms are making changes, too. Another small tech company in Portland, Treehouse, has also adopted a four-day week for productivity reasons, while consulting giant KPMG made 32-hr weeks a regular option for employees after first introducing the idea as a cost-cutting measure. Even Goldman Sachs, the Wall Street investment bank, recently told its summer interns not to come into the office between midnight and 7 A.M., after a 22-year-old analyst was found dead in the parking lot outside his San Francisco apartment building. He had committed suicide after complaining about the bank's long hours and pressure-cooker culture.

However, the trend is not to be confused with one that's seen employers granting all manner of perks in the name of "work–life balance." Google's headquarters, for example, has nap pods and free gourmet meals. Facebook's new campus boasts a barbershop. In Canada, Chubb Insurance Co. touts an in-house yoga studio, while FlightCentre held a global employee event in Macau that featured singers William and Jessie J. Experts caution that such freebies risk exacerbating the overwork problem by giving employees more reasons to stay at the office. In fact, Cha says it's often the companies touted as being the most progressive in this area, including the ones that ostensibly offer "flexible" work-from-home schedules that have the most overworked employees. "The overwork culture is so prevalent it actually hinders workers from taking advantage of the work–life balance policies available to them," Cha says. "That's the most depressing thing about this overwork problem. It's so built into people's psyche that it's hard to take it apart."

Meanwhile, at the other end of the spectrum, is Amazon. The Times said the company was one of several leading the charge toward a data-driven workplace designed to systematically suck every last bit of output from employees. And while it might be tempting to assume the hard-driving attitude has yielded unassailable results—Amazon just surpassed Wal-Mart as the world's biggest retailer—it should be noted Amazon has earned only meagre profits despite 20 years of business. It also has one of the highest employee turnover rates in the tech sector.

Attitudes won't change overnight. Even Fang admits she's unable to honor her own less-is-more policy. "I honestly still work 24-7," she says. "I can't really commit to it because it's my company and I need to ensure everything's being managed." She has, however, blocked off Sundays to catch up on laundry and grocery shopping. On Sunday evenings, meanwhile, she explores the company's new home in Austin (SchooLinks recently relocated from Los Angeles to take advantage of a start-up accelerator program) along with her small staff. "It's still also kind of working, I guess, doing team-building," she says. "But I like my team—they're also my friends—so it's okay."

Critical Thinking

1. How does working more actually undermine our productivity?
2. What are some potential human costs of overwork? Why do we still do it?
3. What types of programs and policies are some companies instituting in order to help employees restore work–life balance? Is what they're doing enough? What else might be needed to change corporate to make it more family-friendly?

Internet References

Families and Work Institute
http://www.familiesandwork.org/

Mental Health America: Work Life Balance
http://www.mentalhealthamerica.net/work-life-balance

Organisation for Economic Cooperation and Development: Employment
http://www.oecd.org/employment/

Article Prepared by: Patricia Hrusa Williams, *University of Maine at Farmington*

In Whose Best Interests? A Case Study of a Family Affected by Dementia

RACHAEL WEBB AND KAREN HARRISON DENING

Learning Outcomes

After reading this article, you will be able to:

- Describe the prevalence of and challenges for relatives and caregivers of those diagnosed with dementia.
- Understand the role that medical ethics, laws, policies, and family dynamics play in making decisions for patients with dementia.
- Discuss what it means for families to make decisions in the best interest of the patient with dementia.

People aged 60 years and over make up the most rapidly expanding segment of the international population. Their number is expected to treble from 605 million to 2 billion by 2050 (World Health Organization, 2012).

It is estimated that, worldwide, over 135 million people will have some form of dementia by 2050 (Alzheimer's Disease International, 2013), with increasing age being the strongest risk factor for developing the condition (O'Connor, 2010). An estimated 835,000 people are living with dementia in the United Kingdom, which is expected to rise to over two million by 2050 (Alzheimer's Society, 2014). In the United Kingdom, it has been estimated that as many as 25 million people (42 percent of the UK's population) will know a close friend or family member affected by dementia (Luengo-Fernandez et al., 2010).

Family Carers

An estimated 670,000 family members and friends are the primary carers of someone with dementia (Newbronner et al., 2013). Carer distress is all too common in people caring for someone with dementia, whether they are living with the person with dementia or trying to maintain their independence when they are living alone (Harrison Dening and Hibberd, 2016).

Much is known about the needs of carers of people with dementia; research into the issues spans many decades (Newbronner et al., 2013). We know that education for the carer on the illness, symptoms, communication, managing behavioral concerns, finances, legal issues, and planning can all help to reduce some of the anxieties around caring (Yuhas et al., 2006; National Institute for Health and Care Excellence and Social Care Institute for Excellence, 2006; Brodaty and Donkin, 2009; Harrison Dening and Hibberd, 2016).

While carer research, arguably, has not moved the evidence base of knowledge significantly on from previous seminal work, there is now enquiry into how approaches in broader mental health and technology interventions may support this group of people. For example, Ho et al. (2016) investigated if carers' biomarkers had any influence on building resilience and reducing psychological distress using a mindfulness-based stress reduction (MBSR) training course of eight weeks' duration. The study sample was small—20 carers underwent the course and the results were inconclusive—but Ho et al. assert that MBSR may provide a basis for developing a personalized approach to supporting carers.

The use of assistive technology to support family carers is also a growing research field. Rialle et al. (2008) surveyed 270 family carers regarding 14 innovative technologies to aid care and alleviate the burden; the research was carried out because of the severe physical and psychological stress induced by dementia care and the slow uptake in use of these technologies. Results indicated two almost equal and opposing views between those who found them useful and those with very adverse views of their utility.

The elements of the caring role that generate the most distress and the greatest sense of burden are around making the

Case Study Part 1. The Dilemma

Phillip has cared for his father, George, for approximately five years. George was diagnosed with Alzheimer's disease nine years ago and has lived alone since the death of his wife Emily 10 years ago.

George's needs have increased over time and he now receives a social care package of three visits a day to assist with his personal care and meal preparation. However, he often attempted to wash and dress himself for the carers coming and often attempted to prepare his own meals as he felt this was helping them.

Recently, Phillip has begun to express concerns to the community mental health team (CMHT) about whether his father was safe living alone. The CMHT reviewed George's mental state and found his mental state and level of functioning had deteriorated since the last assessment, due to his Alzheimer's disease.

An occupational therapist assessed his care package and activities of daily living skills and the psychiatrist undertook a capacity assessment, which found George to lack capacity in relation to decision-making. However, overall it was felt there were no risks that precluded him from continuing to live alone in his own home.

Phillip continued to contact the CMHT expressing his concerns, stating that he felt his father was not coping. The team felt that Phillip was experiencing considerable carer-related stress so referred him to the Admiral nurse service.

Phillip is an only child and has a demanding job. Some days, he visits his father before and after work; his line manager has expressed some concern that his level of functioning within his job has recently been affected. He has a wife and two teenage children.

During assessment by the Admiral nurse, Phillip said his main concern was that his father was telephoning him frequently at all times of the day and night with small worries or problems, such as losing the remote control for the TV and asking what the time was and when he was coming to see him. Phillip felt the CMHT were not listening to his concerns regarding his father living at home alone.

When Phillip's mother Emily was dying, she made Phillip promise her that he would look after his father and not send him into a care home; they were both worried about his memory at that time.

Although Emily and George had not formalized their "pact" to each other in a lasting power of attorney, Emily felt it would be in George's best interests to live in his own home. Phillip had made a promise to her that he would look after his father.

day-to-day decisions that caring for a person with dementia involves (Harrison Dening et al., 2012). It is essential to offer support and guidance on the many day-to-day decisions and issues that arise, as these can involve ethical dilemmas for families (Carers Trust, 2012).

Ethical Issues Around Care

An ethical dilemma is a problem without a satisfactory resolution in that neither choice will be a "right" or "wrong" decision (Fant, 2012).

Ethical dilemmas often occur when caring for a person with dementia; some can be overcome by a family carer and/or a professional carer without much thought or distress. However, sometimes such ethical dilemmas can cause significant distress, causing family carers to neglect their own needs when faced with the overriding desire or compulsion to meet the needs of the person with dementia for whom they care. This may result in a family carer struggling to balance their own needs, those of other family members, and the needs of the person with dementia they care for. This can often have a reverberating impact on a carer's psychological as well as physical health or, perhaps worse, begin to negatively affect relationships between family members.

This paper presents a case study approach to consider best interests decision-making for families affected by dementia.

Family Decision-making

There is a wealth of literature on family involvement in decision-making in health care.

Family carers of people with dementia often experience increasing demands around making decisions as the illness progresses. Hansen et al. (2004) stated that patterns of decision-making differ according to a carer's experiences, education, and social and cultural background. Not surprisingly, carers often find decision-making difficult, and studies have reported on practical issues, including difficulties in deciding what to do about day-to-day care and distress in making health-related decisions (Vig et al., 2007) and having insufficient information about possible alternatives and their effects (Mezey et al., 2000; Hirschman et al., 2006).

In the case study, Phillip was finding it increasingly difficult to make decisions in respect of his father's care. He was seeking help in the dilemma that was facing him, trying to support his father to remain living at home according to his mother's expressed wish while fearing that this was unsafe. Family carers can struggle to support autonomy for the person with dementia and enable their wishes to be met, especially when in direct conflict with their own.

Autonomy and Dementia

Autonomy is an important concept in relation to the philosophy of the self and with regard to decision-making. A dictionary definition of autonomy is the ability of the person to make his or her own decisions (Oxford University Press, 2011), which includes in a medical context. German philosopher Immanuel Kant argued that autonomy is demonstrated by one who is able to decide on a course of action (Kant, 2008).

However, as the disease progresses, people with dementia may not be able to decide on the best course of action and be autonomous. Respect for a person's personal autonomy is considered one of many fundamental ethical principles in dementia care, and supporting autonomy wherever possible is the central premise of the concept of consent when considering care required in the future (Beauchamp and Childress, 2013). The four principles of medical ethics, devised by Beauchamp and Childress, are considered the standard theoretical framework from which to consider ethical situations in health care:

- **Autonomy:** The right for an individual to make his or her own choice.
- **Beneficence:** The principle of acting with the best interest of the other in mind.
- **Nonmaleficence:** The principle that "above all, do no harm," as stated in the Hippocratic oath.
- **Justice:** A concept that emphasizes fairness and equality among individuals.

Dementia confounds this perspective on autonomy because, as dementia progresses, the ability to consider future thoughts and actions becomes compromised, thus affecting decision-making abilities (Fratiglioni and Qiu, 2013); however, balancing this against the other principles enables a more considered view of an individual within the wider context of their social world.

Family carers often feel bound to support care for the person with dementia that is in conflict with their own needs (Wendler and Rid, 2011) and to honor their expressed wishes, such as not to place them in a care home. When reflecting on the ethical framework espoused by Beauchamp and Childress (2013), the perception of "justice" can seem weighted in favor of the individual with dementia at times when, in reality, each person with dementia is embedded within relationships and social systems where each individual has needs that may at times be in conflict. Carers such as Phillip may find themselves increasingly in a position whereby providing such support can harm their own psychological or physical health and perhaps even damaging their relationships with those around them.

In Whose Best Interests?

Mental Capacity

In the United Kingdom, the Mental Capacity Act 2005 (MCA; HM Government, 2005) protects and supports people who do not have the ability to make decisions. At its core is a set of principles that recognize the rights of people with impaired decision-making capacity caused by mental illness, learning disability, head injury, dementia, or other conditions.

The act introduced a radical change to the legal concept of capacity from one that regarded decision-making capacity as all or nothing to one that recognizes that capacity is decision specific, relating to the time when a decision or action needs to be taken.

The principles of the MCA encompass the right of a person (including someone with dementia) to exercise their autonomy as far as possible and requires others to support them to do so. The general legal and ethical rule is that people without capacity are treated in their "best interests." Part of what makes up their best interests are their own wishes and preferences as well as what is clinically viewed as the most appropriate action. Where individuals lack capacity, a fundamental consideration is their past wishes and preferences.

In George's case, he and his wife had discussed their wish to support each other at home and not to allow admission to a care home. Phillip had agreed to this too when his mother had asked him to "take over" her promise to George, even though their "pact" had been a verbal one and no lasting power of attorney had been registered (Office of Public Guardianship, 2016).

Phillip was clearly struggling to balance his own needs with the needs of his family and the needs of his father. This was having an impact on both his physical and mental health. Phillip had to face the difficult decision of whether to place his father into full-time care as trying to maintain George to continue to live in his own home was failing.

As discussed, such decisions are not easy or straightforward, and for Phillip, there were a number of conflicting factors; George's needs and demands were having a distressing effect on the wider family and placing Phillip in a difficult and dichotomous position over whose needs he should prioritize as there was conflict in meeting all.

A study by Lord et al. (2015) found that relatives of people with dementia report proxy decision-making to be difficult and distressing. Phillip felt distress and a huge sense of responsibility to make the right decision. But what was the right decision? The issues around decision-making for people with dementia can become more complex because capacity is progressively lost as the illness advances. Phillip felt guilty over even giving thought to his own needs or those of his wife and children. It is in circumstances such as this that many family carers feel they have failed the person for whom they care and feel they should have been able to cope better (Bramble et al., 2009).

The Admiral nurse could see that the conflict of making decisions and the issue of in whose best interests was becoming very difficult and distressing for Phillip and that he would require specific guidance to ensure that he balanced his own needs and those of his family when considering those of his father.

Balancing the Needs of the Carer

The work of the Admiral nurse is centered on the whole family—the person with dementia and their family carers. A major component of support provided is in empowering decision-making to enable the family to navigate the various transition points along the journey of dementia, such as seeking a diagnosis, access to support services, admission to a care home, and end of life care options. Often, as in Phillip's case, it is important to support the carer to ensure their own needs and wishes are balanced with those of the person they care for.

Older people often trust loved ones to make decisions on their behalf (High, 1994) and want those decisions to be in keeping with their wishes and preferences (Roberto, 1999; Whitlatch et al., 2009). However, they also wish to keep the burden of such decisions upon their family to a minimum (Rosenfeld et al., 2000). Supporting families in successful decision-making, such as on a move into residential care, is multifaceted and may involve giving careful consideration to the balance between the perspectives and wishes of the person with dementia and those of the carer.

Case Study Part 2: Exploring Concerns

Over several sessions with Phillip, the Admiral nurse explored a number of concerns.

Phillip was under a lot of pressure at work, had always enjoyed his job but was now finding it hard at times. He had always take[n] pride in his work but recently had started to make small mistakes.

His children and his wife had expressed that they felt he spent too much time with George and that he should "put him in a home." Although the family had said this as an off-the-cuff remark, it had made Phillip feel very guilty and [unsupported] by the rest of the family, which added to his feelings of a general lack of understanding and support by services.

Phillip was experiencing a lot of the common signs of carer stress—low mood, tiredness, anxiety, and a lack of concentration. He was expressing feelings of guilt in that he was not a good enough son to his father, husband to his wife, or father to his children.

Case Study Part 3: Resolution

Initially, Phillip struggled to understand how the various stressors in all areas of his life were affecting his emotions, decision-making, and thought processes as well as his wider family members.

He agreed that to continue with the current situation would be difficult. George was receiving the maximum level of community care at home, but this still had not reduced the number of telephone calls or his increasing reliance and demands on Phillip.

The Admiral nurse supported and enabled Phillip to see that he had been hoping other people would make the decision for his father to be placed in residential care.

He felt an overwhelming sense of pressure to make the right decision since the death of his mother and being the sole next of kin for his father. He felt a huge sense of guilt at even thinking about putting George into a home given his promise to his mother.

The Admiral nurse explored Phillip's understanding of why his parents had made their pact. It transpired that several years ago they had watched a TV documentary about underperforming care homes and perceived all homes to be of a similar, poor quality.

The Admiral nurse supported Phillip to consider his father's overall values and beliefs and what else might be important to him.

George was a very family-orientated person and would always put his family first. In reflection with Phillip about his situation and what George's thoughts would have been if he had the capacity to express them, Phillip acknowledged that his father would have told Phillip to put himself and his family first.

Similarly, the Admiral nurse helped Phillip to explore the meaning behind George's frequent calls. He felt that George may not have remembered having calling previously and he might be lonely and seeking company.

Phillip was able to consider all aspects of the current situation. This included considering George's values and beliefs, and how his own needs and those of his family were to be balanced with those of his father; this enabled him to come to a decision to place George in residential care.

He understood that there are times when one must make decisions that are balanced and, wherever possible, consider the "best interests" of all affected.

This did not eliminate Phillip's sense of guilt on making the decision, but it no longer felt powerfully overwhelming.

A core competency domain for Admiral nursing is in supporting carers to balance the needs of the person with dementia with their own needs, ensuring that equity remains in the caring partnership wherever possible (Bunn et al., 2015). In practice, it can be challenging to support this balance of interests and needs when caring for a person with dementia.

Admiral nurses strive to make the wishes and preferences of the person with dementia influence the care delivered. When these become at odds with what is in the best interests of the carer, this demands skillful attendance of the nurse involved.

Conclusion

Family carers need much more support in tackling the ethical problems they face. As this case shows, Admiral nurses play a vital role in supporting family carers to do this. As the Admiral nurse developed a good therapeutic relationship and took time to understand Phillip's needs and wishes fully, she explored the presenting problem and conflicting factors, and was able to support Phillip in his decision to place George in a care home, not with an overwhelming sense of guilt but in facing the decision through a best interests approach.

As this case shows, Admiral nurses are able to support family carers through the difficult process of trying to balance their own needs against those of the person with dementia. This case was very complex, and the Admiral nurse was able to support Phillip to recognize and, most importantly, place making a difficult ethical decision into the wider family context.

In a nurse–patient relationship, the nurse is often believed to hold the power but, as Kubsch (1996) argued, this power can be used to positively influence others because of the very knowledge and skills the nurse possesses. As Manojlovich (2010) stated, intuitive professionals closest to carers and people with dementia can enable and empower care for the ultimate good of all concerned.

In this case, the Admiral nurse, while appreciating the best course of action and outcome for all involved, guided, enabled, and empowered Phillip to make a decision that was appropriate for the whole family unit.

Key Points

- Family carers need much more support in tackling the ethical problems day-to-day decision-making presents in caring for a person with dementia.
- Nurses are well placed to recognize and support approaches that balance best interest decision-making in a family context where one person needs cannot always outweigh those of another.
- Admiral nurses are in a key position to provide relationship-centered care for families affected by dementia and support best interests decision-making in complex scenarios.

References

Alzheimer's Disease International. (2013). *Dementia Statistics.* ADI, London. www.alz.co.uk/research/statistics (accessed 23 May 2016).

Alzheimer's Society. (2014). *Dementia UK. Second Edition.* Alzheimer's Society, London.

Beauchamp TL, Childress JF. (2013). *Principles of Biomedical Ethics.* Oxford University Press, Oxford.

Bramble M, Moyle W, McAllister M. (2009). Seeking connection: family care experiences following long-term dementia care placement. *J Clin Nurs* **18**(22): 3118–25.

Brodaty H, Donkin M. (2009). Family caregivers of people with dementia. *Dialogues Clin Neurosci* **11**(2): 217–28.

Bunn F, Goodman C, Pinkney E, Drennan VM. (2015). Specialist nursing and community support for the carers of people with dementia living at home: an evidence synthesis. *Health Soc Care Community* **24**(1): 48–67.

Carers Trust. (2012). *What is a Carer?* https://www.carers.org/what-carer (accessed 23 May 2016).

Fant C. (2012). *Major Ethical Dilemmas in Nursing.* www.nursetogether.com/ethical-dilemmas-in-nursing (accessed 23 May 2016).

Fratiglioni L, Qiu C. (2013). Chapter 31: Epidemiology of dementia. In: Dening T, Thomas A, eds, *Oxford Textbook of Old Age Psychiatry*, 2nd edn. Oxford University Press, Oxford.

Hansen L, Archbold PG, Stewart BJ. (2004). Role strain and ease in decision-making to withdraw or withhold life support for elderly relatives. *J Nurs Scholarsh* **36**(3): 233–8.

Harrison Dening K, Greenish W, Jones L, Mandal U, Sampson EL. (2012). Barriers to providing end-of-life care for people with dementia: a whole-system qualitative study. *BMJ Support Palliat Care* **2**(2): 103–7.

Harrison Dening K, Hibberd P. (2016). Exploring the community nurse role in family-centred care for patients with dementia. *Br J Community Nurs* **21**(6): doi:10.1136/eoljnl-2015-000018.

High DM. (1994). Surrogate decision making. Who will make decisions for me when I can't? *Clin Geriatr Med* **10**(3): 445–62.

Hirschman KB, Kapo JM, Karlawish JH. (2006). Why doesn't a family member of a person with advanced dementia use a substituted judgment when making a decision for that person? *Am J Geriatr Psychiatry* **14**(8): 659–67.

HM Government. (2005). *Mental Capacity Act 2005.* http://www.legislation.gov.uk/ukpga/2005/9/contents (accessed 23 May 2016).

Ho L, Bloom PA, Vega JG, Yemul S, et al. (2016). Biomarkers of resilience in stress reduction for caregivers of Alzheimer's patients. *Neuromolecular Med* 17 Mar [Epub ahead of print].

Kant I. (2008). *Immanuel Kant: Critique of Judgement.* Edited by Walker N, translated by Meredith JC. Oxford University Press, Oxford.

Kubsch SM. (1996). Conflict, enactment, empowerment: conditions of independent therapeutic nursing intervention. *J Adv Nurs* **23**(1): 192–200.

Lord K, Livingston G, Cooper C. (2015). A systematic review of barriers and facilitators to and interventions for proxy decision-making by family carers of people with dementia. *Int Psychogeriatr* **27**(8): 1301–12.

Luengo-Fernandez R, Leal J, Gray A. (2010). *Dementia 2010.* Alzheimer's Research Trust, London.

Manojlovich M. (2010). Predictors of professional nursing practice behaviors in hospital settings. *J Nurs Adm* **40**(10 Suppl): S45–51. doi:10.1097/NNA.0b013e3181f37e7d.

Mezey M, Teresi J, Ramsey G, Mitty E, Bobrowitz T. (2000). Decision-making capacity to execute a health care proxy: development and testing of guidelines. *J Am Geriatr Soc* **48**(2): 179–87.

Newbronner L, Chamberlain R, Borthwick R, Baxter M, Glendinning C. (2013). *A Road Less Rocky: Supporting Carers of People with Dementia.* Carers Trust, London.

National Institute for Health and Care Excellence and Social Care Institute for Excellence. (2006). *Dementia. A NICE–SCIE Guideline on Supporting People with Dementia and their Carers in Health and Social Care. National Clinical Practice Guideline Number 42.* British Psychological Society, Royal College of Psychiatrists and Gaskell, London. http://www.scie.org.uk/publications/misc/dementia/dementia-fullguideline.pdf (accessed 23 May 2016).

Oxford University Press. (2011). *Oxford English Dictionary.* Oxford University Press, Oxford.

O'Connor D. (2010). Prevalence and incidence of dementia. In: Ames D, Burns A, O'Brien J, eds, *Dementia.* Hodder Arnold, London.

Office of Public Guardianship. (2016). *What We Do.* https://www.gov.uk/government/organisations/office-of-the-public-guardian (accessed 23 May 2016).

Rialle V, Ollivet C, Guigui C, Hervé C. (2008). What do family caregivers of Alzheimer's disease patients desire in smart home technologies? Contrasted results of a wide survey. *Methods Inf Med* **47**(1): 63–9.

Roberto KA. (1999). Making critical health care decisions for older adults: Consensus among family members. *Fam Relat* **48**(2): 167–75.

Rosenfeld KE, Wenger NS, Kagawa-Singer M. (2000). End-of-life decision making: a qualitative study of elderly individuals. *J Gen Intern Med* **15**(9): 620–5.

Vig EK, Starks H, Taylor JS, Hopley EK, Fryer-Edwards K. (2007). Surviving surrogate decision-making: what helps and hampers the experience of making medical decisions for others. *J Gen Intern Med* **22**(9): 1274–9.

Wendler D, Rid A. (2011). Systematic review: the effect on surrogates of making treatment decisions for others. *Ann Intern Med* **154**(5): 336–46.

Whitlatch CJ, Piiparinen R, Feinberg LF. (2009). How well do family caregivers know their relatives' care values and preferences? *Dement* **8**(2): 223–43.

World Health Organization. (2012). *World Health Statistics 2012. Indicator Compendium.* http://www.who.int/gho/publications/world_health_statistics/WHS2012_IndicatorCompendium.pdf (accessed 23 May 2016).

Yuhas N, McGowan B, Fontaine T, Czech J, Gambrell-Jones J. (2006). Psychosocial interventions for disruptive symptoms of dementia. *J Psychosoc Nurs Ment Health Serv* **44**(11): 34–42.

Critical Thinking

1. If one of your parents had dementia, what do you think would be the most challenging part of caring for them? Why?
2. What does it mean to make decisions which are in the best interests of the patient with dementia?
3. After reading the case study, what ethical dilemmas did this family face in caring for their parent with dementia? What kinds of supports are needed by this family to ensure the patient is well cared and the needs of both the patient and family are met?

Internet References

Alzheimer's Association
http://www.alz.org/

American Medical Association Code of Medical Ethics
https://www.ama-assn.org/delivering-care/ama-code-medical-ethics

Caregiver Action Network
https://caregiveraction.org/

National Alliance for Caregiving
http://www.caregiving.org/

Rachael Webb is an Admiral Nurse, Small Heath, Birmingham.

Karen Harrison Dening is the Head of Research and Evaluation, Dementia UK, London.

Article

Prepared by: Patricia Hrusa Williams, *University of Maine at Farmington*

Supporting the Supporters: What Family Caregivers Need to Care for a Loved One with Cancer

LEONARD L. BERRY, SHRADDHA MAHESH DALWADI, AND JOSEPH O. JACOBSON

Learning Outcomes

After reading this article, you will be able to:

- Describe the prevalence of challenges of family caregivers of cancer patients.
- Explain the components of a four-part framework for supporting family caregivers.
- Discuss the benefits and challenges experienced by family caregivers and cancer patients.

[I]n the desperate race for cancer cures, I also hope that doctors, politicians, and scientists will remember to look to the dark side of that moon—where the caregivers live—and find a way to ease their journey.[1]

An estimated 4.6 million people in the United States care for someone with cancer at home.[2] Too often, these caregivers—spouses, other family members, or friends—are poorly prepared for this vital but demanding role that takes a toll on them and, by extension, the patient.[3,4] Only 1/3 of all caregivers report being asked by a health care provider what they need to care for the patient; even fewer are asked what they need to care for themselves.[2] That lack of preparation can worsen the anxiety that caregivers already feel about a loved one's health.[5–10]

An at-home caregiver, whom we simply call the family caregiver, typically provides the patient with cancer with at least four types of assistance: (1) daily living activities (e.g., transportation, meals); (2) medical care (e.g., wound care, medication management, injections); (3) social support (e.g., companionship, encouragement, communication with friends and family); and (4) advocacy (e.g., with providers and insurers).[11] If the patient's illness progresses, a caregiver's responsibilities often consume even more time, energy, and emotional resources. The patient may need help with walking, bathing, toileting, and self-feeding, just as hope for disease remission is fading.[10]

A family caregiver's work can be a full-time occupation—an average estimate of 8.3 hr per day for 13.7 months, according to one U.S. study,[12] and of 66 hr per week during the patient's last year of life, as documented in another study.[13] Caregiving also is a high-risk occupation[14] whose effects on the caregiver have been linked empirically to diminished quality of life, depression, impaired immunity, heart disease, and early death.[10,15–21] Many family caregivers also have to quit a paying job or take extended leave, which worsens the financial impact of a cancer diagnosis.[2,22] Lifestyle disruption and social isolation are common, as one family caregiver's comment illustrates[1]:

> Jonathan now has a quality of life that can only be described as poor. And so, truthfully, is mine. The fact that he is incapable of leaving the house and enjoying a movie or a walk in the park means that I no longer can do these things, either. Like other well-spouse caretakers, I am a victim, too, of his illness.

The psychological burden may be even greater for family caregivers than for the patient, especially as the disease advances,[10] and greater for female than for male caregivers.[7] Stress is particularly heavy if caregivers feel ill prepared: a sense of low self-efficacy heightens the perceived burden, so it is important to develop self-confidence for the caregiving role.[16]

As patients with cancer benefit from advances in therapy and extended survival, treatment is shifting from inpatient to outpatient settings, and more daily caregiving now occurs in the home. In-home support may have bidirectional health effects: the patient's health affects the family caregiver's health and vice versa.[23] Nevertheless, family caregivers are often not seen as valuable human resources who themselves require support to give support.[8,11,23] With cancer and other serious diseases, support services must extend beyond the patient to his or her primary source of home assistance, if any. A 2016 report calls for a national strategy on family caregiving that advances the goal of achieving family-centered care.[24]

Evidence on Supporting Cancer Caregivers

Meta-analyses of caregiver interventions reveal positive outcomes for family caregivers and patients alike. As Northouse et al.[16(p1229)] wrote, "[W]hen the patient-caregiver dyad is treated as the unit of care, important synergies are achieved that contribute to the well-being of both patients and caregivers."

Education, skills training, and therapeutic counseling for caregivers favorably affect how they perceive their burden, quality of life, coping skills, and knowledge while lowering their levels of depression and distress.[7,16,25–29] By the same token, patients who are effectively supported by a caregiver are less symptomatic and experience better physical and mental health than are controls.[16,25,27–29]

Most cancer centers and clinics do not offer comprehensive caregiver support programs, despite clear evidence of benefit.[16] One barrier is the lack of a cohesive framework that outlines which types of services to offer—and how to pay for and measure the effects of those investments. We propose such a framework, so that cancer organizations can discuss its merits and adopt the components best suited to their institutions.

A Framework for Supporting Cancer Caregivers

Family caregivers fall into two broad categories. One group cares for patients with an advanced metastatic cancer that is unlikely to be cured but requires chronic management for months to years. Not unlike patients with advanced heart failure or lung disease, many cancer patients experience periods of stability interspersed with high-stress, high-need spikes, ultimately culminating in irreversible decline. A second group cares for patients who undergo curative-intent therapy that is often highly intensive. The physical and emotional toll may be overwhelming for families of patients who receive induction therapy for acute leukemia, allogeneic and autologous stem-cell transplantation, or complex multimodality care (e.g., for osteosarcoma). We have identified four categories of interventions to support both types of family caregivers and, by extension, the patient and clinical-care team.

Assess

The clinical team for the patient with cancer must first identify who (if anyone) will assume primary home-caregiving duties and which other people constitute the wider caregiving circle (because they can periodically assist the patient, the primary family caregiver, and the clinical team). Visually rendering the entire structure of clinical and family caregivers is a practical way to link everyone in the caregiving network so that they can communicate easily.

Just as a comprehensive assessment of the patient is used to formulate a treatment plan, so should the family caregiver be assessed to formulate a caregiver support plan. Ideally, an assigned nurse or social worker navigator would conduct the initial caregiver assessment in person. This early face-to-face contact can help to establish trust between the patient's home-based and outside support networks and reveal what the family caregiver needs to fulfill this role. The caregiver assessment should include the caregiver's availability (employment status, family responsibilities, and community activities); competency (formal education, caregiving experience, medical skills, and mental stability); family dynamics (strength of relationship with the patient, family, and friends); financial situation (insurance status, income, savings, and transportation); and willingness to give care.[16] Salient information from the interview can be entered in the patient's electronic health record (EHR).

Validated scales exist for measuring a family caregiver's needs and evolving burden (e.g., quality of life, social isolation, family impact, financial stress, physical and mental health). These scales include the Caregiver Reaction Assessment[30] and the Cancer Caregiving Tasks, Consequences, and Needs questionnaire.[31] The selected scale, administered to the caregiver soon after the patient's cancer diagnosis, would provide baseline data. It can then be administered every three to six months (more often, if indicated), with data recorded in the EHR so that the clinical team can track the caregiver's changing needs. Administering the scale electronically is feasible if the caregiver can access a computer, tablet, or smartphone—and if the EHR can capture the data. All of these steps may seem cumbersome, but in the long run, they offer the potential to improve clinical outcomes; lessen the patient's, caregiver's, and clinical team's burdens; and save money.

Educate

Preparing family caregivers for their role must involve explicit education, including skills training.[16,32–36] Larger cancer centers should consider developing a caregiver curriculum with standard general offerings (e.g., medication management, treatment adverse effects, symptom management, nutrition, stress management) and specialized offerings tailored to individual caregivers' needs (e.g., family communication, financial/insurance guidance, community resources, behavioral counseling). An interdisciplinary faculty could include community volunteers, such as clergy, clinical psychologists, and nutritionists (if not already on staff). A combination of in person and remote (telephone, online, and videoconferencing) approaches can be used with both the patient-caregiver dyad and the caregiver separately.

One example, a pilot project at the Dana-Farber/Boston Children's Cancer and Blood Disorders Center, trains family caregivers of children with cancer to safely manage central venous catheters at home. The project includes structured education and teach-back, simulation using a mannequin, and longitudinal knowledge and skills assessment. Another approach is to integrate prerecorded educational material into the care process. For example, MD Anderson offers patients and caregivers educational videos during the unavoidable wait time between rooming by the nurse and the physician encounter. Financial concerns also burden many cancer families.[22,37–39] Lacks Cancer Centers offer financial navigation services, tailored to a family's circumstances, that save the family money and reduce Lacks' use of charity care and its burden of bad debt.[11,40]

Although some educational offerings must be delivered one-on-one to ensure privacy, others work in group settings. The group appointment model, commonly used to educate patients who share a newly diagnosed chronic disease, can be used with cancer caregivers.[11,25]

Preparing caregivers should be an ongoing process so that benefits are sustained and educational services evolve as needed.[19,32] Investment in a caregiver curriculum can be a shared responsibility among cancer practices, professional cancer and caregiver organizations, and community organizations, particularly in communities lacking a large health system. In addition, just as many cancer centers match newly diagnosed patients with volunteer mentors (e.g., posttreatment patients who have the same type of cancer), they could match new cancer caregivers with experienced ones. Research shows that when patients with advanced cancer receive early (rather than delayed) palliative care that involves the family, caregivers experience significantly less depression and stress.[26]

Empower

The concept of empowerment is typically used in employment contexts,[41,42] but it is relevant to any ongoing role in which someone needs to feel confident; in control of his or her tasks; responsible for performing well; included, respected, and listened to by a larger group; and appreciated for contributing to the mission at hand. Feeling empowered also requires being well informed about what is occurring and what lies ahead. Family caregivers are more likely to be effective and less likely to feel overwhelmed if both they and their ill loved ones are empowered as full-fledged members of a care team working toward a common goal. Cancer, more than most other illnesses, demands ongoing formal care in medical facilities and informal care where the patient lives. The formal and informal providers, as well as the patient, must coordinate with one another and pool resources to reach the best possible outcome, just as a team does. Each team member's expertise is integral to achieving the goal. Consider these examples:

- A nurse, who was the primary caregiver for her father and husband, made this statement at a 2015 Institute for Healthcare Improvement forum: "Caregivers have so much to tell. The clinicians need to hear from them." She identified her most important caregiving roles as protecting, advocating for, and ensuring respectful, dignified treatment of her family members.
- A woman whose husband had bladder cancer said in a personal interview, "I would say to the nurses, 'Give him saline with that.' They would say, 'It is not needed,' and I would reply, 'It makes him feel better'."

Because many caregivers are not as proactive as these family members, an explicit invitation to join forces with the formal care team—and processes that facilitate involvement—are essential. Investing in teamwork empowers caregivers by fostering transparency, responsiveness to team members' needs, open discussion and problem-solving, mutual learning and appreciation, and, of course, trust.[42,43]

Assist

Any caregiver-support program must strengthen caregivers' sense of control over their lives and provide greater peace of mind. That happens when family caregivers know that they can receive assistance when they need it, ranging from getting a medication question answered to dealing with an emergency.

Current practices are mostly reactive (i.e., the caregiver initiates contact and the provider organization responds). To offer proactive assistance, a provider must anticipate issues, monitor patients, and intervene early. At Michigan's Henry Ford Health System Cancer Center, for example, pharmacists use a standard checklist to proactively phone the households of all of the center's patients who are receiving oral chemotherapy so that they can intervene when needed.

Cancer centers could also consider using low-cost, high-speed technology proactively. In a 2015 national study, 71 percent of caregivers reported being interested in using technology to support them in their caregiving roles.[44] Imagine a family caregiver consulting videos on an organizational YouTube channel,[45] lessons on an e-Learning website, or interactive media via a take-home CD[46] when facing a challenge, or using the EHR patient portal to regularly report the patient's symptoms and access contact information for support personnel.[47] Caregivers also could benefit from enhanced real-time assistance from national organizations (e.g., American Cancer Society, National Cancer Institute, National Alliance for Caregiving, and Family Caregiver Alliance) through mobile applications with credible references and educational media (akin to the physician resource UpToDate), thereby replacing cold searches online.[48]

Reactive assistance is also needed, of course, but it often comes with delays, such as when an anxious caregiver calls the physician's office only to land on the busy staff's long list of return calls. During off hours, delays are even worse. Patient navigation services (now a cancer center accreditation standard of the American College of Surgeons) can offer timely, reliable assistance to family caregivers and patients. An effective navigator (usually a nurse or social worker) or navigation team (nurse plus social worker) can be a go-to resource for patient and caregiver needs, such as clarifying a doctor's instructions, scheduling appointments, resolving transportation difficulties, and managing medications.[49,50] These triage services could even be offered as an online chat feature on the EHR patient portal, which could help staff assist multiple individuals more quickly.

Providing off-hours care at a cancer urgent-care clinic, where staff access a symptomatic patient's EHR to assist the patient and the worried caregiver, is one option for high-volume practices. Arizona-based Hospice of the Valley offers another choice: an off-hours call center staffed by nurses who have EHR access. If indicated, a nurse is sent to the patient's home within 2 hr. Almost all of the incoming calls on a Saturday when one of us (L.L.B.) was listening were from spouse caregivers. Consider the potential benefits for patients, families, providers, and payers if an experienced call center nurse were available to all cancer families, not just patients receiving hospice care.[11] Many emergency room visits and subsequent hospitalizations could be avoided.[51–53]

Veterans Affairs centers are exemplary in providing caregiver education and assistance. In 2016, 23,000 caregivers used Veterans Affairs services developed specifically for them, including support phone lines, support coordinators, peer-support mentoring programs, online training, in-home skilled nursing care, and up to 30 days per year of respite care.[54]

How to Fund the Support

Now for the elephant in the room: money. Health systems and cancer centers make money treating people who are sick. Fee-for-service reimbursement effectively blocks robust investment in caregiver services. If a patient with cancer uses more health care because informal, in-home care is lacking, more fee income is generated. This unintended but serious consequence of an outdated reimbursement system ignores the real value that family caregivers of seriously ill patients provide.

A common mistake of corporations is to be blind to invisible, long-term costs while pursuing clearer short-term gains. A cancer practice that ignores the hidden value of caregiver services reduces its short-term costs while raising the risk that the patient will need more-formal, higher-cost services down the road. In short, the practice is not fully leveraging the resources that could be provided by unpaid caregivers if they are well prepared for the caregiving role. All stakeholders, including the payer, should have an interest in changing that reality.

The Center for Medicare & Medicaid Innovation's Oncology Care Model, which bundles payments for all provided services, includes a shared-savings component,[55] thereby making long-term costs more visible to the provider organization and shifting risk from the payer to the provider.[56] Risk transfer can work, however, only if the provider can control (or at least influence) the assumed risks.[56] If a health system is going to accept risk, it must keep its patients as healthy as possible, and family caregivers help to achieve that goal.[16,25]

Because caregivers are more vulnerable to becoming sick (or sicker) themselves, well-designed value-based payment systems that encourage investment in caregiver services strengthen the business case for such programs. One model worth testing by the Centers for Medicare & Medicaid Services and commercial payers is a value-based system that incorporates two care-management fees for cancer practices. One fee would fund patient services, such as patient navigators, who are not typically reimbursed because they are not coded treatments; the other would fund caregiver support services. Both fees could be paid several times a year on a sliding scale, according to prespecified benchmarks of performance using documented metrics.

Bigger, forward-thinking employers are potential allies in funding family caregiver programs if they work directly with cancer centers that treat employees or family members or if they partner with an insurer. After all, employers suffer losses when employees who have a seriously ill family member miss work.[57,58] For many companies, presenteeism (when workers are less productive because they or someone in their family is ill) represents a much larger (although less visible) cost than that of health insurance benefits.[59,60]

Serving the Patient-Caregiver Dyad

Research consistently shows the benefits of well-planned services that support family caregivers in a role for which they often are ill prepared cognitively and emotionally.[16,25] A cohesive program of caregiver support can mitigate that burden, yet a considerable gap remains between what is known to benefit cancer caregivers and what actually gets implemented.[16,24] Prioritizing the acute medical needs of a patient with cancer makes sense, but evidence reveals the upside for the patient if the focus of care expands to the patient-caregiver dyad.[23] Making the family caregiver an afterthought or a peripheral concern is a missed opportunity in cancer care. It is time to move beyond the concept of merely patient-centered care and place both the patient and the family caregiver at the center of care that benefits all stakeholders in the complex task of serving patients with cancer.

References

1. Stern KP: My husband is dying. Caring for him is an emotional roller coaster. Washington Post, June 2, 2016
2. National Alliance for Caregiving, AARP: Caregiving in the US. http://www.caregiving.org/wp-content/uploads/2015/05/2015_CaregivingintheUS_Final-Report-June-4_WEB.pdf
3. Reinhard SC, Levine C, Samis S: Home Alone: Family Caregivers Providing Complex Chronic Care. Washington, DC, AARP Public Policy Institute, 2012
4. van Ryn M, Sanders S, Kahn K, et al: Objective burden, resources, and other stressors among informal cancer caregivers: A hidden quality issue? Psychooncology 20:44–52, 2011
5. Lutgendorf SK, Laudenslager ML: Care of the caregiver: Stress and dysregulation of inflammatory control in cancer caregivers. J Clin Oncol 27:2894-2895, 2009
6. Kurtz ME, Kurtz JC, Given CW, et al: Depression and physical health among family caregivers of geriatric patients with cancer-a longitudinal view. Med Sci Monit 10: CR447-CR456, 2004
7. Kim Y, Baker F, Spillers RL: Cancer caregivers' quality of life: Effects of gender, relationship, and appraisal. J Pain Symptom Manage 34:294-304, 2007
8. Hodgkinson K, Butow P, Hunt GE, e t al: Life after cancer: Couples' and partners' psychological adjustment and supportive care needs. Support Care Cancer 15:405-415, 2007
9. Grov EK, Dahl AA, Mourn T, et al: Anxiety, depression, and quality of life in caregivers of patients with cancer in late palliative phase. Ann Oncol 16:1185-1191, 2005
10. Williams AL, McCorkle R: Cancer family caregivers during the palliative, hospice, and bereavement phases: A review of the descriptive psychosocial literature. Palliat Support Care 9:315-325, 2011
11. Berry LL, Mate KS: Essentials for improving service quality in cancer care. Healthcare 10.1016/j.hjdsi.2016.01.003 [epub ahead of print on March 22, 2016]
12. Yabroff KR, Kim Y: Time costs associated with informal caregiving for cancer survivors. Cancer 115:4362-4373, 2009 (18, suppl)
13. Rhee Y, Degenholtz HB, Lo Sasso AT, et al: Estimating the quantity and economic value of family caregiving for community-dwelling older persons in the last year of life. J Am Geriatr Soc 57:1654-1659, 2009
14. Rosenthal MS: A piece of my mind. Caregiver-centered care. JAMA 311: 1015-1016, 2014
15. Cameron JI, Chu LM, Matte A, et al: One-year outcomes in caregivers of critically ill patients. N Engl J Med 374:1831-1841, 2016
16. Northouse L, Williams AL, Given B, et al: Psychosocial care for family caregivers of patients with cancer. J Clin Oncol 30:1227-1234, 2012
17. Beesley VL, Price MA, Webb PM: Loss of lifestyle: Health behaviour and weight changes after becoming a caregiver of a family member diagnosed with ovarian cancer. Support Care Cancer 19:1949-1956, 2011
18. Palos GR, Mendoza TR, Liao KP, et al: Caregiver symptom burden: The risk of caring for an underserved patient with advanced cancer. Cancer 117:1070-1079, 2011
19. Kim Y, Given BA: Quality of life of family caregivers of cancer survivors: Across the trajectory of the illness. Cancer 112:2556-2568, 2008 (11, suppl)
20. Gouin JP, Hantsoo L, Kiecolt-Glaser JK: Immune dysregulation and chronic stress among older adults: A review. Neuroimmunomodulation 15:251-259, 2008
21. Lee S, Colditz GA, Berkman LF, et al: Caregiving and risk of coronary heart disease in U.S. women: A prospective study. Am J Prev Med 24:113-119, 2003
22. Zafar SY, Peppercorn JM, Schrag D, et al: The financial toxicity of cancer treatment: A pilot study assessing out-of-pocket expenses and the insured cancer patient's experience. Oncologist 18:381-390, 2013
23. Wittenberg E, Prosser LA: Health as a family affair. N Engl J Med 374: 1804-1806, 2016
24. National Academies of Sciences, Engineering, and Medicine: Families caring for an aging America. http://www.nationalacademies.org/hmd/Reports/2016/familiescaring-for-an-aging-america.aspx
25. Northouse LL, Katapodi MC, Song L, et al: Interventions with family caregivers of cancer patients: Meta-analysis of randomized trials. CA Cancer J Clin 60:317-339, 2010
26. Dionne-Odom JN, Azuero A, Lyons KD, et al: Benefits of early versus delayed palliative care to informal family caregivers of patients with advanced cancer: Outcomes from the Enable III randomized control trial. J Clin Oncol 33:1446-1452, 2015
27. Sorensen S, Pinquart M, Duberstein P: How effective are interventions with caregivers? An updated meta-analysis. Gerontologist 42:356-372, 2002
28. Hartmann M, Bazner E, Wild B, et al: Effects of interventions involving the family in the treatment of adult patients with chronic physical diseases: A meta-analysis. Psychother Psychosom 79:136-148, 2010

29. Martire LM, Lustig AP, Schulz R, et al: Is it beneficial to involve a family member? A meta-analysis of psychosocial interventions for chronic illness. Health Psychol 23: 599-611, 2004
30. Given CW, Given B, Stommel M, et al: The caregiver reaction assessment (CRA) for caregivers to persons with chronic physical and mental impairments. Res Nurs Health 15:271-283, 1992
31. Lund L, Ross L, Groenvold M: The initial development of the 'cancer caregiving tasks, consequences and needs questionnaire' (CaTCON). Acta Oncol 51: 1009-1019, 2012
32. Hendrix CC, Bailey DE Jr, Steinhauser KE, et al: Effects of enhanced caregiver training program on cancer caregiver's self-efficacy, preparedness, and psychological well-being. Support Care Cancer 24:327-336, 2016
33. Bahrami M, Farzi S: The effect of a supportive educational program based on COPE model on caring burden and quality of life in family caregivers of women with breast cancer. Iran J Nurs Midwifery Res 19:119-126, 2014
34. Grbich C, Maddocks I, Parker D: Communication and information needs of caregivers of adult family members at the diagnosis of terminal cancer. Prog Palliat Care 8:345-350, 2000
35. Wilkes L, White K, O'Riordan L: Empowerment through information: Supporting rural families of oncology patients in palliative care. Aust J Rural Health 8:41-46, 2000
36. Beaver K, Witham G: Information needs of the informal carers of women treated for breast cancer. Eur J Oncol Nurs 11:16-25, 2007
37. USA Today, Kaiser Family Foundation, Harvard School of Public Health: USA Today/Kaiser Family Foundation/Harvard School of Public Health National Survey of Households Affected by Cancer, http://kff.org/health-costs/poll-findirtg/usatodaykaiser-family-foundationharvard-school-of-public-2/
38. Stump TK, Eghan N, Egleston BL, et al: Cost concerns of patients with cancer. J Oncol Pract 9:251-257, 2013
39. Chino F, Peppercorn J, Taylor DH Jr, et al: Self-reported financial burden and satisfaction with care among patients with cancer. Oncologist 19:414-420, 2014
40. Sherman D: Oncology financial navigators: Integral members of the multidisciplinary cancer care team, https://www.accc-cancer.org/oncology_issues/articles/S014/S014-Oncology-Financial-Navigators.pdf
41. Bowen DE. Lawler EE III: The empowerment of service workers: What, why, how, and when. Sloan Manage Rev 33:31-39, 1992
42. Berry LL: On Great Service. New York, NY, Free Press, 1995
43. McChrystal S, Collins T, Silverman D, et al: Team of Teams: New Rules of Engagement for a Complex World. New York, NY, Portfolio/Penguin, 2015
44. AARP Project Catalyst: Caregivers & technology: What they want and need. http://www.aarp.org/content/dam/aarp/home-and-family/personal-technology/2016/04/Caregivers-and-Technology-AARP.pdf
45. Wittenberg-Lyles E, Parker Oliver D, Demiris G, et al: YouTube as a tool for pain management with informal caregivers of cancer patients: A systematic review. J Pain Symptom Manage 48:1200-1210, 2014
46. Reis J, McGinty B, Jones S: An e-learning caregiving program for prostate cancer patients and family members. J Med Syst 27:1-12, 2003
47. DuBenske LL, Gustafson DH, Shaw BR, et al: Web-based cancer communication and decision making systems: Connecting patients, caregivers, and clinicians for improved health outcomes. Med Decis Making 30:732-744, 2010
48. Gustafson DH, DuBenske LL, Namkoong K, et al: An eHealth system supporting palliative care for patients with non-small cell lung cancer: A randomized trial. Cancer 119:1744-1751, 2013
49. Palos GR, Hare M: Patients, family caregivers, and patient navigators: A partnership approach. Cancer 117:3592-3602, 2011 (15, suppl)
50. Berry LL, Davis SW, Wilmet J: When the customer is stressed. Harv Bus Rev 93: 86-94, 2015
51. Mayer DK, Travers D, Wyss A, et al: Why do patients with cancer visit emergency departments? Results of a 2008 population study in North Carolina. J Clin Oncol 29:2683-2688, 2011
52. Leak A, Mayer DK, Wyss A, et al: Why do cancer patients die in the emergency department? An analysis of 283 deaths in NC EDs. Am J Hosp Palliat Care 30: 178-182, 2013
53. Fortner BV, Okon TA, Portenoy RK: A survey of pain-related hospitalizations, emergency department visits, and physician office visits reported by cancer patients with and without history of breakthrough pain. J Pain 3:38-44, 2002
54. Kabat M: VA caregiver support, http://www.caregiver.va.gov/support/support_services.asp
55. Kline RM, Bazell C, Smith E, et al: Centers for Medicare and Medicaid Services: Using an episode-based payment model to improve oncology care. J Oncol Pract 11: 114-116, 2015
56. Polite B, Ward JC, Cox JV, et al: A pathway through the bundle jungle. J Oncol Pract 12:504-509, 2016
57. Mazanec SR, Daly BJ, Douglas SL, et al: Work productivity and health of informal caregivers of persons with advanced cancer. Res Nurs Health 34:483-495, 2011
58. Johns Hopkins Medicine: Managing cancer at work. https://www.johnshopkinssolutions.com/solution/managing-cancer-at-work/
59. Loeppke R, Taitel M, Haufle V, et al: Health and productivity as a business strategy: A multiemployer study. J Occup Environ Med 51:411-428, 2009
60. Berry LL, Mirabito AM: Partnering for prevention with workplace health promotion programs. Mayo Clin Proc 86:335-337, 2011

Critical Thinking

1. What do you think would be the greatest challenges experienced by families when someone is diagnosed with cancer? As they care for a family member with cancer?
2. As a family caregiver, what services and supports would be needed in order to adequately care for the patient and avoid overwhelming amounts of stress and psychological, physical, and financial burden?
3. How might providing family care in the home benefit both the patient and the family caregiver?

Internet References

American Cancer Society
https://www.cancer.org/

Caregiver Action Network
https://caregiveraction.org/

National Alliance for Caregiving
http://www.caregiving.org/

Article Prepared by: Patricia Hrusa Williams, *University of Maine at Farmington*

The Challenges of Change: How Can We Meet the Care Needs of the Ever-evolving LGBT Family?

The meaning and construction of family are evolving, and this evolution drives caregiving challenges—and solutions.

NANCY A. OREL AND DAVID W. COON

Learning Outcomes

After reading this article, you will be able to:

- Define the terms lesbian, gay, bisexual, and transgender (LGBT) families and families of choice.
- Understand the support needs and sources of support available for older LGBT adults.
- Explain how contextual issues and service barriers need to be considered in developing individual, family, organizational, community, and policy solutions to better support members of the LGBT community as they age.

To fully comprehend the changing American family, it is important to recognize that there continue to be cultural, political, and religious debates over defining the word "family." Researchers in the social sciences suggest that families not only are a biological construct but also a social construct because the roles and functions families perform are in relationship to a particular social, economic, cultural, political, geographical, and historical context (Demo, Allen, and Fine, 2000). Historically, the nuclear (or traditional) family (father, mother, and biological children) lived in close geographical proximity to older family members, who were instrumental to the survival of society.

But by the 1960s, geographical distances between relatives, divorce rates, and remarriages were increasing. And, during the latter half of the twentieth century, cohabitation, childlessness, nonmarital fertility, interracial, and interethnic unions, as well as same-sex relationships, were more common. These trends illustrated that there were multiple and diverse forms of families (Scherrer and Fedor, 2015). Although there has always been diversity in family structure and function, because of older family members' recent gains in longevity, familial relationships now are extended across multiple generations, increasing this structural diversity.

Only recently has research focused on families and social support systems of lesbian, gay, bisexual, and transgender (LGBT) older adults and, to date, this research is limited (Erosheva et al., 2016). This article highlights new findings and insights about the changing American family, with an emphasis on LGBT families and caregiving. Included in this discussion are ways in which LGBT families are changing, and an exploration of the importance of recognizing the diversity in family types and roles, especially when considering the care provided by and for LGBT individuals.

Forging a New Definition of Family

LGBT communities are redefining family. Given the recent U.S. Supreme Court ruling that legalizes same-sex marriages (*Obergefell v. Hodges*, 14-556, U.S. 23 [2015]), long-term relationships between same-sex partners are more visible. To illustrate the demographic significance of LGBT families, in 2010 there were approximately 594,000 same-sex partner households in the United States, which is 1 percent of all American households (Krivickas and Lofquist, 2011). Within the 594,000 households, 19.3 percent reported having children living with them, and the number of lesbian and gay households with children has increased since 2000 (Krivickas and Lofquist, 2011).

Because data only are available on same-sex partner households, statistics on bisexual and transgender households are not available. It can be assumed that LGBT individuals belong to families that include LGBT parents and heterosexual children and grandchildren, LGBT couples with no children, and LGBT couples who have either formalized their relationships through a civil union or, more recently, through legal same-sex marriages (Fredriksen-Goldsen, 2009). Although LGBT individuals actively participate in familial roles, "defining LGBT families is difficult because it is individuals—not families—[who] have sexual orientation" (Baca, Eitzen, and Wells, 2011).

Mazey (2015) defines LGBT families as "two or more people related by birth, law, or intimate affectionate relationships, who may or may not reside together, and where the LGBT identity of at least one family member impacts other family members in some meaningful way." This is the preferred definition of family because it is broad and inclusive. It is, however, important to recognize that this definition requires that at least one member of the family not only self-identify as LGBT but also disclose this LGBT identity. Due to continued discrimination and stigma related to sexual and gender identity, many LGBT individuals do not disclose their LGBT identity for fear of being estranged from their families of origin. The likelihood of remaining secretive is especially evident with LGBT older adults.

Families of Choice

Those LGBT older adults who came out to family members and faced the negative consequence of becoming estranged from their families of origin created "families of choice," or chosen families. This term describes kin networks that LGBT individuals developed out of necessity when they were estranged from their biological families and-or if their biological families did not provide needed support and care. Families of choice usually include partners, friends, coworkers, neighbors, and ex-partners—individuals who provide the same supportive functions (e.g., emotional and instrumental support) as would be expected from one's family of origin (de Vries and Megathlin, 2009).

Families of choice continue to be a key source of support for LGBT older adults because these adults are twice as likely to live alone, twice as likely to be single, and three to four times less likely to have children than older adults in the broader community (Erosheva et al., 2016). Current research indicates that younger LGBT older adults (i.e., baby boomers) are more likely to have been accepted by their families of origin (MetLife Mature Market Institute, 2010) and biological families, but they consider the LGBT community to be an important source of social support. Families of choice, biological families, families of origin, and the LGBT community all are important sources of social support for LGBT older adults and are instrumental when LGBT older adults require informal or formal care in their homes or in institutional settings.

Nuances of LGBT Family Caregiving

LGBT caregivers and LGBT allies (e.g., heterosexual people who support equal civil rights) caring for LGBT older adults provide the same types of care as heterosexual caregivers (Cantor, Brennan, and Shippy, 2004), so why focus especially on LGBT caregiving? First, the exponential growth of our aging population includes increasing numbers of LGBT older adults and LGBT family caregivers. Mazey's definition of family (2015) helps us define LGBT family caregivers not only as LGBT-identified individuals caring for LGBT or heterosexual older adults, but also as straight allies who are caregiving for LGBT older adults. Moreover, these caregivers are adults of any age who may balance multiple roles, face their own health concerns, and experience numerous barriers to caregiving.

Second, lesbian, gay, and bisexual older adults appear to have a higher risk of disability and poor mental health when compared to heterosexuals (Fredriksen-Goldsen et al., 2013). And, the impact of HIV/AIDS on the gay community is evident, with HIV-positive older adults possibly more susceptible to chronic conditions like dementia that require both paid and unpaid care (Cahill and Valadez, 2013), warranting additional research.

Third, LGBT caregiving has received little attention in the literature, particularly in terms of developing effective interventions to meet LGBT family caregiver needs, and despite the realities of sexual orientation–based and gender identity–based discrimination. This lack of focus likely is due to few funding streams to support such work, as well as research design challenges that often affect research with smaller, dispersed minority groups facing discrimination. Examples include recruitment barriers (e.g., concerns that self-identifying as LGBT for a study might impact employment, access to services, or family support) that negatively impact sample size and identification of reasonably cost-effective, feasible, and acceptable modes of intervention delivery that reach LGBT caregivers and care recipients.

Finally, LGBT family caregivers and LGBT older adults experience discrimination that impedes the provision and receipt of competent care. This discrimination manifests in some health-care systems' and insurance companies' implicit or explicit discriminatory policies, unwelcoming senior centers and nursing homes, and loss of employment through being "outed" as an LGBT caregiver. Until LGBT caregiving partnerships no longer experience such discrimination and related barriers, we believe that the ethical standards of many professions (e.g., social work, psychology, counseling) still should demand that practitioners, administrators, and policy makers increase their understanding of the issues LGBT older adults and LGBT caregivers face, develop competence in providing LGBT caregiver referrals and services, and advance policies that remove barriers to competent care (Coon and Burleson, 2006).

Challenges Offer Opportunities to Learn, Respond, and Serve

Frameworks for evaluation and other such resources already exist to help address diagnostic and care issues for LGBT older adults and LGBT caregivers (e.g., see Coon and Burleson, 2006; National Resource Center on LGBT Aging, 2016); they include contextual considerations (e.g., cultural, legal, spiritual), service barriers, and intervention opportunities at various societal levels, from individuals and families to organizations, communities, and policies.

Opportunities to use these frameworks abound: for example, though gay marriage has been legalized, many LGBT families still lack legal protections at work and experience discrimination from providers. In response, organizations working at individual and interpersonal levels need to respect different degrees of "outness" within a caregiving dyad, openly discuss limits to confidentiality, and collaborate on ways to protect both care recipient and caregiver privacy.

At the organizational or system levels, providers can adopt inclusive language in all communications, display "safe place" symbols to indicate that staff have received training to increase their competence in helping LGBT caregivers, support continuing education on LGBT care and caregiving-related issues, and adopt a zero-tolerance policy for discrimination. At the community and policy levels, they can promote the use of "safe place" symbols throughout their catchment areas, advance policy changes within their own organizations that help to protect LGBT caregiver employees, and take advantage of the National Family Caregiver Support Program's inclusive language to build relationships with other organizations to establish a network of LGBT-friendly services (Coon and Burleson, 2006).

There also is the opportunity to learn from the resilience of LGBT caregivers and their experiences. Even in the face of discrimination, many LGBT caregivers report that caregiving gave them a sense of purpose, made them a better person, or provided spiritual and emotional nurturance (Cantor, Brennan, and Shippy, 2004). Historical factors also may have fostered older LGBT caregiver resilience through the women's and gay liberation movements and the impact of the AIDS epidemic—all of which may have facilitated the relaxation of rigid sex roles and divisions of labor in caregiving (Coon, 2007). Other societal shifts continue to affect family caregiving on the whole, including divorce and blended families, economic downturns and the need for multiple wage earners, multigenerational households with multiple care recipients, and the geographic dispersion of families. Here again, we might learn from the resilience of LGBT families of choice as they are described above.

The lack of attention to LGBT older adults and LGBT caregivers provides unique opportunities to advance research, share insights from research findings and practice-based evidence, and translate those findings into more effective practices and policies. While a growing number of useful evidence-based or evidence-informed approaches appear in the literature (Coon, 2007; Coon and Burleson, 2006) that may be applicable to LGBT caregivers, critical gaps remain in our understanding of successful ways to address health disparities for LGBT older adults and family caregivers. As a result, opportunities exist for developing effective interventions across multiple levels (individual and interpersonal, systems and organizations, community, and policy) to meet their needs.

How does LGBT-based discrimination and stigma impact the stress and burden of caregiving? How might we adapt existing empirically supported caregiver interventions to meet the needs of LGBT caregivers and address discrimination and stigma? What individualized, group-based, or web-supported interventions need to be developed and tested to expand and enhance the support for LGBT caregivers, while keeping costs affordable for organizations to deliver these services? What role does resilience play in adapting to LGBT caregiving? What key strategies at the community and policy levels best reduce barriers to LGBT caregiver and care recipient participation in caregiving research and service use?

Toward Useful and Positive Change

When considering the diversity of LGBT families with respect to gender, ethnicity, geographic region, national origin, and socioeconomic status, it is clear that one size will not fit all. Intervention research will need to find effective ways to serve the diversity of the LGBT caregiving community. For administrators, program planners, and providers currently looking for next steps to better serve LGBT caregivers and care recipients in their communities, the websites of national LGBT nonprofits or professional organizations (e.g., the National Center for Lesbian Rights, www.nclrights.org; the National Resource Center on LGBT Aging, www.lgbtagingcenter.org/) and local LGBT community centers, HIV service organizations, and area agencies on aging all can be useful places to start.

Even if local community organizations do not have programs specifically targeting LGBT older adults or LGBT caregivers, they may have staff with established networks—connections that can positively impact LGBT families. And they can take steps to offer enhanced staff training, use "safe place" symbols, maintain a sensitive, competent referral network, and reach out to other local organizations with LGBT-identified needs. All of these positive actions can advance positive change.

References

Baca, Z., Eitzen, D., and Wells, B. 2011. *Diversity in Families* (9th ed.). Boston, MA: Allyn & Bacon.

Cantor, M. H., Brennan, M., and Shippy, R. A. 2004. *Caregiving among Older Lesbian, Gay, Bisexual and Transgender New Yorkers.* New York: National Gay and Lesbian Task Force Policy Institute.

Cahill, S., and Valadez, R. 2013. "Growing Older with HIV/AIDS: New Public Health Challenges." *American Journal of Public Health* 103(3): e7–e15.

Coon, D. W. 2007. "Exploring Interventions for LGBT Caregivers: Issues and Examples." *Journal of Gay & Lesbian Social Services: Issues in Practice, Policy & Research* 18(3–4): 109–28.

Coon, D. W., and Burleson, M. H. 2006. "Working with Gay, Lesbian, Bisexual, and Transgender Families." In G. Yeo and D. Gallagher-Thompson, eds., *Ethnicity & the Dementias* (2nd ed.). New York: Routledge Taylor & Francis Group

Demo, D., Allen, K., and Fine, M. 2000. *Handbook of Family Diversity.* New York: Oxford University Press.

de Vries, B., and Megathlin, D. 2009. "The Meaning of Friendship for Gay Men and Lesbians in the Second Half of Life." *Journal of GLBT Family Studies* 38(1): 98–123.

Erosheva, E., et al. 2016. "Social Networks of Lesbian, Gay, Bisexual, and Transgender Older Adults." *Research on Aging* 38(1): 98–123.

Fredriksen-Goldsen, K. 2009. "Older GLBT Family and Community Life: Contemporary Experience, Realities, and Future Directions." *Journal of GLBT Family Studies* 5(1–2): 2–4.

Fredriksen-Goldsen, K., et al. 2013. "Health Disparities among Lesbian, Gay, and Bisexual Older Adults: Results from a Population-based Study." *American Journal of Public Health* 103(10): 1802–9.

Krivickas, K., and Lofquist, D. 2011. *Demographics of Same-Sex Couple Households with Children.* Retrieved December 28, 2015, www.census.gov/hhes/samesex/files/Krivickas-Lofquist%20PAA%20 2011.pdf.

Mazey, N. 2015. *LGBT Families.* Los Angeles, CA: SAGE Publications, Inc.

MetLife Mature Market Institute. 2010. *Still Out, Still Aging: The MetLife Study of Lesbian, Gay, Bisexual, and Transgender Baby Boomers.* Westport, CT: MetLife Mature Market Institute.

National Resource on LGBT Aging. 2016. "Best Practices Guides from the NRC." Retrieved December 28, 2015, www.lgbtagingcenter.org/resources/index.cfm?s=35.

Scherrer, K., and Fedor, J. 2015. "Family Issues for LGBT Older Adults." In N. Orel and C. Fruhauf, eds., *The Lives of LGBT Older Adults: Understanding Challenges and Resilience.* Washington, DC: American Psychological Association.

Critical Thinking

1. Why is it so important to examine family caregiving in the LGBT community? How and why might the dynamics and issues be different for this group than the heterosexual community? How might they be similar?
2. What contextual issues and service barriers are important to consider in developing strategies to support members of the LGBT community as they age?
3. The article suggests that at one size fits all approach to helping supporting aging adults and their caregivers will be ineffective in meeting the needs of LGBT families. Why? Do you agree?

Internet References

American Psychological Association: Lesbian, Gay, Bisexual and Transgender Aging
http://www.apa.org/pi/lgbt/resources/aging.aspx

American Society of Aging: LGBT Aging Issues Network
http://www.asaging.org/lain

National Center for Lesbian Rights (NCLR)
http://www.nclrights.org/

National Resource Center on LGBT Aging
https://www.lgbtagingcenter.org/

Nancy A. Orel, Ph.D., is professor and associate dean of the College of Health and Human Services at Bowling Green State University in Bowling Green, Ohio.

David W. Coon, Ph.D., is associate dean and professor at Arizona State University in Phoenix, Arizona.

Article

Prepared by: Patricia Hrusa Williams, *University of Maine at Farmington*

Why Do Marriages Fail?

JOSEPH N. DUCANTO

Learning Outcomes

After reading this article, you will be able to:

- Identify some common reasons why couples divorce.
- Consider strategies to decrease the frequency of divorce in the United States.

After 56 years as a divorce lawyer, people may assume that I know a lot about marriage and, therefore, can easily answer the inevitable question "why do marriages fail?" Indeed, a divorce lawyer can relate much about his/her personal observation respecting this issue, anticipating that many will take exception to at least one or more of the following views.

Increased Life Span

I blame medical science for a significantly large percentage of failed marriages! During the past 100 years, the average life span of humans in the Western world has increased nearly 60 percent from the start of the 20th century (average 49 years) to 2010 (average 78 years). This increase alone has had an overpowering impact upon marriage, which is a static institution remaining unchanged from the dawn of time. It remains to be seen what civil union marriage will do to both the state of marriage (now at an all-time low) and the absolute numbers of divorce (without reference to customary marriages—as opposed to civil unions), which have fallen in recent years because of increasing disinterest by the young to legally engage in such relationships.

In past centuries, the young married very young, paralleling the onset of puberty, produced numerous children (many of whom died during their infancy), and departed life in their 30's and 40's. Perhaps the greatest love story of all time, Romeo and Juliet, exemplifies this phenomenon with Juliet 14, and Romeo 16, yearning for the nuptial couch. They clearly were not unique in their era, and in many places throughout the world, such early teenage marriages continue as acceptable and are endorsed by cultural principals and religious adherence.

Quite clearly, a marriage duly made "until death do us part," that could be reasonably expected to endure 20 to 25 years at most, is a far different commitment made today, where joint lifespan can see marriages endure for 50, 60, and even 70 years! Clearly, then, medical science, which has so effectively increased the lifespan of people, must bear some responsibility for the proven fact that marriages of long duration enlarge inordinately the number of prospective clients who ultimately find their way to a divorce lawyer's office. Divorce among the "Metamucil Generation" is no longer an unusual event.

Individual Changes Over the Years

Accompanying the incredibly long duration of marriages today is the unhappy fact that married people do not always mature and grow at the same rate and quality over the longer period of years people are married today. She is involved in her career and he is consumed by his occupation. Inevitably—particularly as the kids age and leave home—the parties metamorphose in their interest, attitudes, and aspiration in ways that do not necessarily correlate with the essential unity of the original underlying basis of the marriage. For example, her involvement with professional requirements could create conflicts with the lifestyle adopted over time by him and his colleagues as sports become a passion. Conflict here is inevitable and divorce often a certainty, as neither can abandon the pillars of support each has erected in terms of his or her own individual desires and concerns.

Exacerbation of Pre-Existing Strains

Kids are beautiful and, for many, life would not be worth living without them. Little is said, however, of the disruptive problems that the appearance of children may inflict upon a marriage already experiencing some irritation and doubts. Over my years of practice, I have observed that pre-existing strains in a marriage are strongly exacerbated by additional adverse events which, surprisingly, can often be the appearance of a newborn or, worse, the death of a child, the loss of a job or a business, or the purchase of a new home. Any existing cracks in an otherwise placid marriage will often produce significant fractures when such events occur, thus leading to divorce. These customary strains upon a marriage are intensified when one or both of the parents begin to indulge in escape from drudgery by excessive use of alcohol or drugs, or seek out others to escape from marital unhappiness.

Boredom

Boredom in a relationship is often insidious and corrosive of the marriage bonds. Repetitive behavior, even if initially enjoyed, can soon pale and become irritating. Think, I tell my friends, of eating oatmeal every morning for 40 years and tell me what you believe your reaction would be? Indeed, many marriages are destroyed by boredom and the need or necessity by one of the parties to exit the doldrums of their life for some excitement—any excitement—good or bad—known or unknown.

Life Changes

Virtually nothing has been written relating to the role that menopause plays in leading ultimately to a divorce. Much is known and published that describes the onset and symptoms of menopause in women, which appears around the age of 50 in normal development. With menopause there are numerous psychological and emotional symptoms that present themselves, which can include rapid mood shifts, irritability, and loss of libido.

Many men find these newly-emerging symptoms difficult, and their presence in a wife of many years may lead to emotional and physical withdrawal by both parties. From the female's point of view, many former "quirks" possessed by her husband or supposed personal strengths and long-held opinions may become intolerable during this period, leading to increasing tension and endless arguments between the parties. The husband, if experiencing his wife's coldness or withdrawal altogether from sex, could find easy excuses for infidelity with younger women who "understand and appreciate me" when his wife has failed to do so.

Any meaningful change in the marital relationship coincidentally occurring with the arrival of menopause, such as becoming "empty nesters," a change of occupation or retirement, unemployment, financial instability, plus the unavoidable onset of old age may tip the marital scales toward separation and, inevitably, a mid-life divorce.

Another Man or Woman

The often-supposed "reason" for divorce attributed to the appearance or presence of the other man or woman in the life of one of the partners is simply a symptom of a pre-existing desire to escape the malaise of a moribund relationship. One may seek solace in the other man/woman relationship with the prime purpose of re-injecting life or purpose in an existence that may seem to have become barren. It is not uncommon in my experience that one of the parties to a meretricious relationship will operate with a certainty of detection by the other party, thus motivating the otherwise "innocent" spouse to move for the courthouse door!

Personality Changes

As life goes on, we all undergo personality changes. None of us by age 50 can truthfully believe we are the same person we were at 25. We learn, educate, grow, and change at uneven rates that are heavily dependent upon many variables—including intelligence, receptivity, and intensity of experiences. Uneven growth between spouses is common, and unless great pain is taken to assure continuing effective communication, the marriage can fail. A mother with a high-school education who is housebound for 20 years talking to three-foot-high people over those years may not be expected to maintain a close communion and relationship with an ever-working husband who has acquired several advanced degrees, travels the world over in his occupation, and consorts with the intellectual opinion makers of the world.

Limited Marriage Contract

I have in the past, partially in jest, suggested that there actually be a "marriage contract"—as opposed to a prenuptial one—in which the marriage has a finite term; say five years. At or near the end of that time, the parties are called upon to renew or rewrite their agreement or proceed to divorce. Such a shocking requirement requires a balancing of what is good in the relationship as opposed to that which is destructive. A "time out" to reconstitute the ongoing basis of the marriage is clearly preferable to an inevitable drift toward ending the relationship. Remember, a "civil union" complete written contract is not limited to homosexual relationships, but can be extended to a man/woman relationship that falls outside of the usual bounds of matrimony.

It is imperative, if the marriage is to continue, that both parties commit themselves to a course of re-bonding and enhancement of communication with each other. With kids, it is often difficult but essential that there be frequent "time outs" where a couple can recommit to one another, compare notes so to speak, and plan for their future as a couple in addition to that as a family. A failure to work on the changing nature of a relationship over time is to be confronted by the inescapable fact that the marriage may be dead and, unfortunately, in need of a decent burial!

Critical Thinking

1. With our increased life spans, is it realistic to think that marriages will last "until death do us part?"
2. Of the factors listed as contributing to divorce, which do you see as more important? Why?
3. Given the list of factors that the author states contribute to divorce, what can be done to help couples sustain marriages?
4. What can be done as couples enter marriage to better prepare them for the challenges ahead?

Internet References

HelpGuide: Children and Divorce
www.helpguide.org/mental/children_divorce.htm

HelpGuide: Divorce and Remarriage
www.helpguide.org/topics/breakup_divorce.htm

Article

Prepared by: Patricia Hrusa Williams, *University of Maine at Farmington*

Breaking Up is Hard to Do in Arkansas: Why Divorce Laws Are Getting Stricter

TRACEY HARRINGTON MCCOY

Learning Outcomes

After reading this article, you will be able to:

- Understand couple dynamics during the course of divorce proceedings.
- Discuss differences in divorce laws across the United States and why there have been changes.
- Examine supports needed to help members of the couple during and after the divorce process.

At a time when millions of people are fighting for the right to get married, others are having to fight for the right to get divorced—in a more timely and affordable way. It's certainly become a more arduous task in recent years: over a dozen states have recently introduced bills making it more difficult to get a divorce.

For example, there's a new measure in Oklahoma requiring parenting classes for couples with children seeking a divorce, and Arizona and Utah have passed laws in the past three years mandating counseling courses or longer waiting periods. Seeking a divorce in Massachusetts and have kids under the age of 18? You'll have to attend a six-hour parenting education course. Arkansas has a 540-day standard processing time for divorce, and a couple needs to have an 18-month separation before they can even file. From start to finish, a divorce there can take almost three years. Maryland, South Carolina, and North Carolina aren't much better; each has a mandatory one-year separation or waiting period before you can even file.

Some attorneys and judges think parenting classes and waiting periods help diffuse highly charged situations and protect the children involved. But others think that in many cases, laws requiring waiting periods and mandated marriage counseling can have a negative impact. When there are issues like abuse, adultery, abandonment, or other serious problems in a divorce, says Bari Z. Weinberger, a New Jersey divorce lawyer, "it's an insult to say to someone, hold on, I know you say you're going through hell, but here in our state, you will first need to wait for a very long time just so that we can make sure you really are."

There are plenty of people behind the new laws making divorce more difficult: The same groups and politicians that tend to come out against same-sex marriage are now taking on "divorce prevention" as another family-values issue to rally around. Several politicians, including Michele Bachmann, Rick Perry, and Rick Santorum, signed the controversial "Marriage Vow" document, drafted in 2011 by the conservative organization Family Leader. The vow called for "prompt reform of uneconomic, antimarriage aspects of welfare policy, tax policy, and marital/divorce law, and extended 'second chance' or 'cooling-off' periods for those seeking a 'quickie divorce.'"

New York attorney Matthew Reischer supports the new laws and thinks divorce should be difficult. "I would prefer divorce were more arduous and cumbersome so that due care when marrying would be more intelligently practiced," he says.

Colleen Sheehy Orme, a national divorce columnist, doesn't blame the laws. She thinks the people getting divorced drag out the process because of spite or greed. "I believe it's the contentious divorces that tie up the legal system. In those uglier cases, divorce is essentially what I refer to as 'legalized bullying.' A spouse who is like a cat playing with a mouse."

Divorce typically churns up a lot of emotions, and even if the soon-to-be exes are on good terms, it's almost always a sobering event. "Perhaps more than any other area of the law, divorce invokes the most basic of human emotions: fear, anger, and pain," says Peter Gladstone, a family law attorney in South Florida.

And that's a fundamental problem with divorce: The process dictates that two people who've decided they don't work well together must now attempt to peacefully divvy up every part of their lives: money, assets, and children. No wonder it's so combative. Which is why many believe that the new laws in Oklahoma, Utah, and Arizona aren't helping. Instead of trying to make a highly charged scenario easier to navigate, such legislation does the opposite. Lawmakers and advocates keep positioning waiting periods and parenting classes as beneficial to families, but in practice it just forces two unhappy people to stay together longer.

The good news: Not all lawmakers and states are attempting to save your marriage. California recently launched a pilot program, One Day Divorce, that helps couples finalize their divorces quickly, cheaply, and, most importantly, out of the courtroom. According to attorney Rackham Karlsson, the cost of a contested divorce is around $15,000. "And that's just for one of the spouses," he points out. When you use the One Day Divorce program in Sacramento, the only costs are filing fees of $435 per party.

The program has been running effectively in Sacramento for two years. "Whereas divorce court frequently experiences negative vibrations, the litigants in One Day Divorce are universally smiling and overflowing with joy to the point of high-fiving and hugging their volunteer attorneys—and just as frequently their newly divorced ex," says James Mize, a supervising judge in the family law division at Sacramento Superior Court.

Getting divorce out of the courtrooms benefits everyone involved. The courts want it as much as the soon-to-be-divorced, so they can focus on the cases that truly need judicial intervention. And the couples just want to move on.

States aren't the only entities trying to make divorce easier. Web Divorce Prep is an online divorce documentation and record-keeping software platform that saves time by making spousal communication less antagonistic and simplifying the legal process. Through the app and online platform, users can keep track of children's custody and event schedules, alimony and child support payments, and reimbursable finances. The app also provides easy access to legal documents to streamline the divorce process.

Then there's Divorce Resort, which is exactly what it sounds like: mediation and arbitration conducted at a fancy resort. Founder Daryl Weinman, who has been a divorce lawyer for 17 years, hopes his concept will help make divorce less expensive for couples and a little more pleasant. The total cost for a two-day weekend is $10,000, including the hotel. The unyoking spouses stay in separate suites and throughout mediation never come into contact. After a few days, they leave the weekend with legally binding documents and a timeline they've set to execute the divorce. Dr. Barbara Greenberg, a clinical psychologist who specializes in family and parenting, is a fan of the concept. "Anything that can be done to ease the stress and conflict associated with this lengthy and life-altering process is not only quite wonderful but may also preserve the emotional and physical well-being of all involved," she says.

Tara Eisenhard calls herself a "divorce encouragist." She and her husband of two years recently got divorced in Pennsylvania, where the waiting period is 90 days. "My ex and I separated our assets between ourselves before I hired a lawyer to file," she says. "My divorce was simple and cheap. A few months, a few phone calls, some signatures and I was free!"

Critical Thinking

1. Is it too easy or perhaps not easy enough to get a divorce in the United States? Why are some states putting in place legislation to make divorces harder to obtain?
2. Why are some states putting in place legislation to make divorces harder to obtain? Do you agree with these efforts? What may be some positive and negative aspects of doing this?
3. What is the rationale they present for getting divorce out of the courtroom? How and why might this move make the process smoother and less conflict-ridden?

Internet References

American Psychological Association: Marriage and Divorce
http://www.apa.org/topics/divorce/

Divorce in the United States
https://en.wikipedia.org/wiki/Divorce_in_the_United_States

Divorce Laws by State
http://www.divorcesource.com/ds/main/state-divorce-laws-656.shtml

Article

Prepared by: Patricia Hrusa Williams, *University of Maine at Farmington*

Children of Divorce: 82% Rather Parents Separate Than "Stay for the Kids"

Poll by Resolution also finds nearly a third would have liked if divorcing parents did not criticize each other in front of them

OWEN BOWCOTT

Learning Outcomes

After reading this article, you will be able to:

- Compare the pros and cons of parents staying together for the sake of the children.
- Identify parent behaviors and family dynamics which are damaging to children when parents are considering divorce.
- Understand the support needs of children when their parent's divorce.

Most young people who have experienced divorce do not believe parents should stay together for the sake of the children, according to a survey by the family law organization Resolution.

The poll found that 82 percent of those aged 14–22 who have endured family breakups would prefer their parents to part if they are unhappy. They said it was ultimately better that their parents had divorced, with one of those surveyed adding that children "will often realize, later on, that it was for the best."

Asked what advice they would give divorcing parents, another said: "Don't stay together for a child's sake, better to divorce than stay together for another few years and divorce on bad terms."

The survey, released before the latest annual divorce figures from the Office of National Statistics, show that children want greater involvement in decisions made during the divorce process. More than 60 percent of those polled felt their parents had not ensured they were part of the decision-making process in their separation or divorce.

Half of young people indicated they did not have any say as to which parent they would live with or where they would live. An overwhelming majority—88 percent—agreed it was important to make sure children do not feel like they have to choose between parents.

Feelings of confusion and guilt are commonplace. About half admitted not understanding what was happening during their parents' separation or divorce, while 19 percent agreed that they sometimes felt like it was their fault.

Resolution's research suggested that many parents handle their separations well: 50 percent of young people agreed that their parents put their needs first.

In the survey, carried out by ComRes, 514 young people aged 14–22 with experience of parental divorce or separation from a long-term cohabiting relationship were interviewed.

The findings are released before the parliamentary launch of an online advice guide developed by Resolution for divorcing parents to help manage relationships with their children and with each other.

When asked what they would most like to have changed about a divorce, 31 percent of young people said they would have liked their parents not to criticize each other in front of them and 30 percent said they would have liked their parents to understand what it felt like to be in the middle of the process.

The research also suggested that young people's relationships with their mother and wider family members are likely to stay the same or improve after divorce whereas their relationship with their father is likely to worsen.

The survey results come before the publication on Monday of the latest available annual divorce statistics, for 2013, by the ONS.

The number of divorces in England and Wales declined consistently between 2003 and 2009, reflecting the overall fall in the number of marriages. Since then it has fluctuated. In 2012, there were 118,140 divorces—an increase of 0.5 percent over the previous year.

Jo Edwards, Resolution's chair, said: "Despite the common myth that it's better to stay together for the sake of the kids, most children would rather their parents' divorce than remain in an unhappy relationship.

"Being exposed to conflict and uncertainty about the future are what's most damaging for children, not the fact of divorce itself. This means it is essential that parents act responsibly, to shelter their children from adult disagreements and take appropriate action to communicate with their children throughout this process, and make them feel involved in key decisions, such as where they will live after the divorce.

"We should be supporting parents to choose an out of court divorce method, such as mediation or collaborative practice. This will help parents to maintain control over the divorce and ensure their children's needs are, and remain, the central focus."

Denise Knowles, a counselor with the relationship support group Relate, said: "Evidence suggests that it's parental conflict which has the most damaging effect on children and we see this played out in the counseling room everyday. Children usually find their parents' separation extremely upsetting but as this research demonstrates, eventually many come to terms with the situation and adjust to changes in family life."

Sue Atkins, a parenting expert and author, said: "Children want to feel involved and empowered with relevant information about their parents' divorce and what it means for them. They also want to see their parents behaving responsibly, such as to not argue in front of them."

"That so many children report their relationships with family members remain unchanged after a divorce shows the value in parents seeking advice to support them to find positive solutions to their disputes."

Bob Greig, the founder of the single fathers support organization Only Dads, pointed out that nearly half of children reported that their relationship with their father worsened after divorce. "Although not surprising, [it] is always heartbreaking to hear. It doesn't need to be like this," he said.

"The reasons are well known. Some dads walk away. Other dads and their children are prevented from having a meaningful relationship because mum, for whatever reason, doesn't encourage or even allow one to flourish. Other dads struggle with confidence and health issues postdivorce—these reasons are not perhaps not so well known."

Critical Thinking

1. Should parents stay together for the sake of the kids?
2. Why did the children surveyed feel it was often better if their parents divorced? This study was done in Britain. Do you think the study's findings might be different in the United States or Canada?
3. What supports are needed for children of divorce so they can thrive in the face of this difficult transition? What are three things parents can do to help their children?

Internet References

American Association of Marriage and Family Therapy: Children and Divorce
https://www.aamft.org/iMIS15/AAMFT/Content/consumer_updates/children_and_divorce.aspx

Dr. Emery, Ph.D. on Children and Divorce
http://emeryondivorce.com/

Resolution UK: First for Family Law
http://www.resolution.org.uk/

Article Prepared by: Patricia Hrusa Williams, *University of Maine at Farmington*

Helping Children Endure Divorce

MARLENE ESKIND MOSES

When in the midst of a divorce, it is understandable for a party to become entrenched in what is felt to be a personal battle and preoccupied with details such as where to live, how to maximize the financial settlement, and how to pay the legal fees. Sometimes, this preoccupation leads to losing sight of what is going on with one's children, who are unquestionably also directly affected by that parent's decision to divorce.

Learning Outcomes

After reading this article, you will be able to:

- Describe the impact of divorce on children.
- Summarize how the parent–child relationship survives divorce.
- Explain how divorce can happen without devastating the children involved.

If the divorce practitioner receives little feedback from a client about the children, it is all too easy to focus exclusively on meeting the client's personal goals with minimal awareness of how doing so will truly affect the client's children. However, it is up to us to actively solicit feedback from our clients about their children and educate our clients about how to help their children navigate the transition. We should remain mindful that our clients' children are "shadow clients,"[1] and we should strive to fine-tune our advice and strategies accordingly.

The Effects of Divorce on Children

There has been an abundance of research concluding that growing up in a single-parent household is less than ideal and can be detrimental to a child's well-being. Even in low-conflict divorces, children can suffer in a myriad of ways. The obvious immediate repercussion is the disruption of life as they have known it. Children not living with both biological parents are more likely to experience psychological struggles and academic problems.[2] Long-term effects of divorce on children can include increased susceptibility to substance abuse. Teenagers with divorced parents are 50 percent more likely to drink alcohol than those with married parents.[3] Children of divorce also are more likely to experience divorces of their own down the road.[4]

Research shows that the effects of divorce on a child depend to some extent on the age of the child at the time of divorce, the child's gender and personality, and the degree of conflict between the parents. Infants may react to changes in parents' energy level and mood by losing their appetite or spitting up more. Preschool-aged children often blame themselves for their parent's divorce, viewing it as the consequence of their own misbehavior. They may regress and exhibit behavior such as bedwetting and may become uncooperative or aggressive. School-aged children are old enough to understand that they are hurting because of their parents' separation. They may feel rejected by the parent who left. It is not uncommon for children in this age group to exhibit psychosomatic symptoms such as headaches or stomachaches. Adolescents may become excessively moody, withdrawn, depressed or anxious. They may favor one parent, blaming the other for the divorce.[5]

Some research even suggests gender differences. Certain studies have found that children raised primarily by a parent of the same sex tend to have greater success adjusting to the divorce than those who are raised primarily by a parent of the opposite sex.[6] Although there is little correlation between the sheer amount of time that divorced fathers spend with their children and those children's overall adjustment, children of divorce whose fathers spend quality time actively engaged in their lives and activities tend to perform better in school and exhibit fewer behavioral problems.[7] Father involvement has been linked to children feeling less at the mercy of the world and more willing to behave responsibly.[8]

The quality of a child's relationship with the primary parent is a particularly strong indicator of the child's successful adjustment following a divorce. It also goes without saying that day-to-day involvement of both parents lets a child know that he or she is loved. This does not mean, however, that an equal or near-equal division of parenting time is necessarily the best option. For instance, preschool-aged children may feel they are being punished when they are moved from one household to another. Older children, too, may dislike this type of arrangement if it intrudes on their daily lives. Some parents with equal or near-equal division of time, or who engage in multiple transfers of the children back and forth in a short period of time, fight more often because they are in constant contact, which in turn causes the children to suffer.[9] A child's well-being is particularly affected by the amount and intensity of conflict between the parents. Marital conflict is associated with increased anxiety and depression, and poorer overall social and academic adjustment in children.[10]

So, how can we use this research to educate our clients with the goal of helping ensure that their children adjust with minimal side-effects to the divorce?

Guidelines for Helping Children

1. *Telling children about the divorce:*
   Ideally, children should be told about the divorce as soon as a definite decision has been made to get divorced. Children need to be told before any changes occur, and they should be informed of the changes to expect, such as moving to a new house or school, or beginning a parenting schedule. If possible, both parents should tell the children together, with the parents agreeing on the details of the explanation ahead of time. It is important to present a united front as much as possible.[11]

   Children are entitled to know why their parents are divorcing, and the reasons given should be simple and honest. Telling children that it is too complicated to explain or that they would never understand the reasons could leave them wondering whether they might be able to change their parents' plans. Blanket reassurances do not always work, and children will likely need an opportunity to talk about why they feel at fault for the divorce, oftentimes on more than one occasion. Parents need to acknowledge the reasons for the child's concerns, such as "Yes, you are right that your father and I do argue about how much time we each feel you should spend on the computer or with friends or watching television, and I can see why this makes you worried that the divorce is your fault." Then, words of reassurance need to follow immediately, such as: ". . . but you didn't cause the breakup . . ." If a child's concerns are not cavalierly dismissed but are instead truly heard and discussed, without the parents becoming defensive or dismissive, the child is more likely to feel assured that indeed he or she was not the cause of the parents' divorce. The child who feels at fault could also feel responsible for fixing the problem. Therefore, children need a clear statement from each parent that they cannot prevent or reverse the divorce.[12] They also need to be reassured that while parents and their children do not always get along, they do not stop loving each other and do not get divorced from each other.[13]

   Finally, it may be tempting to place blame on the other parent for the divorce, but such defensiveness sends a message that the children need to take sides, which only serves to increase their anxiety, guilt and stress.[14]

2. *Encouraging a relationship with the other parent:*
   Because of the inherently adversarial nature of divorce, it may seem counter-intuitive to a litigant not to seek to limit the other parent's time with the children. The "winner" gets the kids, and the "loser" does not. In fact, a better legal strategy may be to encourage and facilitate time and a continuing relationship with the other parent. Tennessee's custody statute requires the court to consider, in making a custody determination, "each parent's past and potential . . . willingness and ability . . . to facilitate and encourage a close and continuing parent–child relationship between the child and both of the child's parents, consistent with the best interest of the child. In determining the willingness of each of the parents . . . to facilitate and encourage a close and continuing parent–child relationship between the child and both of the child's parents, the court shall consider the likelihood of each parent . . . to honor and facilitate court ordered parenting arrangements and rights, and the court shall further consider any history of either parent or any caregiver denying parenting time to either parent in violation of a court order."[15]

   In addition to what the law tells us, social research tells us that children are better off with the influence and presence of both parents in their lives, absent extraordinary circumstances. It is important for both parents to be mindful of this and to strive to create a parenting plan that provides this for their children.

   Hand-in-hand with encouraging and facilitating a meaningful relationship with the other parent is showing respect for the other parent. It is harmful to a child for either parent to make derogatory remarks about the other parent. The child can be made to feel as if he or she is expected to take the side of the parent who is disparaging the other parent. This behavior by a parent violates the statutory standard parenting rights set forth in all Tennessee parenting plans. Such rights include "the right to be free of unwarranted derogatory remarks made about the parent or his or her family by the other parent to the child or in the presence of the child."[16] Acting contrary to this mandate can lead to a finding of contempt and sometimes even a change of custody in extreme circumstances.

3. *The parenting schedule.*
   It is usually best for each parent's time with the children to be scheduled at regular and predictable times.[17] Once the schedule is created, it is important that it be honored. Children may see missed visits, especially without notification, as rejection.[18] Children crave consistency, and routines provide a sense of security and may help ease fears of abandonment. If possible, the parents should work together to ensure that the same routines and rules are followed at each home. It is important to resist the temptation to spoil the children during or following a divorce by not enforcing limits or allowing children to break rules.[19]

   Handovers between the two households can be particularly stressful for children, let alone parents. Children often feel guilty and are reluctant to admit to one parent that they are thinking about or missing the other parent. As a result, children are often anticipating the emotional turmoil of the handover back to the other parent instead of enjoying the time remaining before the transfer.[20] The divorce practitioner can counsel clients to minimize the number of handovers each week. Furthermore, it may help for the handovers to occur at a neutral location such as the child's school, as this is likely to cause less stress than handovers occurring on either parent's home turf. The parents will need to commit to making handovers free of arguments and hostility.

   Although the typical parenting plan mentions only in passing that each parent has the statutory "right to unimpeded telephone conversations with the child at least twice a week at reasonable times and for reasonable durations,"[21] it may be worthwhile to be proactive and help clients work through the logistics. For instance, it can be wise to avoid phone calls at emotionally charged and more intrusive times such as meal time or bedtime.[22] It is not uncommon for a parent to feel that the ex-spouse is interfering with the phone calls in a multitude of ways, so a word to the wise: address these potential issues before they arise.

   Finally, in crafting the parenting schedule, thinking outside the box can make for much more meaningful periods of parenting time. When children have been asked what they would change about their scheduled times with each parent, some have responded that they do not necessarily care to be shuffled back and forth with their siblings as a group. Children enjoy and benefit from one-on-one time with each parent. However, frequently, for the purposes of organizing the schedule, children are indeed "lumped together as a homogenous group, irrespective of their ages and needs."[23] Tennessee's standard parenting plan form treats the children as a group, so we lawyers need to be more proactive and consider suggesting to our clients that separate parenting times for each child be carved out if feasible for the family.

Conclusion

Given the proof that parents have the power to affect their children's reactions to divorce, it is necessary that parents put their children's welfare ahead of their own conflict with their spouse or former spouse. We as divorce practitioners also have the power to influence our clients' behavior by educating them and helping them craft parenting plans that minimize as much as possible the negative effects of divorce on our clients' children.

Notes

1. Sammons, William A.H., and Lewis, Jennifer M. (1999), *Don't Divorce Your Children.*
2. Pendergrast, Val (1997), "Sheathing Solomon's Sword," http://www.weeklywire.com/ww/08-04-97/knox_feat.html.
3. *Family Matters: Substance Abuse and the American Family,* The National Center on Addiction and Substance Abuse at Columbia University (March 2005), http://www.casacolumbia.org/articlefiles/380-Family percent20Matters.pdf.
4. Nuri, Banister, "Children of Divorced Parents Are More Likely to Themselves Divorce," *Journal of Young Investigators,* vol. 23, issue 3, March 2012, http://www.jyi.org/news/nb.php?id=352.
5. Temke, Mary (1998), "The Effects of Divorce on Children," University of New Hampshire, Cooperative Extension, http://extension.unh.edu/Family/Documents/divorce.pdf.
6. *Id.*
7. Nowinski, Joseph (2011), "The New Grief: Helping Children Survive Divorce: Three Critical Factors," http://www.psychologytoday.com/blog/the-new-grief/201110/helping-children-survive-divorce-three-critical-factors.
8. Biller H., Solomon R.S. (1986), *Child Maltreatment and Paternal Deprivation: A Manifesto for Research, Treatment, and Prevention.*
9. Temke, *supra.*

10. Nowinski, *supra.*
11. Ferrer, Millie and McCrea, Sara (2002), *Talking to Children about Divorce,* University of Florida, IFAS Extension.
12. Sammons, *supra.*
13. Block, Jocelyn; Kemp, Gina; Smith, Melinda; Segal, Jeanne (2012), "Children and Divorce: Helping Kids Cope with Separation and Divorce," http://www.helpguide.org/mental/children_divorce.htm.
14. Sammons, *supra.*
15. *Tenn. Code Ann.* § 36-6-106(a)(10).
16. *Tenn. Code Ann.* § 36-6-101(a)(3)(A).
17. Sammons, *supra.*
18. Gold-Bikin, Lynne Z. and Kolodny, Stephen (2003), *The Divorce Trial Manual: From Initial Interview to Closing Argument.*
19. Block, *supra.*
20. Sammons, *supra.*
21. *Tenn. Code Ann.* § 36-6-101(a)(3)(A).
22. Sammons, *supra.*
23. *Id.*

Critical Thinking

1. Do you think divorce is always something children merely endure? What do you think they are aware of during the process?
2. Can divorce ever be beneficial or helpful to children? Are the results always negative?
3. The author makes several recommendations regarding how parents can help their children through a divorce. Do you agree with them? Why or why not?
4. Using information gained from this article, describe an intervention or support program that could be developed to facilitate the positive development of children from families where parents are divorcing.

Internet References

HelpGuide: Children and Divorce
www.helpguide.org/mental/children_divorce.htm

HelpGuide: Divorce and Remarriage
www.helpguide.org/topics/breakup_divorce.htm

Marlene Eskind Moses is the principal and manager of MTR Family Law PLLC, a family and divorce law firm in Nashville. She is currently serving as a vice president of the International Academy of Matrimonial Lawyers. She has held prior presidencies with the American Academy of Matrimonial Lawyers, Tennessee Board of Law Examiners, Lawyer's Association for Women, and the Tennessee Supreme Court Historical Society. She has also served as vice president for the United States Chapter of the International Academy of Matrimonial Lawyers and first vice president of the Nashville Bar Association. Selected as a Diplomate in the American College of Family Trial Lawyers, she is the only one in the College from Tennessee. The Tennessee Commission on Continuing Legal & Specialization has designated Moses as a Family Law Specialist; she is board certified as a Family Law Trial Specialist in addition to holding certifications in mediation, arbitration, and collaborative law.

Article Prepared by: Patricia Hrusa Williams, *University of Maine at Farmington*

The Effects of Co-Parenting Relationships with Ex-Spouses on Couples in Step-Families

CLAIRE CARTWRIGHT AND KERRY GIBSON

Learning Outcomes

After reading this article, you will be able to:

- Identify stresses experienced in families when a divorced spouse remarries.
- Evaluate the strengths and weaknesses in a study examining step-families.
- Utilize research findings in developing ideas about needed interventions and supports for step-families.

According to the Australian Bureau of Statistics (ABS, 2007) approximately one in ten couple families contain resident step-children. In Wave 3 of the Household, Income and Labour Dynamics in Australia (HILDA) survey, 13% of households had either residential or non-residential step-children, or both (Qu & Weston, 2005). In the United States, approximately 9% of married couple households, and 12% of cohabiting households contain resident step-children (Teachman & Tedrow, 2008). Step-family data are not collected in the New Zealand Census. However, 19% of the 1,265 child participants in the longitudinal Christchurch Health and Development Study had lived in a step-family between the ages of 6 and 16 years (Nicholson, Fergusson, & Horwood, 1999).

The majority of step-families are formed after divorce through the repartnering or remarriage of a parent (Pryor & Rodgers, 2001). As newly formed step-couples begin to live together, they must manage a complex family transition through which they establish a new household and bring together a number of adults and children, some of whom are unrelated (step-parents, step-children and step-siblings). Unlike first-marriage couples, newly repartnered couples do not have the luxury of getting to know each other before becoming parents and step-parents. Instead, they begin life together facing the challenges associated with developing their new couple's relationship and new step-relationships, at the same time as having to deal with multiple changes in their lives and those of their children.

Step-families are also closely linked to other households because of children's relationships with parents in other residences. When parents repartner, former spouses must continue to deal with each other over issues to do with child care, including parenting arrangements and financial support of children (Braithwaite, McBride, & Schrodt, 2003). How well parents manage these co-parenting issues affects both the step-couple and the children (Braithwaite et al., 2003).

This paper comes from the Couples in Repartnered (Step-) Families study, conducted in New Zealand (Cartwright, 2010). The study consisted of an online questionnaire completed by 99 adults living in step-families; and interviews, both individual and joint, with 16 step-couples. The step-couples reflected back on the processes associated with repartnering and establishing a step-family. The effects of co-parenting issues with former spouses emerged as a source of stress for many step-couples, so the decision was made by the authors to examine this area of step-family life. The results present a thematic analysis of the qualitative data from the interviews that are relevant to ongoing co-parenting relationships and interactions with former spouses and the effects of these on the step-couple.

Co-parenting Relationships Following Separation and the Effect on Step-Couples

In a review of the step-family research conducted in the previous decade, Coleman, and Fine (2000) talked about the importance of extending step-family research beyond the step-family household. However, few researchers have since made this move. As Schrodt (2011) noted, co-parenting has been investigated in first-marriage families and divorced families, but researchers have generally neglected the investigation of co-parenting relationships and their effects in the step-family context.

To do so is important, as the remarriage of one parent brings about another family transition and its associated stressors (Coleman et al., 2000). As Christensen & Rettig (1996) noted, systems theory suggests that co-parenting relationships established between parents following divorce are likely to be disrupted with the addition of a new parental partner, and require adjustments to accommodate the presence of the step-parent. There is evidence that some former spouses struggle to accept the development of new relationships, and the arrival of new parental partners is a common stressor for divorced individuals (Hetherington & Kelly, 2002). This may be particularly difficult, for example, for those who did not want to divorce and have remained single, and those who have settled into a comfortable co-parenting arrangement. American clinicians (e.g., Papernow, 2006) and researchers (e.g., Hetherington & Kelly, 2002) have noted that some former spouses feel threatened by new partners. For example, in an interview study with 35 divorced adults, the men and women talked about feeling that they were being replaced, both as a partner and a parent (Miller, 2009). Hence, having one's former spouse repartner may lead to feelings of insecurity and either disrupt settled arrangements or exacerbate ongoing difficulties.

There is evidence from studies in the United States that co-parenting relationships can deteriorate after the addition of a step-parent to the family, leading to increased stress for all family members (Coleman, Fine, Ganong, Downs, & Pauk, 2001). Christensen & Rettig (1996) examined the effects of remarriage on co-parenting relationships in a sample of 372 women and 277 men contacted three years after their divorce. The researchers found that both the women and men in the study reported having less frequent co-parental interaction, less parenting support from former spouses, and more negative attitudes towards their former spouses. Further, in a study of 327 divorced adults' attitudes to co-parenting, Ganong, Coleman, Markham, and Rothrauff (2011) found that repartnered mothers reported a lower level of intention to co-parent in the future compared to mothers who remained single. The authors suggested that repartnered women may have seen their new partners as being potential father replacements and that this may have affected their attitudes to co-parenting with their former spouses. Alternatively, the authors posited that the change in attitude could be as a result of increased conflict that occurred following remarriage.

On the other hand, a recent study of the interactions of 22 parenting teams including both of the former spouses and a step-parent, found that the participants expressed moderate satisfaction with their interactions with the other household, and interactions were generally not conflicted (Braithwaite et al., 2003). Interactions were mainly child-focused, were between parents, and were rarely initiated by a step-parent. The researchers concluded that this group of volunteer participants, who had been together on average 6 years, had reached a position of equilibrium. This suggests that given time a number of former spouses and their new partners can develop functional ways of interacting around the children that are satisfactory to them. There is also some evidence that contact with a former spouse who is supportive and engages in cooperative co-parenting can have a positive effect on the repartnered parent in the step-family (Weston & Macklin, 1990).

It is also important to note that some researchers believe that fathers whose children are primarily in the care of mothers can lose further contact with their children when the father remarries. However, Ganong and Coleman (2004) concluded in their review of the step-family literature that the small number of studies on the effects of remarriage on father–child contact have shown mixed results. Some studies have found no change in contact between children and fathers (Stephen, Freedman, & Hess, 1994) while other studies have found a decrease in contact (McKenry, McKelvey, Leigh, & Wark, 1996). Given the evidence of the disruption to co-parenting relationships caused by repartnering, it seems likely, as Smyth (2004) concluded, that some children will have less contact with parents who remarry or repartner, but it [is] also possible that some children will have increased contact, and contact for others will remain unchanged.

Finally, some of the problems that arise between divorced co-parents after remarriage relate to financial issues, including support of the children. Just as men fare better economically after divorce than women, women fare relatively better economically after remarriage than men (Ozawa & Yoon, 2002). Fathers who remarry are potentially placed under greater financial stress due to expectations that they will support children from the previous union, step-children, and children born to the new partnership (Hans & Coleman, 2009). Following remarriage, a father's income may thus be further stretched while a mother's is potentially added to. Further, in Hans' (2009) study of social beliefs around child support modification following remarriage, the majority of their sample of 407 people believed that it was appropriate to modify child support following remarriage to maintain an equitable agreement. It seems likely therefore that in such circumstances disagreements over child care payments may re-emerge or, if disagreements are ongoing, be exacerbated following remarriage as there is potentially more competition for economic resources.

Ganong and Coleman (2004) pointed out that many step-couples come together with "an audience of interested and powerful third parties" (p. 76), some of whom (such as former spouses and, in some instances, children) may have an investment in the relationship not succeeding. As discussed, researchers (e.g., Hetherington & Kelly, 2002) and step-family therapists (e.g., Papernow, 2006) have found that some former spouses engage in behaviours that have a negative effect on step-couples. Papernow observed that resentful or jealous former spouses can make managing child care issues difficult for parents and step-parents. Some former spouses also respond to the repartnering as a competition over the children's affection (Ganong & Coleman, 2004), fearing that they might lose their children. This potentially increases the emotional distress associated with child care arrangements; hence, former spouses who are struggling themselves can have a significant psychological presence in the step-family (Ganong & Coleman, 2004), which in turn is likely to affect the step-couple's relationship.

Method

Participants

Participants were recruited from among 99 participants who had taken part in the study's online survey. At the completion of the online questionnaire, participants could volunteer to take part in a couple's interview. Sixteen couples (32 participants) were recruited in this manner. All couples were living in Auckland. Two participants were in the 30–34 age range; 16 were 35–39; 13 were 40–44; and one was over 50 years.

The couples had been living in a step-family household for between one and nine years, with a mean of 3.9 years. Ten of the couples had remarried, the remainder were cohabiting with new partners. They had between one and four children from previous unions living in their households, with a mean of 2.5 children. All the couples had children with them at least one-third of the time, and the majority had step-children in the household for at least two-thirds of the time. Four couples had children born to their relationship and one was expecting. The children from previous unions ranged in age between 4 and 14 years, with a mean of approximately 10 years.

In the group of participants, there were 12 mothers, 12 fathers, and 9 adults who did not have children from a previous marriage. Between them, they had 25 former spouses. Five of these families were step-father families, five were step-mother families, and six were complex step-families in which both adults had children of their own. However, two of the complex step-families were living mainly as step-father families due to them having irregular contact with the step-fathers' children.

Interviews

The couples were interviewed together and then separately. The joint interviews lasted between an hour and an hour and a half, and the individual interviews each lasted around 20 minutes. In the joint interviews, the couples were asked for the story of their relationship and how it began and developed. They were then asked to talk about their children's experiences and how they had responded to the formation of the new relationship and step-family living. The couples were asked to talk about how they had worked out the care arrangements for the children; what they agreed and disagreed about; how they looked after their own relationship; what worked and what did not. They were asked to talk about the positive aspects of their relationship, and any recommendations they would give to couples considering repartnering.

In the individual interviews, the participants were asked if there was anything else that was important to them that they would like to talk about. They were also asked to talk about the greatest challenges they had experienced in their family situation, and the most positive aspects of their experiences.

Data Analysis

The interviews were transcribed and a number of datasets were created to allow for further analysis. These included the challenges internal to the couple's relationship, the responses of children, influences external to the step-family household, positive experiences, and the parenting of children. This paper presents the analysis of the body of data taken from the interviews in regard to ongoing contact with former spouses that was in the dataset relating to influences from outside the step-family. A thematic analysis was conducted on the data using the methods described by Braun and Clarke (2006). This included the process of re-reading the data, and recording a summary of the comments made by participants in regard to interactions with former spouses and the effects of these. These comments were then examined and grouped into sets of related data. From this process, a number of themes were proposed. These proposed themes were then checked against the data to see if they fit and represented the main ideas that were present. The themes were further examined by the second author for their fit to the data and the final themes were defined. These themes are presented in the next section.

Before presenting the themes, it is important to acknowledge that this analysis is based on the step-couples' interviews. The former spouses' stories of their experiences are not included. It is also important to note that the majority of the data is about negative experiences with former spouses. Eight of the 25 parents in the group did not talk about relationships with former spouses in any significant way and four step-couples' experiences did not include issues with spouses. Hence, 12 couples (17 parents) were negatively affected by the nature of the co-parenting relationship and the data presented in the results come from these participants.

Results of the Thematic Analysis

The results section presents four themes that were established from the data analysis process described above. These include: battles over children's residence and financial matters; not pulling their weight; lack of cooperation; and the other parent's negativity towards the step-parent or the new step-family. The effects that these areas had on the step-couples will be examined throughout each theme.

Battles over Children's Residence and Financial Matters

As has been well documented by previous research (Amato, 2000; Pryor & Rodgers, 2001), separated and divorced parents often continue to engage conflictually as they deal with each other over issues concerning their shared children and shared property. In this group of participants, six step-couples described conflict with former spouses over child care and support and/or joint property, which was associated with high levels of stress or distress. For five of the six couples, the discord was between fathers and their ex-wives. For some participants, the conflict with former spouses had mostly resolved at the time of the interviews, for others it was current and ongoing. Participants described a range of feelings they experienced during periods of conflict with former spouses, including feeling frustrated, anxious and exhausted, and sometimes hopeless or desperate. They also described a range of effects on the couple's own relationship. Some couples had conflict between themselves over how to handle difficulties with former spouses, others became united, and one couple considered separating. As might be expected, some also disagreed some of the time and were supportive and felt united at other times.

Three fathers who repartnered quickly after separating, including one whose new relationship pre-dated the separation from his spouse, experienced severe levels of stress that involved legal "battles" over children's residence and financial arrangements. The couples' stories of the beginning of their relationships were dominated by descriptions of these problems. As one step-mother said about the effects of the conflict between her partner and his ex-wife over joint property and, to a lesser extent, contact with the children:

> The fact that for the first two years it was a battleground. And just constantly in your face everyday. . . . You never had the courting and the dating type scenario. You just go, bang, and you're straight in and we had two and a half, three years of just absolute battle and grief.

The father talked about his experiences in similar terms, describing "a lot of nasty conflict and a lot of expensive lawyers" and two years of "war". He also talked about his perception that his ex-wife was driven by a desire for revenge, as the quote below suggests:

> I guess some of it was, I know the whole of that thing was she was out to sort of ruin me personally and there was no way that was going to happen. . . . For the first two years she was just irrational. Her actions were just irrational and it was driven by vengeance and anger, and trying to rationalise that with someone just doesn't work.

Another father, who had repartnered within six months of separating, had lost regular contact with his pre-adolescent and adolescent children at the time of the interviews. He moved towns and hoped that his ex-spouse would cooperate with transporting the children, but this had not happened. For this couple, the first half of the interview was dominated by the story of his attempts to see his children, his ex-wife's unwillingness to assist with travel, and their contact through lawyers. They talked about trying to "be united as a couple as you have so many things against you". However, the relationship came under pressure over time, as the father missed his children more. The step-mother talked about her frustration, how she tried to assist by talking to the children's mother, and also her annoyance at times with her partner. She had difficulty understanding why it was so difficult, given that her interactions with her own former spouse were uncomplicated:

> I guess the longer it went on, the harder it became. . . . I'd get wound up or I'd have a knot in my stomach. I think the stress side of things came more from frustration. . . . I have such a simple arrang[e]ment with my son's dad . . . and I couldn't understand why we couldn't have that with their mother, because I knew it could be simple. Then I'd say, you know, they're your kids, you can sort it out because she [mother] is not listening to me.

Another couple, who repartnered shortly after their former relationships had ended, had three ex-partners between them, and they experienced difficulties with all of them when they repartnered. While none of the situations were as difficult as the ones described above, the effect of having three ex-partners made their first two years together stressful. The father talked about the challenges of this over the first year, which illustrates the complexity of the issues that some step-couples face:

> When we first met, the children only went to their mother's on a Saturday night, every fortnight. . . . Then she [ex-wife] split up from her husband and then after that she didn't want to work, so went for custody—shared care of the boys—so she could get the benefit. And we fought it for a year, but in the end it was too stressful, and the kids wanted to go to their mother half the time. . . . Just creating your own family unit to fit in with them [his ex-partners] as well, and then we had to do it with my wife's daughter and iron that side out as well!

Two couples talked about their experiences of mothers who complained that the step-mothers were mistreating their children and how these claims were linked with attempting to have increased time with the children. As an example, one of the fathers told the story of his former spouse, who left to live overseas when the children were preschoolers. As the children grew older, they visited their mother occasionally. After the father and the step-mother married some years later, the mother accused the step-mother of mistreating the children. The step-mother talked about the effects on her at the time and how she coped with it:

> I wanted out. I thought, I am not going to do this. We'd only just got married, and then I was worried because she'd sent us a copy, she'd sent the school a copy, she's sent the courts a copy. . . . I raised above it. I knew it wasn't true. The kids knew it wasn't true and denied it. . . . She was just jealous and she still is jealous because I'm bringing up her biological kids.

Finally, one mother was frightened about the welfare of her infant son. The mother separated from her ex-husband when their child was a baby, because of her concern for their physical safety, but the father attempted to gain shared care of the young child. As she said, talking about her ex-husband:

> He's got a hatred for me, has a total hatred for me. . . . He hates the fact that [step-father] is in [son's] life.

The step-father also talked about the effects of this and his caution about getting involved:

> Yeah, whether I really wanted to get myself tangled up in what was happening, a custody dispute, taking on a toddler. . . . So whether I was willing to adjust to that, whether I wanted to get involved in all of that and the baggage, I suppose you would call it.

This custody dispute continued for four years and was coming to an end at the time of the interviews. The mother commented, "It's gone on for four years. So now that's dealt with, I am finding it a bit hard to believe that this is it". The step-father also spoke about his approach over the recent years and how he tried to be supportive:

> [Partner] was pretty highly strung there for a while. And I just had to keep telling myself I know what's causing this mess. I couldn't possibly understand how she feels, going through a custody battle, and just had to wait for it all to finish really, so at times it was pretty hard.

Hence, these couples came under what could be considered severe levels of stress, often during the early stages of their relationships, because of conflict with former spouses over children's residence and/or financial arrangements. The parents in this group appeared to feel threatened by the former spouses' attitudes towards them, the potential loss of custody of the children, or issues related to joint property. The conflict between the former spouses, including the ongoing legal "battles", sometimes affected the step-couples' relationships, becoming a source of disagreement for some of them, and making it harder for them to develop their relationship and the step-family while they were feeling under a state of "siege".

Not Pulling Their Weight!

Another experience that some participants talked about were the ongoing feelings of frustration or sense of unfairness that arose when some former spouses' demands or lack of contribution led to a sense of increased pressure for the step-couple. These experiences were less severe than those in the previous theme, but were an ongoing source of stress. A number of participants felt that the other parent was not pulling their weight, whether financially, in provision of child care, or both. One mother talked about her frustration at her child's father and her concern for her child that her father was not meeting his parenting responsibilities:

> There's this person who's never grown up and they're not going to. . . . And it frustrates me, for [daughter's] sake as well. It's just that kind of responsibility thing when somebody just doesn't fundamentally get that as a parent they have a responsibility. He's never organised a holiday. He's never paid me a cent of maintenance. He's never been to any of [daughter's] important dates at school!

Couples also talked about the financial pressures they were under, and perceived that these were exacerbated by the demands of former spouses. One couple talked about the stress associated with each of them having an ex-spouse whom they perceived placed a financial burden on their household. They reported that one of the former spouses, a father, contributed nothing financially for his child; and the other former spouse, a mother, made ongoing requests for financial support for her child over and above the monthly support payment. As the couple said about the woman's former spouse:

> We won't go into character assassination, but his father basically told [son], you know, he was not his responsibility. He was entirely my responsibility and not to expect anything from him. (Step-father)
>
> He's the type of parent who won't go out and get a job to support his other two children and his [new] partner because it means paying me more child support. (Mother)

This couple also felt that the mother of his child, who was on a benefit, was also demanding. He talked about the pressure he was under and his guilt about his daughter, and appeared to feel torn between his former spouse, daughter and wife:

> It was like I was paying out this money [child support], and she would say, "Our child wants to go on a schoo[l] trip". I can't afford to do it and I'd be like, "What do I do now?", because I don't want any more money going out, but its affecting my child and it would really become difficult. And then I would have my wife saying, "We can't afford to do much" . . . and I would think, "I know, but my daugher is missing out", and I used to feel like I was in the middle of everything.

Another father talked about feeling similarly torn and resentful towards his ex-wife for not working and not contributing more to the financial support of their sons:

> I feel resentful sometimes about forking out, because she treats us like the bank. But I don't want the children to go without. Don't get me wrong, but it does piss me off, excuse my language.

Finally, one couple talked about a mother who had given up much of the responsibility for her children, both in terms of child care and economic support, because of her changed personal circumstances. As a result, the step-mother, who was at home with her young children born to her new marriage, had become, by default, the main caregiver for her step-children, and talked about the difficulties of fulfilling a parenting role for them:

> I'm not saying that [father] doesn't take responsibility, but at the moment because of what's been going on, it's just even more highlighted the fact that I'm actually the primary caregiver and making these decisions [about the step-children] and trying to feel my way through this. . . . I find it hard to actually understand and believe that she's just about dropped them like hot potatoes.

While this step-mother appeared to be managing well with her step-children and the couple reported the children were happy in their home, for her it came as an unexpected shock that she should become the primary caregiver for the step-children, and this was also a source of tension between the couple.

Lack of Cooperation

A number of participants talked about their disappointment or frustration at what they perceived to be an ongoing lack of cooperation from the other parent, usually over care of the children. This lack of cooperation took many forms. It included an unwillingness of some spouses to allow some flexibility in care arrangements to fit in with contingencies, to communicate or negotiate, and/or to cooperate with a step-parent, when this was required. For some participants, this lack of cooperation began or was exacerbated when the parent repartnered.

One father, for example, described how he and his ex-spouse had developed a workable routine for handing over the children from one home to the other and how this had changed since he repartnered:

> It'd gone from being businesslike, where we would occasionally, at hand-over time, meet in a café and have a morning tea together with the children and try to normalise things. The kids would say goodbye to me, kiss and cuddle, and off they'd go. . . . [Now] we'll meet outside Burger King. You park on one side of the place, I'll park on the other, and the kids can walk over the carpark. And, you know, back to deep freeze, sort of frosty. We are back to that.

Another couple talked about problems with former partners on both sides. The father had child care issues with an ex-wife and the couple also perceived a lack of cooperation from her ex-husband (as each is both a parent and step-parent, they are referred to by gender):

> *Female:* But then we had other issues on the other side, just trying to make everything fit, and that person [ex-husband], I don't know why, being difficult!
>
> *Male:* Her dad being difficult!
>
> *Female:* Just over school holidays really.
>
> *Male:* Yeah, and other stuff. When he's got one person to think about, we don't understand why he was difficult.
>
> *Female:* He doesn't care!
>
> *Male:* Doesn't care what we do!
>
> *Female:* As far as he's concerned, our family unit is none of his business.

One couple with parents living overseas had difficulty gaining permission from the children's mother to allow the children to visit their grandparents. As the step-mother said:

> When we wanted to go on a holiday, and she had agreed to it, and then she withdrew her agreement. And we'd already

bought the overseas tickets and the kids thought they were going. And then she's saying they th[at] couldn't go, or it had to go through the court for the court to say, "Yes, they could go to see their grandparents". And I just hate that!

Another couple also experienced a lack of cooperation from the children's step-mother. This couple had moved house in the early stages of repartnering, and the oldest child, who normally got on well with his step-father, was objecting to the new living situation. The couple told the story of what happened when the mother rang the children's father to ask for support while they worked through the issues with the teenager:

Mother: I asked for the dad's support, which he gave me, but the woman that he's married used the opportunity to undermine us. . . .

Step-father: They went to their dad's that night, so we weren't there to talk about it that evening. Then the following night they came back with these questionnaires that the step-mum had written out, like, what do they feel about living here?

Mother: And using the same questionnaire to ask the children about what it was like at their place as well. Yeah, that wasn't useful.

Another mother talked about her frustration and disappointment with her daughter's father and his unwillingness to help out, especially during the school holidays. This couple did not have any extended family support:

For us as a family, we don't have people that help us with our kids. . . . There's just us, so that really is where it kind of bites. You get six weeks of summer holidays and you're both working and there's this other person who's just gone. They're not there for six weeks every summer.

Hence, some of the participants talked about their disappointment and frustration at the lack of cooperation that they experienced with the other parent, or in one case, step-parent. This added to their stresses and appeared to put pressure on them as a couple. Over time, some also appeared to learn to live with the lack of cooperation and were less frustrated by it. As one mother said, referring to the decrease in the effects of problems with the former spouse, "Once it was an elephant in the room, now it's a little mouse in the field".

The Other Parent's Negativity towards the Step-Parent or the New Step-Family

A number of parents and step-parents talked about their concerns or worries that the former parents' negativity towards the step-parent or step-family situation might adversely affect the children and the children's attitude towards the step-parent or living in a step-family, thereby undermining the efforts they were making to build the step-family and care for the children.

One mother did not allow the children to visit the new step-family household for the first few months. Over time, the step-mother became involved in picking the children up from school, assisting them with homework, helping to make lunches for them, and found the mother's treatment of her difficult to accept. This situation came to a head and improved after the step-mother stood up for herself. Following a call where the mother had spoken rudely to her, she said:

I'm not the nanny. I'm not the receptionist. I'm bringing your children up whether you like it or not. They're with us nearly 50% of the time. . . . You can't even have the decency to be civil to me when I ring up or to acknowledge that fact that I'm picking them up from school! . . . I said I spend my good earned money on them buying them clothes and food, and you've got the nerve to treat me like this! . . . And I said we have the decency to treat [your new partner] with respect and talk to him directly!!

While this type of response might have been followed by ongoing conflict or difficulty between the mother and the step-mother, in this instance, the mother apologised and the relationship became more civil. It is also important to note that in this instance, the young children did not appear to develop any negative attitutides towards their step-mother and were reported to be moving between houses quite happily.

Another couple talked about their worries about the mother's negative attitude towards the step-mother and their concerns about how this affected the children. This couple had a relatively smooth transition into step-family life, and the greatest challenge was the ex-wife's response to the remarriage. The father talked about his ex-wife's reaction to his new partner and his concerns about this:

My ex-wife hasn't reacted at all well to [step-mother] being on the scene, and insinuated in the early part of our relationship that the girls completely disliked [step-mother]. . . . She wrote this vitriolic email saying about how insensitive it was for me considering marrying someone who the girls obviously disliked so much. . . . The data didn't match what I was seeing. . . . I'm not paranoid about it, but I still worry to an extent what she will feed the girls about us.

A step-father also spoke about what he perceived as interference from the step-mother in the children's other home. He talked about his perceptions that the step-mother acted as if she was the mother of the children but failed to accept his role as a step-father:

> I've met her a few times and she blanked me completely. . . . There's a couple of things she has done that I've felt have been against me . . . Her interference seems to be a lot, and thinking she's the mother, whereas although I've been around less time, I don't think I'm the dad. That's been difficult.

Finally, a mother's story of her preschool child's experience provides some insight into how loyalty issues affect children. She talked about the effects on her son of the non-residential father's attempts, as she perceived it, to turn the child against his step-father. The mother talked about her concerns for her partner's feelings and for the wellbeing of her son:

> The only time we've really had difficulties with [step-father] and [son] is when he's come back from his father's and, "Me and my dad hate you", this sort of stuff. . . . I said to [step-father] at the time, "You need to remember that this is [my ex-] talking. That is not my son because he absolutely idolises [his step-father]". [Later] I said to [my son], "Why did you say that about [step-dad]? You don't hate him", and he said, "Because my dad said". And he was so young!

Hence, some parents and step-parents experienced the other parent(s) as competing for the children, and attempting to turn the children against them or to win the children over to their side. In only one instance, a step-mother was seen as the main instigator of the difficulties. The other instances concerned former spouses' lack of acceptance and angry responses to the step-parent or the new step-family situation.

Discussion

Previous research suggests that co-parenting relationships can deteriorate when a former spouse repartners (Christensen & Rettig, 1996; Coleman et al., 2001). This study provides insights into how this can occur and the effects it has on step-couples. A number of the parents observed an increase after they repartnered in the conflict they experienced with former spouses over the children's residence, child support and/or joint property. This appeared to be heightened for couples where one of them had repartnered early during the post-separation period, when issues around child contact and joint property were not yet resolved, and feelings on both sides were still running high. On the other hand, disturbance in some co-parenting relationships also occurred after repartnering when the divorce had taken place some years earlier. A small number of parents perceived that former spouses were being deliberately difficult in response to their repartnering.

For some parents, the conflict over child contact and financial issues was associated with high levels of stress and added a great deal to the pressure that couples were experiencing as part of their adjustment to step-family living. It also placed stress on their relationships with each other, and this was exacerbated if they disagreed over how to manage the issues with the former spouse. It was also difficult at times for the step-parents to accept and deal with the stress associated with the conflict between their partners and former spouses. On the other hand, it is important to note that around a third of the parents who participated in the study did not talk about experiencing problems in their co-parenting relationships with former spouses as part of their adjustment to step-family living.

These results support the notion discussed earlier that remarriage and the entrance of new parental partners can destablise family systems (Christensen & Rettig, 1996), either by exacerbating difficulties that exist or leading to new problems that need to be resolved. It also provides indirect support for previous evidence that the entrance of a new parental partner into the extended family system can lead to feelings of insecurity and a fear that the parent is not only being replaced as partner but also being replaced as a parent (Miller, 2009). This may be particularly difficult for former spouses who observe step-couple closeness and attractive step-parent qualities. It may also be difficult for individuals who are struggling emotionally. This appeared to be so in a small number of instances discussed in the thematic analysis, in which the participants talked about the attitude of the former spouse to the step-parent and had a sense that their ex-partner was attempting to turn the children against the step-parent and perhaps the remarriage. This supports Papernow's (2006) conclusion that some former spouses engage in jealous behaviour that makes co-parenting difficult and places stress on the step-couple. In a small number of instances, couples perceived that the former spouse's negativity was directed at the step-parent. In some instances, this lead to increased tensions between the step-couple and/or feelings of insecurity for the step-parent.

As found previously (Braithwaite et al., 2003), however, step-parents did not appear to deal with or negotiate with former spouses on anything but an occasional basis. This was left mainly to parents. An exception to this was a wife of a former spouse who was seen as interfering directly with the management of the children, and one step-mother who attempted to assist with resolving disagreements. She stepped back from this, however, when it was unsuccessful.

It is also important to note that some of the stressors associated with former spouses were not severe, but were an ongoing source of stress or irritation that made life more difficult for the couples at times. Some former spouses were experienced as being inflexible or refusing to negotiate special requests or one-off changes to routines to allow for special arrangements or events. Some ex-spouses were experienced as not meeting their responsibilities, either through child care (such as assisting with holidays), or in providing financial support of the children. Some parents thought that the other parent was not pulling his or her weight financially and found this added to the financial stessors they were already experiencing. There was also some evidence to support previous finding[s] that some fathers in step-family situations feel torn between former spouses, their children and current partners, in regard to financial support (Hans & Coleman, 2009).

As researchers, we were surprised to note that five of the six co-parenting relationships that we considered came under severe levels of stress, were between repartnered fathers and their ex-wives. On the other hand, it has been found consistently that men tend to repartner more quickly than women (Cartwright, 2010) and some men in this study repartnered within six months of separating, at a time when issues around child care and finances were still under negotiation and the relationship between the two former spouses was still emotionally fraught. Early repartnering is likely to lead to heightened distress for former spouses, especially when they have not wanted to divorce.

American researchers (e.g., Hetherington & Kelly, 2002) and step-family therapists (e.g., Papernow, 2006) have observed that repartnering parents often have unrealistally positive expectations of step-family life, believing, for example, that step-children will love their new partners as much as they do. Some step-couples in this study also appeared surprised or taken aback by their former spouses' responses to them or their new partner following repartnering, including those who repartnered quickly. It may be that some step-couples are not cognisant of the problems that can arise with former spouses if repartnering occurs quickly after a separation, before the necessary period of adjustment has taken place. The likelihood of step-couples having realistic expectations may also be affected by the lack of research in the area of co-parenting following remarriage, and also the lack of norms to guide parents and step-parents in how to relate to each other (Weston & Macklin, 1990). It might be helpful for those considering repartnering to understand that relating to former spouses can become an obstacle course if the former spouse feels threatened or believes that they have not been treated fairly. It may also be helpful for former spouses to be aware of the strong emotions that are evoked by their exes repartnering, and to have guidance about how to manage themselves during this stressful period.

It is important to acknowledge the limitations of this study and briefly discuss future research directions. First, this sample of participants volunteered to be interviewed and may not be representative of step-couples generally. The sample may have included a greater proportion of people who had experienced considerable difficulty and wanted to talk about this to a researcher. Second, the views of former spouses were not included in this study and hence their experiences and viewpoints are missing. Research that includes all the adults involved is likely to provide greater insights into the dynamics of co-parenting within step-family situations. Third, because of the nature of the interviews, participants who told the story of the development of their relationships tended to talk only about the problems and challenges they experienced with former spouses. Hence, this study is informative about the types of problems that step-couples experience, but not of positive co-parenting relationships following repartnering. Around a third of the participants appeared to have non-problematic relationships with former spouses, but little data were collected about these relationships because of the focus on the step-couples' challenges and the experiences they regarded as important to them.

In terms of future research, it is important that family transition researchers in Australia and New Zealand focus more on the areas of co-parenting following remarriage, and the relationships between former spouses, parents and step-parents. No previous research has been conducted in either country in this area. The lack of research in this area may also exacerbate a lack of norms to guide repartnering parents and former spouses. In line with this, in order to better understand how co-parenting relationships work, it is also important to study well-functioning co-parenting relationships and how these develop or are maintained following the repartnering of at least one former spouse. Finally, given that the majority of separated parents will eventually repartner, and some will do so quickly, it may be desirable for educational programs and literature aimed at separated couples to include information about the stressors associated with the transition into step-family life and their potential effects on co-parenting relationships between former spouses.

References

Amato, P. (2000). The consequences of divorce for adults and children. *Journal of Marriage and the Family, 62* (4), 1269–1287.

Australian Bureau of Statistics. (2007). *2006 Census of Population and Housing* (Cat. No. 2008.0). Canberra: ABS.

Braithwaite, D. O., McBride, M. C., & Schrodt, P. (2003). Parent teams and the everyday interactions of co-parenting in stepfamilies. *Communication Reports, 16* (2), 93–111.

Braun, V., & Clarke, V. (2006). Using thematic analysis in psychology. *Qualitative research in psychology, 3,* 77–101.

Cartwright, C. (2010). Preparing to repartner and live in a stepfamily: An exploratory investigation. *Journal of Family Studies, 16* (3), 237–250.

Christensen, D. H., & Rettig, K. D. (1996). The relationship of remarriage to post-divorce co-parenting. *Journal of Divorce & Remarriage, 24* (1–2), 73–88.

Coleman, M., Fine, M. A., Ganong, L. H., Downs, K. J. M., & Pauk, N. (2001). When you're not the Brady Bunch: Identifying perceived conflicts and resolution strategies in stepfamilies. *Personal Relationships, 8* (1), 55–73.

Coleman, M., Ganong, L., & Fine, M. A. (2000). Reinvestigating remarriage: Another decade of progress. *Journal of Marriage and the Family, 62* (4), 1288–1307.

Ganong, L., & Coleman, M. (2004). *Stepfamily relationships: Development, dynamics and interventions.* New York: Kluwer Academic/Plenum Publishers.

Ganong, L. H., Coleman, M., Markham, M., & Rothrauff, T. (2011). Predicting postdivorce co-parental communication. *Journal of Divorce & Remarriage, 52* (1), 1–18.

Hans, J. D. (2009). Beliefs about child support modification following remarriage and subsequent childbirth. *Family Relations, 58* (1), 65–78.

Hans, J. D., & Coleman, M. (2009). The experiences of remarried stepfathers who pay child support. *Personal Relationships, 16* (4), 597–618.

Hetherington, E. M., & Kelly, J. (2002). *For better or for worse: Divorce reconsidered.* New York: W. W. Norton and Company.

McKenry, P. C., McKelvey, M. W., Leigh, D., & Wark, L. (1996). Nonresidential father involvement. *Journal of Divorce & Remarriage, 25* (3–4), 1–14.

Miller, A. E. (2009). Face concerns and facework strategies in maintaining postdivorce co-parenting and dating relationships. *Southern Communication Journal, 74* (2), 157–173.

Nicholson, J. M., Fergusson, D. M., & Horwood, L. J. (1999). Effects on later adjustment of living in a step-family during childhood and adolescence. *Journal of Child Psychology and Psychiatry, 40,* 405–416.

Ozawa, M. N., & Yoon, H.-S. (2002). The economic benefit of remarriage. *Journal of Divorce & Remarriage, 36* (3–4), 21–39.

Papernow, P. (2006). Blended family relationships: Helping people who live in stepfamilies. *Family Therapy Magazine,* May, 34–42.

Pryor, J., & Rodgers, B. (2001). *Children in changing families: Life after parental separation* (Understanding Children' Worlds). Oxford, UK: Blackwell.

Qu, L., & Weston, R. (2005). Snapshot of couple families with stepparent–child relationships. *Family Matters, 70,* 36–37.

Smyth, B. (2004). Postseparation fathering: What does Australian research tell us? *Journal of Family Studies, 10* (1), 20–49.

Stephen, E. H., Freedman, V. A., & Hess, J. (1994). Near and far. *Journal of Divorce & Remarriage, 20* (3–4), 171–191.

Teachman, J., & Tedrow, L. (2008). The demography of step-families in the United States. In J. Pryor (Ed.), *The international handbook of step-families: Policy and practice in legal, research, and clinical environments* (pp. 3–29). Hoboken, NJ: John Wiley.

Weston, C. A., & Macklin, E. D. (1990). The relationship between former-spousal contact and remarital satisfaction in stepfather families. *Journal of Divorce & Remarriage, 14* (2), 25–48.

Critical Thinking

1. What do you see as the biggest challenges faced when a step-family is formed?
2. If this study were conducted in the United States, do you think the findings would be the same and why? Are there things about this study that could be strengthened or which limit the generalizability of its findings about step-families?
3. How could the findings of this study be used in developing interventions and supports designed for step-families?

Internet References

HelpGuide: Children and Divorce
www.helpguide.org/mental/children_divorce.htm

HelpGuide: Divorce and Remarriage
www.helpguide.org/topics/breakup_divorce.htm

National Stepfamily Resource Center
http://www.stepfamilies. info

Stepfamilies Australia
http://www.stepfamily.org.au

Claire Cartwright and **Kerry Gibson** are both at the Doctor of Clinical Psychology Programme, School of Psychology, the University of Auckland, New Zealand. This paper is based on a presentation made at the 12th Australian Institute of Family Studies Conference, 25 July 2012, Melbourne.

Unit 5

UNIT

Prepared by: Patricia Hrusa Williams, *University of Maine at Farmington*

Families, Now and into the Future

What is the future of the family? Where do we go from here? Many people have made dire predictions regarding the health, well-being, and sanctity of the family as a social structure in society. As previous units of this volume have shown, the family is an institution which continues to evolve and change. Still, certain elements of family appear to be constant. The family is and will remain a powerful influence in the lives of its members. This is because we all begin life in some type of family, and this early exposure carries a great deal of weight in forming our social selves—who we are and how we relate to others. From our biological families, we are given our basic genetic makeup. In the context of daily routines and rituals, we also learn how to care for ourselves and others. In families, we are given our first exposure to values, and it is through families that we most actively influence others. Our sense of commitment and obligation begins within the family as well as our sense of what we can expect of others.

Much that has been written about families has been less than hopeful, focusing on ways of avoiding or correcting "maladaptive" behaviors and patterns. The articles in this unit take a positive view of family and how it influences its members. Through its diversity, rituals, traditions, history, and new ways of establishing connections, the family still remains a vital and important structure in which we work, play, love, and adapt.

The articles in this unit explore the different shapes and forms families come in and the ways they linked together. Articles also consider how technology and changes in societal norms and values are altering how we procreate, relate, marry, and parent the next generation. A goal is to explore the family now and as it might be as we venture into the future, considering its role as a healthy, supportive place for personal growth.

Article

Prepared by: Patricia Hrusa Williams, *University of Maine at Farmington*

The Changing American Family

NATALIE ANGIER

Learning Outcomes

After reading this article, you will be able to:

- Describe shifts in family characteristics and structure in the United States.
- Explain how demographic, social, political, and economic forces have contributed to changes in the family in the United States.

Kristi and Michael Burns have a lot in common. They love crossword puzzles, football, going to museums and reading five or six books at a time. They describe themselves as mild-mannered introverts who suffer from an array of chronic medical problems. The two share similar marital résumés, too. On their wedding day in 2011, the groom was 43 years old and the bride 39, yet it was marriage No. 3 for both.

Today, their blended family is a sprawling, sometimes uneasy ensemble of two sharp-eyed sons from her two previous husbands, a daughter and son from his second marriage, ex-spouses of varying degrees of involvement, the partners of ex-spouses, the bemused in-laws and a kitten named Agnes that likes to sleep on computer keyboards.

If the Burnses seem atypical as an American nuclear family, how about the Schulte-Waysers, a merry band of two married dads, six kids and two dogs? Or the Indrakrishnans, a successful immigrant couple in Atlanta whose teenage daughter divides her time between prosaic homework and the precision footwork of ancient Hindu dance; the Glusacs of Los Angeles, with their two nearly grown children and their litany of middle-class challenges that seem like minor sagas; Ana Perez and Julian Hill of Harlem, unmarried and just getting by, but with Warren Buffett-size dreams for their three young children; and the alarming number of families with incarcerated parents, a sorry byproduct of America's status as the world's leading jailer.

The typical American family, if it ever lived anywhere but on Norman Rockwell's Thanksgiving canvas, has become as multilayered and full of surprises as a holiday turducken—the all-American seasonal portmanteau of deboned turkey, duck and chicken.

Researchers who study the structure and evolution of the American family express unsullied astonishment at how rapidly the family has changed in recent years, the transformations often exceeding or capsizing those same experts' predictions of just a few journal articles ago.

"This churning, this turnover in our intimate partnerships is creating complex families on a scale we've not seen before," said Andrew J. Cherlin, a professor of public policy at Johns Hopkins University. "It's a mistake to think this is the endpoint of enormous change. We are still very much in the midst of it."

Yet for all the restless shape-shifting of the American family, researchers who comb through census, survey and historical data and conduct field studies of ordinary home life have identified a number of key emerging themes.

Families, they say, are becoming more socially egalitarian over all, even as economic disparities widen. Families are more ethnically, racially, religiously and stylistically diverse than half a generation ago—than even half a year ago.

In increasing numbers, blacks marry whites, atheists marry Baptists, men marry men and women women, Democrats marry Republicans and start talk shows. Good friends join forces as part of the "voluntary kin" movement, sharing medical directives, wills, even adopting one another legally.

Single people live alone and proudly consider themselves families of one—more generous and civic-minded than so-called "greedy marrieds."

"There are really good studies showing that single people are more likely than married couples to be in touch with friends, neighbors, siblings and parents," said Bella DePaulo, author of *Singled Out* and a visiting professor of psychology at the University of California, Santa Barbara.

But that doesn't mean they'll be single forever. "There are not just more types of families and living arrangements than there used to be," said Stephanie Coontz, author of the coming book *Intimate Revolutions,* and a social historian at Evergreen State College in Olympia, Wash. "Most people will move through several different types over the course of their lives."

At the same time, the old-fashioned family plan of stably married parents residing with their children remains a source of considerable power in America—but one that is increasingly seen as out of reach to all but the educated elite.

"We're seeing a class divide not only between the haves and the have-nots, but between the I do's and the I do nots," Dr. Coontz said. Those who are enjoying the perks of a good marriage "wouldn't stand for any other kind," she said, while those who would benefit most from marital stability "are the ones least likely to have the resources to sustain it."

Yet across the divide runs a white picket fence, our unshakable star-spangled belief in the value of marriage and family. We marry, divorce and remarry at rates not seen anywhere else in the developed world. We lavish $70 billion a year on weddings, more than we spend on pets, coffee, toothpaste and toilet paper combined.

We're sappy family romantics. When an informal sample of 52 Americans of different ages, professions and hometowns were asked the first thought that came to mind on hearing the word "family," the answers varied hardly at all. Love! Kids! Mom! Dinner!

"It's the backbone of how we live," said David Anderson, 52, an insurance claims adjuster from Chicago. "It means everything," said Linda McAdam, 28, who is in human resources on Long Island.

Yes, everything, and sometimes too many things. "It's almost like a weight," said Rob Fee, 26, a financial analyst in San Francisco, "a heavy weight." Or as the comedian George Burns said, "Happiness is having a large, loving, caring, close-knit family in another city."

In charting the differences between today's families and those of the past, demographers start with the kids—or rather the lack of them.

The nation's birthrate today is half what it was in 1960, and last year hit its lowest point ever. At the end of the baby boom, in 1964, 36 percent of all Americans were under 18 years old; last year, children accounted for just 23.5 percent of the population, and the proportion is dropping, to a projected 21 percent by 2050. Fewer women are becoming mothers—about 80 percent of those of childbearing age today versus 90 percent in the 1970s—and those who reproduce do so more sparingly, averaging two children apiece now, compared with three in the 1970s.

One big reason is the soaring cost of ushering offspring to functional independence. According to the Department of Agriculture, the average middle-class couple will spend $241,080 to raise a child to age 18. Factor in four years of college and maybe graduate school, or a parentally subsidized internship with the local theater company, and say hello to your million-dollar bundle of oh joy.

As steep as the fertility decline has been, the marriage rate has fallen more sharply, particularly among young women, who do most of the nation's childbearing. As a result, 41 percent of babies are now born out of wedlock, a fourfold increase since 1970.

The trend is not demographically uniform, instead tracking the nation's widening gap in income and opportunity. Among women with a bachelor's degree or higher, 90 percent adhere to the old playground song and put marriage before a baby carriage. For everybody else, maternity is often decoupled from matrimony: 40 percent of women with some college but no degree, and 57 percent of women with high school diplomas or less, are unmarried when they give birth to their first child.

More than one-quarter of these unwed mothers are living with a partner who may or may not be their child's biological father. The rise of the cohabiting couple is another striking feature of the evolving American family: From 1996 to 2012, the number jumped almost 170 percent, to 7.8 million from 2.9 million.

Nor are unmarried mothers typically in their teens; contrary to all the talk of an epidemic of teenage motherhood, the birthrate among adolescent girls has dropped by nearly half since 1991 and last year hit an all-time low, a public health triumph that experts attribute to better sex education and birth-control methods. Most unmarried mothers today, demographers say, are in their 20s and early 30s.

Also démodé is the old debate over whether mothers of dependent children should work outside the home. The facts have voted, the issue is settled, and Paycheck Mommy is now a central organizing principle of the modern American family.

The share of mothers employed full or part time has quadrupled since the 1950s and today accounts for nearly three-quarters of women with children at home. The number of women who are their families' sole or primary breadwinner also has soared, to 40 percent today from 11 percent in 1960.

"Yes, I wear the pants in the family," said Ana Perez, 35, a mother of three and a vice president at a financial services company in New York, who was, indeed, wearing pants. "I can say it brings me joy to know I can take care of my family."

Cultural attitudes are adapting accordingly. Sixty-two percent of the public, and 72 percent of adults under 30, view the ideal marriage as one in which husband and wife both work and share child care and household duties; back when Jimmy Carter was president, less than half of the population approved of the dual-income family, and less than half of 1 percent of husbands knew how to operate a sponge mop.

Mothers are bringing home more of the bacon, and of the mortarboards, too. While most couples are an even match scholastically, 28 percent of married women are better educated than their mates; that is true of just 19 percent of married men. Forty years ago, the asymmetry went the other way.

Some experts argue that the growing legion of mothers with advanced degrees has helped sharpen the already brutal competition for admission to the nation's elite universities, which stress the importance of extracurricular activities. Nothing predicts the breadth and busyness of a child's after-school schedule better, it turns out, than the mother's level of education.

One change that caught many family researchers by surprise was the recent dip in the divorce rate. After many decades of upward march, followed by a long, stubborn stay at the familiar 50 percent mark that made every nuptial feel like a coin flip, the rate began falling in 1996 and is now just above 40 percent for first-time marriages.

The decline has been even more striking among middle- and upper-middle-income couples with college degrees. For them, fewer than one in three marriages is expected to end in divorce, a degree of stability that allows elite couples to merge their resources with confidence, maximally invest in their children and otherwise widen the gap between themselves and the struggling masses.

There are exceptions, of course. Among baby boomers, the rate of marriage failure has surged 50 percent in the past 20 years—perhaps out of an irritable nostalgia, researchers said, for the days of free love, better love, anything but this love. Nor do divorce rates appear to have fallen among those who take the old Samuel Johnson quip as a prescription, allowing hope to triumph over experience, and marrying again and again.

For both Mike and Kristi Burns, now in their 40s, the first marriage came young and left early, and the second stuck around for more than a dozen years.

Kristi was 19, living in South Carolina, and her Marine boyfriend was about to be shipped to Japan. "I wasn't attached to him, really," she said, "but for some reason I felt this might be my only chance at marriage."

In Japan, Kristi gave birth to her son Brandon, realized she was lonely and miserable, and left the marriage seven weeks after their first anniversary. Back in the States, Kristi studied to be a travel agent, moved to Michigan and married her second husband at age 23.

He was an electrician. He adopted Brandon, and the couple had a son, Griffin. The marriage lasted 13 years.

"We were really great friends, but we weren't a great husband and wife," Kristi said. "Our parenting styles were too different."

Besides, she went on, "he didn't verbalize a lot, but he was mad a lot, and I was tired of walking around on eggshells."

After the divorce, friends persuaded her to try the online dating service Match.com, and just as her free trial week was about to expire, she noticed a new profile in the mix.

"Kristi was one of the first people to ping me," said Mike Burns, an engineer for an e-commerce company. "This was at 3 in the morning."

They started chatting. Mike told Kristi how he'd married his first wife while he was still in college—"definitely too young," he said—and divorced her two years later. He met his second wife through mutual friends, they had a big church wedding, started a software publishing company together, sold it and had two children, Brianna and Alec.

When the marriage started going downhill, Mike ignored signs of trouble, like the comments from neighbors who noticed his wife was never around on weekends.

"I was delusional, I was depressed," he said. "I still had the attitude that divorce wasn't something you did."

After 15 years of marriage, his wife did it for him, and kicked him out of the house. His divorce papers hadn't yet been finalized, he told Kristi that first chat night. I'll help you get through it, she replied.

Mike and Kristi admit their own three-year-old marriage isn't perfect. The kids are still adjusting to one another. Sometimes Kristi, a homemaker, feels jealous of how much attention her husband showers on his daughter Brianna, 13.

Sometimes Mike retreats into his computer. Yet they are determined to stay together.

"I know everyone thinks this marriage is a joke and people expect it to fail," said Kristi. "But that just makes me work harder at it."

"I'd say our chances of success are better than average," her husband added.

In America, family is at once about home and the next great frontier.

Critical Thinking

1. Would you say you grew up in a typical American family? What does the typical American family look like today?
2. Consider three ways families are different than they were 50 years ago. Why have these changes occurred? How have they served to change American society in both positive and negative ways?
3. Where do you see the future of the family in America going? What trends and changes in families do you anticipate seeing in the next 50 years?

Internet References

Kearl's Guide to the Sociology of the Family
www.trinity.edu/MKEARL/family.html

U.S. Census: Families and Living Arrangements
http://www.census.gov/hhes/families

U.S. Department of Health and Human Services: Families
http://www.hhs.gov/children/index.html

World Family Map
http://worldfamilymap.org/2014/about

Article

Prepared by: Patricia Hrusa Williams, *University of Maine at Farmington*

What Will the Family of the Future Look Like?

Technology, immigration, and the gender revolution—What are these trends doing to the traditional family model?

ANN BERRINGTON AND AGNESE VITALI

Learning Outcomes

After reading this article, you will be able to:

- Define terms such as family structure, fertility rate, gender roles, and gender equality.
- Compare and contrast trends in families in the United States and Europe.
- Understand how socioeconomic factors, gender roles, technology, and international migration influence how families will look in the future.

As we approach UN International Day of Families, only the foolhardy would try and predict the future of family groups. Previous attempts have, in fact, failed. William J Goode, writing in the early 1960s during the "golden age of marriage," saw convergence toward the western-style conjugal family as an inevitable consequence of industrialization. No sooner had his seminal book World Revolution and Family Patterns been published than divorce rates started increasing, and married women began moving into the labor force.

Nothing ventured, nothing gained, however. And there are some clear clues we can draw on to guess at how family life might change in Europe over the years.

From the early 1970s, marriage and childbearing began to be postponed and cohabitation and nonmarital childbearing started to increase. The trend is clear in the chart below.

Demographers Dirk Van de Kaa and Ron Lesthaeghe interpreted these changes as the consequence of changing values, increased self-fulfillment, and individualism. They suggested that all European countries would experience a "second demographic transition." Marriage, sex, and parenthood would be separated, and we would see a convergence to sustained low fertility and a new set of family forms: nonmarital fertility, lone parenthood, and cohabiting couple families.

There has been movement in most countries towards new family forms such as cohabitation and nonmarital childbearing. Even in what are generally considered to be more religious countries in Southern Europe. In Spain, births outside marriage rose from 2 percent in 1972 to 39 percent in 2012.

Countries still differ, though, in the way in which cohabitation, marriage, and childbearing are related. The extent to which governments have acted to recognize and regulate nonmarital cohabiting unions and same-sex couples suggests that the acceptance of new family forms will continue to vary greatly between countries.

Poverty Effects

As family biographies have become destandardized, so there has been a "convergence toward diversity." In other words, people today experience a greater range of ways to organize their family lives, and we expect such diversity to characterize future families. However, according to US scholar Sara McLanahan, socioeconomic differences in the types of parenting structures

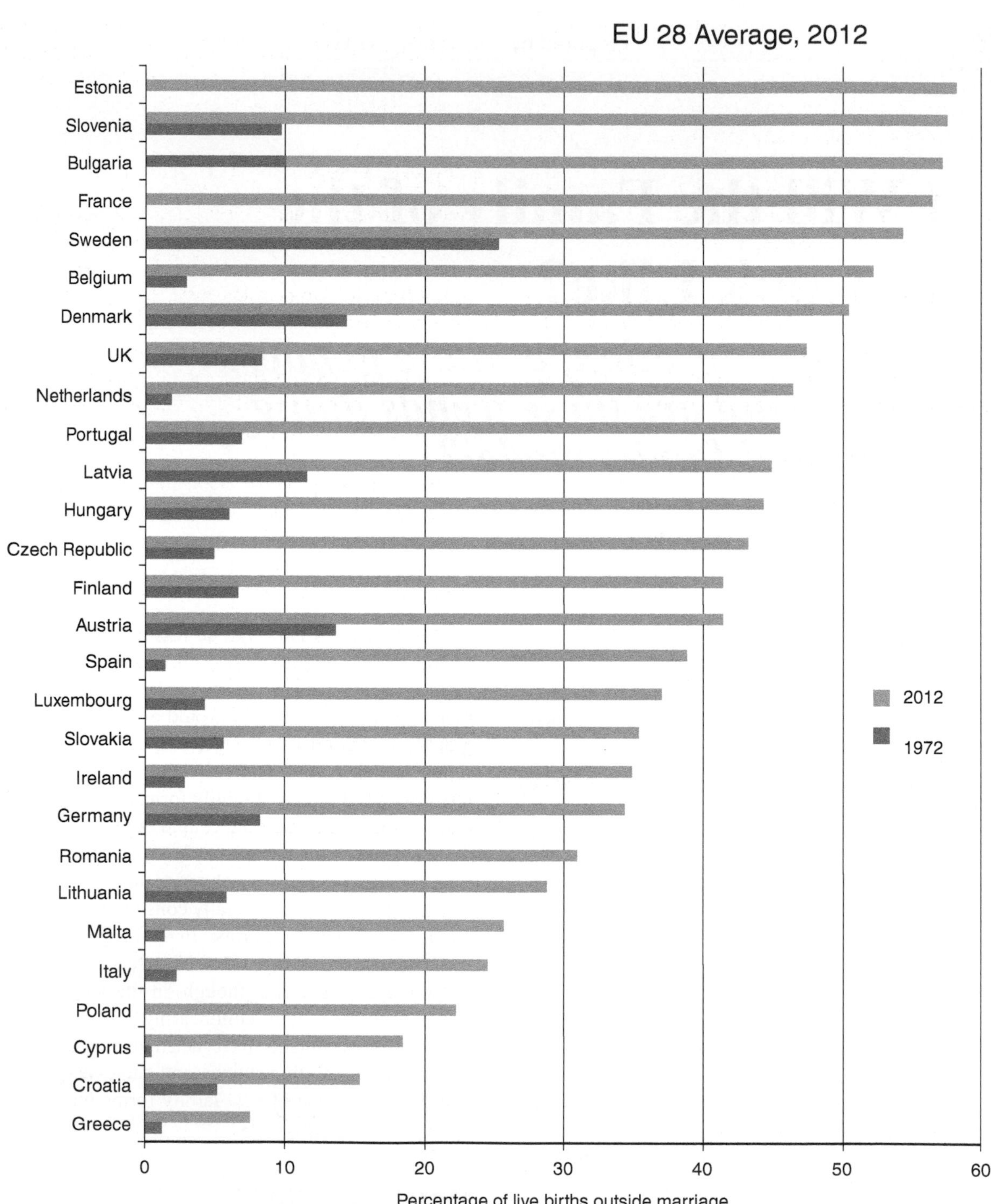

Figure 1 Percentage of births outside of marriage, 1972 and 2012 in EU 28

and behavior in evidence can be seen as fueling poverty by creating "diverging destinies" for children.

Partly in response to economic precariousness and reduced gains to marriage, less well-educated people are more likely to enter partnerships at an earlier age and to have children outside marriage. They are also more likely to see their relationships fail, or to go through pregnancy with multiple partners, compared to those with higher levels of education in the United States and possibly also in the United Kingdom.

You can also see the evidence of persistent diversity in large cross-national differences in the level of childbearing. As can be seen in the chart below, there is persistently low fertility (around 1.3 to 1.4 births per woman) in Southern Europe and the German-speaking countries, compared to much higher fertility (between 1.8 and 2 children per woman) in Nordic countries and Western Europe.

Childbearing is higher in countries with higher levels of female labor force participation, economic development, generosity of paid parental leave provision for mothers, and paternity leave.

Drivers of Change

There are several factors likely to affect how families are structured and organized and which could impact on shaping the future families. These include increasing longevity which has important implications for how we plan our lives, care needs, and intergenerational relations.

Increased international migration will create more transnational families—especially since for the first time women account for more than 50 percent of all international migrants. Technology is likely to influence the future of families too. As mobility increases, family members are increasingly geographically separated, but more connected via mobile technologies. Flexible working becomes more possible, allowing men and women to better combine their work and family roles.

Home Life

Another driver of change in future families is gender equality. The United Nations 2030 Agenda for Sustainable Development sets, among others, the goal of achieving gender equality and empowering all women and girls. But which type of gender equality matters for the future of families?

The adaptation of women to their new role in traditionally male activities in the public sphere and the acceptance of their new roles as equal or primary earners has been faster than the adaptation of men to traditionally female roles as care providers.

Men's share of housework and childcare is highest in gender-egalitarian countries such as the Nordic ones, and lowest in areas of low gender equality such as Southern and Eastern Europe.

However, look at the chart above and you can see that in all countries women still devote more time than men in housework activities. The gender revolution is far from being fully completed, even in the gender-egalitarian Nordic countries.

Sharing the Load

Proponents of the gender revolution theory predict a happy ending for the family of the future. Once gender equality in all spheres of life is reached, a new model of the family will become widespread, with higher fertility and more stable unions.

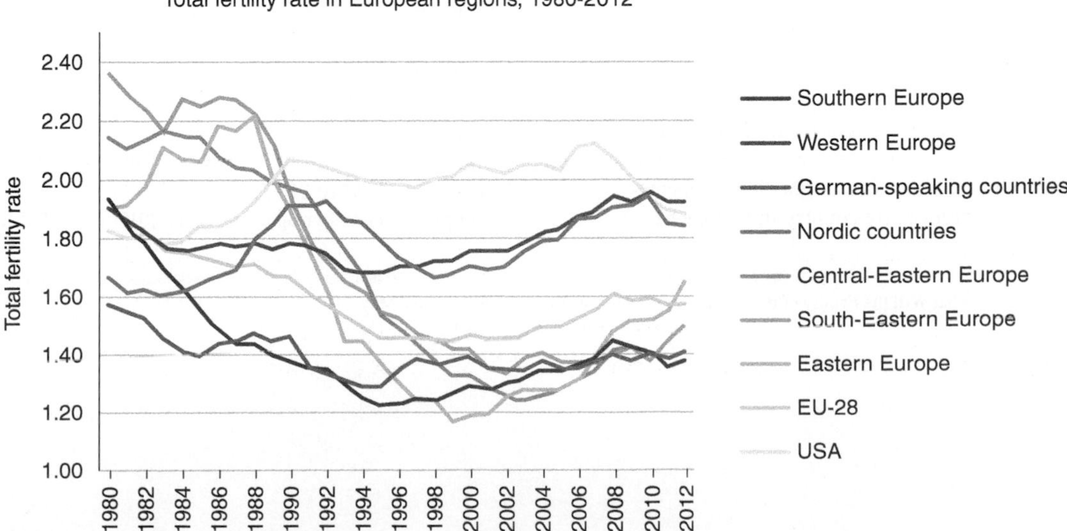

Figure 2 Total fertility rate in European regions, 1980-2012

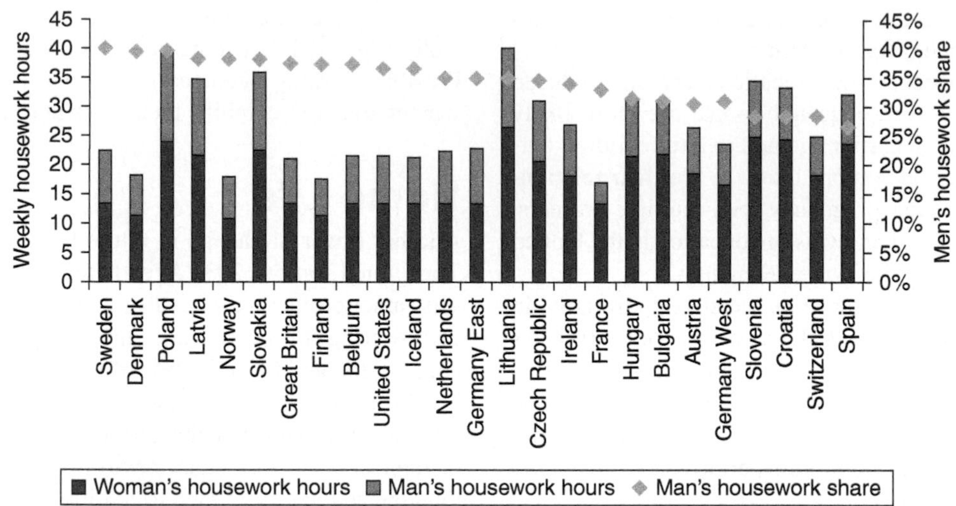

Figure 3 Weekly housework hours by gender and country and men's housework share

However, current data highlight striking differences across social classes: gender-egalitarian ideologies and decreased risk of divorce are a prerogative of the highly educated. Whether the gender revolution will translate into a positive outcome for families in the future may depend on whether and how fast men, especially from lower social classes, embrace gender equality in the home.

This is the equality that seems to matter most for promoting more stable families and higher fertility. The hope has to be that attitudes toward an equal division of tasks in and outside the home will continue to spread until we arrive at a new model of the family where partners become increasingly more similar in terms of their employment and caring responsibilities.

Critical Thinking

1. This article focuses on trends in families in Europe. How similar are these trends to what is occurring in the United States? Since the United States is a large, diverse country might some of the differences by country in Europe be similar to the differences we may see geographic region in the United States?
2. The authors state that family trends show a "convergence toward diversity." What do they mean by this? Do you agree with their perspective? Why or why not?
3. How do factors such as income, educational level, religion, and viewpoints regarding gender roles shape childbearing decisions and family structure? How might these factors as well as innovations in technology and increasing longevity bring about changes in families in the future?

Internet References

Council on Contemporary Families
https://contemporaryfamilies.org/

Institute for Family Studies
https://ifstudies.org/

Social Trends Institute: Family
http://www.socialtrendsinstitute.org/about-sti/what-we-do/family

World Family Map 2017
https://worldfamilymap.ifstudies.org/2017/files/WFM-2017-FullReport.pdf

Article

Prepared by: Patricia Hrusa Williams, *University of Maine at Farmington*

Why Are Fewer People Getting Married?

JAY L. ZAGORSKY

Learning Outcomes

After reading this article, you will be able to:

- Identify trends in marriage rates over time.
- Discuss how factors such as economics, social policies, and societal attitudes contribute to marriage rates.
- Consider whether a bias toward couples exists in society.

June kicks off the U.S. wedding season. Whether you love nuptials or hate them, an astounding trend is [occurring]: fewer couples are tying the knot.

The number of U.S. marriage ceremonies peaked in the early 1980s, when almost 2.5 million marriages were recorded each year. Since then, however, the total number of people getting married has fallen steadily. Now, only about two million marriages happen a year, a drop of almost half a million from their peak.

As a result, barely more than half of adults in the United States say they're living with a spouse. It is the lowest share on record, and down from 70 percent in 1967.

What's behind this trend? Is marriage becoming obsolete? Why should we care?

Marriage Rates Are Dropping Too

The drop in marriages is even more dramatic when the rapid growth in the U.S. population is taken into account. In fact, the marriage rate is the lowest in at least 150 years.

The figure below shows the number of marriages per 1,000 people for the last century and a half. It does not matter if it is a person's first, second, or even third marriage. The rate simply tracks the number of weddings that occurred adjusted by the population.

Record-low Marriage Rate

This graph charts the rise and fall of the U.S. marriage rate. The figure shows how many marriages per 1,000 people.

In the late 1800s, about nine of every 1,000 people got married each year. After rising in the early 1900s through World War I, the marriage rate plummeted during the Great Depression, when fewer people were able to afford starting a family. The rate shot up again at the end of World War II as servicemen returned home, eager to get hitched and have babies.

But since the early 1980s, the marriage rate has steadily dropped until it leveled off in 2009 at about seven per 1,000.

A Global Trend

It's not just the United States where this is happening.

The United Nations gathered data for roughly 100 countries, showing how marriage rates changed from 1970 to 2005. Marriage rates fell in ⅘ of them.

Australia's marriage rate, for example, fell from 9.3 marriages per 1,000 people in 1970 to 5.6 in 2005. Egypt's declined from 9.3 to 7.2. In Poland, it dropped from 8.6 to 6.5.

The drop occurred in all types of countries, poor and rich. And it clearly wasn't based on geography, since one of the biggest declines occurred in Cuba (13.4 to 5), while one of the biggest increases occurred in the neighboring island of Jamaica (4.9 to 8.7).

Among countries that experienced a reduction, the average rate fell from 8.2 marriages per 1,000 to just 5.2, which is an even lower rate than what the United States is now experiencing.

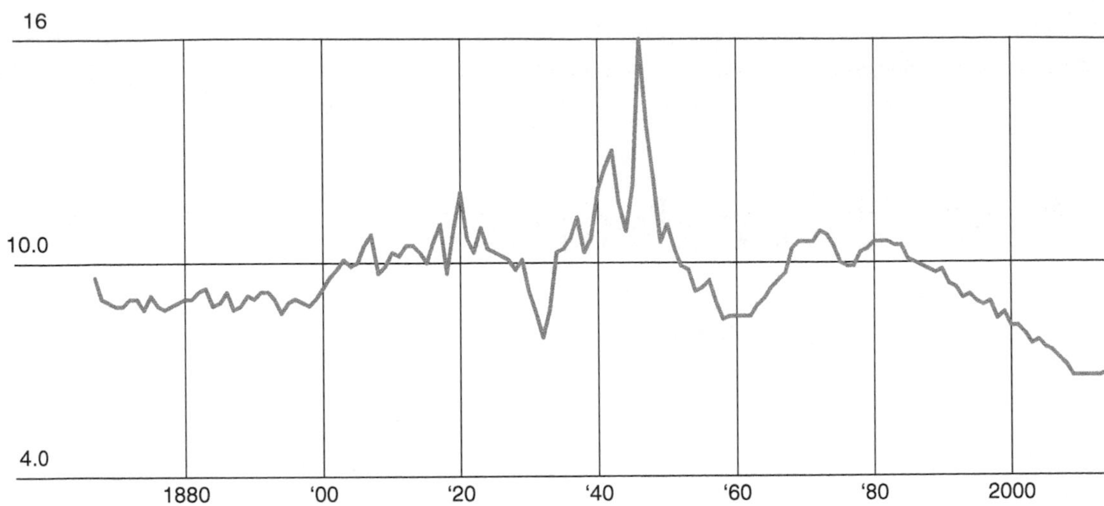

Source: Author created based on data from the Center for Disease Contrors National VItal Statistics System

Why Has the Drop Occurred?

The range of culprits is quite large.

Some blame widening U.S. income and wealth inequality. Others point the finger at the fall in religious adherence or cite the increase in education and income of women, making women choosier about whom to marry. Still others focus on rising student debt and rising housing costs, forcing people to put off marriage. Finally, some believe marriage is simply an old, outdated tradition that is no longer necessary.

But given that this is a trend happening across the globe in a wide variety of countries with very different income, religious adherence, education, and social factors, it's hard to pin the blame on just a single culprit.

Don't Blame the Government

Moreover, this drop in marriages is not occurring because of adverse legal or public policy changes. Governments across the globe continue to provide incentives and legal protections that encourage marriage.

For example, the U.S. federal government has over 1,000 laws that make special adjustments based on marital status. Many of these adjustments allow married couples to get preferential tax treatment and more retirement benefits and bypass inheritance laws.

Moreover, government legalization of same-sex marriages around the world has boosted the number of individuals able to enter into legally sanctioned unions.

While legalizing same-sex marriages has boosted the number of marriages, this increase has not been enough to reverse the declining trend.

Is It a Switch to Cohabiting?

Another popular explanation for why fewer people are getting married is that more couples prefer to live together informally, known as cohabitation.

It is true that the percentage of people living with a partner instead of marrying has risen over time. In 1970, just half-of-one-percent of all adults were cohabiting in the United States. Today, the figure is 7.5 percent.

However, this trend fails to explain the whole story of falling marriage rates. Even when we combine the share of adults who are married with those who are cohabiting, the picture still reveals a strong downward trend. In the late 1960s, over 70 percent of all U.S. adults were either married or cohabiting. The most recent data show less than 60 percent of adults are living together in either a marriage or cohabiting relationship.

This means over time, a smaller percentage of people are living as a couple. The number of people living alone, without a spouse, partner, children, or roommates has almost doubled. The number of people living by themselves in the United States was less than 8 percent in the late 1960s. Today, it's almost 15 percent.

Costs and Benefits of Marriage

So why have marriage rates declined around the world, while the number of people living on their own has exploded? In my mind, the simple answer is that for more people, the current costs of marriage outweigh the benefits.

The benefits of marriage are numerous and well-known. Researchers have linked marriage to better outcomes for children, less crime, an increase in longevity and happier lives,

Marital bliss?

More and more Americans are choosing to live alone or with a partner rather than get married. The chart shows the share of U.S. adults (18 and up) living with a spouse, a partner, on their own or with their parents (child of a householder – a college donn is considered in this category).

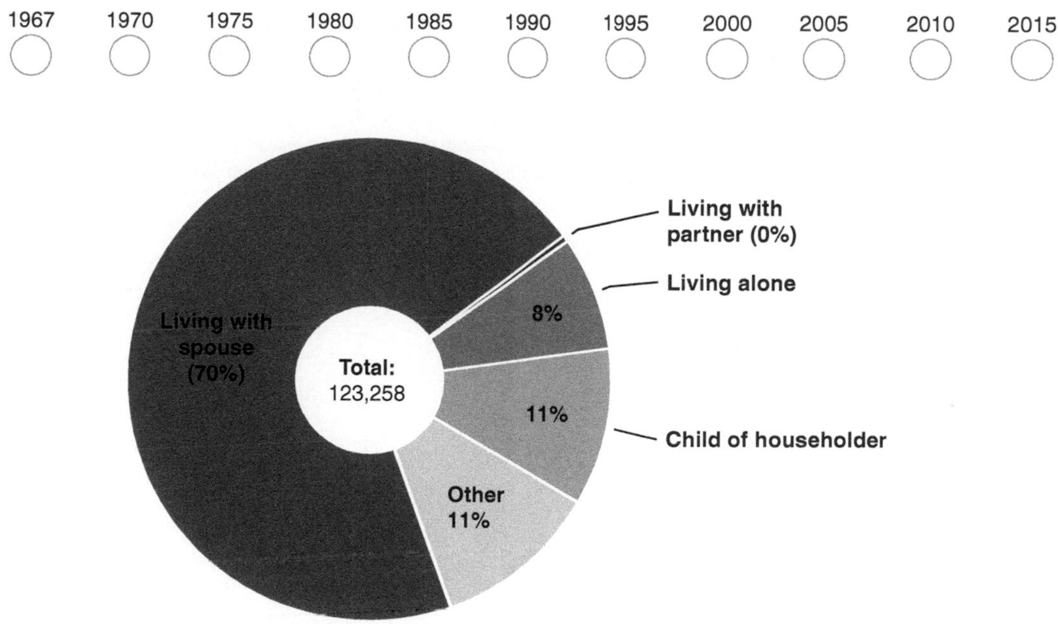

among many factors. My own research revealed that marriage is associated with more wealth.

Nevertheless, as Gary Becker pointed out in his widely used theory of marriage, these benefits don't come for free. Marriage is hard work. Living with someone means taking into account another person's feelings, moods, needs, and desires instead of focusing just on your own. This extra work has large time, emotional, and financial costs.

While decades ago many people believed the benefits of marriage outweighed these costs, the data around the world are clearly showing that more people are viewing the benefits of being married, or even cohabiting, as much smaller than the costs.

Why Do We Care?

As the wedding season takes hold, I have already been invited to a few nuptials, so it is clear marriage is not actually becoming obsolete.

Society today is geared toward couples. However, if the trends continue, then the growing number of single people will presumably begin to exert political pressure to eliminate the laws that favor and reward marriage and implicitly discriminate against them.

The question is: how large will this policy shift be and how soon until it occurs?

Critical Thinking

1. Why do you think fewer people are getting married? Do you think marriage becoming obsolete in modern society?
2. What factors did the author find which appear to discourage or contribute to the decline in marriage rates? How strong is their case and the data they present to support these factors? What other factors might be at play?
3. The author suggests that in modern society, the costs of marriage often outweigh the benefits. What do you see as the costs and benefits of marriage? In what ways might the benefits outweigh the costs? Do you think our society

discriminates against those who choose not to marry, as the author suggests?

Internet References

Council on Contemporary Families
https://contemporaryfamilies.org/

Institute for Family Studies
https://ifstudies.org/

Social Trends Institute: Family
http://www.socialtrendsinstitute.org/about-sti/what-we-do/family

World Family Map 2017
https://worldfamilymap.ifstudies.org/2017/files/WFM-2017-FullReport.pdf

Jay L. Zagorsky is an economist and research scientist in The Ohio State University.

Article Prepared by: Patricia Hrusa Williams, *University of Maine at Farmington*

Relationships in the Melting Pot

TINA LIVINGSTONE

Learning Outcomes

After reading this article, you will be able to:

- Define terms such gender identity terms as trans-identified, trans-historied, transvestite, transgendered (male-gendered, female-gendered), and transsexual.
- Describe challenges faced by female-gendered trans' people and their partners as their trans-identity is disclosed.
- Discuss the five stages of bereavement as they apply to trans-identity disclosure in couples.

Trans-identified people may experience themselves as male gendered, female gendered, bigendered, intergendered, or agendered; they may be born male bodied, female bodied, or intersex. However, for diverse reasons, society's attention has focused on female-gendered trans' people—those born male bodied. This group has been publicly demonized more than the others; indeed, some parts of society still struggle to accept them.

Perhaps it is for these reasons that it tends to be their partners presenting for counseling, and therefore, this is where this article will focus. This is not to say that partners of female-bodied and intersex-bodied people have no issues—it simply affords me space to explore issues at some depth rather than surface skim within the word limits of an article.

Similarly, trans' emergence and/or transition previously seemed associated with middle years. This was due in part to the fact that the population was heavily stigmatized and subject to severe regulatory discourse, and in part because the minority were well scattered through the rest of the population. However, improved communication systems, equalities legislation, and an ever-growing body of knowledge have enabled those who are born differently gendered to speak up at a younger age. Consequently, the United Kingdom now has a specifically designated unit for the support and treatment of transgender youth—the Gender Identity Development Service at the Tavistock and Portman NHS Foundation Trust. Again, it is not to be assumed that partner issues are irrelevant for trans' youth. However, though there will be some similarities, these relationships are more often set in the sphere of knowing and therefore somewhat different.

Thirdly, it feels important to note that not all partners go into relationship with trans-identified and trans-historied people unwittingly. As society settles its struggles with diversity and becomes more open, it has become more common for people to knowingly enter into a relationship with trans' people—both populations have become less socially anxious around each other. As with trans' youth, there will be some similarities and some differences in the issues arising, but in writing an article rather than a book, I must focus in order to achieve some detail.

Female Partners in Existing Relationships

When trans-identity is disclosed, natural human fascination with the unusual tends to direct curiosity toward the person concerned; the attention given to those in relationship with trans-identified and trans-historied people is miniscule in comparison. Indeed, it has been frequently considered understandable, and often presumed unavoidable, that any existing intimate partnership with a trans-identified person will fracture and fall away once trans' nature has been disclosed or exposed. The regulatory discourse that silenced gender diversity for so long has had an equally silencing effect on those in relationship with them. The partner population thus suffers from not only being queered by association, but also from prejudice by proxy—in so far as a society that regards the trans' population as disordered assumes their partners must be too!

Historically, divorce was a prerequisite for gender reassignment—treatment protocols categorized marriage as "a contra-indication to cross-sex surgery."[1] This derived partly from the heteronormative assumption that men are naturally attracted to, and partnered by, women, and vice versa; so somebody who was genuinely female would want a male partner, and similarly no married female would wish to stay with a woman. It also concerned professional liability, one treatment protocol clearly stating the requirement for "proof of divorce to protect the surgeon and referring physicians from possible lawsuits from alienated spouses."[2] For sometime, it was not possible to study the effect of gender transition in existing marriages simply because those marriages ended. Trans-identified male-bodied people not seeking clinical treatment were relegated to the category of transvestite and regarded as sexually deviant; consequently, their wives and partners were similarly described. Therapists at this time were encouraged to "help such women . . . develop sufficient insight and information to intelligently manage the dilemma,"[3] with accepted outcomes being either the wife accepting her husband as perverted or severance of the relationship.

Clinicians pondered the flaws and weaknesses of those who partnered transvestites for many years. Their findings indicated the prevalence of obesity, childlessness, alcoholism, and psychiatric disorder; even the simple incidence of being first born in their family was correlated to neurotic tendency. This somewhat depressing perspective seems to have been developed from the work of Stoller in the 1960s, who created a binary model of "transvestites" women' as comprising "malicious male-haters," all having in common "a fear of and a need to ruin masculinity."[4] In a later study of transvestites' wives and partners, Wise[3] similarly observed that "depression, hostility, sadism, and alcohol abuse were methods utilized to cope with their perverse mate," and that "subjects were often demoralized and agitated." He further indicated high rates of major affective disorders, borderline personality disorders, and a prevalence of acute sadomasochistic themes within this client group.

Until very recently, negative attitudes toward the trans' population were also very prevalent in the press and media, parallel to which was a dearth of reporting any positive outcomes. Without some body of knowledge, there can be no reference points for any journey; thus, it becomes something approached with anxiety, misgiving, and doubt. Without some understanding of potential and possibility, there's little incentive to make any effort, thus it becomes easier to avoid or give up. Moreover, if we are designated unnameable, our very existence becomes taboo. It is small wonder that the partners of trans-identified and trans-historied people have been conspicuous by their absence in the counseling room for so long . . . but they are coming. They are coming because cyberspace is teaching them that they are not alone, that it is possible to find support in their struggle, and, perhaps most importantly, that positive outcomes are possible.

Virginia Erhardt champions those who stay in relationship with trans-identified people as "willing to investigate and cultivate open-minded attitudes about gender variance." She reports that they "often have high levels of ego-strength . . . capacity to self-soothe and self-validate, regardless of the opinions of others," and that they have "good emotional boundaries."[5] I would say that they are as equally human as any other sector of the population, that they have diverse strengths and weaknesses, as do all individuals, and that their journeys are as unique and varied as anyone else's. As with most client groups, they approach counseling full of fear, uncertain of both self and outcomes, and doubtful that they have the strength to survive. My hope for them, and you, is that whatever path they end up taking, whether a relationship ends or continues, they move forward knowing that they have been truly heard, did their best, and are as valid and valued as anyone else.

Exposure and Disclosure

Whatever the trans' nature of an individual—transvestite/transgender/transsexual—the first encounter for the majority of partners of male-bodied trans' people generally concerns cross-dressing. Whether this is disclosed in conversation or discovered by accident or design, the partner concerned usually experiences some degree of shock, rapidly followed by a bombardment of doubts and fears. Common areas of concern include security, inadequacy, homosexuality, and identity. Anxieties about security often emanate from awareness of social stigma and a consequent cascade of questions such as: "What will other people think and how will they behave toward me/toward you/toward us?' Fears of inadequacy rumble along the lines of: "Why am I not enough?" Concerns about homosexuality rise up in the enquiry: "Do you really want to be with a man?" Consideration of identity comprises diverse strands including the enquiry: "If you take the female role, what do I do?" And statements of assertion may include: "I am not a lesbian," and "I married a man."

The nature of disclosure obviously affects the person receiving it, and unfortunately, disclosure frequently feels extremely ill-timed for the partner. Midlife changes are frequently precipitated by increased awareness of our mortality, and disclosure of trans-identity is no exception. Zamboni reports that, "death of a parent or another family member can prompt a transgendered person to 'come out'."[6] I have found that the emergence of cancer, or other life-threatening conditions, in a family member or a friend, similarly heralds change. Conversely, happy events that also mark the passage of time, such as the birth of a child, an older child's graduation, or a major anniversary, can also precipitate disclosure. While, for some, the timing for disclosure seems to coincide with a notion that "things are so bad, it can't make it worse," others seem to think that the best time is when all is well, such as during a family holiday or romantic weekend away. My experience is that there is never a good time, but sometimes are worse than others.

Whether accidental discovery or exposure is deliberate, conscious or unconscious, is debatable. It certainly seems strange that someone who has been dressing secretly for years suddenly forgets to put away their stockings, or leaves their wife's worn clothes in a heap. It is also strange that people well experienced in private use of computers suddenly forget to hibernate them while on a trans' website or gallery. While genuine forgetfulness may be the reason, it could also be that engineering a discovery feels like a good way of at least sharing responsibility for it, if not totally transferring the weight.

Whatever the nature of the disclosure, one of the hardest things for the couple to manage at this time is their mutually heightened sense of vulnerability. As the partner's world is well and truly turned upside down, the trans-identified person will be desperate for acceptance, emotionally fragile, and extremely fearful of loss. Both sides are likely to feel a burden of guilt for the distress of the other as circumstances unfold, and both may be unable to engage anywhere near the topic without distress. Commonly, what promotes one partner's happiness causes the other upset, both become prone to launch grenades of emotional blackmail at the other, and neither is able to hear much beyond their own turmoil.

Almost every other eventuality in life will have been rehearsed; the "what ifs" of life that arise when someone is inexplicably late, or we hear of someone else's misfortune, will have played out over and over again. All except for this one. The profound sense of helplessness and isolation for a partner in such a situation is thus overwhelming, and frequently compounded by the need to sustain secrecy, since at this stage it is usual for other family members and the closest of friends to be outside the circle of disclosure.

At this time, partners are also subject to intense feelings of betrayal, as with the disclosure of any large secret.[7] The fact that other people within the trans' communities are likely to know about the situation before they do, and that things will have been going on behind their back, often exacerbates both the sense of being alone and hopelessness.

Perhaps hardest of all, neither partner has all the answers that the other wishes to hear—on the one side because while trans' nature is submerged, it can only be partially known, and on the other because, in facing the unknown, we have no measure of how we will cope, let alone a picture of outcomes. The nature of adjustments the partner will need to make in order to sustain the relationship will depend very much on the trans' status of her partner. Parameters will vary, from the hope that she will participate in erotic cross-dressing and allow her husband freedom to participate in the trans' scene, through wishing for her acceptance of her husband living part time as a female, to her acceptance of full gender transition. At the point of disclosure, the fact that this is likely to be an unknown exacerbates the sense of precariousness.

Processing Panic

Partners in existing relationships are likely to feel a sense of deep loss, akin to bereavement, because this feels like the point when their future dies. What is known cannot be unknown and therefore their picture of a future relationship, however nebulous, is duly shattered. Ellis and Eriksen[8] recognized the emotional process for partners as being similar to the five stages of bereavement: denial, anger, bargaining, depression, and acceptance.[9] As with all models, not every person will be subject to every aspect, nor will stages necessarily occur sequentially, or without repetition. Characteristically, the partner will first deny what is happening. This may be as simple and direct as refusing to look or listen—avoiding contact being one of the most common ways to sustain denial. At other times, people desperately try to tag the events with an alternative cause—such as work-related stress or midlife crisis—thus suggesting the situation is temporary and can be stopped. Anger is frequently fueled by a sense of betrayal and may initially be directed at full force at the trans' person. It is quite likely to ricochet onto others, including helping professionals, and, of course, the self too. Notions of failure and seeking out fault and blame can become all consuming. At such times, Emerson and Rosenfeld[10] advocate the importance of validating feelings and normalizing thoughts. At the bargaining stage, attempts to restrict, if not reverse, the situation often escalate to the level of threat, rather than negotiation, and here experience in conflict resolution and mediation can hold the counselor in good stead. Depression accumulates as the permanence of trans' nature dawns and emotional exhaustion takes its toll.

If it's not gone already, it is here that sexual dysfunction often occurs. People who are hurting seldom feel like being touched when what was once warmly familiar feels like a cold lie. Where sexual intimacy has already ceased, the situation merely confirms a partner's fears of undesirability and sense of impending doom. Where a sexual relationship exists, it becomes a minefield of doubts. Whether sexual intimacy continues or not, the therapist working with a relationship at this level of risk should be able to hold real fear and deep distress. Here, it can be really useful to enable the client to recognize any signs of affection and care remaining, as these can be crucial stepping-stones in affording the necessary space not to act in haste.

Once loved ones are able to start their grieving, it is reported that peer support or social contact with other SOFFAs (significant others [spouses and partners], family, friends, and allies) can be helpful.[11] Much, of course, depends on the nature of the individuals and their situations—for example, hearing about the joys of nonmonogamy is cold comfort to the wife who has just found her husband's frilly knickers collection. Similarly, when one's own desirability is in question, it is not always helpful to know that other people are happily living as sisters or soul mates. What can be useful is to know that one is truly not alone with such experience, that people not only survive but eventually thrive, both together and separately, and that all one's doubts, fears, and feelings are truly understandable. Resonance may not contain all the answers, but for some it can ease the grip of desolation.

Loss has many dimensions, and so far as partners are concerned, it is not simply the potential loss of their partner that is at stake (as if that weren't more than enough to handle), but also the potential loss of self, that feels under threat. Identity exists in relationship rather than in a vacuum, and when someone transitions in an existing relationship, the change is not solely about them. Whether the couple are heterosexual or not, a change of sex automatically impacts on partner identity. Most people's sense of identity includes sexual identity, and most sexual identity is not simply about what happens in the bedroom, it is also about who we are in the world, and how society relates to that. One of the most devastating conundrums partners face is that any acceptance of their partner's identity feels like a betrayal of their own; in being asked to change perception of the other, they feel they are asked to change themselves at a fundamental level. Most heterosexual women have no inclination to partner another female, and similarly neither gay men nor lesbian women readily welcome the notion of being converted to heterosexual. Here, labels can strangle away the very will to continue, and counselors can ease the knot by sharing information. For example, in a gay relationship, it can be helpful to ascribe relationship as differently queer, while in a heterosexual relationship, a focus on the love of the person rather than usual labels can be helpful.

A major part of who we are comprises our roles in life. While couples in a same-sex relationship tend not to ascribe gender role to their everyday living, gender stereotypical roles are often absorbed into heterosexual partnership. Cultural constructs around one's place in home and society may comprise cornerstones of identity, even evoke a true sense of pride and purpose—thus feeling one's identity as a husband or wife is at risk can be deeply threatening. Worries about who now fixes the car may seem trivial, but when a husband can no longer do his chores lest she break a nail, or refuses to take the lads to football practice, lest she be thought a man, domestic routines can soon become a nightmare.

Negotiating Boundaries

Whether or not transition is intended, wives and partners are often expected to catch up with trans' issues at a frightening pace. Those who show any signs of possible acceptance are bombarded with books, articles, and websites—often experiencing information overload. The fact is that when we are shocked, it can take time to work out our feelings, and when in distress and panic, it can be very difficult to think. Lev notes that in transgender emergence, subjects resemble a coiled spring, ready to pop, and that in their exuberance, "some do not think clearly about jobs, careers, spouses, and children, and sometimes take risks that may entail grave consequences."[12] Examples given include fathers "cross-dressing at home and in front of their children, who are confused and frightened" and "discussing hormone therapy with wives who are still bitter and angry over the disclosure." Often, if the relationship is to stand a chance, boundaries must be negotiated; a truly difficult thing to achieve against such an emotive backdrop.

When partners do assert boundaries, or try to negotiate pace, they often face accusations of being cruel and lacking understanding. Many report cases of "infantile tantrums" and the sense of "dealing with a child," experiencing their other halves as suddenly selfish and self-absorbed. Unfortunately, "narcissistic self-obsession can be recognized as part of the normative emergence process for a transgender person who has repressed or hidden these issues for many years."[12] This doesn't make such behaviors any easier to live with, but understanding that it is both common, and a phase, can help people find the strength to stick it out, especially when their relationship is founded on genuine love. Indeed, when founded on sincere and deep affection, the childlike qualities of the repressed self-emerging can trigger protectiveness in partners; as they remember that children have an endearing side, and that sometimes life can actually be fun.

This brings me to the point that, despite being one devil of a roller coaster, a partner's journey is not necessarily all bad. The majority of trans-identified and trans-historied people hold acceptance, and those who are prepared to try to reach it, in the highest esteem. Often a deliberate disclosure denotes great hopefulness and immense trust. Sometimes, counseling partners is not simply about giving them space to air their struggles and process problems, it is about being able to share the good times and celebrate. One of my clients once explained that, unlike other wives, she felt obliged to have a huge smile slapped on her face all the time, and that it ached. It was not that she wasn't happy—but she felt the loss of having a simple moan and grumble about her spouse, as people do from time to time. She confided that if she so much as looked glum, let alone expressed any discomfort, friends and family seemed to think her marriage was inevitably falling apart, and any denial simply resulted in them labeling her brave!

Being beside Visible Difference

Acceptance does not eradicate every issue. Indeed, where trans-identity is concerned, it can actually add other layers of difficulty. Whether full transition occurs or not, partners are often expected to adjust to visible and tangible changes at an alarming rate as their other half explores femininity. Even those who partner part-time girls, or where the boundary is set at not seeing the female side, may find the disappearance of familiar facial and body hair distressingly different. Manicured nails (even unpainted) and plucked eyebrows can be equally alarming. Aside from personal discomfort, these signals also trigger fear of exposure within the wider family, within social circles, and at work. Potential for ridicule, and even rejection, is often keenly felt, making it difficult for partners to be supportive even when they want to be. Moreover, when a spouse dresses in female clothes anywhere in public, many wives find themselves unable to hold hands or show the simplest signs of affection, lest they be thought lesbian; this is not necessarily about prejudice, it is simply about identity. Having acclimatized to who we are in the world, it can be devastating to feel that identity reframed from outside ourselves; good counsel not only holds that devastation but also enables co-construction of a more acceptable and truly grounded self.

Where acceptance is sufficient to go out together socially, with the trans' partner cross-dressed, non-trans' partners are often surprised at the high levels of protectiveness that emerge. One recounted: "We were in the chippie and I noticed a group of lads looking. I found myself putting myself between them and her, and giving them such a look! I swear if they had said anything, I would have punched one." First outings can be exhausting for both sides because of the fear of being outed or ridiculed, and even when all goes well, adrenaline at the ready is very tiring.

Where dressing occurs in the home, despite the most carefully negotiated strategies to sustain privacy, the doorbell can suddenly become a direct signal for panic, and even doing laundry can become problematic. One client reported her anxiety rocketing when, as she unloaded the washing machine, her daughter noticed a rather short colorful skirt and asked who owned it. Trying to claim it as her own backfired when the daughter responded that it was too small, to which the mother countered that she was on a diet. The daughter then pushed her to say when she had worn it, and she snapped: "When you are in bed and I get some peace!" While the humor in this and other situations did not escape this client, she struggled with being untruthful—to her children, to her parents, and to her close friends.

Relationship Reframed

While asexual couples exist, and can be deeply happy, most people do not go into marriage or partnership with a platonic relationship in mind. Where trans' emergence occurs, sex can be a major stumbling block in diverse ways, regardless of orientation. It often takes time for people to become comfortable and confident sexually, and once settled in sexual routine, however fabulous, notions of having sexual intimacy in alternative ways can be scary and repulsive, even unthinkable. Mechanics aside, the simple realization that one's partner has been fantasizing about being in your role during sex, rather than being truly with you, can evoke shock, humiliation, and despair. To see the light of hopefulness extinguished by such revelations in the counseling room can be truly hard to be with; understanding that it is not necessarily "game over" enables one to hold that hopefulness for the client, in case it can be picked up again.

While acknowledging that the positioning of sex in any partnership varies, and accepting that for some, "practices of emotional care and the values of honesty and trust are emphasized above sexual desire,"[13] it feels crucial that counselors hold in awareness the possibility that such narratives can be simply avoidant.

Because they have previously been stigmatized as perverted, there is huge pressure on trans-identified and trans-historied people to present themselves as asexual; indeed, those transitioning to female frequently stereotype sex as a masculine pursuit to assert their femininity. Digging for such hidden truths, especially where a relationship seems comfortable for those in it, would be questionable. However, assumptions around sex being less important in trans' relationships can be equally wrong. While genuinely respecting the clients, wherever they are, I would advocate we always hold in awareness potential and possibility. It was once my deep privilege to receive a breathlessly excited call from a wife whose marriage to a transsexual woman had previously transitioned happily into the platonic plane over a decade previously. The call was to let me know that, on holiday, after a good day and good wine, she and her lady had enjoyed great sex as never before. She told me that she had no one else who would understand, and the laughter in her closing words was wonderful: "I do hope we can remember how it went."

The possibility of engaging in alternative sexual practices, whether in terms of activity or relationship configurations, is not something I would recommend bringing to the counseling room too early. Lacking knowledge is sometimes a blessing until it's relevant to your own circumstance. However, it is without doubt useful to hold a nonjudgmental attitude and have information to hand should this become relevant to the client. Sometimes, a wider vocabulary of sexual practice or honestly negotiated nonmonogamy opens up positive possibilities, where elsewhere contemplating such things would simply have caused a meltdown. Sometimes expanding horizons heals; my experience is that open marriage, polyamory, and stable triads are all possible positive outcomes.

Final Thoughts

Self-discovery and change are inevitable consequences of a partner's journey. The changes in their life partner, whether or not that involves transition, will make them more conscious of themselves in the world. Depending on outcomes, the final level of acceptance may be when the partner truly and wholeheartedly joins the journey of the trans-identified partner, when the relationship transitions to something more in line with siblings than lovers, or when they part without malice. I know couples who have revisited their wedding vows in church, both wearing dresses, people who still enjoy a fully sexual marriage, and others who live happily in sisterly union, as well as ex-partners, comfortable in their own lives, who happily take their children on holiday together every year. All things are possible—with time, respect, and love. It is simply that when we are devastatingly hurt, we cannot even contemplate the possibilities. Somewhere, there is a legally female lady who dresses male again once a year to take her wife out on their anniversary—no emotional blackmail, no regret, and no embarrassment, on either part, just love. There are also at least three female fathers who have proudly given away their respective daughters at the marriage altar. To have accompanied people on such journeys is a great privilege. My hope is that this article enables you to contemplate enjoying such a privilege too. Many of us understand the space where the possibility of laughter is forgotten—we should never lose sight of the possibility of its return.

References

1. Randall JR. Indications for sex reassignment surgery. Archives of Sexual Behavior 1971;1(2):153–161.
2. Clemmensen LH. The 'real life' test for surgical candidates. In: R. Blanchard R, Steiner BW (eds). Clinical management of gender identity disorders in children and adults. Washington, DC: APA; 1990 (pp 212–135).
3. Wise TN. Coping with a transvestitic mate: clinical implications. Journal of Sex & Marital Therapy 1985; 11(4): 293–300.
4. Stoller RJ. Sex and gender. New York: Science House; 1968.
5. Erhardt V. Head over heels. Wives who stay with cross-dressers and transsexuals. Binghamton, NY: The Haworth Press Inc; 2007.
6. Zamboni BD. Therapeutic considerations in working with the family, friends, and partners of transgendered individuals. The Family Journal. Counseling and Therapy for Couples and Families 2006; 14(2): 174–179.
7. Reynolds A, Caron S. How intimate relationships are impacted when heterosexual men cross-dress. Journal of Psychology and Human Sexuality 2000; 12(3): 63–77.
8. Ellis KM, Eriksen K. Transsexual and transgenderist experiences and treatment options. The Family Journal 2002; 10(3): 289–299.
9. Kübler-Ross E. On death and dying. New York: Macmillan; 1969.
10. Emerson S, Rosenfeld C. Stages of adjustment in family members of transgender individuals. Journal of Family Psychotherapy 1996; 7(3): 1–2.
11. Weinberg TS, Bullough VL. Alienation, self image, and the importance of support groups for the wives of transvestites. Journal of Sex Research 1988; 24(1): 262–268.
12. Lev AI. Transgender emergence: therapeutic guidelines for working with gender-variant people and their families. Binghamton, NY: Hayworth Clinical Practice Press; 2004.
13. Hines S. Intimate transitions: transgender practices of partnering and parenting. Sociology: The Journal Of The British Sociological Association 2006; 40(2): 353–371.

Critical Thinking

1. If your partner revealed their trans-identity to you, how would you feel? Could you or would you want to maintain your relationship with you? What questions would you have?
2. The author suggests that in prior generations, doctors' protocols required those seeking gender reassignment to show proof of divorce. Why do you think this was done? What might be some consequences of this practice?
3. What are some ways counseling may assist couples where one partner has recently disclosed their trans-identity? Possible?

Internet References

GLAAD: Transgender Frequently Asked Questions
https://www.glaad.org/transgender/transfaq

Human Rights Campaign: Transgender Resources
http://www.hrc.org/

National Center for Transgender Equality
http://www.transequality.org

Tina Livingstone is a client-centered counselor and Pink Therapy Advanced Accredited Sex and Gender Diversities Therapist working in private practice. An experienced supervisor, consultant, and trainer, she has 15 years' experience of working with gender diverse clients and their families. She gained an MSc in Counseling at Strathclyde University in 2013, based on quantitative research into trans-identified and trans-historied clients' experience of everyday counseling. Further details of her work can be found at: http://www.positivebeams.com.

Article

Prepared by: Patricia Hrusa Williams, *University of Maine at Farmington*

Family Diversity Is the New Normal for America's Children

A Briefing Paper Prepared for the Council on Contemporary Families

PHILIP COHEN

Learning Outcomes

After reading this article, you will be able to:

- Identify demographic changes in families in the past 50 years.
- Analyze how societal, political, technological, and cultural changes are contributing to changes in the demographic characteristics of families in the United States.

People often think of social change in the lives of American children since the 1950s as a movement in one direction—from children being raised in married, male-breadwinner families to a new norm of children being raised by working mothers, many of them unmarried. Instead, we can better understand this transformation as an explosion of diversity, a fanning out from a compact center along many different pathways.

The Dramatic Rearrangement of Children's Living Situations Since the 1950s

At the end of the 1950s, if you chose 100 children under age 15 to represent all children, 65 would have been living in a family with married parents, with the father employed and the mother out of the labor force. Only 18 would have had married parents who were both employed. As for other types of family arrangements, you would find only one child in every 350 living with a never-married mother!

Today, among 100 representative children, just 22 live in a married male-breadwinner family, compared to 23 living with a single mother (only half of whom have ever been married). Seven out of every 100 live with a parent who cohabits with an unmarried partner (a category too rare for the Census Bureau to consider counting in 1960) and six with either a single father (3) or with grandparents but no parents (3). The single largest group of children—34—live with dual-earner married parents, but that largest group is only a third of the total, so that it is really impossible to point to a "typical" family.

With two-thirds of children being raised in male-breadwinner, married-couple families, it is understandable that people from the early 1960s considered such families to be the norm.[i] Today, by contrast, there is no single family arrangement that encompasses the majority of children.

To represent this diversity simply, we can calculate the chance that two children live in the same work-family structure. In 1960 you would have had an 80 percent chance that two children, selected at random, would share the same situation. By 2012, that chance had fallen to just a little more than 50–50.

The diversity masks an additional layer of differences, which come from the expanding variety of pathways in and

[i] Interestingly, the dominance of the male-breadwinner nuclear family was not always as great as it was at mid-century. As historian Stephanie Coontz has shown, up until the 1920s, most households contained more than one wage earner—mothers working on the family farm or business, and/or children working for pay as well.

out of these arrangements, or transitions from one to another. For example, among the children living with cohabiting parents in 2012, the resident parent is divorced or separated in about a third of cases. In those cases, the cohabiting-parent family often is a blended family with complex relationships to adults and children outside the household. Many more parents have (or raise) children with more than one partner over their lives than in the past, and many more children cycle through several *different* family arrangements as they grow up.

The children in America's classrooms today come from so many distinct family arrangements that we can no longer assume they share the same experiences and have the same needs. Likewise, policy-makers can no longer design family programs and regulations for a narrow range of family types and assume that they will pretty much meet the needs of all children.

The Decline of Married Couples as the Dominant Household Arrangement

The diversification of family life over time is also shown in the changing proportions of all household types, including ones without children. I put each household into one of five types, using Census data from 1880 to 2010. The largest category is households composed of married couples living with no one except their own children. If there was any other relative living in a household, I counted it as an extended household. The third category is individuals who live alone. Fourth are single parents (most of them mothers) living with no one besides their own children. In the final category are households made up of people who are not related (including unmarried couples).

The married-couple family peaked between 1950 and 1960, when this arrangement characterized two-thirds of households. This was also the peak of the nuclear family, because up until the 1940s, extended families were much more common than they became in the 1950s and 1960s. After that era, the pattern fans out.

By 2010, the proportion of married-couple households had dropped to less than half (45 percent) of the total. The proportion of individuals living alone rose from 13 to 27 percent between 1960 and 2010, and single-parent households rose from 6 to 12 percent. The result is that households composed of lone individuals and single parents accounted for almost 40 percent of all households by 2010. Extended households are less common than they were a century ago, mostly as a result of the greater independence of older people, but their numbers have increased again in the last several decades. In sum, the dominant married-couple household of the first half of the twentieth century was replaced not by a new standard, but rather by a general increase in family diversity.

How Did We Get Here? Market Forces, Social Welfare Reform, and Family Rearrangements

As the market economy generated new products and services that can supplement or substitute for many of the core functional tasks that families had to perform in the past, people became more able to rearrange their family lives. For example, technological innovations made women's traditional household tasks, such as shopping, preserving food, house-cleaning, and making clothes, far less time-consuming, while better birth control technology allowed them to control the timing or number of their births. After 1960, employment rates for both married and unmarried women rocketed upward in a 30-year burst that would finally move women's work primarily from the home to the market.

The shift to market work reinforced women's independence within their families, but also, in many cases, *from* their families. Women freed from family dependence could live singly, even with children; they could afford to risk divorce; and they could live with a man without the commitment of marriage.

In the aftermath of the Depression and World War II, social reformers increased their efforts to provide a social safety net for the elderly, the poor, and the disabled. The combination of pension and welfare programs that resulted also offered opportunities for more people to structure their lives independently.

For older Americans, Social Security benefits were critical. They helped reduce the effective poverty rates of older people from almost 60 percent in the 1960s to 15 percent by 2010, freeing millions of Americans from the need to live with their children in old age. At the beginning of the twentieth century, the Census counted only 1 in 10 people age 55 or older living with no relative. By the end of the century, the proportion was more than 1 in 4. Most of that change occurred between 1940 and 1980.

For younger adults, the combination of expanding work opportunities for women and greater welfare support for children made marriage less of a necessity. In the 1960s and 1970s, Aid to Families with Dependent Children grew rapidly, eventually supporting millions of never-married mothers and their children. Welfare did not create single-mothers—whose numbers rose partly in response to poverty, economic insecurity, and rising incarceration rates, and have continued to rise even after large cutbacks in public assistance—and it always carried a shameful stigma while providing a minimal level of monetary support. But it nevertheless allowed poor women to more easily leave abusive or dangerous relationships.

Market forces were most important in increasing the ability of middle-class and more highly educated women to delay, forego, or leave marriage. Poor women, especially African-American women, had long been more likely to work for pay, but their lower earnings did not offer the same personal independence that those with better jobs enjoyed, so welfare support was a bigger factor in the growing ability of poor women to live on their own. Nevertheless, the market has contributed to the growth of single mother families in a different way over the past 40 years, as falling real wages and increasing job insecurity for less-educated men have made them more risky as potential marriage partners.

As a result of these and other social trends such as women's increasing educational attainment, diversity of family arrangements increased dramatically after the 1950s.

Changes in Women's Work-Family Situations

The work-family situations of both women and children show the same pattern of increasing diversity replacing the dominant-category system that peaked in the 1950s. For women aged 30–34, the rise in education and employment is most dramatic, while marriage and motherhood have become markedly less universal.

Rather than simply see each of these as separate trends, we can create profiles by combining the four characteristics (educational, employment, marital, and parental status) into 16 different categories—employed college graduates who are married mothers on one extreme; non-employed non-graduates who aren't married or mothers on the other. Data indicates there has been a decline in a single profile—the married, non-college educated, not-employed, mother—and the diversity in statuses that have replaced that single type. In 1960, almost 80 percent of women in their early 30s and had not completed college and were married with children. Now such women comprise less than a third of the total—and no category includes more than 18 percent of women. In terms of diversity, in 1960 the chance that two women picked at random would be from from the same category was 40 percent. Today that chance has fallen to 11 percent.

Diversity and Inequality

Some of the new diversity in work-family arrangements is a result of new options for individuals, especially women and older people, whose lives are less constrained than they once were. But some of the new diversity also results from economic changes that are less positive, especially the job loss and wage declines for younger, less-educated men since the late 1970s.

In and of itself, however, family diversity doesn't have to lead to inequality. In the Nordic countries of Finland, Norway and Denmark, for example, unmarried-mother families have poverty rates that barely differ from those of married-couple families—all have poverty rates less than 10 percent. Similarly, many countries do a better job of minimizing the school achievement gap between children of single mothers versus children of married parents—a study of 11 wealthy countries found the gap is largest in the United States.

Different families have different child-rearing challenges and needs, which means we are no longer well-served by policies that assume most children will be raised by married-couple families, especially ones where the mother stays home throughout the children's early years. As we debate social and economic policy, we need to consider the needs of children in many different family situations, and how they will be affected by policy changes, rather than privileging one particular family structure or arrangement.

Critical Thinking

1. The author states that diversity in families is the new normal. What does he mean by this? Do you agree with him and why?
2. Of the statistics presented on children and families in the article, identify the one that surprised you the most. Why?
3. Why are these changes occurring in the family in our society? What do you see as the biggest change in families which will occur in the next 50 years? Will there be a "typical" family? Why/why not?

Internet References

Administration for Children and Families
www.acf.hhs.gov

Child Trends
www.childtrends.org

U.S. Census Bureau
www.census.gov

For further information, contact Professor Cohen at pnc@umd.edu; (301) 405-6414. Most of data can be found in Professor Cohen's new book, The Family: Diversity, Inequality, and Social Change, available now from W.W. Norton: http://books.wwnorton.com/books/978-0-393-93395-6/.

Article

Prepared by: Patricia Hrusa Williams, *University of Maine at Farmington*

Family Strengths and Resilience:

Insights from a National Study

The Search Institute conducted a study of family assets by surveying parents and adolescents on family strengths and challenges. Remarkably, family strengths, particularly relational factors, are powerfully related to the ability to surmount adversity.

EUGENE C. ROEHLKEPARTAIN AND AMY K. SYVERTSEN

Learning Outcomes

After reading this article, you will be able to:

- Define resilience.
- Explain the Search Institute's Framework of Family Strengths.
- Identify the major findings from the American Family Assets Study.

We often have opportunities to talk with practitioners in education, youth development, family services, and other fields about today's families. When asked about their own families, they will most often admit their quirks and challenges—but they generally express great appreciation for their families and how they add meaning, purpose, and joy to their lives. In contrast, when asked about the families they serve or the families of the young people they seek to teach or engage, they often share quite a different story. There is general consternation with the perceived state of today's families and a defeatist attitude about the chances that they can effectively engage and work with families in ways that improve the well-being of the family, its children, and the broader community. Emerging research is stimulating new understanding about the strengths of families. These strengths emphasize relationships and practices of family life that are malleable and may represent untapped leverage points for engaging with families.

Study Methodology

The American Family Assets Study (Syvertsen, Roehlkepartain, & Scales, 2012) focused on families with young adolescents (a critical period of transitions in family relationships), surveying one parenting adult and one young person (age 10 to 15) in about 1,500 families nationwide. The survey was developed based on a review of the research on family processes, strengths, resilience, interviews and focus groups with youth and parents, and input from a national advisory board. Data were collected online in collaboration with Harris Interactive. Quotas were set to ensure the socioeconomic and cultural diversity of families and the final dataset was weighted to reflect the U.S. Census.

Search Institute's Framework of Family Strengths

Through the years, qualitative researchers have identified more than 80 different strengths that are valued in families around the world (e.g., DeFrain & Asay, 2007). This new study from Search Institute focused on 21 strengths that are relevant to diverse families, widely valued, and measurable through online quantitative surveys. The family strengths we identified (shown in detail in Table 1) are organized in five categories:

- **Nurturing Relationships**—Healthy relationships begin and grow as we show each other we care about what each has to say, how we feel, and our interests.
- **Establishing Routines**—Shared routines, traditions, and activities give a dependable rhythm to family life and help to imbue it with meaning.

Table 1 Search Institute's Framework of Family Strengths

Search Institute has identified 21 research-based family strengths that directly relate to positive outcomes for parenting adults and youth. The percentages indicate how many families experience each asset, based on a study of 1,511 diverse families including at least one parenting adult and one child between the ages of 10 and 15 from across the United States.

Family Strength	%
Nurturing Relationships	
1. *Positive Communication*—Family members listen attentively and speak in respectful ways.	56%
2. *Affection*—Family members regularly show warmth to each other.	71%
3. *Emotional Openness*—Family members can be themselves and are comfortable sharing their feelings.	54%
4. *Support for Sparks*—Family members encourage each other in pursuing their talents and interests.	64%
Establishing Routines	
5. *Family Meals*—Family members eat meals together most days in a typical week.	58%
6. *Shared Activities*—Family members regularly spend time doing everyday activities together.	41%
7. *Meaningful Traditions*—Holidays, rituals, and celebrations are part of family life.	51%
8. *Dependability*—Family members know what to expect from one another.	27%
Maintaining Expectations	
9. *Openness about Tough Topics*—Family members openly discuss sensitive issues, such as sex and substance use.	60%
10. *Fair Rules*—Family rules and consequences are reasonable.	44%
11. *Defined Boundaries*—The family sets limits on what young people can do and how they spend their time.	28%
12. *Clear Expectations*—The family openly articulates its expectations for young people.	84%
13. *Contributions to Family*—Family members help meet each other's needs and share in getting things done.	57%
Adapting to Challenge	
14. *Management of Daily Commitments*—Family members effectively navigate competing activities and expectations at home, school, and work.	41%
15. *Adaptability*—The family adapts well when faced with changes.	28%
16. *Problem Solving*—Family members work together to solve problems and deal with challenges.	33%
17. *Democratic Decision Making*—Family members have a say in decisions that affect the family.	53%
Connecting to Community	
18. Neighborhood Cohesion—Neighbors look out for one another.	33%
19. *Relationships with Others*—Family members feel close to teachers, coaches, and others in the community.	22%
20. *Enriching Activities*—Family members participate in programs and activities that deepen their lives.	56%
21. *Supportive Resources*—Family members have people and places in the community they can turn to for help.	45%

Note. Cut-off criterions were selected to best reflect the ideal we strive for in family well-being. The exact cut-off point for each family strength was determined based on a literature review and previous Search Institute research. In general, individuals scoring 75% or higher on a family strength—measured using a Likert-type scale—were considered to have satisfied the criterion for each strength.

- **Maintaining Expectations**—Each person participates in and contributes to family life. Shared expectations require talking about tough topics.
- **Adapting to Challenge**—Every family faces difficulties, large and small. The ways families adapt to those changes together helps them through adversity.
- **Connecting to Community**—Community connections, relationships, and participation sustain, shape, and enrich how families live their lives together.

A Portrait of Families with Young Adolescents

How are families with young adolescents doing? We created a composite Family Assets Index, ranges from 0 to 100. On average, U.S. families scored 47 out of 100. Dividing families into quartiles produced this distribution:

- Struggling [Index Score: 0 to 25] 17 percent
- Challenged [Index Score: 26 to 50] 39 percent

- Adequate [Index Score: 51 to 75] 34 percent
- Thriving [Index Score: 76 to 100] 11 percent

What is surprising to many who have seen the data is that the overall level of family strengths *does not differ significantly* by parent education, single-parent versus two-parent families, immigration status, parents' sexual orientation, or household income. At the same time, there are slight differences by race-ethnicity and different types of communities. However, the study's major conclusion is that there are *more similarities than differences in overall family strengths across demographic groups.* This reinforces the message that all types of families have strengths to tap and challenges to overcome.

Why Family Strengths Matter

Most of the family strengths identified in this research are common sense. This study, though, begins to show the relationship between these everyday strengths and key aspects of well-being for both youth and families. The more of these strengths youth and parents experience, the better off they are in many areas of life.[I] These general patterns are illustrated with the measures shown in Table 2. We found the following:

- Young people in families with more strengths are more engaged in school, take better care of their health, express positive values, and develop the social competencies they need to thrive.
- When parents experience these strengths in their families, they also take better care of their physical and mental health and they contribute more to their communities.

A key finding is that the levels of family strengths generally have a much stronger relationship to positive outcomes than many "fixed" or demographic factors, such as family structure, socioeconomic status, and race-ethnicity. For example, depending on the measure of well-being in question, family strengths account for between 20 and 30 percent of the variance in youth well-being, compared to less than 10 percent of the variance that can be attributed to 10 different demographic measures for the family and the youth (Roehlkepartain, 2013). That is

Table 2 Percent of Youth and Parenting Adults Who Maintain Good Health and Exhibit Positive Behaviors and Values, by Levels of Family Strengths

a. Youth

	Level of Family Strengths			
	Struggling	**Challenged**	**Adequate**	**Thriving**
Health Behavior Index[a]	39	48	75	79
Depression[b]	83	76	72	54
Regulates Emotions and Behaviors[c]	31	43	60	76
Responsible[c]	37	58	71	85
Civically Engaged[c]	24	38	62	86
Socially Responsible[c]	47	63	81	92

b. Parenting Adults

	Level of Family Strengths			
	Struggling	**Challenged**	**Adequate**	**Thriving**
Health Behavior Index[a]	22	32	52	68
Depression[b]	71	69	55	25
Stressed as a Parent[c]	17	13	12	1
Politically Engaged[c]	5	14	27	35
Family Serves Community[d]	43	54	70	88
Satisfied with Life[c]	72	87	94	99

Notes. [a] Percent who engage in a range of healthy behaviors 4–5 days in the average week.
[b]Percent who reported feeling sad or depressed once in a while or more often in the past month.
[c]Percent who averaged 75% or higher on a measure.
[d]Percent of families who spend time together helping other people 1–2 times in the typical month.

[I] Because this is a cross-sectional and correlational study, we cannot establish causality.

good news, because we have the power to build these strengths, which are malleable even if circumstances do not change.

Family Strengths in the Face of Adversity

Family resilience involves the capacity to withstand adversity and overcome challenges. To examine resilience, we focused our analysis on a subset of 207 families (about 1 percent of the sample) that reported the highest levels of family stress based on a new measure of 13 different challenges such as the death of a parent, a separation or divorce in the family, having an accident, being unemployed, being the victim of crime, dealing with substance abuse in the family, or imprisonment of a family member (Roehlkepartain, 2013). We then calculated the odds that the young people would experience high levels of well-being based on whether they were in families with high or low levels of family strengths. Simply, do family strengths offset the potential negative effects of stresses on family life so youth become more resilient in the face of adversity?

What we found is that the odds of youth from highstressed families achieving the high level of six measures of well-being are significantly greater if they experience high levels of family strengths when compared to their peers in high-risk families that do not experience high levels of family strengths. Thus, for example, youth in high-stressed families who experienced high levels of family strengths were compared with those experiencing low levels of strengths. Those with family strengths were nine times more likely to exhibit personal responsibility, seven times more likely to show self-regulation and school engagement, and five times more likely to show caring behavior.

These findings provide important, if preliminary, evidence of the role of family strengths in young people's resilience in the face of challenges. Family relationships, processes, and practices may contribute to well-being for young people whose families face sustained challenges (Walsh, 2006). One does not have to have a perfect, challenge-free life in order to flourish, and many families facing adversity have the capacities needed to survive, regenerate, and do well.

Strategies for Enhancing Family Strengths

Search Institute is seeking opportunities to explore the impact of this study on families in greater depth with partners in communities and organizations, recognizing that the research only points the way toward innovation, which requires ongoing dialogue, experimentation, and refinement over time to discover what really works. In the meantime, here are some initial thoughts on the opportunities this research presents.

Emphasize relationships more than structure. Research, rhetoric, policy, and practice have often focused on the structure and form of families while deemphasizing the relational, affective dimensions of family life. This evidence emphasizes *relational mechanisms* as foundational, often underdeveloped, pathways for positive growth.

In contrast to the dominant evidence-based programs, Li and Julian (2012) propose designing interventions in which building and strengthening developmental relationships—"the active ingredient upon which the effectiveness of other program elements depend" (p. 163)—is a primary focus. Thus, "in program design, the focal question ought to be 'How does a (practice, program, system, or policy) help to strengthen relationships in the developmental setting?' " (p. 163).

Recognize both strengths and challenges. Too often, research on families has been framed in terms of their risks or vulnerabilities. Without denying the challenges families face, a shift to understanding strengths can increase the self-efficacy in families, highlighting the potential of resilience in the face of adversity. This shift in emphasis has tremendous implications for how programs are designed, how professionals are equipped, and how funding and policies are shaped to strengthen rather than label or shame families because of their risks.

Start with families' priorities, passions, and capacities. Too often work with families focuses on how to transfer expertise and knowledge to them. Whereas parent education and family support have historically been expert-driven (Thomas & Lien, 2009), recent years have seen a shift toward parentcentered, empowerment-oriented strategies that emphasize "the role of parents as members of communities and the larger world" (Doherty, Jacob, & Cutting, 2009, p. 303). The professional task shifts from the expert holder of knowledge to facilitating democracy and shared action. Perhaps it is time to shift our focus from engagement as "family support" toward engagement as "family citizenship." This not only benefits the community, but also strengthens families' self-efficacy, their ties in the community, and, as a result, their resilience.

Tapping the Power of Families

There is agreement on the importance of engaging families but this can be an exasperating process, particularly beyond early childhood. None of the strategies to reach, engage, and support parenting adults and families seem to work. Families just do not show up. Thus, family engagement efforts become trivialized. So we have a lot of work to do and innovation to try to break through. Despite entrenched, sometimes generational challenges and the lack of clear approaches, it is critical to the wellbeing of society to find ways to strengthen families. We also must recognize and celebrate the strengths that are present, the qualities that make us smile about our own families, and those that would make us smile if we knew other families better, too.

References

DeFrain, J., & Asay, S. M. (Eds.). (2007). *Strong families around the world: Strengths-based research and perspectives.* New York, NY: Haworth Press.

Doherty, W. J., Jacob, J., & Cutting, B. (2009). Community engaged parent education: Strengthening civic engagement among parents and parent educators. *Family Relations,* 58(3), 303–315. doi:Io.IIII/j.I74I3729.2009.00554.x

Li, J., & Julian, M. M. (2012). Developmental relationships as the active ingredient: A unifying working hypothesis of "what works" across intervention settings. *American Journal of Orthopsychiatry,* 82(2), 157–166. doi:Io.IIII/j.I939-0025.20I2.0II5I.x

Roehlkepartain, E. C. (2013). *Families and communities together: Strength and resilience during early adolescence* (Doctoral dissertation). University of Minnesota, Minneapolis, MN.

Syvertsen, A. K., Roehlkepartain, E. C., & Scales, P. C. (2012). *The American family assets study.* Minneapolis, MN: Search Institute. Retrieved from www.search-institute.org/research/family-strengths

Thomas, R., & Lien, L. (2009). Family education perspectives: Implications for family educators' professional practice and research. *Family & Consumer Sciences Research Journal,* 38(1), 36–55- doi:Io.IIII/j.I552-3934.2009.00004.x

Walsh, F. (2006). *Strengthening family resilience* (2nd ed.). New York, NY: Guilford.

Critical Thinking

1. Looking at the results of the study, what are the top three family strengths identified in the study? What are the bottom three areas identified?
2. How do the authors define resilience? Do you agree or disagree with their definition and why?
3. For families experiencing high stress, which family assets or strengths were most important in helping youth be successful? How can we work to build these skills or strengths through policies and programs in our own community?

Internet References

National Clearinghouse on Families and Youth, Family and Youth Services Bureau
www.ncfy.acf.hhs.gov

Reclaiming Child and Youth Journal
www.reclaimingjournal.com

Search Institute
www.search-institute.org

Eugene C. Roehlkepartain, PhD is vice president of research and development for Search Institute, Minneapolis, Minnesota, where he served in leadership since 1991. Contact him by e-mail at gener@search-institute.org **Amy K. Syvertsen, PhD** is a research scientist at Search Institute and was principal investigator on the American Family Assets Study. She may be reached by e-mail at amys@search-institute.org. Search Institute is a nonprofit organization dedicated to discovering what young people need to succeed in their families, schools, and communities. For more information, visit www.search-institute.org

Article

Prepared by: Patricia Hrusa Williams, *University of Maine at Farmington*

Strengthening Ties: The Case for Building a Social Policy Centered on Families

PHILLIP LONGMAN ET AL.

Learning Outcomes

After reading this article, you will be able to:

- Identify changes in families in the United States.
- Discuss factors that lead to decreased mobility and social inequality among families.
- Consider programs and services needed to strengthen the next generation of families.

As the 19th century drew to a close, many social observers noted—some with alarm and others with approval—that families were playing a diminishing role in shaping the next generation. With the spread of public education, urban living, and popular culture, parents' influence over children's lives waned, while that of teachers, dime novels, Saturday matinees, and comic books increased. As the family farm or crafts shop gave way to mass production and consumption, the historical unity of work and family life also began to fray. Most people no longer made a living where they lived, and parents and children were rarely bound together in common enterprise.

The economic and social importance of the family seemed to diminish further during much of the 20th century. With the rapid increase in living standards, young men no longer needed to wait to inherit the family farm or business in order to become independent from their parents. They could earn more than fathers by simply joining the wage economy. For women, unequal wages and barriers to workplace advancement ensured that marriage—and family life—remained the chief means of achieving security and social status, but this, too, was increasingly taking place in suburban isolation, away from extended family networks. The spread of private pensions and other means of financial savings, along with the coming of Social Security, made support in old age far less contingent on the strength of family ties.

Yet while many of these trends continue, the family, it turns out, is hardly the vestigial institution many social theorists predicted. Indeed, owing to deepening inequality and other broad economic and social changes, who gets ahead and who does not in American life has come to depend, arguably more than ever, on the strengths and weakness of one's family network. Perhaps because this reality is so at odds with the future predicted by leading social thinkers over the last two centuries—and because it tilts against the bedrock notion that ours is an up-by-the-bootstraps country where anybody with pluck and determination can get ahead, regardless of family resources or background—our social policies have hardly begun to adjust to its implications.

Most of the social and economic policies in the United States do not explicitly address, or take into account, the growing importance of families as sources of human capital and determinants of individual success. And even the small subsets of programs that we conventionally frame as part of "family policy" are often based on long-defunct assumptions about the actual structure of modern families, including the evolving roles of men and women, the advent of families headed by same-sex couples, and the increasing class-based disparities in marriage and divorce rates. In designing and implementing social programs, policymakers routinely fail to account for the enduring impact of the family, its fast-changing composition, or the pressures created by economic and technological change. Policy "silos" prevent the strategic coordination of support systems and social programs, which range from childcare to early and higher education to workforce and small business development to ensuring access to digital technologies.

It is time to correct this failure to adapt—to think of innovative ways to strengthen families and help them thrive and prosper. In response to the new set of realities and large-scale trends, policymakers must develop new ways to support families across generations. To do so effectively will require bringing together expertise from many policy realms. We need new frameworks for analyzing the increasingly critical role of the family in modern America, examining the influence of technology on families and social networks, and exploring ideas for policies and programs that will more effectively support the modern American family in all its diversity.

Families in an Age of Increasing Inequality and Diminishing Opportunity

Many factors are contributing to the increasing importance of the family as a determinant of both individual and national well-being, but the broadest and perhaps most important are the decline in upward mobility and the stark increase in inequality that have occurred since the 1970s. Over the last two generations, fewer than one out of ten children born to parents in the bottom fifth of income distribution in the United States managed to rise to the top fifth as adults.[1] At the same time, the gap between those at the top of the income scale and those at the bottom has widened to a degree not seen since the 19th century.[2] A straightforward consequence has been that the financial, economic, and social cost of losing the "birth lottery" has increased, while the lifetime benefits of being born into a stable, financially secure, and socially well-connected family have arguably never been better.

Critically related to these trends has been the rising cost of securing the job skills and other endowments in human capital that are increasingly demanded by today's economy. In the 1950s and into the 1970s, for example, the consequences of not graduating from college, or even high school, were largely benign. Low-skilled, blue-collar jobs were comparatively plentiful, and for men belonging to unions, generally paid enough to support a family. While racial discrimination made this far from a universal experience—in African American families, mothers have historically been obliged to work to supplement men's earnings—the majority of families in the middle of the 20th century could get by with just one wage.

Today, by contrast, a family wage for blue-collar work is exceedingly rare, and most low-skilled jobs pay substantially less, adjusted for inflation, than they did in the late 1960s. Meanwhile, nearly ⅔ of jobs today require some postsecondary education and training, compared to just 30 percent of jobs in the early 1970s.[3] Most also require sophisticated social skills as well as access to and appropriate use of rapidly changing information technologies and complex and ever-evolving social networks.

The social and financial advantages required to obtain these endowments further underscores the importance of the family. Children born into families rich in both money and social capital have an increasing advantage over children whose families lack the social knowledge and financial means to navigate the world of quality early childhood settings, extracurricular learning activities, higher education, advanced technology, and complex professional networks.

Also powerfully underscoring the growing importance of the family in determining the life outcomes of today's children is the emergence of a two-tier family system, one that is both a cause and a consequence of deepening inequality and declining economic mobility. Among the 60 percent of the population that lacks a college degree, family formation, and family stability have declined drastically. As recently as the 1980s, only 13 percent of the children of mothers with only a high school degree were born outside of marriage. By the late 2000s that number had risen to 44 percent.[4]

It is not just that parents are not getting married; it is that parents often are not forming long-term unions of any kind. Partners are replaced by new partners, creating a kind of household churning, a coming and going of cohabiting adults.[5] Meanwhile, the college-educated are not only more likely to marry one another—often in unions in which both partners hold well-paying jobs—but to stay married, with consequences that further widen the income and mobility gap across generations. As a politically diverse set of family policy experts put it in a recent joint article published in the *Washington Monthly*:

> American marriage today is becoming a class-based and class-propagating institution. In upscale America, marriage is thriving: most people marry, fewer than 10 percent of children are born to unmarried mothers, and most children grow up through age eighteen living with their two married parents. Among the more privileged, marriage clearly functions as a wealth-producing arrangement, a source of happiness over time, and a benefit to children.[6]

Conversely, the steep decline in marriage rates among the rest of the population correlates strongly with downward mobility among both children and adults. For example, according a study by the Pew Charitable Trusts, women who are divorced, widowed, or separated are between 31 and 36 percentage points more likely to fall down the economic ladder than women who are married.[7]

Meanwhile, the age structure of the U.S. population also is changing, placing new importance—and pressures—on family ties. Owing primarily to falling birthrates since the 1950s, and to a lesser extent to increasing lifespans, America is becoming an aging society, with more dependent elders and proportionately fewer children and working-aged adults. Families face daunting challenges in providing for the long-term care needs of aging relatives. Within the last two years of life, fully 28 percent of Americans suffer from one or more serious disabilities that typically require long-term nursing home care or extensive caregiving by family members.[8] At the same time, stagnant and declining real wages mean an increasing number of families depend on inheritances and other forms of financial support from older family members. Recent years have seen a huge increase in the share of 18- to 34-year-olds living with their parents, which reached 31 percent in 2014.[9] Reflecting the growing interdependence within extended families, multigenerational households, which sociologists in the 1950s considered a relic of a preindustrial past, are making a significant comeback.

To be sure, historically high rates of immigration over the last several decades have helped to arrest the aging of the U.S. population and substantially changed its composition. One in seven children entering kindergarten in the United States today speaks a primary language other than English.[10] But the number of people moving to the United States has dropped sharply in recent years and is likely to drop much more in the future, owing to a combination of plunging birthrates and rising living standards throughout the developing world. Media accounts and political agendas notwithstanding, net migration between the United States and Mexico both legal and illegal, for example, has been approximately zero, or even slightly negative, since 2005.[11] At the same time, birthrates among Hispanic Americans have been plunging rapidly, resulting in a two-child family norm for Hispanic women now in their 40s. Birthrates among Asian Americans are well below replacement rates.[12] In 2013, following trends found throughout the world, the American birthrate hit another low, with the average number of lifetime children per woman falling to 1.86, or well below the 2.1 needed to replace the population over time.[13]

In a broader sense, as children become relatively scarcer, their contribution in human capital becomes more essential not only to government finance—and Social Security payments—but to employers and the economy, further underscoring how the strength and stability of the family is an increasingly crucial key to sustainable, broad prosperity, even for people who do not have children themselves. It is critical to see inequality as both a cause, and a condition, of family-centered pressures today. Demographic shifts and the erosion of the "traditional" family unit are occurring against a backdrop of changing opportunity structures.

Even as the family itself undergoes deep changes in its size, structure, and diversity, the challenge of framing effective social policy is further complicated by a series of enormously important megatrends. Policymakers will need to recognize these changing conditions before they are able to help craft an effective policy response. These trends are reshaping how families live together, participate in the economy, and interact with the world around them.

Changing Role of Women—and Men—in the Workplace

The past half-century has brought a massive entry of women, including mothers of young children, into the paid workforce. The proportion of women ages 25 to 54 who are working or looking for work stands at 75 percent, up from 35 percent in 1950.[14] Of the 66 million women who are employed—up from 30 million in 1970—three-quarters work full-time.

On average, today's working women earn significantly more than did working women a generation ago, primarily as a result of rising educational attainment and the increasing share of women in higher paid professions. For women without a college degree, who constitute the majority, wage and salary increases have been hardly measurable from one generation to the next. For example, among women age 25 to 34 who lack a college degree and who work full time, median annual wage and salary income, adjusted for inflation, increased by barely more than $2,000 between 1969 and 2005.[15] Even before the Great Recession, women without a college degree who worked full time earned not much more than their counterparts did two generations before.

At the same time—even though full-time female wage and salary workers still earn only 82 percent of what full-time male earners do,[16]—women bear an ever-larger share of the burden of the family breadwinning. Wives are breadwinners or co-earners in about ⅔ of American marriages. Among families with working wives, the percentage in which the wife out-earns the husband has risen from 23.7 percent in 1987 to 38.1 percent in 2012. Almost 7 percent of wives—nearly four million women, up from 1.7 percent in 1967—are in the paid labor force while their husbands are not.[17]

Men's workplace standing has meanwhile been moving in the opposite direction. Between 1969 and 2009, a period in which U.S. GDP per capita more than doubled after adjusting for inflation, the real median annual earnings of working-aged

American males declined by 28 percent. The steepest downward mobility was among male high school dropouts, who in 2009 earned 66 percent less than their counterparts did in 1969. The slide for men with only a high school degree was a staggering 47 percent. Even for prime-aged male college graduates, real earnings were 12 percent below that enjoyed by their counterparts 40 years before.[18]

This decline in male earnings has been accompanied by a huge decline in the percentage of men who remain in the workforce. In the late 1960s, only about five out of every 100 working-aged men did not have a job in any given week. By 2000, this figure had more than doubled, to 11 out of every 100 men. By the end of 2014 it reached 16 percent.[19]

Including men who are in jail reveals an even sharper drop in the male labor force participation rate. Four times as many American men, per capita, are incarcerated today as was the case in 1975. Among African Americans, the change is even more dramatic.[20] African American men are more likely to go to prison than to graduate from college with a four-year degree. In 2010, more young black male high school dropouts were behind bars (37 percent) than were employed (26 percent).[21] One in nine African American children (11.4 percent) has an incarcerated parent.[22]

Rise of Single Parenthood

The number and proportion of families headed by a single parent has increased dramatically, particularly among working-class whites. In 1979, unmarried parents accounted for 22 percent of families with children; by 2012, their share jumped to 34 percent.[23] Forty percent of mothers with children under 18 are the primary earners in their families, up from 11 percent in 1960.[24] While most single women say they want to get married, many are deciding to go it alone when they have children, preferring life as a single parent to a life in which they are supporting not only children but also a male partner.

Continuing high rates of divorce among working-class parents add to the number of children being raised by single parents. Though causation can be difficult to determine, one study from the American Enterprise Institute finds that "at least 32 percent of the growth in family-income inequality since 1979 among families with children . . . can be linked to the decreasing number of Americans who form and maintain stable, married families."[25] At the same time, the declining economic fortunes of working-class Americans, particularly men, has depressed marriage rates to all-time lows and become itself a source of increasing family instability.

With all these changes in family structure, less than ⅕ of American children today live in a "traditional" family with a sole male provider. Yet our current policies fail to address this reality, or address it awkwardly. For example, the emphasis on "work first" in our welfare policies forces mothers of young children back into the labor market. While this can be source of stability, too often erratic hours, lack of childcare, low wages and the general precariousness of work mean the effect on the family is stress and chaos.

Rising Cost of Living for Families

While the cost of many items in our economy, such as consumer electronics, is growing cheaper, the cost of the particular goods and services parents most need to help themselves and their children get ahead has grown much faster than family wages or general inflation. Between 2005 and 2015, the cost of attending a public or private college, for example, rose 40 percentage points more than the Consumer Price Index.[26] The cost of higher education is increasing at the same time that the labor prospects of those without a college credential grow ever bleaker. Parents and children are increasingly relying on debt to finance their own and their children's postsecondary education, creating drag on the economy and stress on families. The share of young adults with student loans rose from 26 percent in 2001 to 40 percent in 2013.[27] Sadly, much of this debt is held by people who never finished college, and who have often been victimized by predatory lending practices.

Meanwhile, health-care costs rose nearly 20 percentage points more than general inflation.[28] The total annual cost of health care for a family of four covered by a typical employer-sponsored plan reached $23,215 in 2014, or roughly the equivalent cost of buying a new Honda Accord LX every year.[29] The growing burden of health care costs is a major reason why employers are so reluctant to hire and wages remain stagnant.

Even after passage of the Affordable Care Act, health-care costs continue to grow much faster than wages and salaries, putting extreme pressure on family budgets. A higher percentage of Americans is uninsured today than in 2001. And despite a massive increase in Medicaid spending and insurance premium subsidies offered under Obamacare, a recent Commonwealth Fund survey finds that a higher share of Americans (35 percent) now report difficulties in paying medical bills or had medical debt than in 2005.[30]

This huge increase often affects families directly. Economic theory holds that the price of manufacturing the same product should decline over time. Yet when it comes to children's vaccines, for example, the exact opposite is true. Between 1986 and 2014, the price for the basic five vaccines soared 434 percent, from $215 to $937 per child, adjusted for inflation. As a July 2014 *New York Times* article explained, this hike appears to be the result of consolidation and monopolization among pharmaceutical companies.[31]

Childcare expenses have also surged far faster than either family wage or general inflation. In many places, families are paying more for childcare than for rent and food, especially when their children are younger than three years old. In 2012, in 31 states and the District of Columbia, the average annual average cost for an infant in center-based care was higher than a year's tuition and fees at a four-year public college. Even at these prices, waiting lists are common and families report not being able to find high-quality, affordable options, leaving them scrambling to find any care at all.[32]

Generational Downward Mobility

Throughout most of American history, despite vast disparities across various racial, ethnic, and other demographic groups, almost all American families realized a rising material standard of living from one generation to the next. This is a relationship that still largely holds for today's older Americans, who typically have enjoyed, at each stage of life, a higher net worth than people their age a generation before. For example, Americans who were 74 years or older in 2010 had an average net worth that was 149 percent higher (after adjusting for inflation) than that enjoyed by Americans in 1983 who were the same age.

But starting with those born in the early 1950s, this pattern disappeared, and for younger Americans as a whole, it has been thrown into steep reverse. So, for example, the net worth of Americans who were 29- to 37-years-old in 2010 was more than ⅕ lower (adjusted for inflation) than was the net worth of people that age in 1983.[33]

This trend of intergenerational downward mobility is particularly pronounced among members of minority groups. Among African Americans who were raised in middle-class families in the late 1970s, for example, 37 percent fell out of the middle class by the time they reached middle age. The corresponding number for their white counterparts was 25 percent.[34]

Whether today's young adults will experience a permanently lower standard of living than their parents' generation remains unclear. Most Millennials have at least the good fortune of having been too young to have bought into the top of the last decade's housing bubble, unlike so many members of Generation X. But Millennials do face continued exposure to predatory lending, and low real wages in the aftermath of the Great Recession, in addition to their record levels of student debt. According to a recent report by the Kauffman Foundation, though Millennials have high levels of education and lifelong exposure to information technology, their shaky finances mean that most "can't afford to become entrepreneurs."[35] The median family headed by someone under 35 earned $35,300 in 2013, down 6 percent from 2010 and down nearly 20 percent from 2001.[36] Young adults today are more likely to have a college degree than their counterparts in 1980 but also more likely to be in poverty.

This pattern of cross-generational downward mobility amplifies the importance of inherited wealth, and with it, the importance of family ties in determining the future of success in America.

The same trend also presents challenges for programs, such as Social Security, that transfer income from young to old, since such programs cannot rely on rising real wages among each new generation of taxpayers to finance the benefits for each new generation of retirees. The fact that the next generation of elders is likely, on current trends, to be less well off than the one before, and therefore more dependent on government support—and/or more likely to stay in the workforce longer—only adds to the financial, as well as the moral challenge.

Families and the Decline in the Number and Quality of Jobs

When industrialization first began undermining the economic basis of the family as a holistic unit in which all parties worked together in common enterprise, the response of many reformers was to press for child labor laws and for labor contracts that would guarantee working-class fathers a "family wage." That way, progressive-era figures such as Mary Harris "Mother" Jones reasoned, children and their mothers could be saved from capitalists who sought to exploit their labor in the mills and mines.[37] The upshot, by the middle of the 20th century, was a middle-class family that some people today inaccurately think of as the classic traditional family: a male breadwinner employed outside the home in the formal economy who leaves behind each morning a "homemaker" wife and several nonworking children. Historians such as Stephanie Coontz have convincingly demonstrated that this "Father Knows Best Family," with its unique division of labor, was, however, little more than a historical blip.

By the 1970s, it, and the last vestiges of the old family wage regime, largely gave way to the two-paycheck family. This dramatic change offered many women unprecedented opportunities to develop their skills, seek professional advancement and fulfillment, and free themselves from financial dependence. By deploying both spouses to the paid workforce, many families were able to cope with the long-term decline in real male wages and with the escalating fixed cost of family life.

Still, this strategy had its downsides: the lack of childcare and paid family leave place enormous pressures on parents trying to combine work and parenting. Leisure time vanished. And, as (now U.S. Senator) Elizabeth Warren and her daughter,

Amelia Warren Tyagi, pointed out in their 2003 book, *The Two Income Trap*, families in which both partners must work to meet their fixed expenses face inherent financial risks. If one partner becomes sick or laid off, or must tend to an aging relative, the other cannot make up for the loss of income by joining the workforce. At the same time, Warren and Tyagi noted, in many areas two-paycheck families may bid up the price of housing, childcare, and other goods and services related to raising children beyond what most one-paycheck families can afford.

Even as employers and government policy have failed to accommodate to the emerging two-paycheck family norm, that norm itself has begun to give way to a variety of transitional, often fragile, and unstable arrangements. The most basic problem is that, relative to the size of the workforce, there are fewer formal jobs than in the 1970s, and these jobs pay less than before. There are many reasons for this change. One that has been widely noted is the decline in the power of labor unions. Among men in private sector jobs, the percent who belong to unions fell from 35 percent in 1973 to 8 percent in 2007, while among women the figure declined from 16 percent to 4 percent.[38]

Growing evidence shows that consolidation among employers is further reducing the relative bargaining power of the employee. This is true for professional workers; the Justice Department recently won a case against some of Silicon Valley's richest employers, for forming an illegal cartel in which they promised not to hire one another's workers. It is even more true for workers at the lower end of the employment spectrum. For instance, the rise of supergiant retailers that combine many lines of business under one roof can often dramatically reduce the total number of potential employers competing for workers in a given community.[39]

Even as the quality and security of jobs decline, the entry requirements of many occupations are increasing. Jobs that were once accessible to individuals without a college degree—those of bookkeepers, office managers, human resource professionals, for example—increasingly require a postsecondary degree. The growth of the service sector and the decline of manufacturing have generated significant increase in the number of licensed occupations. Between 1950 and 2008, the percentage of the U.S. workforce with an occupational license grew from five percent to almost thirty percent.[40] Obtaining an occupational license often requires some form of postsecondary education, which aspiring workers have to pay for themselves. As job security declines, Americans are also far more likely than previous generations to need access to job training or skill-upgrading opportunities throughout their lifetimes.

Then, there are the growing numbers of men and women who no longer hold full-time jobs at all, but instead work two or more part-time jobs, often at odd hours and on weekends. In many cases, these workers perform duties that not long ago were handled by formal full-time employees, albeit now as "independent contractors," "freelancers," or "contingent workers." Here too, much of the problem appears to stem from the growing imbalance of power between the individual and the large corporations that increasingly dominate business activity. It is often the largest firms that choose to subcontract so extensively, in some cases for all but their core business activities. This can destroy career ladders for entry level and low-skilled workers. It can also significantly destabilize family life.[41]

In a growing number of instances, upstart firms are taking advantage of new technologies to disrupt entire lines of work—like taxi driving—in ways that reduce the number of people who can earn a living wage in that sector. According to a 2012 report by the McKinsey Global Institute, technology is enabling employers to "unbundle" occupations into discrete tasks and skills, which they can buy on a contract basis, eliminating the need to hire employees. Companies such as Federal Express, Uber, or the cleaning service "platform" Handybook escape employer mandates by classifying those who work for them as contractors.[42] Such contingent workers increasingly make do not only without the benefit of a regular paycheck but without any employer-provided benefits whatsoever.

Even high-skilled workers are now increasingly threatened by automatization, outsourcing, and by the workplace trend toward "on demand" relationships. New technologies, or more precisely, the patterns of ownership and control that restrict how certain new technologies are used, seem to destroy more living-wage jobs than they create.[43] And "just in time" scheduling technologies cause workers to lose what little control they once had over their schedules, from week to week or even day to day, wreaking havoc on their ability to find safe and stable childcare.[44]

To be sure, for some parents, the ability to work as freelancers or home-based entrepreneurs is welcome. But the general pattern across America is that workers are losing market power, so their vulnerability to exploitation is increasing, whether they be janitors, delivery drivers, copywriters, or ad hoc professors.

. . .

Families and the Pressures of Digital Technologies

The advent of the personal computer and the Internet has changed society profoundly—and the family no less, as households face significant new threats and opportunities. Widespread diffusion of information communication technologies has helped quicken the pace of globalization; disrupted 19th and 20th century labor practices, including divisions between work and leisure time; embedded new kinds of automation in all facets of public and private decision making; and escalated the need for Americans to be able to comprehend and filter a constant stream of information to participate fully in work and community life. Within homes, technologies such as television, video games, and smartphones have ushered in daily routines that affect, for better and worse, how parents and children interact with each other and with extended family members. These changes affect families of all income levels, but the downsides are especially challenging for families already buffeted by unemployment and destabilizing cultural shifts.

As the U.S. economy transitioned from traditional family businesses and old hierarchical industrial models, getting even a low-level job increasingly requires access to, and understanding of, digital technology. Eighty percent of Fortune 500 companies, including Walmart, Comcast, and McDonald's, now only accept job applications online.[45] Internet use is prevalent among 94 percent of jobholders across industries, including nontechnology firms, big corporations, and small businesses in urban and rural settings, and places in between, according to Pew Research Center.[46]

This increasing reliance on digital technologies has created intense pressures and opportunities for families. Digitization, for example, presents new threats to the financial security of many families by making them more vulnerable to surveillance and discrimination in the marketplace. Take automated prediction and targeting: credit unions and banks are using automated computer decision systems to remotely disable the cars of people who owe money on subprime loans, sometimes stranding borrowers in the middle of their drive to work or school.[47] And educational software companies now offer end users—from young students to lifelong learners—data-driven products that track and adapt content based on user behavior and ability. For young students, that might mean educational content that pegs them to a lower social stratum, and hence, content that carries a lower expectation for the user. That is, beyond traditional concerns for narrow- or niche-targeting, advanced technologies are producing new forms of data-driven, automated discrimination.[48]

At the same time, technologies are providing important connections, as families scattered across the globe stay connected and engage in "remote caregiving." The Bureau of Economic Assistance estimates that in 2009, foreign-born individuals sent $38 billion in remittances—something that would have been nearly impossible prior to the advent of electronic payments and information infrastructures—to households abroad.[49] Money aside, members of "transnational" and "commuter" families use social technologies like Skype and Facebook as connective tissue, to reach out to children or aging parents abroad, keep relationships current, and pass on familial knowledge.[50]

Researchers, policymakers, popular pundits, and journalists often note that digital technologies have the power to disrupt personal relationships and deliver uninvited content. This anxiety centers on the impact that new technologies can have on the well-being of children and the strength and social cohesion of families. Child development experts worry that cell phones and personal computer devices—now common fixtures at the dinner table—distract parents from their children (and vice versa) and prevent them from engaging in positive, nurturing conversations. In a study of caregivers and smart phones in a fast-food restaurant, researchers observed nearly ⅔ of participants using mobile devices during meals, eating and talking while engrossed in their screens, only putting them down briefly to engage in other activities.[51]

The "anytime anywhere" access of Internet-enabled technologies has produced a thicket of benefits and dangers that families struggle to navigate. The same information technology that allows today's children and young adults to trade friendly emails with grandparents and "kick start" micro investments in worthy causes also exposes them to a range of content and activities, including violent video games, "sexting," pornography, cyberbullying, and other forms of online harassment.[52]

The effects of new technology vary widely across socioeconomic and other divides. Children from low-income families, for example, spend more time with TV and videos than children from affluent families, and are three times more likely to have a television in their bedroom.[53] There are also great disparities in how families use technology, whether merely for entertainment, or for social and educational betterment. Parents in low-income families struggle to acquire digital literacy and often do not have easy access to teachers, librarians, mentors, and other educated professionals to help.[54]

While researchers are unlikely to come to consensus about the beneficial or harmful effects of digital technologies, these technologies will continue to play an integral role in families' life choices and opportunities. Today, families have no choice but to use digital communication to interact with the many public institutions that no longer accept paper applications or other communications. Public assistance programs have increasingly become "smart," meaning participants are now more likely to interact with an algorithmically trained virtual assistant rather than a human caseworker.[55] Caregivers must also contend with digital systems in schools and elsewhere, as learning processes become computer-driven. In short, technology is becoming the primary medium through which people gather, do schoolwork, shop, apply for jobs, schedule childcare, communicate with teachers, read to their children, share neighborhood news, and spread the word about family celebrations and hardships.

Families that lack adequate access to and understanding of modern information technology are now at risk of falling prey to technology's threats while missing its opportunities. Yes, access has improved: between 1984 and 2011, the number of households that reported having a computer increased from 8.2 percent to 75.6 percent. The number of households accessing the Internet increased from 18 percent in 1997 to 71.7 percent in 2011.[56] But despite this rapid diffusion of computer-driven technology, poorer families still struggle to join the information age. The U.S. Department of Commerce reported that among low-income households ($25,000 or less), computer use stands at 57 percent, while Internet use is at 49 percent. For the wealthiest households ($100,000 or more), 97 percent have computers, and 96 percent have Internet access.[57] Many rural areas lack broadband infrastructure, and even in some cities, up to 50 percent of families do not have access to broadband services at home.[58] Local library systems—many under severe budget constraints—are overloaded with patrons, often children and job seekers, seeking Internet access.[59] It is crucial for students to be able to use tech tools and different types of social media; yet in some regions, commercial establishments such as McDonald's, Starbucks, or other restaurants with WiFi are the only places for low-income students to do their homework.

Building a Family-centered Policy Framework

New America has convened experts from a variety of programs—ranging from early education to workforce development to our Open Technology Initiative—who will focus on issues and policies affecting the family at both a macro and micro level. At the macro level, we are exploring how diverse policies, not normally conceived of as "family" policy, are nonetheless profoundly affecting the family as an institution. These include policies involving asset-building and consumer finance; open access to and regulation of digital technology and e-commerce; trade, antitrust, and competition policy; as well as a broad range of other policy realms. Over the next year, New America will visit some local communities hardest hit by the Great Recession that have attempted to rethink the programs and services they offer to better meet the needs of families. We will use takeaways from those visits and from our conversations with others working in the field to create a new federal policy framework, a vision, even, for what might be called a family-centered social policy.

In addition to a general failure to address or even acknowledge the effects of the megatrends discussed above, family policy in the United States today is also often poorly designed technically. In our initial survey, we have identified four types of common structural challenges:

1. **The silo challenge:** Interventions focus on distinct areas (housing assistance, food, income, workforce training) without coordinating and integrating support systems.
2. **The diversity challenge:** Families are diverse (number of adults, relationship of caregivers to children), but many nontraditional family arrangements are not supported by policy.
3. **The intergenerational challenge:** Policy interventions often focus only on either children or adults, even though they may be more effective if they supported the family as a whole across generations.
4. **The gender challenge:** Even when policies are designed to support parents and children together, many focus only on the relationship between the mother and the child, and offer little or no support to fathers, despite the fact that research confirms the positive impact that fathers can have on children's emotional and even language development.

Our approach is to reject explanations that treat abstractions such as "globalization," "free markets," "technology," or even "demographics" as if they were unalterable laws of the universe. Instead, we view the problems facing the family as matters of political economy, of being wholly within the power of humans and human institutions to mold and shape.

At the micro level, we are seeking to craft innovations that offer better coordinated, evidence-based, up-to-date family-centered policies and programs. We will examine, for example, the many policy interventions that ignore prevailing household dynamics, such as those that focus on adults or children rather than the whole family. We will also examine programs to see how they account for the power of social media and new communication technologies that could enable families to support each other while also connecting them to resources that match their unique needs.

Finally, we seek to ensure that the design of programs fits the real world in which families live, and that rules or eligibility requirements do not undermine program goals. The problems of the American family are solvable. By applying a cross-cutting perspective, we can foster alternative frameworks for social policy that recognizes the centrality of the family in American life while crafting programs that better address the needs of the family as a whole.

Endnotes

1. Raj Chetty, Nathaniel Hendren, Patrick Kline, Emmanuel Saez, and Nicholas Turner, *IS The United States Still a Land of Opportunity? Recent Trends in Intergenerational Mobility*, NBER Working Paper 19844, January 2014.
2. Thomas Piketty, *Capital in the Twenty-First Century*, trans. Arthur Goldhammer (Cambridge, MA: Belknap Press, 2014).
3. Anthony P. Carnevale, Nicole Smith, and Jeff Strohl, *Help Wanted: Projections of Jobs and Education Requirements*

Through 2018 (Washington, DC: Georgetown University Center on Education and the Workforce, 2010), https://cew.georgetown.edu/wp-content/uploads/2014/12/fullreport.pdf.

4. Elizabeth Marquardt, David Blankenhorn, Robert I. Lerman, Linda Malone-Colón, and W. Bradford Wilcox, *The State of Our Unions: The President's Marriage Agenda for the Forgotten Sixty Percent* (Charlottesville, VA: The National Marriage Project and the Institute for American Values, 2012), http://www.stateofourunions.org/2012/SOOU2012.pdf.
5. Kathryn Edin and Maria J. Kefalas, *Promises I Can Keep: Why Poor Women Put Motherhood Before Marriage* (Berkeley, CA: University of California Press, 2005).
6. David Blankenhorn, William Galston, Jonathan Rauch, and Barbara Dafoe Whitehead, "Can Gay Wedlock Break Political Gridlock?" *Washington Monthly*, March/April, 2015, http://www.washingtonmonthly.com/magazine/marchaprilmay_2015/features/can_gay_wedlock_break_politica054228.php.
7. Gregory Acs, *Downward Mobility From the Middle Class: Waking Up From the American Dream* (Washington, DC: The Pew Charitable Trusts, Economic Mobility Project, September 2011).
8. Alexander K. Smith, Louise C. Walter, Yinghui Miao, W. John Boscardin, and Kenneth E. Covinsky, "Disability During the Last Two Years of Life," *JAMA Internal Medicine* 173, no. 16 (September 2013): 1506–1513.
9. The Council of Economic Advisors, *15 Economic Facts About Millennials*, Executive Office of the President of the United States, October, 2014, p. 37, http://m.whitehouse.gov/sites/default/files/docs/millennials_report.pdf.
10. Gail M. Mulligan, Jill Carlivati McCarroll, Kristin Denton Flanagan, and Daniel Potter, *Findings From the First-Grade Rounds of the Early Childhood Longitudinal Study, Kindergarten Class of 2010–11 (ECLS-K:2011): First Look* (Washington, DC: U.S. Department of Education, Institute of Education Sciences, National Center for Education Statistics, 2014), http://nces.ed.gov/pubs2015/2015019.pdf.
11. Jeffrey S. Passel, D'vera Cohn, and Ana Gonzalez-Barrera, *Net Migration from Mexico Falls to Zero—and Perhaps Less* (Washington, DC: Pew Research Center, April 23, 2012), http://www.pewhispanic.org/files/2012/04/Mexican-migrants-report_final.pdf.
12. Lindsay M. Monte and Renee R. Ellis, *Fertility of Women in the United States: 2012: Population Characteristics* (Washington, DC: U.S. Census Bureau, July 2014), Table 2.
13. Joyce A. Martin, Brady E. Hamilton, Michelle J. K. Osterman, Sally C. Curtin, and T. J. Mathews, "Births: Final Data for 2013," *National Vital Statistics Reports* 64, no. 1 (Hyattsville, MD: U.S. Department of Health and Human Services, January 15, 2015), http://www.cdc.gov/nchs/data/nvsr/nvsr64/nvsr64_01.pdf.
14. *Women in the Labor Force: A Databook*, Report 1049 (Washington, DC: U.S. Bureau of Labor Statistics, May 2014), http://www.bls.gov/opub/reports/cps/womenlaborforce_2013.pdf.
15. Jeff Madrick and Nikolaos Papanikolaou, *The Stagnation of Male Wages*, Table 2.1 (New York: Schwarz Center for Economic Policy Analysis, The New School, May 2008).
16. U.S. Bureau of Labor Statistics, "Usual Weekly Earnings of Wage and Salary Workers: Fourth Quarter 2014," Economic News Release, January 21, 2015, http://www.bls.gov/news.release/pdf/wkyeng.pdf.
17. *Women in the Labor Force: A Databook*, Report 1052 (Washington, DC: U.S. Bureau of Labor Statistics, December 2014), http://www.bls.gov/opub/reports/cps/women-in-the-labor-force-a-databook-2014.pdf.
18. Michael Greenstone and Adam Looney, "Trends: Reduced Earnings for Men in America," *Milken Institute Review*, Third Quarter 2011. These trends were well in place before the coming of the Great Recession. Between 1969 and 2005, real earnings for men with only a high school degree declined from $34,682 to $30,000 (in 2005 dollars). Among full-time male workers with a college degree, real wage and salary income increased at an annual growth rate of just .1 percent between 1969 and 2005. See, for example, Jeff Madrick and Nikolaos Papanikolaou, *The Stagnation of Male Wages* (New York: Schwarz Center for Economic Policy Analysis, The New School, May 2008).
19. Amanda Cox, "The Rise of Men Who Don't Work, and What They Do Instead," *New York Times*, December 11, 2014, http://www.nytimes.com/2014/12/12/upshot/the-rise-of-men-who-dont-work-and-what-they-do-instead.html?abt=0002&abg=0.
20. E. Ann Carson, *Prisoners in 2013* (Washington, DC: Bureau of Justice Statistics, 2014), http://www.bjs.gov/content/pub/pdf/p13.pdf.
21. Bruce Western, "Incarceration, Inequality, and Imagining Alternatives," *The ANNALS of the American Academy of Political and Social Science* 651, no. 1 (January 2014): 302–306. http://scholar.harvard.edu/files/brucewestern/files/incarceration_inequality_and_imagining_alternatives.pdf.
22. Bruce Western and Becky Pettit, *Collateral Costs: Incarceration's Effect on Economic Mobility* (Washington, DC: The Pew Charitable Trusts, 2010).
23. Robert I. Lerman and W. Brad Wilcox, *For Richer, For Poorer: How Family Structures Economic Success in America* (Washington, DC: American Enterprise Institute, Institute for Family Studies, October 28, 2014), http://www.aei.org/publication/for-richer-for-poorer-how-family-structures-economic-success-in-america/.
24. Wendy Wang, Kim Parker, and Paul Taylor, *Breadwinner Moms* (Washington, DC: Pew Research Center, 2013), http://www.pewsocialtrends.org/files/2013/05/Breadwinner_moms_final.pdf.
25. Robert I. Lerman and W. Bradford Wilcox, *For Richer, for Poorer: How Family Structures Economic Success in America*

(Washington, DC: AEI and Institute for Family Studies, 2014), http://www.aei.org/publication/for-richer-for-poorer-how-family-structures-economic-success-in-america/.

26. Bureau of Labor Statistics Data, cited by Annie Lowrey, "Changed Life of the Poor: Better Off, But Far Behind," *New York Times*, April 30, 2014.
27. Miller, Ben. 2014. The student debt review-analyzing the state of undergraduate student borrowing. Washington, DC: New America- Education Policy Program, http://www.newamerica.org/downloads/TheStudentDebtReview _2_18_14.pdf.; Student loan debt by age group. in Federal Reserve Bank of New York [database online], 2013Available from http://www.newyorkfed.org/studentloandebt/index.html.
28. Bureau of Labor Statistics data, cited by Annie Lowrey, "Changed Life of the Poor: Better Off, But Far Behind," *New York Times*, April 30, 2014.
29. Christopher S. Girod, Lorraine W. Mayne, Scott A. Weltz, and Susan K. Hart, *2014 Milliman Medical Index* (Seattle, WA: Milliman, 2014), http://www.milliman.com/uploadedFiles/insight/Periodicals/mmi/pdfs/2014-mmi.pdf.
30. Sara R. Collins, Petra W. Rasmussen, Michelle M. Doty, and Sophie Beutel, *The Rise in Health Care Coverage and Affordability Since Health Reform Took Effect: Findings from the Commonwealth Fund Biennial Health Insurance Survey, 2014* (Washington, DC: The Commonwealth Fund, 2015), http://www.commonwealthfund.org/publications/issue-briefs/2015/jan/biennial-health-insurance-survey.
31. Elisabeth Rosenthal, "The Price of Prevention: Vaccine Costs are Soaring," *New York Times*, July 2, 2014, http://www.nytimes.com/2014/07/03/health/Vaccine-Costs-Soaring-Paying-Till-It-Hurts.html.
32. Child Care Aware of America, *Parents and the High Cost of Child Care: 2013 Report* (Arlington, VA: Child Care Aware, 2013), http://usa.childcareaware.org/sites/default/files/cost_of_care_ 2013_103113_0.pdf.
33. Eugene Steuerle, Signe-Mary McKernan, Caroline Ratcliffe, and Sisi Zhang, "Lost Generations? Wealth Building Among Young Americans," The Urban Institute, March 2013, Fig. 3, http://www.urban.org/publications/412766.html.
34. Gregory Acs, *Downward Mobility From the Middle Class: Waking Up From the American Dream* (Washington, DC: The Pew Charitable Trusts, Economic Mobility Project, September 2011).
35. "The Future of Entrepreneurship: Millennials and Boomers Chart the Course for 2020," Ewing Marion Kauffman Foundation, February 2015, http://www.kauffman.org/~/media/kauffman_org/resources/2015/soe/2015_state_of_entrepreneurship_address.pdf.
36. "2013 Survey of Consumer Finances," Board of Governors of the Federal Reserve System, http://www.federalreserve.gov/econresdata/scf/scfindex.htm.
37. Bonnie Stepenoff, "Keeping It in the Family: Mother Jones and the Pennsylvania Silk Strike of 1900–1901," *Labor History* 38, no. 4 (Fall 1997): 432–449.
38. Bruce Western and Jake Rosenfeld, "Unions, Norms, and the Rise in U.S. Wage Inequality," *American Sociological Review* 76, no. 4 (2011): 513–537.
39. Barry C. Lynn and Phillip Longman, "Who Broke America's Jobs Machine?" *Washington Monthly*, March/April 2010, http://www.washingtonmonthly.com/features/2010/1003.lynn-longman.html; and Paul Krugman, "Robots and Robber Barons," *New York Times*, December 9, 2012, http://www.nytimes.com/2012/12/10/opinion/krugman-robots-and-robber-barons.html?ref=todayspaper.
40. Morris M. Kleiner and Alan B. Krueger, "Analyzing the Extent and Influence of Occupational Licensing on the Labor Market," *Journal of Labor Economics* 31, no. 2 (2013): S173–S202, http://www.nber.org/papers/w14979.
41. Weil, David, *The Fissured Workplace: Why Work Became So Bad for So Many and What Can Be Done to Improve It* (Cambridge, MA: Harvard University Press, 2014).
42. Lydia DePillis, "New Tech Companies Say Freelancing is the Future of Work. But There's a Downside for Workers," *Washington Post*, February 3, 2015, http://www.washingtonpost.com/news/storyline/wp/2015/02/03/new-tech-companies-say-freelancing-is-the-future-of-work-policy-needs-to-catch-up/.
43. John Komlos, *Has Creative Destruction Become More Destructive?* CESifo Working Paper No. 4941, August 2014, http://www.econstor.eu/bitstream/10419/102176/1/cesifo_wp4941.pdf; and Robert J. Gordon, *The Demise of U.S. Economic Growth: Restatement, Rebuttal, and Reflections*, National Bureau of Economic Research, Working Paper 19895, February 2014, http://www.nber.org/papers/w19895.
44. Liz Watson, Lauren Frohlich, and Elizabeth Johnston, *Collateral Damage: Scheduling Challenges for Workers in Low-Wage Jobs and their Consequences* (Washington, DC: National Women's Law Center, 2014), http://www.nwlc.org/sites/default/files/pdfs/collateral_damage_scheduling_fact_sheet.pdf
45. U.S. Department of Commerce, "A Look Ahead to 2012: NTIA by the Numbers," The Commerce Blog, December 30, 2011, http://2010-2014.commerce.gov/blog/2011/12/30/look-ahead-2012-ntia-numbers (accessed June 24, 2013). See also *Science* Career Blog, "Online Job Ads Report vs. Bureau of Labor Statistics Report: Half-Full, Half-Empty," July 6, 2012, http://blogs.sciencemag.org/sciencecareers/2012/07/online-job-ads-1.html.
46. Kristen Purcell and Lee Rainee, *Technology's Impact on Workers* (Washington, DC: Pew Research Center, 2014), http://www.pewinternet.org/2014/12/30/technologys-impact-on-workers/.
47. Michael Corkery and Jessica Silver-Greenberg, "Investment Riches Built on Subprime Auto Loans to the Poor," *New York Times*, January 26,

2015, http://dealbook.nytimes.com/2015/01/26/investment-riches-built-on-auto-loans-to-poor/?_r=0.

48. Seeta Peña Gangadharan, "Introduction," in *Data and Discrimination: Collected Essays*, ed. Seeta Peña Gangadharan (Washington, DC: New America, 2014), http://www.newamerica.org/downloads/OTI-Data-an-Discrimination-FINAL-small.pdf.

49. Congressional Budget Office. *Migrants' Remittances and Related Economic Flows,* Publication 4038, February 2011, https://www.cbo.gov/sites/default/files/02-24-remittances_chartbook.pdf.

50. Gonzalo Bacigalupe and Susan Lambe, "Virtualizing Intimacy: Information Communication Technologies and Transnational Families in Therapy," *Family Process* 50, no. 1 (March 2011): 12–26, https://www.academia.edu/460646/Virtualizing_Intimacy_Info rmation_Communication_Technologies_and_Transnational_Fa milies_in_Therapy; and David Kleeman, "Kids in the Middle: Media's Unique Roles for Children of Immigrants," *Huffington Post* blog, July 18, 2014, http://www.huffingtonpost.com/david-kleeman/kids-in-the-middle-medias_1_b_5597096.html.

51. Jenny S. Radesky, Caroline J. Kistin, Barry Zuckerman, Katie Nitzberg, Jamie Gross, Margot Kaplan-Sanoff, Marilyn Augustyn, and Michael Silverstein, "Patterns of Mobile Device Use by Caregivers and Children During Meals in Fast Food Restaurants," *PEDIATRICS* 133, no. 4 (April 2014): e843–e849, http://pediatrics.aappublications.org/content/early/2014/ 03/05/peds.2013-3703.full.pdf+html.

52. Michele L. Ybarra, Kimberly J. Mitchell, Janis Wolak, and David Finkelhor, "Examining Characteristics and Associated Distress Related to Internet Harassment: Findings From the Second Youth Internet Safety Survey," *Pediatrics* 118, no. 4 (October 2006): e1169–e1177, http://pediatrics.aappublications.org/content/118/4/e1169.shor.

53. Victoria J. Rideout, Ulla G. Foehr, and Donald F. Roberts, *Generation M^2: Media in the Lives of 8- to 18-Year-Olds* (Menlo Park, CA: Kaiser Family Foundation, 2010).

54. Susan B. Neuman and Donna C. Celano, *Giving Our Kids A Fighting Chance: Poverty, Literacy, and the Development of Information Capital* (New York: Teachers College Press, 2012).

55. Virginia Eubanks, "Digital Dead End" and "Big Data and Human Rights," in *Data and Discrimination: Collected Essays*, ed. Seeta Peña Gangadharan (Washington, DC: New America, 2014), http://www.newamerica.org/downloads/OTI-Data-an-Discrimination-FINAL-small.pdf.

56. Thom File and Camille Ryan, "Computer and Internet Use in the United States: 2013," American Community Survey Reports, U.S. Census Bureau, November 2014.

57. *Exploring the Digital Nation: Embracing the Mobile Internet* (Washington, DC: National Telecommunications and Information Administration and U.S. Department of Commerce, 2014), http://www.ntia.doc.gov/files/ntia/publications/exploring_the_digital_nation_embracing_the_mobile_internet_10162014.pdf.

58. "America's worst-connected big cities," November 3, 2014, http://redistributingthefuture.blogspot.com/2014/11/americas-worst-connected-big-cities.html; "Worse Connected = Poorest Cities," November 7, 2014, http://redistributingthefuture.blogspot.com/2014/11/worst-connected-poorest.html.

59. Dharma Dailey, Amelia Bryne, Alison Powell, Joe Karaganis, and Jaewon Chung, *Broadband Adoption in Low-Income Communities* (Brooklyn, NY: Social Science Research Council, March 2010).

Critical Thinking

1. What do the authors mean by the term "two-tiered family system"? How is it related to social and economic inequality in the United States?
2. What are some of the big changes in families and challenges to their well-being that family policy experts need to be ready to address in the next 10 years?
3. How can we better meet the needs of modern families—what programs and services might be needed to help the next generation of families to thrive?

Internet References

Center for Law and Social Policy (CLASP)
http://www.clasp.org/

Center for the Study of Social Policy
http://www.cssp.org/

Council on Contemporary Families
https://contemporaryfamilies.org/

New America: Family-Centered Social Policy
https://www.newamerica.org/family-centered-social-policy/